Contact Englishes of the Eastern Caribbean

Varieties of English Around the World

General Editor

Edgar W. Schneider
Department of English & American Studies
University of Regensburg
Universitätsstraße 31
D-93053 REGENSBURG
Germany
edgar.schneider@sprachlit.uni-regensburg.de

Editorial Assistants

Alexander Kautzsch, Magnus Huber (Regensburg)

Editorial Board

Laurie Bauer (Wellington); Manfred Görlach (Cologne);
Rajend Mesthrie (Cape town); Peter Trudgill (Fribourg);
Walt Wolfram (Raleigh, NC)

General Series

Volume G30
Contact Englishes of the Eastern Caribbean
Edited by Michael Aceto and Jeffrey P. Williams

Contact Englishes of the Eastern Caribbean

Edited by

Michael Aceto
East Carolina University

Jeffrey P. Williams
Cleveland State University

John Benjamins Publishing Company
Amsterdam/Philadelphia

™ The paper used in this publication meets the minimum requirements
of American National Standard for Information Sciences – Permanence
of Paper for Printed Library Materials, ANSI z39.48-1984.

Library of Congress Cataloging-in-Publication Data

Contact Englishes of the Eastern Caribbean / edited by Michael Aceto and
      Jeffrey P. Williams.
            p.   cm. (Varieties of English Around the World, ISSN 0172–7362 ; v.
G30)
            Includes bibliographical references and indexes.
            1. English language--Caribbean Area. 2. English language--Variation-
-Caribbean Area. 3. Creole dialects, English--Caribbean Area. 4. Languages in
contact--Caribbean Area. 5. Caribbean Area--Languages. I. Aceto, Michael. II.
Williams, Jeffrey P. (Jeffrey Payne), 1958- III. Series.

      PE3302 C66 2003
      427'.9729-dc21   2002033021
      ISBN 90 272 4890 7 (Eur.) / 1 58811 363 9 (US) (Hb; alk. paper)

John Benjamins Publishing Co. · P.O. Box 36224 · 1020 ME Amsterdam · The Netherlands
John Benjamins North America · P.O. Box 27519 · Philadelphia PA 19118-0519 · USA

Contents

Map

The Caribbean Basin

map courtesy of http://www.lib.utexas.edu/maps/americas/caribbean.gif

Preface

The 1998 Society for Pidgin and Creole Linguistics meeting in New York City was important to me for both personal and professional reasons. It was there that I met my co-editor, Jeff Williams, in person for the first time and we began to consider how we might fill the existing fieldwork gaps in the Anglophone Eastern Caribbean. Both Williams and I had been trained by the Department of Linguistics at the University of Texas at Austin (albeit at different times) and studied under the same dissertation supervisor, Ian Hancock, a seminal if not retiring figure in Creole studies these days. (Today, Hancock's interests are in the field of Romani studies, but his work in Creole studies inspired both Williams and me as graduate students. Thus this volume is dedicated to him and his model of excellent scholarship.) It was in NYC in the chairs outside the presentation rooms that we decided to begin two projects. One was a large-scale grant proposal to begin to study ten of the understudied Caribbean islands in the Eastern Caribbean: five islands for each researcher over a period of five years. That goal has unfortunately not yet been realized, but we have hopes for the future. The other equally active approach was to try to call on colleagues to research and write chapters for this book. That goal has been accomplished and the results are open before you.

I would like to thank the Dept. of English at East Carolina University, Bruce Southard, James Holte, and Maura Pizarro for providing me with a research assistant in order to carry out this project. I would like to thank Kris Ketcham for his editorial assistance and knowledge of computer programs. His expertise pushed this book toward completion. I would also particularly like to thank Dean W. Keats Sparrow, Associate Dean Scott Snyder, and the College of Arts and Sciences for granting me a College Research Award. This generous award allowed me complete course release for one semester and afforded me the time required to finish the work at hand. Finally, I would like to thank Edgar Schneider for his support and interest in this volume from the beginning of its conception.

Michael Aceto

Introduction

Michael Aceto and Jeffrey P. Williams

East Carolina University / Cleveland State University

1. Research on Eastern Caribbean English-derived dialects and creoles

In the following chapters, readers will find a range of papers on the English dialects and English-derived creoles of the Eastern Caribbean. The genesis of this volume began in 1997 when Glenn Gilbert, then editor of the *Journal of Pidgin and Creole Languages*, invited Aceto to participate in a symposium on the goals of creolistics in the twenty-first century at the meeting for the Society for Pidgin and Creole Linguistics (SPCL) in New York City in January 1998. As Aceto considered the theme of the symposium, which was to designate high priority research for the coming century, and what he might offer, he looked over his library, various bibliographies, and field notes. Since he was living on the Caribbean island of Puerto Rico, Aceto was perhaps more geographically-inclined in his considerations than focused on specific language-oriented phenomena from various theoretical perspectives whether they be cognitive, sociolinguistic, diachronic, etc. Of course, a task of this nature — i.e. in trying to figure out what needs to be done — is an odd endeavor since one must look at the work that has been completed (and/or published) and then subtract that aggregate research from a larger abstract picture of the total possible work that *could* be done out there in the world. The difference that remains is the work that needs to be completed in order to give researchers and scholars a more comprehensive picture of the general subject at hand, which, in this case, is English-derived Caribbean languages. The subject of the present volume is one of several topics that revealed themselves to Aceto as neglected by researchers (topics that other researchers found equally compelling can be found in Gilbert 2002).

As a region, the Eastern Caribbean has been left virtually untapped as a source of fieldwork data in Anglophone dialectology and Creole studies. Of course, there are individual pieces of research derived from some islands of the Eastern Caribbean, some of which are noted below, and at least two geographical exceptions to these generalizations are Barbados, Guyana, and perhaps Trinidad. Barbados has been central to previous discussions and debates in trying to determine its possible role in the diffusion of shared features heard throughout the Anglophone Caribbean as well as in answering questions related to the concept of "decreolization" as to whether Barbados once contained significant communities of speakers of a "deeper" Creole than typically seems to be spoken today (Cassidy 1980; Hancock 1980; Rickford 1992; see Van Herk, this volume). Trinidad has received significant attention from Winer (1993) and is important as a case study for reasons discussed below. These cases aside, the Eastern Caribbean is still largely absent from contemporary research and fieldwork in creolistics. Neumann-Holzschuh & Schneider (2000), one of the most recent additions to the excellent Creole Language Library series published by Benjamins, contains scant references to the Anglophone Eastern Caribbean. For reasons discussed in Aceto (2002a) and below, the "action" in Creole studies is not centered in the Eastern Caribbean, except perhaps as represented by Guyana in South America. Researchers have largely ignored the approximately one dozen other Anglophone islands in the Eastern Caribbean chain.

The paper presented at the SPCL conference in 1998 appears as Aceto (2002a) and it designates specific islands of the Eastern Caribbean (among other areas of the Americas as well) as sites for future research by compiling the relatively few bibliographic references that have been published on English-derived Caribbean varieties other than Jamaican and Guyanese and by indicating which specific islands or areas have received little or no attention from linguists. A summary list of the conclusions reached in that paper is as follows:

1.   There are no individual pieces of published or available research (i.e. M. A. theses or Ph.D. dissertations) describing the English-derived languages spoken on Barbuda, Turks and Caicos Islands, St. John, St. Thomas, Tortola, Virgin Gorda, Anegada, Anguilla, St. Eustatius, the Grenadine Islands of St. Vincent (Bequia, Mustique, Canouan, Union Island, & Mayreau).

2.   The English Creoles spoken on Grenada, Montserrat, St. Croix, Nevis, St. Martin, and St. Vincent are represented by a single piece of linguistic research each.

3. The following locations are represented by one title but fewer than four each: Dominica, Saba, St. Kitts, and St. Lucia.

4. Many islands or nations have only received the attention of a single researcher: Carricaou, Grenada, Montserrat, Saba, Nevis, St. Martin, and St. Vincent.

The point is clear: more work by more researchers would greatly improve our understanding of specific linguistic and sociohistorical features which one lexically-related Creole or English variety may or may not share with another. Two geographical areas of high priority are St. Eustatius and St. Kitts.[1] Both are considered important sources for the local (i.e. Caribbean) purchase of slaves during the slave trade and thus might have been sites responsible for dispersing language features throughout the Caribbean and possibly the Americas.[2] Of course, some of the goals which prompted Aceto (2002a) have been rectified to some degree by the present volume (e.g., see Cutler's article on the English of Grand Turk; Sabino, Diamond and Cockcroft's paper about plural marking on St. Thomas, St. John, Anegada and Tortola; Williams's chapter on Anguilla; and Aceto's article on Barbuda). Nonetheless, even after the publication of this volume, most of the islands listed above are still wide open for researchers interested in pursuing future fieldwork in Anglophone West Indian locations for which we have relatively little data.[3]

The general goal of Aceto (2002a) as well as the present volume is simply to stimulate more field-based linguistic research and, more specifically, fieldwork in neglected Anglophone areas of the Americas in order to broaden our base of knowledge about these language varieties. The following remarks undoubtedly reflect our own biases towards field-based linguistic and sociolinguistic research, and our feeling that linguistic researchers should not let the convenience of archival research lull them into forgetting the importance of obtaining corroborating linguistic data from living speakers. Diachronic work based on archival sources is certainly important, but it should always be correlated with data derived from contemporary fieldwork since this contemporary data will provide the foundation for the diachronic analyses of future scholars interested in these same languages. Dixon (1997: 132–148) also reminds us that fieldwork is really at the heart of linguistics and even the important work performed by those who view themselves as "theoreticians" depends crucially upon fieldwork carried out by others. Newman and Ratliff (2001) also stands as evidence for the importance of the fieldwork enterprise in linguistics.

2.   Overview of the contents of the volume

The region of the Eastern Caribbean has been defined broadly for this volume in an effort to be as inclusive as possible regarding neglected Caribbean Basin English-derived language varieties. That is, we view the Eastern Caribbean as a curiously neglected area of research from the perspective of Anglophone studies and thus, from the outset of the call for papers, have wanted to include other such contiguous, under-represented areas of the Caribbean such as the Virgin Islands (both American and British), the Bahamas, and the Turks and Caicos islands, which are most often not considered part of the Eastern Caribbean, despite their geographical proximity. We would have even welcomed a paper on the English of Bermuda, but no researcher stepped forward to provide us with one.

Several themes reveal themselves in the present volume. One is the familiar and recurring need to define what a Creole is from either a structural or a historical perspective. Aceto's chapter presents original data on Barbudan Creole English, a heretofore undocumented English-derived language (see also Aceto 2002b), which is used as a case study to present three broad classes of English language emergence: Immigrant, Dialect, and Autonomous varieties. His contribution is an effort to move beyond largely reified notions such as the so-called creole continuum (which only compares local varieties against their lexifiers) to a perspective that focuses more on the historical and sociolinguistic processes responsible for local language emergence. Garrett's contribution insists that not all English-derived Caribbean vernaculars should be considered as Creole languages.

Several of the chapters in the present volume present research from islands we know little or nothing about. Cutler's contribution on the English of Grand Turk island suggests that this language has more in common with other North American varieties such as African American Vernacular English and Bermudian than with varieties in the Caribbean. Sabino, Diamond, and Cockcroft examine plural marking in the British and American Virgin Islands. (See also the chapters by Williams on Anguilla, Aceto on Barbuda, and Garrett on St. Lucia; more below.)

We may put to the side strictly cognitive issues since none of the papers here addresses this topic directly from a language acquisition perspective (see DeGraff [1999] for an excellent treatment of these points), although the contribution by McPhee treats the grammar of Bahamian English briefly within the context of extended X-bar theory. Her paper is a fairly exhaustive treatment of

TMA combinations heard in Bahamian (see Childs, Reaser and Wolfram's chapter for an investigation into the phonology of two enclave communities in the Bahamas; more below).

Suffice it to say, one should object strenuously to the suggestion that speakers of so-called Creole languages (however these languages are ultimately defined) are cognitively any different in terms of their linguistic processes from human beings who speak non-Creole languages. This objection should be maintained even if it can ever be satisfactorily demonstrated that Creole languages are structurally different from other natural human languages. In the last several years, it has been asserted that so-called Creole languages manifest structural characteristics different from non-Creole languages (McWhorter 1998, 2000; Parkvall 2001), but most researchers have dismissed these assertions/alleged diagnostic structural features as not being exclusive to this group of languages researchers call Creoles (Plag 2001; also cf. Mufwene 2000). Rizzi (1999: 453) tries to answer the following question: "Does the study of language development, language change, and creolization offer privileged windows for the study of the language faculty?" He concludes that "creoles do not look different from other natural languages in any qualitative sense" (466), but they do contain "a relatively high concentration of unmarked options, plausibly a consequence of the special genesis of creoles" (467). What a Creole language is will not definitively be cleared up here, but Garrett's contribution to the volume suggests that English-derived varieties displaying features similar to those found in so-called Creoles can emerge in social contexts very different from the slavery/plantation scenario associated with many Creoles. In other words, restructured English varieties are still emerging today on islands of the Caribbean and these varieties are not related to the same social contexts and environments which may have defined the emergence of earlier varieties of languages such as Jamaican or Sranan. This point is discussed in detail in Aceto's contribution on Barbuda.

Several papers in the present volume (Bryan and Burnette, Garrett, Fayer, Kephart) discuss the emergence of English-derived varieties in territories where French-derived creoles were (and still are in many cases, especially among older residents) the first-language vernacular of island citizens: St. Lucia, Dominica, and Carriacou. Clearly the historical emergence of these English-derived varieties is qualitatively different from the more traditional plantation scenarios assumed in, for example, Jamaica, Guyana, and Suriname. Bryan and Burnette present the results of a survey they conducted among teachers about their attitudes towards language varieties in Dominica. This multilingual area has at least four languages spoken: English, a French-derived creole, a variety of English influenced by the French creole, and an earlier variety of Creole English called Kokoy imported into the island in the nineteenth century largely from Antigua and Montserrat. Their research suggests teachers are recognizing these languages and becoming more tolerant of their use in a range of social contexts. Garrett's chapter is the most comprehensive investigation in print as to the origins of vernacular English in St. Lucia. What is startling is the number of features that are similar to other Creole languages (the language also has many features unique to it), even though he makes the strong case that this language emerged initially in educational settings beginning in the twentieth century due to contacts between teachers using English varieties for instruction and students who were originally monolingual speakers of a French-derived Creole variety. Fayer's chapter also suggests the possible role that education played in the emergence of the Shakespeare *Mas'* performance in Carriacou. Kephart's contribution provides a grammatical sketch of Carriacou Creole English, a variety we know relatively little about except through his work.

The subsequent and largely post-emancipation emergences of current English-derived languages in these earlier Francophone locations in the Eastern Caribbean are not the only varieties to emerge apart from a plantation setting. The cases of Creole English in Trinidad and the English-derived creoles spoken along the Caribbean coast of Central America should also be added to this group. However, what are clearly significant differences in the social context for language emergence (i.e. the slave plantation versus other settings) may in fact obscure similar general patterns of restructuring from a second language acquisition perspective.[4] For example, in early Suriname, there were native speakers of African languages in contact with regional varieties of British English and perhaps an English-derived pidgin; in St. Lucia, there were (and still are) native speakers of French Creole in contact with local English-derived varieties used in educational contexts. Out of these language contact scenarios arose, respectively, Sranan and St. Lucian Vernacular English. The role of second language acquisition in the emergence of Creole languages has largely been ignored in Creole studies since the work of Andersen (1981, 1983), except as it pertains generally to substrate languages spoken by the ancestors of Afro-Caribbeans. DeGraff (1999) has highlighted the importance of understanding patterns in both first and second language acquisition for all areas of Creole and language studies, and recent work by researchers suggests the field is beginning to explore seriously the contribution of second language acquisition beyond a strict substratist approach to the emergence of Creole languages (see Winford

2000 and Plag & Uffmann 2000 as two of the most recent examples). In the present volume, the papers examining or describing English-derived varieties (or cultures) that have emerged in contact with (or calqued on) French-derived creoles form a plurality of the papers and may broaden some received notions in Creole studies as to how these languages (whether one chooses to label a specific variety a "creole" or not; see specifically Garrett, this volume) may emerge in a range of social contexts.

The contributions by Childs, Reaser and Wolfram, and Williams examine non-creolized, local varieties of English that are spoken in the Eastern Caribbean. These varieties, spoken primarily by those of European descent, are important in the development of a sociohistorical scenario of language change and genesis in the Anglophone Caribbean. Childs, Reaser and Wolfram look specifically at the differences and similarities between the speech of black and white Bahamians in two isolated, enclave communities. Williams documents the dialect of English that is spoken by a single, extended European-descended family-group in the village of Island Harbour on Anguilla — the northernmost of the Leeward Antilles. These two studies add to the small, but growing body of data on non-creolized forms of English in the Caribbean (if the purported distinction between creolized and non-creolized languages can ultimately be validated and maintained; see Mufwene 2000).

The final two papers in this volume present research on Bajan, Trinidadian and Guyanese varieties. As mentioned above, these three English-derived varieties are probably the most studied of all the English-derived languages of the Eastern Caribbean. What is so special about these chapters is the in-depth investigation by Van Herk of a single elderly woman who displays more "deep" Creole features than are typically associated with Barbados. Phonology is a neglected linguistic topic in general in Creole studies (thankfully, many of the chapters here raise phonological issues, e.g., see the chapters by Childs, Reaser and Wolfram; Cutler; Williams; and Van Herk for some considerable discussion of phonology in the Eastern Caribbean). However, Sutcliffe's chapter examines the severely neglected topic of suprasegmentals in Creole languages in his examination of Barbadian, Trinidadian, and Guyanese data.

There are many polemical topics of great interest to creolists (e.g. the nature of the creole continuum, the possible effects of decreolization, possible loci of creole genesis and language diffusion, the structural features and historical processes shared by the group of languages called Creoles by linguists, et al.) and most conclusions based upon English-derived data are largely drawn from Jamaican, Guyanese, and, most often, one of the several English-derived creoles of Suriname. This reductionist attitude is insufficient since the sociolinguistic profiles of many of the locations noted above have never even been documented. Once we have documented the languages spoken in these neglected locales, only then, will researchers be able to accurately and precisely discuss — with an extensive set of attested data in hand — how these varieties fit into a larger linguistic and sociohistorical view of English-derived creole genesis in the Caribbean and the Atlantic region in general. We view this book as a first step down the path towards representing these languages and their speakers among discussions in creolistics, English dialectology, and sociolinguistics.

Notes

1. Baker & Bruyn (1998) raise many of the important diachronic issues associated with St. Kitts.

2. Due to their importance to the entirety of the West Indian slave trade, it is also likely that these islands played a part in the diffusion of linguistic features from other European languages, such as Dutch and French, throughout the creoles of the region.

3. Aside from those geographically designated topics, Creole studies is conspicuously lacking in phonological and semantic treatments of many of these language varieties.

4. Reinecke (1937) made similar claims regarding a typology of social contexts that can give rise to different types of linguistic codes.

Defining ethnic varieties in the Bahamas

Phonological accommodation
in black and white enclave communities*

Becky Childs, Jeffrey Reaser, and Walt Wolfram
North Carolina State University

Introduction

One of the persistent sociolinguistic questions about language variation in the Bahamas, as in other regions of the Caribbean, is the historical and current relationship between black and white varieties. Long-term, mono-ethnic enclave communities are particularly illustrative of this ethnolinguistic dynamic, as they highlight a number of questions about language contact and sociolinguistic development. How do white enclave communities surrounded by majority black populations accommodate to the speech of these cohort speech communities, given the demographic dominance of a black population that historically has been socially subordinate? How are local black vernacular norms reconciled with the broader historical base of dominant colonial white speech norms in enclave white communities? Do enclave communities nurture ethnolinguistic distinctiveness, and if so, through what linguistic configurations?[1] Recent studies of Bahamian speech have arrived at conflicting conclusions with respect to the direction of language accommodation (Holm 1980; Sellers 1999; Wolfram, Childs, and Torbert 2000; Sabino 2000), showing both resistance and accommodation to local black Bahamian norms by whites.

In this account, we compare the phonological relationship of two enclave speech communities in The Great Abaco Island region of the Bahamas, Cherokee Sound and Sandy Point. Cherokee Sound is an exclusively white community of approximately 150 residents and Sandy Point is an exclusively black community of approximately 300 residents located 35 miles southwest of Cherokee Sound. Figure 1 gives the location of Cherokee Sound and Sandy Point, as well as the location of Abaco Island in relation to Florida.

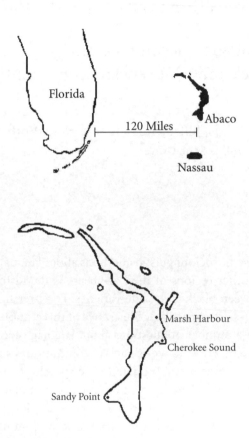

Figure 1. Location of Abaco, Cherokee Sound and Sandy Point

In this description, we consider a diagnostic set of phonological variables to determine the relationship of these ethnically contrastive enclave communities. Included in the analysis are several salient phonological traits such as syllable-initial *h*- deletion (e.g. *'ear* for *hear*) and insertion (e.g. *heggs* for *eggs*), [*v*/*w*] alternation (e.g. *vatch* for *watch*), as well as a less salient phonotactic pattern, the reduction of syllable-coda consonant clusters (e.g. *wes'* for *west*). We also consider the overall vowel systems of these two communities based on an acoustic analysis of the vowel systems for representative speakers from the respective communities. An examination of these features should reveal the extent to which ethnolinguistic distinctiveness and accommodation persist in these communities. More importantly, this comparison provides insight into the intersection of linguistic, sociohistorical, and sociopsychological factors in explaining language convergence and divergence in enclave dialect communities.

Sociohistorical background

In this section, we provide the sociohistorical background of Great Abaco Island in general and the enclave communities of Cherokee Sound and Sandy Point in particular. Both of these contexts are essential to understanding the past and the present dynamics that have molded the sociolinguistic situation in the respective communities under investigation here.

Abaco Island

Abaco, the second largest of the Bahamas Islands with a landmass of 649 square miles, is located in the northern part of the Bahamas, approximately 120 miles east of the Florida peninsula (see Figure 1). Abaco is known as an "out island" due to its relative sociohistorical isolation from the more urban areas of the Bahamas such as Nassau and Freeport; in fact, its history is tied to its isolation. It was one of the last regions settled in the Bahamas, as the British loyalists who arrived in 1783 found it empty. Previously, Lucayan Indians had inhabited the island until the Spanish conquest at the end of the fifteenth century brought about the destruction of the Native American population through disease and enslavement. After removing the natives of Abaco, the Spanish left the island deserted. This was followed by a failed French attempt at settlement in 1625. Later in the seventeenth century, the British also attempted to colonize Abaco, but this attempt was aborted and the island remained relatively empty, aside from pirates who used the island as a shelter, until 1783 when a group of British loyalists fled the newly formed United States for Abaco (Dodge 1995).

The British loyalists settled at Carleton, located north of present-day Marsh Harbour. It is estimated that about two-thirds of the loyalists came to Abaco via boats leaving from New York, the other third from boats leaving from St. Augustine, Florida. Although the loyalists departed primarily from

New York and Florida, the refugees themselves could have come from any-where in the US during the war, since loyalists from throughout the colonies fled either to New York or to Florida as the American Militia occupied more land. In fact, Bethel (1995) suggests that the residents of Cherokee Sound originally came to the Bahamas from the Carolinas via Florida.

Most of the wealthy loyalists returned to England within ten years of their settlement in Abaco, but those too poor to return stayed and relied on the resources of the land (such as the pine forest and plentiful water supply) and the rich marine resources of the sea to maintain a subsistence living on the island. By 1785, Marsh Harbour was already the largest city on Abaco, inhab-ited by nearly 44% of the island's population, with an additional 25% residing in nearby Maxwell (Dodge 1995). Many loyalists brought slaves with them in hope of setting up a plantation colony similar to those found in the American South, but the aspiration for large cotton plantations quickly died as settlers realized that the thin Bahamian soil would not support the crop. It is estimated that approximately 5,000 to 8,000 loyalists in all came to the Bahamas in the years following the American Revolutionary War, making them an important demographic group to consider in reconstructing the history of the language of Bahamians.

As noted, blacks from the US were also part of the early migration to Abaco, both as slaves and ex-slaves. During the Revolutionary war, the British encouraged blacks to abandon their white masters and join the British cause. A detailed record called the *Book of Negroes* gives the list of names of the blacks who came to Abaco as part of this movement. The book describes 88 former slaves, 22 of whom claimed to be free, who came to Abaco in 1783. The free slaves were assigned to white plantation families, but when the plantation system collapsed by the end of the eighteenth century, many of the blacks found themselves without overseers. From their arrival until emancipation in 1838, the black population, although the majority, was widely subjected to the rule of the white loyalists. This subordination eventually led to a series of revolts, which started in 1788 (Dodge 1995). During this period, many of the white plantation families deserted the island and returned to England while those who stayed found themselves in an increasingly uncomfortable and unstable situation. Also, diseases such as malaria chased many of the less-resistant white inhabitants off the mainland to isolated cays leaving the black population as the dominant Abaco population. The eventual rise to political control culminated in 1953 with the formation of the Progressive Liberal Party, which has become the controlling political party on Abaco and in the Bahamas.

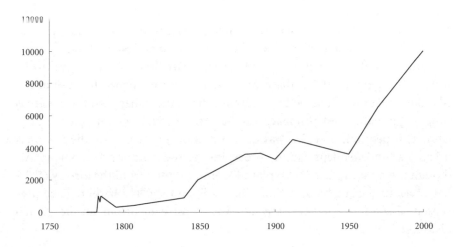

Figure 2. Population growth in Abaco

The population grew slowly during the nineteenth century, as indicated in Figure 2, and Abaco remained on the periphery of Bahamian life. However, during this time of relative stasis, Abaco was important to the rest of the Bahamas since it was a major shipbuilding island, accounting for almost half of Bahamian boat production from 1855 to 1864. The majority of the construction took place in Marsh Harbour and Cherokee Sound.

Farming in Abaco has been quite unstable, with various booms and recessions that included pineapple farming, citrus fruits, and sisal, a fibrous plant used to make rope and twine. Another industry that significantly changed the complexion of Abaco was the lumber industry early in the twentieth century, bringing modern conveniences such as electricity to the island. Like other periods of economic prosperity, the lumber industry set off a period of immigration to Abaco in the 1960s. This time, however, Haitians were fleeing to Abaco to escape the poverty of their native county, and it is estimated that Haitians made up as much as 20% of the population of Abaco during that period. Today, Haitians still constitute a demographic force on Abaco, making up as much as 44% of the population of Marsh Harbour (Dodge 1995). But the prosperity from logging was short-lived as the industry had exhausted the timber supply by 1969 and the economy again declined (Dodge 1995). Throughout the repeated history of economic gain and decline, the only steady industries were boat building, conching, fishing, and lobstering (called *crawfishing* by islanders). These livelihoods dominated and continue to dominate the outlying communities that are the focus of our study. On one level, then, the economic cycles that the island as a whole experienced were not felt quite as harshly in outlying settlements like Cherokee Sound and Sandy Point.

Throughout its relatively short history, Abaco has remained loyal to its British overseers. In 1971, Abaco presented a petition signed by 75% of the island population that asked for separation from the Bahamas if the Bahamas sought "premature independence" so that Abaco could remain a part of England. This petition, however, was denied and on July 10, 1973, the Bahamas became an independent nation — despite the resistance of Abaconians. Although it may seem that Abaco played an important part in the history of the Bahamas, its geographic isolation, poor soil, and shallow harbors have prevented Abaco from participating fully in mainstream Bahamian life. Abaco historian Steve Dodge (1995: vi–vii) writes:

> It is obvious that Abaco is a small place outside the mainstream. It has contributed little to the momentum of the modern world. In fact, much of this history describes the impact of the modern world on Abaco rather than vice versa.

We observe that the general setting of Abaco is somewhat isolated from other islands of the Bahamas, thus creating a broader context of isolation for the enclave communities of Cherokee Sound and Sandy Point.

The local setting: Cherokee Sound and Sandy Point

Although there is no evidence as to the exact date of settlement or where precisely the settlers came from, Cherokee Sound was apparently established not long after the British loyalists began arriving in 1783. Though the residents of Cherokee Sound were unable to provide specific details, the Carolinas are cited as the source of the original settlers. Cherokee Sound historian, Patrick Bethel (1995), notes that there were two settlements on the south coast of Abaco as early as 1784, Cherokee Sound and Crossing Rocks, with the first documented visit to the settlement by a minister in 1815. Given this historical background, it can be assumed that the British loyalists were almost certainly the first settlers.

The name of the community, Cherokee Sound, is also of disputed origin. Most members of the community we have spoken to, as well as local historian Patrick Bethel (1995), believe that the name comes from a link to the Cherokee Indians of North Carolina. As recounted in Bethel (1995), Colonel Brown, the

King's liaison to the Cherokee Indians in North Carolina, brought a congrega-
tion of expatriates first to Florida and then to Abaco after Florida was ceded
back to Spain. It is speculated that Colonel Brown was in love with one of
several Cherokee Indians included in the group, and thus named the new
settlement in her honor (Bethel 1995).[2] The true history of settlement and the
naming of the community, however, may be lost forever to legend as the
history of the community has been passed on almost exclusively by oral
tradition.

Cherokee Sound exists in a situation of compounded isolation. It is located
on the southern part of Abaco (see Figure 1), about 35 miles from Marsh
Harbour, and did not have a road connecting it to the rest of the mainland or
electricity until 1994.[3] In addition to its geographical detachment over land, the
lack of an adequate harbor, the presence of a coral reef that cuts it off from the
eastern shore of Abaco, and an inland creek that separates it from the rest of
mainland Abaco, make navigation to the settlement difficult. Until recently, the
community was difficult to reach by land or by sea. The community has thus
existed as a self-contained settlement, known to the outside world primarily for
their boat-building expertise and distinctive dialect. Throughout Abaco, Cherokee Sound is known for having an identifiable speech pattern, and it is often cited
by long-term Abaconians as possessing one of the most distinctive dialects on
the islands.

Although no official census data existed for Cherokee Sound, Bethel (1995)
claims that there were approximately 400 people living in the settlement in the
early nineteenth century. He describes a slow decline in population that has
continued through modern time as the population dropped to about 180 by the
early 1990s and even further since then. Cherokee Sound has been affected very
little by the immigration that has affected the rest of Abaco in recent decades.
The settlement still reflects a past era in that it lacks medical facilities and police
or fire stations, but it has a school (through eighth grade), a small store that
carries some food and other essentials, a gas pump, a mail room (the mail comes
once a week), and two churches: a Methodist Church and an Assembly of God
Church. Although many houses are now equipped with satellite dishes and
video games, the social life of the community is still closely centered around
church. Children play outside, swimming, fishing, riding bikes, and helping
their parents work. Adults, particularly men, are often found in the late after-
noons socializing under a cabana that overlooks the water, and residents visit
with each other regularly.

The history of Cherokee Sound as a predominately white community does not seem unlike that of other Anglo-Bahamian settlements. Since the early history of Abaco, white people have often isolated themselves from the black settlements by moving off the mainland island to the cays around Abaco (Craton and Saunders 1992). This was done in part to escape the malaria-carrying mosquitoes, but also to escape the turbulent situation that had arisen on occasion between the races. While Cherokee Sound is currently all white, it was not exclusively white until quite recently. There were six black families living in Cherokee Sound as recently as 1945 (Bethel 1995). Race relations have never been a source of major confrontation in Cherokee Sound in the way that they have been in other parts of the Bahamas, but some of the underlying attitudes about race eventually led to total segregation. According to Bethel, "The Blacks knew their place and accepted it" (1995: 37). Despite their overall minority status in the Bahamas, residents do not feel like a subjected population; they are proud of who they are and take pride in the things that they feel most set their community apart from other communities such as cleanliness, self-sufficiency, and even dialect. Furthermore, they do not exhibit the ideology of subordination sometimes exhibited by minority populations in which the language varieties of socially subordinate groups are viewed as linguistically deficient (Lippi-Green 1997, Wolfram fc.). In a situation of compounded isolation, members of the settlement have developed a sense of identity that is distinctly that of Cherokee Sound.

In contrast to Cherokee Sound, Sandy Point is an exclusively black community of approximately 300 residents located on a peninsula on the western shore of southern Abaco (see Figure 1). Like Cherokee, Sandy Point has a school, a convenience store, a post office, and three churches, but it also has a hardware store, a medical clinic staffed by a local nurse, and a couple of fishing lodges that offer tourists guided fishing excursions. And like Cherokee Sound, it remains an outlying area on an isolated island.

Sandy Point was probably founded around 1838 by emancipated slaves, although it is not known how many slaves originally settled in Sandy Point, or even where they came from. Mailboat captain Ernest Dean (1997) describes the community in 1929 as containing about two dozen houses, so it has grown considerably in the last half-century because of marriage to outsiders who moved there and substantial birth rates in the community. Figure 3 indicates the population growth for Sandy Point as compared with the decline in the population of Cherokee Sound during the twentieth century.

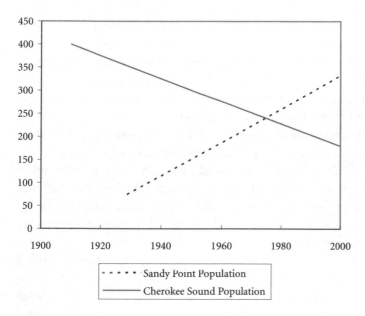

Figure 3. Population estimates for Sandy Point and Cherokee Sound in the twentieth century

Children actively swim, fish, ride bikes, climb trees, and help their parents, in addition to enjoying modern luxuries such as satellite TV and video games. Virtually all of the residents we have spoken with view it as a good, safe community ideal for raising children. As in Cherokee Sound, the community is largely reliant on the natural resources of the land and sea. Palms with coconuts grace the horizon, as do lime trees, almond trees, fig trees, and seagrapes. The ocean fuels the economy through lobstering and other commercial fishing; Sandy Point also has a number of bonefish guides and is touted as one of the best fishing areas in the Bahamas. Conversations with fishing lodge owners revealed that often an entire month can pass between guests, however, so it seems that tourism has not had a significant influence on the community structure per se.

Historically, Sandy Point has not experienced the extent of social isolation that Cherokee Sound has. The government provided electricity in 1964 and, at the same time, a road was cleared from Marsh Harbour to Sandy Point. However, the unpaved road fell into such disrepair that the 50-mile drive took several hours, with travelers often required to carry numerous spare tires. Prior to pavement of the road in 1995, it was easier to reach Sandy Point by boat, and the mailboat became an important method for obtaining goods as well as for transporting people to other parts of the Bahamas. Before the road was paved, children attended school through the twelfth grade in Sandy Point or went away to live with relatives in Nassau or Freeport. Now, most children from the community attend high school in Marsh Harbour.

The social activities of the community are similar to those found in Cherokee Sound, as the churches in Sandy Point function as an integral part of the social lives. In addition to church, many of the younger residents enjoy other social activities such as a weekly "goombay," a meal served by a community member followed by music, drinking, and dancing on the beach. Most of the free time that the residents enjoy is spent hanging out at the local store or by the piers fishing and talking to friends.

Sandy Point makes an ideal comparison community for Cherokee Sound since its isolated status is much like that of Cherokee Sound. The social dynamics of the community are fairly similar, and people of Sandy Point seem to have a fairly strong sense of identity as Bahamians and Sandy Point residents. Impressionistically, the dialect spoken in Sandy Point is similar to the black Bahamian dialect found in Marsh Harbour, both being a little different from the Nassau dialect, which tends to be a bit more vernacular. Sandy Point is a convenient baseline black Abaconian English variety, especially in terms of our examination of phonological features. Eventually, more research may reveal dialect differences between this variety and other black Bahamian varieties, but for the purpose of this study, Sandy Point is an ideal comparison group for Cherokee Sound, which is located 35 miles to the northeast.

Some comparative phonological structures

In the following sections, we compare some phonological features for Cherokee Sound and Sandy Point. So far, we have interviewed 41 speakers from Cherokee Sound and 42 speakers from Sandy Point, representing a full spectrum of age groups. Although our qualitative observations are based on the tape-recorded interviews with the full set of speakers, our quantitative analysis and acoustic measurements at this point are based on a much more limited subsample of representative speakers, generally from 6 to 10 speakers. Although quantitative analysis is still limited, the emerging trends suggest some important similarities and differences in the communities.

Syllable-coda consonant cluster reduction

From the earliest language variation studies, syllable-coda consonant cluster reduction has served as a benchmark in the analysis of the structurally ordered effects of language variation (Labov, Cohen, Robins, and Lewis 1968; Wolfram 1969; Guy 1980; Wolfram, Childs, and Torbert 2000). Although there is debate about the descriptive and explanatory accounts of consonant cluster reduction (CCR), there is virtual consensus about the observed facts: syllables that end in a stop and share voicing (i.e. both consonants are either voiced or voiceless) may variably delete the final segment of the cluster. As a result, most analyses have agreed that syllable-coda consonant clusters ending in [t], [d], [k], or [p] may be reduced. The list of clusters eligible for CCR is given in Table 1.

Table 1. Clusters subject to syllable-coda consonant cluster reduction

Phonetic cluster	Monomorphemic	Bimorphemic
[st]	*test, post*	*missed, guessed*
[sp]	*wasp, clasp*	
[sk]	*desk, risk*	
[ʃt]		*finished, cashed*
[zd]		*raised, amazed*
[ʒd]		*judged, charged*
[ðd]		*bathed, smoothed*
[ft]	*craft, cleft*	*laughed, stuffed*
[vd]		*loved, paved*
[nd]	*mind, find*	*rained, fanned*
[md]		*named, rammed*
[ld]	*cold, old*	*called, smelled*
[pt]	*apt, adapt*	*rapped, stopped*
[kt]	*act, contact*	*looked, cracked*

Table 1 shows that this process of reduction can occur whether the cluster is composed of one morpheme, i.e., monomorphemic, or created through suffixation, i.e., bimorphemic. This, of course, assumes a standard English norm for suffixation. However, for Bahamian English, the underlying status of clusters is more involved, since past-tense marking on verb forms may be absent because of a grammatical process. Thus, our figures for bimorphemic clusters may be confounded by the grammatical system of basilectal Bahamian English. At this point in our analysis, we simply observe this complexity, which will be examined in detail in our future studies of the Bahamian English tense, mood, and aspect system.

Other studies of variation in CCR have indicated that certain phonetic and functional linguistic factors seem to systematically affect instances of reduction, including the form of the following segment (e.g. consonants favor reduction over vowels, as *bes' kid* > *bes' at*), the phonetic composition of the cluster in terms of sonorancy of the preceding segment (nasal > lateral > sibilant > stop, e.g. *win'* > *wil'* > *wes'* > *ac'*), the prosodic status of the syllable (e.g. stressed syllables > unstressed syllables as in *cóntrac'* > *contrác'*), and the grammatical status of the final stop in the cluster (e.g. monomorphemic > redundant bimorphemic > bimorphemic, as in *gues'* > *crep'* > *guess'*). Numerous studies (e.g. Labov, Cohen, Robins, and Lewis 1968; Labov 1972a; Wolfram 1969, 1974, 1980, 1985; Fasold 1972; Guy 1980) on many varieties of English have confirmed these systematic, variable effects on the relative incidence of CCR, though of course we cannot assume this ordering hierarchy for the varieties of Bahamian English.

Surveys of CCR (Wolfram and Schilling-Estes 1998; Wolfram, Childs, and Torbert 2000) indicate that prevocalic cluster reduction tends to be enhanced in varieties influenced historically by phonological transfer from prior language contact situations rather than from independent development within English due to the fact that syllable-coda clusters are highly marked and relatively rare in most languages of the world. Almost all English dialects have significant levels of cluster reduction in preconsonantal positions (e.g. *tes' case* for 'test case'), especially in monomorphemic clusters, but prevocalic environments differ significantly among dialects. In surveys such as Wolfram, Childs, and Torbert (2000), varieties that have significant levels of CCR including African American Vernacular English, Vietnamese English, varieties of Hispanic English, and Native American English generally do not contain syllable coda consonant clusters. Varieties that do not have significant levels of prevocalic CCR include Standard English, Northern US White Working Class Speech, and Appalachian English. From this vantage point, it seems that Bahamian English varieties like the variety found in Sandy Point, with its extensive syllable-coda, prevocalic consonant cluster reduction, would align with English varieties that have experienced language transfer of some type.

The analysis of CCR for representative Sandy Point and Cherokee Sound speakers follows well-established procedures for data extraction. This includes the elimination of sequences difficult to hear due to phonetic similarity (e.g. clusters following by homorganic stops, as in *test time*), attention to type-token ratios (e.g. no more than five examples of one word type were extracted), and the elimination of function words that seem to reflect lexicalized reduction

(e.g. *an'* for *and*). Table 2 shows the aggregate rates of CCR for several repre
sentative speakers from the Cherokee Sound and Sandy Point communities. Accompanying Table 2 are the results of a VARBRUL analysis. VARBRUL is a probabilistic-based, multivariate regression analysis that shows the relative contribution of various linguistic or social factors to a variable process. VARBRUL determines the input probability as the likelihood of the rule applications apart from the influence of the constraining factors. The factor groups can consist of any of the various linguistic constraints, such as morphemic status and following phonological environments, along with external factors such as ethnicity, age, and gender. Factors in each factor group are assigned a weight by VARBRUL as a number between 0 and 1, with a mid weighting of .5. A value of over .5 indicates a favoring effect while a value under .5 indicates an inhibiting effect. In the VARBRUL analysis accompanying Table 2, three factor groups are considered: community, cluster type (mono-morphemic vs. bimorphemic), and following phonetic environment (following consonant, pause, and vowel).

Table 2. Consonant cluster reduction in Abaco communities

	Monomorphemic						Bimorphemic					
	Prevocalic % Red	N	Prepausal %Red	N	Preconson. %Red	N	Prevocalic %Red	N	Prepausal %Red	N	Preconson. %Red	N
Cherokee Sound English	22.5	102	47.4	78	66.4	140	7.7	65	6.7	15	54.9	71
Sandy Point English	80.4	51	100	24	98.8	67	55.5	18	66.6	6	100	11

VARBRUL Results:

Input probability	=.58
Community:	
Sandy Point	= .89
Cherokee Sound	= .31
Cluster Status:	
monomorphemic	= .57
bimorphemic	= .34
Following Environment:	
prevocalic	= .22
prepausal	= .49
preconsonantal	= .74
Chi square per cell	=.839

The most significant difference in the VARBRUL analysis is based on the community. The incidence of reduction in all environments for the speakers from Cherokee Sound is significantly lower than that of the speakers from Sandy Point. Certainly, it does not seem unusual for white speakers of Cherokee Sound to exhibit lower levels of CCR when compared to the black Bahamian English cohort speakers from Sandy Point, who speak a variety of English that has extensive prevocalic CCR. However, this is not the whole story. While there is a significant difference in the level of CCR for the two communities, it should also be noted that the incidence of CCR for the white community is somewhat higher than that typically found for other Anglo varieties of English.[4] Compare, for example, CCR reduction in prevocalic position — the most diagnostic phonological context for reduction — among Cherokee Sound English and some representative Anglo varieties of English given in Figure 4. The comparison groups, taken from Wolfram and Schilling-Estes (1998) and Wolfram, Childs, and Torbert (2000) include Standard American English, Appalachian English, Northern Working-Class White English, and Coastal North Carolina White speech.

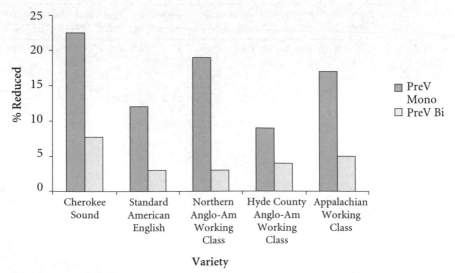

Figure 4. Comparison of consonant cluster reduction in representative Anglo dialects in the US

Figure 4 shows that Cherokee Sound English, by comparison with other Anglo English varieties of English, has accommodated to a limited extent the black Bahamian norm even though there is a significant difference between CCR in Cherokee Sound and Sandy Point. The levels of CCR in Cherokee Sound are routinely higher than those found in comparable Anglo varieties of English, though significantly different from Sandy Point.

Syllable onset *h-* deletion and insertion

Previous descriptions of Bahamian English (Holm 1988) report that *h-* deletion or "*h-* dropping" is much more common among white speakers than among blacks. British Cockney has often been cited as the source of *h-* dropping in Anglo Caribbean varieties, but of course, *h-* dropping is quite common in an array of English dialects (Trudgill 1990). Although there has been limited description of *h-* dropping in the Bahamas, there has been no detailed examination of this linguistic process in out-island communities such as Abaco, particularly a comparative analysis of white and black communities. Holm (1988; 76), however, notes that "on the island of Abaco in the Bahamas *ear* is what you do with your *hear* (or vice versa)." The unique circumstances of the isolated settlements of Sandy Point and Cherokee Sound on Abaco thus provide an opportunity to gain insight into both Bahamian English norms and the role which language contact plays in the evolution of particular dialects that are geographically parallel but ethnically distinct.

For this analysis of *h-* dropping, several factors were considered. In terms of phonetic environment, we considered preceding phonetic environment (consonant as in *stop hitting*, vowel as in *very hot*, or pause as in *Help!*) in an effort to determine whether certain environments systematically constrained dropping. For the purposes of this analysis, all cases of unstressed auxiliaries *have*, *had* and unstressed pronominals such *his*, *her*, and *him* were ignored as all varieties of English tend to drop *h-* in these cases. Thus, in terms of phrasal stress, only cases of primary- or secondary-stressed *h-* were considered. Type-token ratios were also controlled in the extraction process: only seven tokens of each word in a specific environment were counted.

In Table 3, the incidence of *h-* dropping is compared for Cherokee Sound and Sandy Point based on several representative speakers. Accompanying Table 3 is a VARBRUL analysis that considers the factors of preceding environment and community.

Table 3. Syllable onset *h*- dropping in Cherokee and Sandy Point

Community	Preceding Environment					
	Consonant		Pause		Vowel	
	% Red	N	%Red	N	%Red	N
Cherokee Sound	59.3	91	93.0	15	50.5	91
Sandy Point	47.1	70	66.6	18	33.3	51

VARBRUL Results:

Input Probability	= .53
Community:	
Cherokee Sound	= .57
Sandy Point	= .40
Preceding Environment:	
Pause	= .79
Consonant	= .52
Vowel	= .41
Chi-square per cell	= .278

Table 3 indicates that *h*- dropping is a more common process in Cherokee Sound English than in Sandy Point English, though it obviously occurs in both varieties. There is also a systematic hierarchy of phonetic effects in that *h*-dropping is favored at the beginning of an utterance, followed by contexts with a preceding consonant and then by those with a preceding vowel. The inhibition of *h*- dropping intervocalically makes phonetic sense since it prohibits a canonical vowel + vowel sequence. While both communities exhibit considerable *h*- loss and follow the same hierarchy of phonotactic constraints, *h*-dropping is considerably more prominent in Cherokee Sound than in Sandy Point, confirming Holm's (1988) original evaluation of this process on Abaco.

There is another dimension of syllable-onset *h*- that seems to set Cherokee Sound and Sandy Point apart, namely, the insertion of *h*- on items whose lexical representation in other English varieties begins with a vowel, as in *heggs* for *eggs* or *harm* for *arm*. Typically, these productions are considered as a type of hypercorrection, though the assignment of this label entails a specialized social situation as well as a linguistic production that we have not yet examined in detail in these communities. Shilling (1980) notes that this insertion is "much commoner with white speakers than with black." Our analysis thus far confirms Shilling's observation; in fact, all instances of *h*- insertion in our data were collected from lifetime residents of Cherokee Sound. Certainly, the data indicate that the social differences between the communities, primarily ethnicity, are important in discerning significant phonological differences in these out-island dialects.

The alternation of *w* and *v*

The alternation of /w/ and /v/ (phonetically often the intermediate [ʋ] instead of [v]), such as [ʋatʃ] for *vatch* and *watch* and [ʋi] for *we*, is one of the most marked features of Bahamian speech. While this feature, like *h*- dropping and final CCR, is found in both black and white Bahamian speech, Holm (1980) notes that *v* and *w* seem to be interchangeable for many white speakers. This assessment suggests that *w* will often replace *v*, giving rise to situations like *wiolence* for *violence* as well as *v* for *w* in *vatch* for *watch*. However, this pattern is not manifested in the Cherokee Sound dialect; only the use of *v* (i.e., [ʋ] or [v]) for *w* has been found in our analysis of the Cherokee Sound community thus far. On the other hand, the use of *w* for *v* has been observed for the Sandy Point community. Although this difference deserves more careful scrutiny, it may be an essential dichotomy between the two communities with respect to the alternation of *w* and *v*.

For this analysis of *v* for *w*, several factors were taken into account, including ethnicity and the preceding phonetic environment (consonant, vowel, and pause) in an effort to determine systematic constraints on variable alternation. Again, type-token ratios were controlled so that only seven tokens of each word in a specific environment were counted. Table 4 summarizes the quantitative analysis of [v] and [ʋ] for *w* based again on several representative speakers in each community; the accompanying VARBRUL analysis considers the factor groups of community and preceding environment.

Table 4. v/w alternation in Cherokee and Sandy Point

Community	Preceding Environment					
	Consonant		Pause		Vowel	
	% Red	N	%Red	N	%Red	N
Cherokee Sound	18.8	101	36.6	41	28.0	111
Sandy Point	13.6	59	8.3	12	4.0	49

	VARBRUL Results:	
	Input Probability	=.19
	Community:	
	Sandy Point	=.31
	Cherokee Sound	=.59
	Preceding Environment:	
	Pause	=.61
	Consonant	=.46
	Vowel	=.50
Chi square per cell		=.921

The analysis indicated in Table 4 confirms the ethnic divide in the use of this feature. Although both communities participate in the process of *w/v* alternation, it is clearly more prominent in Cherokee Sound than in Sandy Point. This difference is the most transparent constraint in the raw percentage scores and the VARBRUL analysis. The analysis of preceding environment is, however, somewhat more complicated. The VARBRUL analysis eliminated this factor group in the step-up, step-down procedure. This elimination may be due to the fact that this factor group is simply not significant or due to an interactive effect between community and phonetic environment. The figures suggest that there may be an interactive effect, as the hierarchy of phonetic constraints on *v* for *w* in the two communities is different: the order for Cherokee Sound is pause > vowel > consonant whereas in Sandy Point the order is consonant > pause > vowel. If this pattern holds up on the basis of a more extensive data set, then it appears that these two communities may indeed be distinctive from each other in subtle, independent linguistic constraint effects on *w/v* alternation. We have already suggested that the communities differ in frequency and correspondence variants. It may well be that the participation of both communities in the general process of *w/v* alternation may camouflage more subtle quantitative and qualitative differences that are ethnically divisive with respect to this variable.

Vowel systems

One of the most diagnostic dimensions of English varieties often lies in the vowel system. There has been limited acoustic analysis of Caribbean varieties of English (Veatch 1991; Patrick 1996; Thomas and Bailey 1998), but no careful instrumental studies of the vowel systems of Bahamian out-islanders such as the inhabitants of Abaco. In addition to providing clues about the possible origins of Bahamian English, the vowel systems may also show different influences on the distinctive communities. Examining the vowel system allows us to assess the impact of accommodation in isolated locations, as well the potential of independent development. In this analysis, we will first compare the vowel systems of Cherokee Sound and Sandy Point based on three representative speakers in each community. Then we will extend the comparison to other varieties of English in the US, in the Caribbean, and in England. While our comparative set of English varieties is hardly comprehensive, it should be instructive as to some major similarities and differences, and should guide our emerging comparative analysis.

Three generations of Cherokee Sound and Sandy Point residents are represented by the speakers selected for detailed acoustic analysis. Acoustic measurements were taken with a Kay Computerized Speech Laboratory (CSL), model 4300B. Signals were digitized at a rate of 11,025 Hz, with 6 dB/oct pre-emphasis at a factor of 0.8. Measurements were taken in the center of the vowel for monophthongs while diphthongs were measured at least 25 ms into the vowel in a steady state (when possible) and again at least 25 ms from the end of the vowel, again in a steady state part of the vowel if possible. This method eliminates most of the transitional effects of adjacent segments on the vowel while still showing the true spectral change of the diphthong. The first, second, and third formants were measured using linear predictive coding (LPC). The default number of poles for the CSL is 12, but the number of poles used ranged from 10 to 18, depending on which value provided the most appropriate formant estimates. The fundamental frequency was measured using a Fast Fourier Transform. Seven to ten tokens of each vowel, taken from a conversational interview with a member of the North Carolina Language and Life Project, were measured, and no more than two tokens of any one word were used. Pre-nasal environments were avoided, except where treated separately in order to eliminate extra resonances and anti-formants. Also, pre-liquid and post-glide tokens were not used so as not to skew the resulting vowel plots. Some vowels such as [U] and [oi] generally had fewer than seven tokens due to their relative scarcity. Tokens were averaged and then plotted as a point in the case of monophthongs or as a point and an arrow representing the nucleus and glide of diphthongs.

The vowel plots of the white speakers are given in Figures 5.1–3 and those of the black speakers in Figures 6.1–3.

Setting aside prosodic features such as stress, rhythm, intonation, and speech rate, all of which merit study, the different vowel systems of Cherokee Sound and Sandy Point show two distinct configurations. Although some features found here can be found in England, the US, and elsewhere in the Caribbean, no particular source aligns isomorphically with all the features of these varieties. Therefore, we can reasonably conclude that the true history of vowel development in these respective varieties is tied to founder effects, contact, accommodation, and innovation.

A number of specific observations can be made on the basis of Figures 5 and 6. First, we may note some differences for the /au/ diphthong. Some people have mistakenly associated Canadian raising, i.e., the process where the nucleus of the /au/ diphthong is raised before voiceless consonants (e.g., *out* as [ɜʉt])

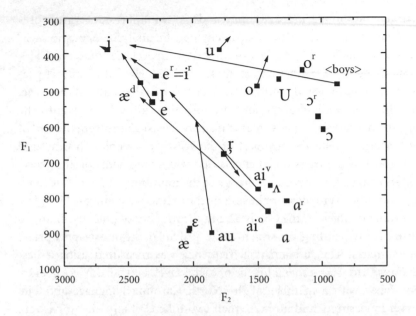

Figure 5.1

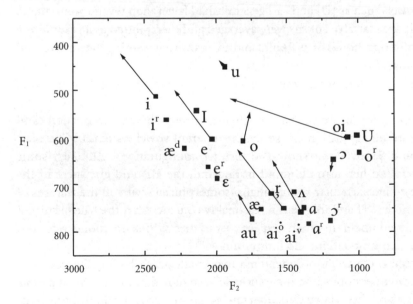

Figure 5.2

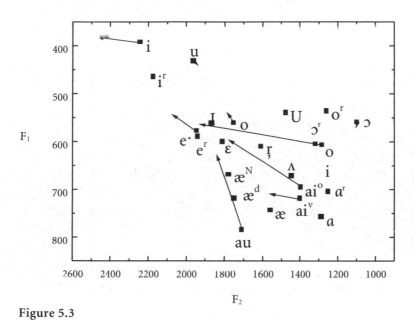

Figure 5.3

Figure 5. Vowel plots for representative Cherokee sound speakers

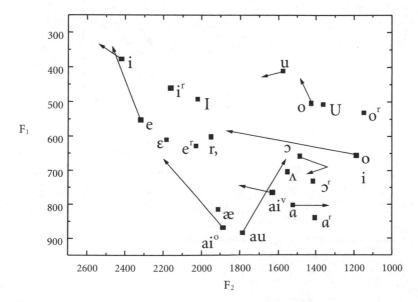

Figure 6.1

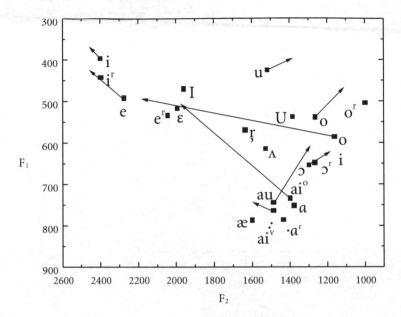

Figure 6.2

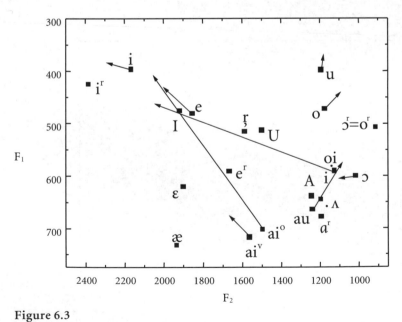

Figure 6.3

Figure 6.   Vowel plots for representative Sandy Point speakers

with the Bahamas. This raising is not found in Cherokee Sound speech, instead, /au/ is front-glided and is produced as [aɛ] or [aö] in all contexts, as can be seen in all three white speakers of different ages in Figures 5.1–3. This front gliding represents a very salient departure from both American and black Bahamian norms, though it shows an affinity to Pamlico Sound English as described in Thomas (2001) and Wolfram, Thomas, and Green (2000). The black speakers from Sandy Point, as well as those from the rest of the Bahamas produce the diphthong with a backing-glide as can be seen in Figures 6.1–3.

Examining the high and middle back vowels reveals another difference between the white and black speakers. The white speakers have a fronted /u/ and /o/ while these both remain backed in the black speakers. The fronting of /u/ is common in white Southern American English varieties, although it has since permeated many Northern communities as well (Ash 1996; Thomas 2001). Although /u/ is not fully fronted to [ü] as is common in the South (see Table 5), it is shifted as far forward as [ʉ]. As previously mentioned, /o/ is also fronted in the white speakers, but it is not lowered as is common in Southern American English varieties: instead, it is realized as [ɵu]. Like the fronting of /u/, this is an innovation that has spread rapidly in American English. Because of this, it is not entirely unreasonable to suspect this variant to have somehow been introduced to the Bahamas from the US. However, the severe isolation of the community leaves questions as to whether this is a product of language contact, an independent innovation of the community, or simply a preservation of the language that settlers brought with them. It is noteworthy that the Pamlico Sound variety spoken on the Outer Banks, which stands apart from other Southern American English varieties, does, in fact, exhibit fronting of /o/ and /u/.

Another feature that seems to separate these two varieties is the diphthong /ai/, as can be seen in the vowel plots in Figures 5.1 and 5.2; the two older white speakers show a strong glide for /ai/ in all environments. The youngest Cherokee Sound speaker, shown in Figure 5.3, shows a weakened glide before voiced consonants, a pattern found in Southern American English varieties. The black speakers show this distinction in all generations, as indicated in Figures 6.1–3. In this, they seem to be closer to modern African American English (AAE) than to other Caribbean Creole varieties (Thomas and Bailey 1998). It is not clear whether the youngest white speaker has accommodated to the majority or to the black norm, or varies for some other reason, such as the imitation of Southern American English varieties.

There are other features that suggest the possibility of accommodation to black Bahamian norms by the white community. In the oldest speaker, [æ] is raised before *d* as in words like *glad* or *bad*. It is found in the vicinity of [ɪ], as seen in Figure 5.1. By the next generation (Figure 5.2), [æ] has receded to a position closer to [ɛ], and by the youngest speaker, it has lowered to the same position as [æ] in other environments, more like it is in Sandy Point. No Sandy Point speaker makes a distinction between [æ] before voiced consonants and elsewhere, so there may be some developing accommodation to the black Bahamian norm by the white community if the Cherokee Sound speakers are reflective of community-wide patterns.

For the two oldest black speakers, [ɑ] is lowered and backed. In this regard, they are more similar to other West Indian varieties than to AAE, a pattern not reflected by other variants. The movement toward a lowered and backed variant for [æ] in the younger speaker, if corroborated by additional data, would indicate that the white community again seems to be moving in the direction of the black norms, accommodating the features of the majority population.

The vowel [ɑ] also shows alignment between the communities. All speakers maintain a distinction between [ɑ] and [ɔ] but have a backed variety of [ɑ]. Although it is tempting to say that this similarity reflects accommodation by the white community, the fact that this variant is found in Southern American English varieties, AAE, and in the Pamlico Sound area leads to questions as to whether this is accommodation as opposed to retention of a form that the first residents of Cherokee Sound and Sandy Point may have brought with them to Abaco. The same can be said for [ɔ]. The fact that both Cherokee Sound speakers and Sandy Point speakers have similar productions for [ɔ] does not necessarily suggest accommodation. The raised, monophthongal [ɔ] is found in many areas of England and in restricted areas of the US, such as the Pamlico Sound region of North Carolina (Thomas 2001; Wolfram, Thomas, and Green 2000) and in Low Country speech of South Carolina (McDavid 1955). As is true in both AAE and other forms of American English, [ɔ] seems to show a fair amount of individual variation. Therefore, it is difficult to make any strong claims about the role this variable has played and continues to play in the dynamic dialect situation found in these communities.

One of the most interesting variants is [ʌ]. Both Cherokee Sound and Sandy Point speakers show a backed variant of [ʌ] that is rounded, realized roughly as [ɔ]. Although this has been well documented in other Caribbean Creoles such as Jamaican English, it is not as common in the US.[5] It is,

however, found (of places cited as possible sources for Bahamian English) in
the Low Country of South Carolina and Georgia (Thomas 2001). Although the
origin of this variant is questionable, it is clearly dissimilar to the lowered
variant that is found in British Cockney and some other varieties of English in
the British Isles. Again, it is possible that either the white community or the
black community could have accommodated this variant either from the other
community or from elsewhere in the Caribbean.

Finally, like /o/, the white speakers of Cherokee Sound do not lower the
nucleus of /e/ in the way that is usually found in the South and in some regions
of England. Instead, the speakers of both Cherokee Sound and Sandy Point
realize /e/ as [ei], as found in AAE and many non-Southern regions of the US.
This represents a significant departure from white Southern American English
varieties as well as from British varieties and other Caribbean varieties. This
variant suggests the strongest case for accommodation; none of the white
varieties that are typically cited as possible sources for white Bahamian speech
contain this variant. This realization, along with those previously mentioned,
suggest the very real possibility for accommodation to black vernacular norms
with respect to some of the less salient phonological features by the white
enclave community.

Although it is impossible to arrive at definitive solutions about vowel
systems based solely on several speakers in each community, there are variants
that are clearly different between the communities. At the same time, there is
evidence for accommodation to black Bahamian norms, some of which resemble AAE, by speakers in a white enclave community. Other features not
described here, such as intonation and other prosodic features, may yet prove
to be the biggest determiners between these two dialects, but this analysis
indicates that there is at least some division based on vowel production.

In Table 5, we compare some of the variants of Cherokee Sound English
and Sandy Point English with other varieties of English. The inventory includes
Cockney English, which has often been cited as having a significant influence
on Bahamian English (Wells 1982) and some American English and Caribbean
varieties. Although it is premature to draw definite conclusions about the role
these dialect forms may have played in shaping the dialects of the Bahamas,
some variants do suggest the possibility of a historical affinity to some of the
varieties that were brought to the Bahamas and influenced Bahamian speech
following the American Revolutionary War. The chart relies heavily on the
profiles of vowels found in Thomas (2001), Patrick (1996), Wells (1982), and
McDavid (1955).

Table 5. Cross-dialectal comparison of diagnostic vowel variants

	Cherokee Sound	Sandy Point	Southern White English	African American	White Low South Car.	British Cockney	Other Caribbean	Pamlico Sound
/au/	[aö~aɛ]	[aɔ~ɑɔ]	[æɔ]	[aɔ~ɑɔ]	[ʌu~ao]	[æʊ~a:]	[ɔu~ʌu]	[aö~aɛ]
/u/	[ʉ:]	[u:]	[ü]	[u:]	[ʉ:]	[ʉ:]	[u:]	[ü]
/o/	[eü]	[ou]	[ou~ȝü]	[ou]	[o:~uə]	[æü~ʌu]	[o:~uə]	[ȝu]
/aiᵒ/	[ɑi]	[ai~ɑi]	[ai]	[ai]	[ʋi~əi]	[ɒi]	[æi]	[ɑi~ɒi]
/aiᵛ/	[ɑi~ɑɛ]	[a:~aæ]	[a:~aæ]	[a:~aæ]	[ai]	[ɒi]	[æi]	[ɑi~ɒi]
/æ/	[a~æ]	[a~æ]	[æ̂~æ]	[ɛ]	[æ~a]	[ɛ]	[a]	[æ]
/ɑ/	[ɑ]	[ɑ]	[ɑ]	[ɑ]	[ɑ~ɒ]	[ɒ]	[a]	[ɑ]
/ɔ/	[ɔ:]	[ɔ:]	[ɔo~ɑɒ]	[ɔ:~ɑɒ]	[ɔ:]	[o:]	[a:~ɔ:]	[ɔ:]
/ʌ/	[ɔ]	[ɔ]	[ʌ~ɔ]	[ʌ~ɔ]	[ʌ~ɔ]	[ɑ]	[ɔ]	[ʌ]
/e/	[ei]	[ei]	[ɛi~æi]	[ei]	[e:~iə]	[ai~ʌi]	[e:~iə]	[ɛi]

Several observations may be made on the basis of Table 5. In an important sense, there are both similarities to and differences from each of the comparative varieties. On one level, Cherokee Sound and Sandy Point share many features that unite them as well as set them apart from other varieties included in the comparison. There are some affinities between Pamlico Sound English in North Carolina and Cherokee Sound English, such as front-glided /au/, monophthongal [ɔ], and fronted /o/ and /u/, but there are also some important differences, such as the variants for [æ]. Cherokee Sound and Sandy Point unite in some of the distinctive vowel productions that set them apart from other varieties, but they also show some divergence from each other, such as whether the /au/ glide is fronted, whether /u/ and /o/ are fronted, and whether the glide of /ai/ is weakened before voiced consonants. We thus see ethnolinguistic diversity at the same time that we see accommodation.

Conclusions

Though still preliminary, our investigation reveals that the white enclave community of Cherokee Sound has been influenced by widespread Bahamian phonological norms while maintaining its dialectal distinctiveness. At the same time, black Bahamians have been influenced by some features that were probably derived from Anglo founder dialects, such as *h*- dropping and *w/v* alternation. Notwithstanding the dynamics of bilateral accommodation historically and currently, there appears to have been, and continues to be, a constant ethnic divide between the communities with reference to salient features such as *h*- dropping, *w/v* alternation, less salient productions such as CCR, and a variety of salient and subtle vowel productions. Although we cannot be certain of the extent of the historical language contact situation involving these distant but neighboring communities, it is clear that ethnolinguistic distinctiveness exists in their phonologies despite substantive overlap.[6] Some of the differences are qualitative, some quantitative, and some combine qualitative and quantitative parameters.

At this point, we obviously do not have all the answers to the question of founder influence, language contact, language diffusion, and independent language change that have molded the dialects of the Bahamas, and we have even fewer answers with respect to enclave communities of white and black Bahamians living on the out-islands. However, it seems clear that there has been mutual influence that reflects changing demographic profiles, shifting social dynamics, and, perhaps most significantly, a persistent ethnolinguistic divide. Isolated out-island communities of Abaco such as Cherokee and Sandy Point demonstrate this complicated dynamic as transparently as any other situation in the Bahamas, the Caribbean, or elsewhere around the world.

Notes

* Research reported here was funded by the National Science Foundation, BCS 99–10224, and by the William C. Friday Endowment at North Carolina State University. The assistance of Jason Sellers, Benjamin Torbert, Amy Caison, Elaine Green, and Marvin Hunt in the collection of data is gratefully acknowledged. Thanks also to Erik Thomas for his assistance with the acoustic analysis and to Jason Sellers (1999) for the sociolinguistic description of Cherokee Sound that guided this study.

1. Some of these questions are addressed for Anguillan society by Williams, this volume.

2. An alternative explanation involves a compound noun derived from *cherry+key* and a respelling. Many of the out island settlements are known as *cays* (e.g. Green Turtle Cay, Great Guana Cay), which is actually pronounced the same as "key." Thus, some conclude that perhaps Cherokee Sound was once Cherry Cay until an orthographic switch led to the fused form Cherokee. Although this hypothesis is not popular among residents we have interviewed, it should be noted that there are, in fact, trees locally called cherry trees at the settlement.

3. Although Cherokee Sound only received access to public electricity in 1994, most individual homes used diesel generators before that time.

4. Our use of the term "Anglo varieties" refers to non-black varieties of English in the Bahamas. Further, the terms locally used for distinguishing the varieties vary between the

communities. In Sandy Point, the local Afro-Caribbean population refers to itself as "Bahamian" and the Cherokee Sound population as "Conchy Joes" whereas the Cherokee Sound population refers to itself as "white" and the Sandy Point residents as "black" or "colored."

5. Thomas (2001) notes that it is common in AAE and Coastal Plain Southern White varieties in the US.

6. Some of the black residents who left Cherokee Sound in the 1940s settled in Sandy Point so there is a historical connection between the communities even if there is little regular contact between the communities.

The grammatical features
of TMA auxiliaries in Bahamian Creole

Helean McPhee
The University of the West Indies, Mona

1.   Introduction

Bahamian is a Caribbean English-lexicon Creole[1] spoken in the Bahamas, an archipelago just southeast of Florida and north of the Greater Antilles. In comparison to other Caribbean Creoles such as Jamaican and Guyanese, Bahamian is under-researched. While some comparative research has been done on TMA auxiliaries in Bahamian and other Caribbean creoles, as far as I am aware no existing works focus on the grammatical properties of these elements in Bahamian except for Hackert (2001). This paper, though limited in scope is intended to provide some insight into the grammatical features of TMA auxiliaries in Bahamian.

Tense, mood and aspect auxiliaries are preverbal elements that are said to play a decisive role in determining creole status (Schneider 1990: 90). According to Comrie (1976: 1–2), "Tense relates the time of the situation referred to to some other time, usually the moment of speaking." Creole languages are said to have relative tense systems. That is, the reference point is the time of the event under discussion and not the time of the utterance (Holm 1988: 151). According to Givón (1984: 272), modality encompasses notions of reality. That is, the possibility, acceptability, necessity or desirability of an event or state. Aspect is a way of "viewing the internal temporal consistency of a situation" (Comrie 1976: 3). Aspect may be habitual, completive, or progressive for example. While most introductory texts on Creole languages present the invariant TMA order for preverbal auxiliaries in Creoles, Alleyne (1980) and Gibson (1986) posit the order MTA, which is more commonly associated with non-Creoles according to Bakker et al. (1995: 248). In this paper, I will take into account semantic and syntactic evidence in assessing the classification of the various TMA auxiliaries in Bahamian.

In Sections 2, 3 and 4, I discuss grammatical properties of TMA auxiliaries in Bahamian in some detail. In Section 2, I discuss the status of *bi:n, dɪd, wʌz,* and *gə* as tense auxiliaries. In Section 3, I examine the syntactic distribution of various types of modals. In Section 4, I discuss the use of *da/a, dʌz, ju:stə, dʌn,* and V-*ɪn* as aspect auxiliaries. This paper refers to some aspects of the Minimalist approach to syntax (Radford 1997). The main assumptions of this approach relevant to this paper are that distributional facts provide insight into the subcategorization of elements, and that strong affixes trigger movement of lexical material to satisfy structural requirements.

2.   The issue of tense in Bahamian

2.1   The status of *bi:n* and *dɪd* as tense auxiliaries

According to Holm (1982: ix), *bi:n* and *dɪd* are preverbal markers that indicate anterior tense, the former used by older Bahamians and the latter by younger Bahamians. This, I contend is not entirely accurate. The markers *bi:n* and *dɪd* are both used in simple past and anterior contexts (see examples below) and, as a young native speaker of Bahamian, I am aware that *bi:n* is used by younger speakers as well.

(1)   aɪ **dɪd** fi:l so: gʊd (LM. A.1999: 7)
       "I felt so good."

(2)   baɪ də taɪm i: ri:tʃ də bʌs **dɪd** li:v
       "By the time he arrived, the bus had left."

(3)   wɪn wi: **bi:n** kʌmɪn ju: dɪn wɔ:ŋ wɔ:k (LP. A.1998: 38)
       "When we were coming, you did not want to walk."

(4)   bi:fɔ wi: gɛt hu:m de: **bi:n** sli:p
       "Before we got home, they had been asleep."

In Bahamian, *bi:n* or *dɪd* may be used to indicate a point in time prior to that of the speaker's psychological reference point. *Bi:n, dɪd,* and *wʌz* signal to the listener that the speaker's psychological reference point is the time of speech.

2.1.1   *The syntax of biːn and dɪd*

Here, I examine the syntactic distribution of *biːn* and *dɪd*, paying particular attention to the occurrence of each with verbs, TMA auxiliaries, and negative markers.

2.1.1.1 *Biːn or dɪd immediately preceding verbs*

Biːn or *dɪd* may immediately precede the main Verb of a matrix clause. Note that the verbal complement of *biːn* or *dɪd* may be inflected (V-*ɪn*) or uninflected.

(5) a.   ʃiː **biːn** tɛl juː dat eː (MD. A.1998: 30)
"She told you that, did she?"

b.   wiː **dɪd** laɪk skuːl (AM.CaI.1999: 7)
"We liked school."

(6) a.   ʃiː **biːn** wʌɪkɪn dɛ fə jɛːz (LP. A.1999: 31)
"She has been working there for years."

b.   ʃiː **dɪd** lʊkɪn fə sʌm stʃrɔː wʌɪk (MD. A.1998: 24)
"She was looking for some straw work."

In addition to Verbal Predicates, *biːn* may immediately precede Noun Phrase Predicates, Locative Predicates, and Adjectival Predicates in Bahamian. *Dɪd* may only precede Locative Predicates, Adjectival Predicates, and Verbal Predicates.

2.1.1.2 *The co-occurrence of biːn and dɪd*

It is widely accepted that *dɪd* is the mesolectal equivalent of *bin* in Caribbean Creoles (Bickerton 1975: 70, Alleyne 1980: 183). Semantically, *biːn* or *dɪd* may indicate a point in time prior to that of the speaker's psychological reference point in Bahamian. However, the co-occurrence of *dɪd* and *biːn* suggests that they do not have the same status at the syntactic level, and that they may in fact occupy different positions in a syntactic tree, at least in some instances. *Dɪd* always precedes *biːn* when the two co-occur.

(7) hiː dɪd biːn wɔʃɪn də kaː wɪn aɪ gɛt dɛ
"He had been washing the car when I got there."

While a number of linguists propose the possibility of co-occurring modals (Bailey 1966: 65) and co-occurring aspect auxiliaries (Gibson 1986: 571), even fewer propose co-occurring tense auxiliaries. Alleyne (1980: 86) posits that in Afro-American dialects, a combination of the "past and future particles" expresses conditional mood. Arguably, the combination to which Alleyne (1980: 86) refers is past marker plus modal (Section 2.2). Note the examples below.

(8)   deː dɪd fɪks də geːt
      "They fixed the gate/they had fixed the gate."

(9)   deː dɪd biːn fɪks də geːt
      "They {came/ went} and fixed the gate/they had been {here/ there} and
      fixed the gate."

The difference in meaning between *dɪd* + uninflected V and *dɪd biːn* +
uninflected V is not one of time. Both examples may be interpreted as simple
past or anterior, depending on context. When *biːn* is inserted in (9), it conveys
the idea of movement from one location to another. This suggests that *biːn* may
function as a verb of motion.

     There is evidence to support the idea that *biːn* may function as a verb in
Bahamian. Note the following examples.

(10)   deː biːn yɛstədeː
       "They went yesterday."

(11)   iː biːn an kɔɪl iː maː
       "She went and called her mother."

It is generally accepted that only lexical items of the same grammatical category
may be conjoined within a clause. In example (11), *biːn* is conjoined with the
verb *kɔːl*, indicating that *biːn* is a verb.

     If in accordance with generative grammar we assume that tense is located
in the head position of TP (Radford 1997: 225), and seek to present the most
economical way of accounting for the example below, the following tree
structure may be postulated. *Dɪd* is the element that appears in Tense in
Diagram 1 below.

(12)   deː dɪd biːn fɪks də geːt
       "They had been (here) and fixed the gate."

Diagram 1

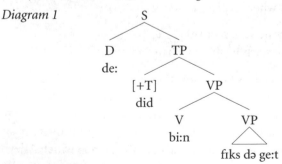

(S = Sentence², TP =Tense Phrase, AP = Aspect Phrase)

2.1.1.3 *The co-occurrence of bi:n and dɪd with modals³*

Bi:n may co-occur with the modals *mʌsi:, mʌs, maɪtɔ, kudə, wudə* and *ʃudə*. With the exception of *mʌsi:,* which may precede or follow *bi:n,* all other co-occurring modals precede *bi:n.* The only modals with which *dɪd* co-occurs are *mʌsi:, gə* and *haftə. Gə* and *haftə* precede *dɪd,* and *mʌsi:* may precede or follow *dɪd.* It is important to note that with the exception of *mʌsi:* which may precede or follow *bi:n* and *dɪd,* the modals that co-occur with *bi:n* precede it, while those that co-occur with *dɪd* follow. Excluding *mʌsi:,* modals precede *bi:n* producing MT ordering, and modals follow *dɪd,* producing TM ordering.

2.1.1.4 *The co-occurrence of bi:n and dɪd with aspect auxiliaries*

Bi:n or *dɪd* may co-occur with any aspect auxiliary excluding *dʌz.* However, there are differences in the syntactic distribution of *bi:n* and *dɪd* with aspect auxiliaries. *(D)a* is the only aspect auxiliary that follows *bi:n* and *dɪd.*

(13)   aɪŋ bi:n a gɛt nʌʔn (AM.CaI.1999: 7)
       "I was not getting anything."

(14)   aɪ du:ŋ no: wɛdə di: gʌvnə **dɪd** a pe: mi: o: wɛdə hi: **dɪd** a pe: mi:
       (AM.CaI.1999: 17)
       "I don't know whether the government {was paying/ used to pay} me or he {was paying/ used to pay} me."

When *bi:n* co-occurs with *ju:stə* or *dʌn, bi:n* must follow.

(15)   ʃi: ju:stə **bi:n** wʌɪkɪn ɔːl di taɪm
       "She used to be working all the time."

(16)   ʃi: dʌn **bi:n** kɔːl ʌm
       "She has already been (there) and called them."

When *dɪd* co-occurs with *ju:stə* or *dʌn, dɪd* must precede.

(17)   no: ju: **dɪd** dʌn lɛf (AM.CaI.1999: 7)
       "No, you had already left."

(18)   de: had wʌn ple:s re:t də **dɪd** ju:stə du: tʃɪkɪn (MD. A.1998: 36)
       "There was a place right there that used to do (prepare) chicken."

It is important to note that with the exception of *(d)a* which follows *bi:n* and *dɪd,* the aspect auxiliaries that co-occur with *bi:n* precede it, while those that co-occur with *dɪd* follow. Excluding *(d)a,* aspect auxiliaries precede *bi:n* exemplifying AT ordering, and aspect auxiliaries follow *dɪd,* exemplifying TA ordering.

When *dɪd bi:n* and *dʌn* co-occur, the ordering established above is maintained. The aspect auxiliary *dʌn* follows *dɪd* and precedes *bi:n.*

(19) hiː dɪd dʌn biːn kʊk wɪn aɪ gɛt huːm
      "He had already been {here/there} and cooked when I got home."

Diagram 2

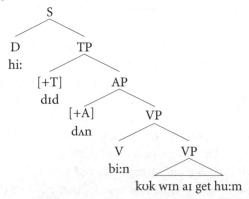

(S = Sentence, TP =Tense Phrase, AP = Aspect Phrase)

Whether one argues for TMA ordering or MTA ordering, the aspect auxiliary is assumed to be nearest to the verb. If one proposes that *biːn* is operating as a tense marker in the example above, one then has to account for the fact that the aspect auxiliary *dʌn* moves to a higher aspectual node with strong aspectual features, by passing the tense marker *biːn*, but for some reason not by-passing the tense marker *dɪd*. On the other hand, if one proposes that *biːn* is a verb in this instance, there is no movement.

2.1.2.5 *Biːn, dɪd, and negation*
A final bit of evidence for a difference in the syntactic classification of *biːn* and *dɪd* comes from their co-occurrence with negative auxiliaries. There are two observed orders for negation and other preverbal material in Bahamian.

(20)   i.   Aux – Neg V   (Neg is a suffix – *n*)
       ii. Neg Aux – V   (Neg is a full form *iː ~ɛːnt; na/noː*)

Dɪd and *biːn* behave differently in negative utterances. Unlike *biːn*, *dɪd* is negated with the suffixed form, -*n*.

(21)   diː tʌɪl dɪdn dʒraɪ an iː slɪp daʊŋ (LB.CrI.1999: 6)
       "The tile was not dry and she slipped."

Biːn can only be negated by the preceding free morpheme such as *na/ noː* or *ɛːnt* often realized as *iː* in Bahamian.

(22) deɪ iː biɪn lɛ də chɪlən haw dɪɪ um wɪɪ (LP. A.1990. 10)
      "They did not let the children have their own way."

Concluding, *dɪd* and *biːn* appear in different positions in the syntactic structure
arguably reflecting their different functions.

Since negation is preverbal in Bahamian, and also precedes many TMA
auxiliaries, it is reasonable to assume the following tree structure for negative
sentences. Here, NegP is assumed to dominate all other preverbal material.

Diagram 3

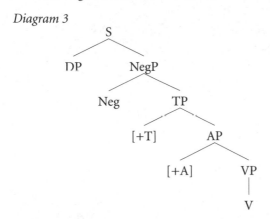

In the minimalist approach to syntax, it is proposed that strong features trigger
movement (Radford, 1997: 108). Thus, one may propose that in Bahamian the
strong negation affix triggers movement. When available, an element in [+T]
moves to Neg to fulfill this requirement; this type of movement constitutes
head to head movement. For example, in negating *hiː dɪdn siːŋ*, *dɪd* may be said
to move upward to a local head in order to satisfy the requirement of the strong
negation affix.

(23) hiː **dɪd**n siːŋ   "He did not sing."
      Diagram 4

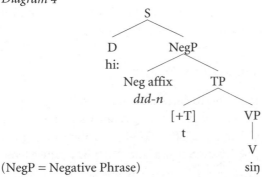

(NegP = Negative Phrase)

On the other hand, a negative utterance which does not include *dɪd* uses the full negative form *íː* or *na/ noː* which appears as the head of NegP as no element is available for attraction into Neg. Note that when preverbal *bɪːn* occurs, there is no movement since the full negative form precedes it.

(24)   juː íː **bɪːn** wɔːŋ wɔːk tə hɛlp miː (LP. A.1998: 38)
        "You did not want to walk to help me."
        Diagram 5

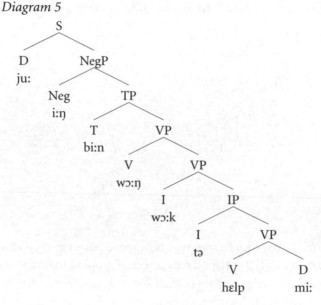

(NegP = Negative Phrase, IP = Infinitive Phrase)

Semantically, *bɪːn* and *dɪd* may be classified as tense auxiliaries. However, upon closer examination, the syntactic distribution of *bɪːn* differs from that of *dɪd*. *Bɪːn* precedes all predicate types, precedes some Modals and follows Tense, Aspect, and negative auxiliaries with which it co-occurs. On the other hand, *dɪd* precedes all predicate types with the exception of Noun Phrase Predicates, and precedes all TMA auxiliaries with which it co-occurs.

2.2   The status of *wʌz* and *gə* as tense markers

Wʌz and *gə* in Bahamian are said to carry anterior tense (Holm 1982: ix) and future tense respectively (Hancock 1987: 290). While most linguists agree that *wʌz* indicates past time, the status of *gə* in the Caribbean English-lexicon Creoles remains a subject of debate. Some argue that *gə* is a future tense marker

(Winford 1993: 57, Gibson 1986: 575), and others, that *gə* is an irrealis modal (Bickerton 1975: 42). In fact, there is a relationship between future tense and irrealis mood. This relationship has been noted by Lyons (1977: 816), Givón (1984: 285) and Heine et al. (1991: 170–1), for languages of the world. Bahamian is no exception. The relationship between the Verb *go:* "go," the Modal *gə* and the "Future" Marker *gə* in Bahamian, requires examination.

2.2.1   *The semantics of gə*

In the examples below, I identify the meaning of *gə*. The pair of sentences is identical except for the presence or absence of *gə*. Note the difference in interpretation.

(25)   a.   aɪ kɔːl ʌm
            "I called her."
       b.   aɪ gə kɔːl ʌm
            "I will call her."

In example (a), the bare verb expresses a state resulting from completion of an event, at the time of speech. However, when *gə* is inserted in example (b), it is perceived that there is a change in the speaker's attitude toward the reality of the event. The event is perceived to be an expectation of the speaker, and unrealized at the time of speech.

Another bit of evidence in support of the fact that *gə* functions as an irrealis modal, is its use in past contexts. In the example below, it is clear that the informant is referring to a past time, since the subject of the conversation (*iy* "he") has been dead for many years prior to the time of speech. *Gə* expresses the informant's expectation at a past time.

(26)   az lɔːŋ az iː biːn dɛ a wʊz gə duː də seːm biːkʊz a wʊz gɛʔn də moniː dɛn
       (AB.CrI.1999: 59)
       "As long as he was there I would have done the same because I was getting the money then."

In decontextualized utterances and in context, *gə* indicates that an event or state is unrealized, and is expected to take place at a time subsequent to that of the speaker's psychological reference point.

2.2.2   *The syntax of gə*

While *biːn gə* is attested in other Caribbean English-lexicon creoles (Winford 1993: 89), there is no evidence of this combination in the Bahamian data. As a native speaker of Bahamian, I am unaware of such a combination. However, the combinations *dɪd gə* and *wʌz gə* are attested in Bahamian.

(27)   an aɪ tɛl dɛm di dʒriːm aɪ had an deː tɛl miː wʌ dɪd **gə** hapʊn
(Donnelly 1996: 14)
"And I told them the dream I had and they told me what would happen."

(28)   hiː wʌz **gə** kʌm ʌiliːə
"He would have come earlier."

With the exception of *mʌsiː*, which may precede or follow *gə*, *haftə* is the only other semantic modal with which *gə* may co-occur. When *haftə* co-occurs with *gə*, *haftə* must follow *gə*.

(29)   deː mʌsiː **gə** kʌm tʊmɔːrə
"They probably will come tomorrow."

(30)   deː **gə** mʌsiː kʌm tʊmɔːrə
"They will probably come tomorrow (or some other time)."

(31)   deː **gə** haftə kʌm tʊmɔːrə
"They will have to come tomorrow."

The only aspect auxiliary with which *gə* may co-occur is *dʌn*.

(32)   deː **gə** dʌn fɪnɪʃ baɪ də taɪm juː gɛt dɛ
"They will already be finished, by the time I get there/they will have already finished, by the time you get there."

The negative marker must precede *gə*, when it negates the unrealized event marked by *gə*.

(33)   noːbɔdiː na **gə** breːk It oːpm (LB.CrI.1999: 10)
"Nobody will break it open."

(34)   dẽː **gə** siː dat (LB.CrI.1999: 9)
"They will not see that."

In Bahamian, *gə* is a semantic modal that marks an unrealized event or state that is expected to come into being at a time subsequent to the speaker's psychological reference point. Like all modals (with the exception of *mʌsiː*), *gə* may only be followed by verbal predicates.

2.2.3   The syntax of *wʌz*

Like *biːn* and *dɪd*, *wʌz* indicates a point in time prior to that of the speaker's psychological reference point and it may take a verbal complement. However, unlike these two markers, ~~was requires~~ an inflected verbal complement.

(35) ʃi **wʌz** kʊkɪn wɪn a kɔ:l
      "She was cooking when I called."

We have already seen that *wʌz* may co-occur with *gə* (Example 28). The only modal auxiliary that may co-occur with *wʌz* is *mʌsi:*, and *mʌsi:* may precede or follow *wʌz*.

(36) a. i: mʌsi: **wʌz** taɪjʊd
          "She probably was tired."
      b. i: **wʌz** mʌsi: taɪjʊd
          "She was probably tired (or experiencing some other feeling)."

The only aspect auxiliary with which *wʌz* may co-occur is *dʌn*. *Dʌn* follows *wʌz* when they co-occur.

(37) de: **wʌz** dʌn fɪnɪʃ wɪn aɪ gɛt dɛ
      "They were already finished when I got there."

Although the syntactic distribution of *wʌz* is not identical to *bi:n* or *dɪd*, it is similar to *bi:n* in some respects and similar to *dɪd* in others. For example, like *bi:n*, *wʌz* may take an adverbial complement and like *dɪd*, *wʌz* takes a negative clitic.

(38) de: **wʌz** hjʌ ɔ:l wi:k
      "They were here all week."

Negation provides evidence that *wʌz* behaves similar to the tense marker *dɪd*. In the following example, the negative clitic may be attached to *wʌz*, suggesting that *wʌz* occupies [+T] and *gə* [+M].

(39) a. hi: **wʌz** gə kʊm
          "He would have come."
      b. hi: **wʌzn** gə kʊm
          "He would not have come."

3. Modal auxiliaries in Bahamian

3.1 Introduction

Most modal auxiliaries in Bahamian are apparently derived from the English lexifier. However, these derivatives do not always have the same meaning as their

English sources. For example, the forms *kʊdə* and *ʃʊdə* may not always be glossed as "could have," and "should have," if accurate translations are to be presented.

(40)   frʌm iː **kʊd** gɛt tə wʌk, iːz wʌk ɪn haʊs (LP. A.1998: 60) [Ability]
"From she was able to work, she worked in houses."

(41)   deː **ʃʊdə** gɛt ə gʌvnə mɪl hjʌ (AB.CrI.1999: 17) [Necessity]
"They should place a government mill here."

A close examination of the distribution of what are traditionally classified as modals in Bahamian reveals that they may be subdivided on the basis of syntactic distribution. Let us take, for example, the modal *mʌsiː*. Like other modals, *mʌsiː* expresses a speaker's notion of reality about an event or state. However, a close syntactic examination of *mʌsiː* reveals that it is distinct from all other modals in Bahamian.

3.2   The status of *mʌsiː*

3.2.1   *The semantics of **mʌsiː***
The sentences below are identical except for the presence or absence of *mʌsiː*. Note the difference in interpretation.

(42)   a.   deː kʌm
"They came."
    b.   deː **mʌsiː** kʌm
"They probably came."

In example (a), the verb expresses a state resulting from completion of an event at the time of speech. However, when *mʌsiː* is inserted in example (b), there is perceived to be a change in the speaker's attitude toward the reality of the event. The event is perceived to be a probability. Semantically, *mʌsiː* also expresses probability in context.

3.2.2   *The syntax of **mʌsiː***
In Bahamian, *mʌsiː* may co-occur with any TMA auxiliary. *Mʌsiː* displays different syntactic behavior from all other modals.

3.2.2.1   *Mʌsiː and tense auxiliaries*
Mʌsiː is the only semantic modal that may either precede or follow the tense elements *biːn*, *dɪd*, and *wʌz*. It should also be noted that *mʌsiː* is the only semantic modal that may precede the undisputed tense auxiliary, *dɪd*.

(43) a. dɛɪ mʌsiː bɪn fɪʃɪnn
          "They probably went fishing."
      b. deː biːn mʌsiː fɪʃnɪn ɔː daɪvɪn
          "They probably went fishing or diving."

(44) a. deː mʌsiː dɪd aftə hɪm ɪniː haʊ (QM.CrI.1999: 6)
          "They probably were chasing him anyhow."
      b. deː dɪd mʌsiː aftə hɪm
          "They were probably chasing him (or doing something else)."

(45) a. iː mʌsiː wʌz aʊtsaɪd wɪn aɪ kɔːl
          "She probably was outside when I called."
      b. iː wʌz mʌsiː aʊtsaɪd wɪn aɪ kɔːl
          "She probably was outside (or elsewhere) when I called."

The English translations provided show that while *mʌsiː* may immediately precede or follow a tense auxiliary, there is a difference in meaning based on its position. When *mʌsiː* precedes a tense auxiliary as in each example (a), it is perceived that the proposition is probable. When *mʌsiː* follows the tense auxiliary and immediately precedes the predicate, it is perceived that the predicate is probable.

3.2.2.2 *Mʌsiː and modal auxiliaries*
In Bahamian, *mʌsiː* may immediately precede or follow all other modals. Some examples are presented below.

(46) a. ʃiː mʌsiː maɪt kʌm tʊmɔːrə
          "She probably may come tomorrow."
      b. ʃiː maɪt mʌsiː kʌm tʊmɔːrə
          "She may probably come tomorrow (or at some other time)."

(47) a. deː mʌsiː kjan fɪks ɪt
          "They probably can fix it."
      b. deː kjan mʌsiː fɪks ɪt
          "They can probably fix it (or do something else)."

(48) a. deː mʌsiː kʊdə fɪks ɪt
          "They probably could have fixed it."
      b. deː kʊdə mʌsiː fɪks ɪt
          "They could have probably fixed it (or do something else)."

(49) a. a mʌsiː gə kʊk leːt sʌpə (HP.CrI.1999: 35)
          "I probably will cook a late supper."

     b.   a gə **mʌsiː** kʊk leɪt sʌpə
         "I will probably cook a late supper (or do something else)."

(50) a.   deː **mʌsiː** ʃʊdə fɪks ɪt
         "They probably should have fixed it."

     b.   deː ʃʊdə **mʌsiː** fɪks ɪt
         "They should have probably fixed it (or do something else)."

(51) a.   deː **mʌsiː** haftə fɪks ɪt
         "They probably have to fix it."

     b.   deː haftə **mʌsiː** fɪks ɪt
         "They have to probably fix it (or do something else)."

In Bahamian, there are two distinct modal positions. A semantic modal may occupy only one of these two modal positions. For example, *maɪt* may only occupy the first modal position, and *kjan* may only occupy the second modal position in Bahamian. Hence, *maɪt kjan* is acceptable in Bahamian, and *kjan maɪt* is not. The fact that *mʌsiː* may precede or follow all types of modals, whether they occupy the first or second modal position indicates that its syntactic distribution is not like that of other modals in Bahamian.

3.2.2.3 *Mʌsiː and aspect auxiliaries*
Mʌsiː may precede or follow all aspect auxiliaries.

(52) a.   iː **mʌsiː** a wʌɪk
         "He is probably working."

     b.   iː a wʌɪk **mʌsiː**
         "He is working probably."

When *mʌsiː* follows (*d*)*a*, it must also follow the complement of (*d*)*a*, as shown in example (b) above.

    Mʌsiː may immediately precede or follow the aspect auxiliaries *dʌz, juːstə* and *dʌn*.

(53) a.   deː **mʌsiː** {dʌz/ juːstə} goː dɛ ɛriː deː
         They probably {go/used to go} there every day."

     b.   deː {dʌz/ juːstə} **mʌsiː** goː dɛ ɛriː deː
         "They {go/ used to go}there probably every day (or with more or less frequency)."

(54) a.   hiː **mʌsiː** dʌn tʃroː dat əweː
         "He probably already threw that away."

b.   hiː dʌn **mʌsiː** tʃroː dat ǝwḛ
     "He already probably threw that away (or did something else with it)."

The English translations provided show that while *mʌsiː* may immediately precede or follow an aspect auxiliary, there is a difference in meaning based on its position. When *mʌsiː* precedes an aspect auxiliary as in each example (a), it is perceived that the proposition is probable. When *mʌsiː* follows the aspect auxiliary, it is perceived that the predicate is probable.

With the exception of *mʌsiː*, a given semantic modal either precedes or follows a given aspect auxiliary. *Mʌsiː* is the only semantic modal that may immediately precede or follow most aspect auxiliaries. (D)*a* is in fact the only aspect auxiliary that may not be immediately followed by *mʌsiː*.

3.2.2.4 *Mʌsiː and Negative markers*
When *mʌsiː* co-occurs with *na* and *iː*, *mʌsiː* must precede them. However, when the negative morpheme is suffixed to a modal or aspect auxiliary, *mʌsiː* may follow or precede the negative modal or aspect auxiliary.

(55)   hiː **mʌsiː** {na/ iː} fɪks ɪt yɛt
         "He probably has not fixed it yet."

(56) a.   hiː **mʌsiː** kʊdn kʌm
           "He probably could not come."
      b.   hiː kʊdn **mʌsiː** kʌm
           "He probably could not come (or could not do something else)."

(57) a.   hiː **mʌsiː** duːŋ kʌm ʌɪliː iːnʌf
           "He probably does not come early enough."
      b.   hiː duːŋ **mʌsiː** kʌm ʌɪliː iːnʌf
           "He probably does not come early enough (or does not do something else)."

While semantically, *mʌsiː* comments on the reality of an event or state, its peculiar syntactic distribution brings into question its modal status. In fact, the syntactic distribution of *mʌsiː* is comparable with that of an adverb. It should be noted that like adverbs, *mʌsiː* may also precede or follow the sentence in Bahamian.

(58) a.   **mʌsiː** ɛdiː muːv ɪt
           "Probably Eddie (was the person who) moved it."
      b.   ɛdiː muːv ɪt **mʌsiː**
           "Eddie moved it, probably."

When *mʌsɪ̈* precedes the subject of a sentence in Bahamian, it is the subject alone that is perceived to be in question. When *mʌsɪ̈* follows the sentence the proposition is perceived to be probable.

4.   Aspect auxiliaries

4.1   Progressive *da/a*

According to Holm (1982: ix), the progressive markers in Bahamian are *da/a* V for older speakers and *V-ɪn* for younger speakers. Donnelly (1996: 13) documents use of the progressive *da* V, but describes it as "rare." Recent fieldwork on Bahamian suggests limited use of the progressive forms *da* and *a* in comparison to *V-ɪn*, among speakers. *Da/a* tends to take uninflected verbal complements for the most part, though there are rare instances of their co-occurrence with *V-ɪn* forms.

(59)   dɛm hʌɪʃn **da** rʌn frʌm hʌɪtiː, bʊt dẽː noː wʊt kjat aɪlən piːpʊl paːs tʃruː
      (AM.CaI.1999: 32) — progressive
      "These Haitians are running from Haiti, but they do not know what Cat Island people have gone through."

(60)   ɪniː taɪm jə paːs hjʌ jə kʊd heː miː **da** tʃap (AB.CrI.1999g 14) — iterative
      "Any time you pass here, you can hear me chopping."

(61)   wɪn mə brʌdə dʌz kʌm hjʌ a da fiːl gʊd jə noː (AB.CrI.1999: 84) — habitual
      "When my brother used to come here, I used to feel good."

The examples above illustrate that the form *da* is used to mark progressive, habitual, and iterative aspect in Bahamian. It is not surprising that an identical form, (*d*)*a* is used to express these aspectual meanings which semantically overlap in Bahamian. Use of an identical form to indicate the aforementioned aspects is not peculiar to Bahamian. The form *a* is identified as a marker of habitual, imperfective and progressive aspects in Jamaican and Guyanese (Christie 1986: 187, Winford 1993: 43).

Holm (1988: 156) identifies *a-V-ɪn* in Bahamian and attributes constructions of this type to influences from archaic and dialectal English. *A* is in fact the only aspect auxiliary that may precede *V-ɪn* in Bahamian.

(62)   jʊ kʊd kiːp **a** iːtɪn dat (AB.CI.1999: 46)
      "You can keep eating that."

4.2 The progressive form, -ɪn

The progressive form, -ɪn is suffixed to verbs and may occur with or without a preceding tense auxiliary, such as biːn, dɪd or wʌz.

(63) hiː wʌɪkɪn fə miː
"He is working for me."

(64) aɪ nɛvə biːn spʌngɪn (MD. A.1998: 18)
"I have never been sponging."

(65) ʃiː dɪd lʊkɪn fə sʌm stʃrɔː wʌɪk (MD. A.1998: 24)
"She was looking for some straw work."

(66) iː wʌz aːksɪn fə juː
"She was asking for you."

The progressive form, -ɪn may not be immediately preceded by any semantic modal except mʌsiː. Some modals may co-occur with V-ɪn only if biːn intervenes. This suggests that biːn acts as some kind of facilitator in such instances.

(67) iː {kʊdə/ʃʊdə/wʊdə/maɪtə} biːn wʌɪkɪn wɪn juː kɔːl
"She {could/should/would/might} have been working when you called."

4.3 Dʌz and juːstə as habitual aspect auxiliaries

Holm (1982: ix) lists "does" dʌz and "is" iz as the habitual markers in Bahamian. Dʌz is said to be used by young and old Bahamians, while iz is said to be used by young Bahamians only. In my estimation, like -əz and in some cases -z, -iz is a phonological variant of dʌz, and is assumed to be so here. I pointed out earlier in Section 4.1, that da is also used to express habitual aspect in Bahamian.

(68) das ɔːl aɪ da iːt (AB.CrI.1999: 47)
"That is all I usually eat."

Holm (1982: ix) proposes that dʌz and juːstə are used in anterior habitual contexts. Unlike juːstə, which is restricted to past contexts, da and dʌz may occur in present and past contexts, as shown in examples below.

(69) dʒɔː da lʊk fə juː biːkʊz iː na nɔː wɪtʃ paːt jʌ de (LB.CrI.1999: 44)
"Joe is looking for you because she does not know where you are."

(70) wɪn mə brʌdə dʌz kʌm hjʌ a dafiːl gʊd jə nɔː (AB.CrI.1999: 84)
"When my brother used to come here, I used to feel good you know."

The syntactic distribution of *dʌz* and *juːstə* is similar in some respects and different in others. Either auxiliary may immediately precede the main V of the matrix clause. While *dɪd* may precede or follow *dʌz* or *juːstə*, the syntactic distribution of *dʌz* and *juːstə* differ with tense auxiliaries and aspectual *dʌn* (Section 4.4.2.3). Unlike *juːstə*, *dʌz* provides no temporal information. *Dʌz* may not co-occur with a tense auxiliary and so utterances in which it is used rely on context for temporal interpretation. On the other hand, *juːstə* may precede *biːn* and follow *dɪd*. When *juːstə* precedes verbal *biːn*, *biːn* must have an inflected verbal complement.

(71)   hiː **juːstə** biːn wʌɪkɪn ɔːl də taɪm
"He used to be working all the time."

(72)   wiː dɪd **juːstə** gɛt wɔːtə frʌm də wɛl
"We used to get water from the well."

4.4   The status of *dʌn*

4.4.1   *The semantics of **dʌn***
The pairs of sentences below are identical except for the presence or absence of *dʌn*. Note the differences in interpretation.

(73)   a.   aɪ fʌgɛt iː neːm
"I forgot his name."
b.   aɪ **dʌn** fʌgɛt iː neːm (QM.CrI.1999: 54)
"I already forgot his name."

(74)   a.   aɪ dʒriːŋk ɪt aʊt
"I drank it (all)."
b.   aɪ **dʌn** dʒriːŋk ɪt aʊt (AB.CrI.1999: 48)
"I already drank it (all)."

In example (73a), the bare stative verb indicates that the state is perceived as prevailing at the time of speech. When *dʌn* is inserted in example (73b), it is perceived that entry into the state is completed and this state of completion is emphasized as being relevant at the time of speech.

In example (74a), the bare non-stative verb expresses a state resulting from completion of an event at the time of speech. When *dʌn* is inserted in example (74b), it is perceived that the state resulting from a completed event is emphasized as being relevant at the time of speech. In Bahamian, *dʌn* is an aspect auxiliary that emphasizes that a state of completion is relevant at the speaker's psychological reference point. *Dʌn* has the same meaning in context.

4.4.2   The syntax of dʌn

In Bahamian, *dʌn* may co-occur with any TMA auxiliary. However, preverbal *dʌn* places certain restrictions on the order in which it may co-occur with certain markers.

4.4.2.1 *Dʌn and tense auxiliaries*
Dʌn must precede *biːn*, follow *dɪd*, and *dʌn* may follow or precede *wʌz*.

(75)   hiː **dʌn** biːn muːv ɪt
         "He has already moved it/he has already been (there) and moved it."

(76)   noː juː dɪd **dʌn** lɛf (AM.CaI.1999: 7)
         "No, you had already left."

(77)   hiː wʌz **dʌn** fɪnɪʃ
         "He was already finished."

(78)   hiː **dʌn** wʌz fɪnɪʃ
         "He already was finished."

Like *juːstə*, *dʌn* must precede *biːn* and follow *dɪd*. On the other hand, unlike all other aspect auxiliaries, *dʌn* may co-occur with many modal auxiliaries. *Dʌn* precedes *haftə*, *kjan*, and *kʊd*, and follows all other modal auxiliaries.

4.4.2.2 *Dʌn and modal auxiliaries*
Dʌn may co-occur with all modals.

(79)   a.   hiː **dʌn** {haftə/gatə} kʊk
               "He already has to cook."
         b.   hiː **dʌn** {kjan/kʊd} kʊk
               "He already can cook/he already knows how to cook."
         c.   aɪ kʊdə **dʌn** fɪnɪʃ
               "I could have already finished."
         d.   aɪ {ʃʊd/ʃʊdə} **dʌn** fɪnɪʃ
               "I should have already finished."
         e.   aɪ {maɪt/maɪtə} **dʌn** fɪnɪʃ
               "I might have already finished."
         f.   aɪ {wʌd/wʌdə} **dʌn** fɪnɪʃ
               "I would already be finished/I would have already finished."

The ability of *dʌn* to precede some modals and follow others indicates that its syntactic distribution is different from that of other aspect auxiliaries in Bahamian.

4.4.2.3 *Dʌn and aspect auxiliaries*

Dʌn may co-occur with the aspect auxiliaries *dʌz* and *juːstə*. This co-occurrence of aspect auxiliaries suggests that *dʌn* does not occupy the same position in a syntactic tree as *dʌz* or *juːstə*. *Dʌn* may precede or follow *dʌz*, but *dʌn* must follow *juːstə*, when they co-occur.

(80) a. iː **dʌn** dʌz kʌm leːt "She already comes late."
     b. iː dʌz **dʌn** kloːzəp baɪ tɛn əklɔːk
         "He usually has already closed up by ten o'clock."

(81)   iː juːstə **dʌn** kliːnəp baɪ də taɪm aɪ gɛt huːm
         "She used to have already cleaned up by the time I got home."

The position of *dʌn* varies depending on the particular tense, modal, or aspect auxiliary with which it co-occurs. When *dʌn* precedes *dʌz* and its complement, *dʌn* modifies the habitual state or event. There is also evidence that *dʌn* may function as a Verb in Bahamian. Note the examples below.

(82) wɛn deː **dʌn** deː goː bak əgɛn (LB.CrI.1999: 30)
      "When they are finished, they go back again."

(83) a de ɪn de tɪl a **dʌn** (AB.CrI.1999: 77)
      "I was there until I was finished."

The verb *dʌn* has the meaning "finish" in Bahamian. Similarity in meaning between the aspect auxiliary *dʌn* and the verb *dʌn* suggests a relationship between the two. Arguably, aspectual *dʌn* is a grammaticalized form of verbal *dʌn*. This relationship requires further examination.

5.   Final remarks

An examination of the grammatical features of Bahamian TMA auxiliaries reveals some of these auxiliaries may be classified differently at the level of semantics and syntax. We have seen that *biːn* or *dɪd* may be used to indicate a point in time prior to that of the speaker's psychological reference point. However, syntactically, *biːn* and *dɪd* are not always interchangeable. Unlike *dɪd*, *biːn* may function as a full verb, and it is perhaps this verbal quality that explains its syntactic distribution with Modal and Aspect auxiliaries, as well as its ability to co-occur with the tense auxiliary, *dɪd*.

Gə may be classified as a modal semantically and syntactically. *Gə* expresses a speaker's expectation of an unrealized event or state to occur at a time subsequent to the speaker's psychological reference point, and its syntactic distribution is comparable with other modals in Bahamian.

We have also seen that *mʌsiː* may be classed as a semantic modal. However, it displays unique syntactic behavior from all other modals, and is more appropriately classified as an adverb at the level of syntax.

Dʌn may function as an aspect auxiliary or as a Verb in Bahamian. Of the aspect auxiliaries in Bahamian, *dʌn* displays peculiar syntactic behavior, combining with tense auxiliaries, modal auxiliaries, and aspect auxiliaries. Arguably, its ability to function as a verb explains its peculiar syntactic distribution.

Notes

* I wish to express gratitude to Silvia Kouwenberg, Mervyn Alleyne, and Hubert Devonish for valuable comments on earlier drafts of this paper. I assume full responsibility for all shortcomings in this paper.

1. The term *creole* is used to refer to varieties of Bahamian other than Standard Bahamian English. I am grateful to the University of the West Indies for sponsorship of fieldwork carried out in Andros, Cat Island, and Crooked Island, Bahamas. Gratitude is also extended to the people of Lowe Sound, Red Bays, Nicholl's Town, San Andros and Mastic Point (Andros), The Bluff, Stephenson, and Bennett's Harbour (Cat Island), Johnny Hill, Colonel Hill, Cabbage Hill, and Church Grove (Crooked Island) who generously provided language data. This data is indicated by references to my personal manuscript. Islands are indicated as follows: Andros (A), Cat Island (CaI) and Crooked Island (CrI). As a native speaker of Bahamian, I have used introspective data to fill data gaps.

2. I have chosen to use the conventional symbol S (Sentence) instead of IP (Inflected Phrase), since inflection is not typical of Creole languages.

3. The following are modals in Bahamian: *mʌsiː, maɪt, maɪtə, kjan, kʊd, kʊdə, mʌs, wʊd, wʊdə, gə, wʊd, wʊdə, haftə,* and *gatə.*

English in the Turks and Caicos Islands

A look at Grand Turk

Cecilia Cutler
New York University

1. Introduction

This chapter presents an overview of the variety of English spoken in the Turks and Caicos Islands in the British West Indies.* No prior linguistic research has been carried out in the Turks and Caicos Islands (TCI) although neighboring varieties in the Bahamas have been described in Holm & Shilling (1982), Holm & Hackert (1996) and others. Holm (1989: 488–89) writes that "[g]eographically — and probably demographically and linguistically — the…TCI forms part of [the Bahamas], but their Creole English has not been studied." We begin with an examination of the historical and sociolinguistic situation in the TCI, highlighting some of the differences between the Turks Islands and the Caicos Islands. The linguistic portion of the paper focuses specifically on the speech of persons living on Grand Turk (referred to from here on as Turks Island English or TIE). Linguistically, there are some important parallels to be made between TIE, other English-derived varieties in the Caribbean, and African American Vernacular English (AAVE).

2. Sociolinguistic situation

The Turks and Caicos Islands (TCI) is a British dependency consisting of some eight major islands and more than forty islets and cays forming the southeastern end of the Bahamas archipelago. The name "Turks" comes from an indigenous cactus called the "Turk's Head," a small globular plant with a fez like cap

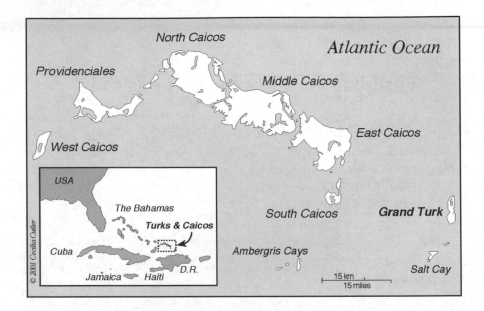

Figure 1. Map of the Turks and Caicos Islands

of whitish hairs from which the red flowers and fruit arise. There are eight major islands in the Turks and Caicos chain (see Figure 1). The Turks Islands are Grand Turk (the capital) and Salt Cay. The Caicos Islands are West Caicos, Providenciales, North Caicos, Middle Caicos, East Caicos, and South Caicos. The population of the TCI in 2000 was 17,502 (U. S. Census Bureau). The official language of the TCI is English. Most of the population is concentrated on Providenciales (Provo) and Grand Turk. Provo, a popular tourist destination, has several large resorts (Club Med, Sandals) and a population of approximately 7,000 (1990 Census Data). Grand Turk, the seat of government, has approximately 4,000 inhabitants (1990 Census Data). The remainder of the population lives in the sparsely populated islands of North Caicos, Middle Caicos, South Caicos, and Salt Cay. Approximately 90% of the population throughout the islands is black. The white population (approximately 5%) is made up of British civil servants and a handful of North Americans who run local businesses. The literacy rate in the TCI is 86.7% (Meditz & Hanratty 1989). The economy of the TCI is increasingly based on tourism and the offshore banking industry.

Migration between the islands since the 1960s has been chiefly uni-directional, i.e., from the relatively undeveloped and agricultural islands of North, Middle and South Caicos to Grand Turk and Provo. Caicos Islanders traditionally came to Grand Turk to find work on military bases or in government, but Provo with its large tourist resorts has proven to be a much better source of employment in recent years.

Historically there was (and still is to a certain extent) a great deal of prestige connected with being from Grand Turk as opposed to the Caicos Islands. Of all the islands, Grand Turk was settled earliest (by Bermudians), and Turks Islanders are proud of their Bermudian heritage. Throughout the colonial history of the islands, Grand Turk has been the seat of government. Turks Island salt was known throughout the West Indies and North America and made the island quite prosperous during the eighteenth and nineteenth centuries. This prosperity, the historically large white population, and substantial intermarriage between blacks and whites made Grand Turk the repository of privilege within the TCI. This prestige continues in the present day although the descendents of the earlier white population have long since moved away. Today, it is common for Turks Islanders to have traveled or spent time living in the Bahamas and U. S. In earlier generations, many young men from Grand Turk found work in the merchant marines and traveled extensively throughout the Atlantic. Many such men, now over fifty, have returned to take up residence in Grand Turk.

The Caicos Islanders, in contrast, have been traditionally somewhat isolated. The inhabitants (except in Provo) still make a living by farming and fishing. No secondary education was available in the Caicos Islands until the 1960s when some Caicos children were brought to Grand Turk for secondary education. Today, there are only three public high schools throughout the TCI, so many Caicos children must still live away from home during the school year to complete their education. Caicos Islanders are reputed to have darker skin than people on Grand Turk and were called "monkeys" by Turks Islanders in past times. The social and economic asymmetries between Grand Turk and the Caicos Islands are shifting as tourism develops in the Caicos Islands. Provo's appeal as a tourist destination is helping to spur tourism on Middle and North Caicos and plans are underway to build a port on South Caicos to accommodate large cruise ships.

Religion also plays a role in defining different social groups in the TCI. Religious affiliation functions as a loose index of island of origin and social class: Traditionally, Turks Islanders were Anglican or Methodist and the Caicos Islanders were Baptist. To this day, the wealthier families on Grand Turk and

Salt Cay with ties to the old white ruling class (often through admixture) are nearly all Anglican; Methodists tend to be middle class and Baptists lower class. Today, Turks Islanders are almost evenly divided between Anglicans (28%), Methodists (28%), and Baptists (31%). Other Christian denominations made up the remaining 12% (CIA World Factbook 1999). The overall breakdown of religious affiliation in the TCI is comparable but Baptists are the single largest group: Baptist (41.2%), Methodist (18.9%), Anglican (18.3%), Seventh-Day Adventist (1.7%), other (19.9%) (CIA World Factbook 1999).

The TCI have been under long-standing political and cultural sway from the United States. Grand Turk was home to two U. S. military bases from World War II until 1983. In the mid 1960s, when the salt industry was shut down, many Turks and Caicos Islanders sought employment in the Bahamas and the United States. Today, young people on Grand Turk often spend holidays and summer vacations with relatives in Miami and return with new words and ways of speaking referred to as "Yankin," i.e., to talk American.

Another significant social change in the TCI in recent years has been the influx of immigrants from Haiti and the Dominican Republic. By some estimates, there are roughly 1,000 legal and 6,000 illegal Haitians living in the TCI (Faul 1996: 24). The newcomers are regarded as harder working and more reliable than the native Turks and Caicos Islanders, which causes some tension between the two groups. The Haitians are also criticized for practicing "obeah" although by all reports, it predates their arrival. Deaths and sickness are often attributed to "a fix" having been put on the person by a Haitian.[1]

3.   Historical Background[2]

3.1   Grand Turk

The islands of the Bahamas and the Turks and Caicos were originally inhabited by Lucayan Indians until the arrival of the Spanish conquistadors sometime in the late 15th century. Some historians have even argued that Grand Turk was Columbus' first landfall in the New World (Sadler 1977). The Spanish immediately began deporting the Lucayans to work in the silver mines on Hispaniola in the early sixteenth century. The islands remained uninhabited until the late 1600s when Bermudian traders recognized the salt potential of the Turks Islands (Grand Turk and Salt Cay) and began sailing there to gather salt during the winter months (Packwood 1975: 46).

Typically, the vessels would land most of the white crews to spend months at the saltponds. The master, meanwhile, with his colored slaves as deckhands, would cruise among the Bahama Islands looking for turtles, wrecks and whatever trade could be found (Wilkinson 1950: 19).

In 1676, the Bermudians established the first settlement on Grand Turk and claimed it as a Bermudian possession (Craton & Saunders 1992: 89). At that time, blacks amounted to only about one quarter of the population of Bermuda (Packwood 1975: 73). These demographics plus the close contact between blacks and whites in the salt raking trade and in other common pursuits such as wrecking meant that the Bermudian blacks who ended up in Grand Turk would have had abundant contact with the white varieties of English found in Bermuda.

> The formation of Bermudian English must have taken place in an environment similar to that found later in the early colonial Bahamas. A low proportion of blacks and occupations such as boatbuilding and sailing brought about close contact between Bermudians of African and British descent; the former presumably had ample opportunity to acquire the latter's varieties (Seymour et al. fc.).

Work in the salt pans was grueling. Although slaves in the Turks Islands fared much better than slaves from the sugar colonies in terms of diet, mortality, and fertility, salt workers suffered from terrible boils on their legs from standing in the salt water for so many hours. "Nowhere [among the salt producing islands] are the effects of diet deficiencies coupled with excessive work under extreme conditions seen more clearly than in the Turks Islands salinas" (Craton & Saunders 1992: 310). The Bermudians exported Turks Island salt to the British colonies in North American from Newfoundland to South Carolina and traded it for grain and salt-fish. This trading sequence became the backbone of Bermuda's economy during the eighteenth century (Packwood 1975; Zuill 1951).

Several events during the eighteenth century challenged the sovereignty of Bermuda over Grand Turk. In 1710, the Spaniards attacked and captured the island. A successful expedition from Bermuda was launched later that year to retake it. Then in 1736, the Governor at Nassau made a request to Whitehall asking that Turks Island be added to the Bahamas, and beginning in 1740, the Bahamas began placing duties on persons engaged in raking salt on Grand Turk. Subsequent attacks by the French launched from Santo Domingo in 1754, 1764, and 1783 led the British Crown to rethink the administration of the island. It was clearly British but there was uncertainty about whether it should be administered from the nearby Bahamas or distant Bermuda.

In 1799, despite the protests of Turks Islanders, the islands were placed under the jurisdiction of the Bahamas. Then, in 1848, "after prolonged agitation," Britain agreed to a separation and the TCI were placed under a local president and council, responsible to the Governor of Jamaica (Albury 1975: 196). When this arrangement proved too costly, the islands were annexed to Jamaica as one of its dependencies in 1873 (Great Britain Colonial Office 1966: 40). But when Jamaica gained its independence in 1962, people in the TCI voted to remain a colony and were placed once again under the governance of the Bahamas. Eventually, when the Bahamas gained its independence in 1972, the TCI received its own Governor. Today, the TCI is one of twelve so-called "Dependent Territories" with British colonial status but whose citizens lack the right to live and work in Britain (Black 1997). Table 1 below shows the population of Grand Turk during the eighteenth and nineteenth centuries. The population data comes from Craton & Saunders (1992: 180). Numbers in italics are estimated.

Table 1. Grand Turk population 1773–1891[3]

	1773	1807	1810	1881	1891
Blacks	110	*1,295*	1,308	1,049	925
Colored	–	–	–	622	686
Freedmen	–	*75*	87	–	–
Whites	40	*500*	540	408	272
Other	–	–	–	–	–
Whites as % of total	27%	*27%*	28%	20%	14%
Total	150	1,870	1,935	2,079	1,883

The white population on Grand Turk began to decline in the nineteenth century and continued to do so through the twentieth century, particularly after the salt industry went into decline in the 1950s. The non-white population increased in the late twentieth century, due in part to the influx of Caicos Islanders and immigrants from Haiti and the Dominican Republic.

Table 2. Grand Turk population 1911–1999

	1911	1921	1943	1960	1975	1980	1999
Blacks	529	759	780	*1,050*	*1,300*	1,588	*2,500*
Colored	244	668	802	*990*	*1,170*	1,353	*2,300*
Whites	169	141	81	*90*	*100*	125	*200*
Other	–	–	–	–	–	52	–
Whites as % of total	18%	9%	5%	*5%*	*5%*	4%	*5%*
Total	942	1,568	1,663	2,180	2,330	3,118	4,000

3.2   The Caicos Islands

The Caicos Islands were uninhabited from the sixteenth century until the arrival of the Loyalist refugees in the 1780s following the American Revolutionary War. These Loyalists, many of whom were wealthy southern planters, initially fled the American Colonies and took refuge in British owned East Florida. Shortly thereafter, in 1783, the Crown signed a treaty in which territory in East Florida was ceded to Spain, forcing the Loyalists to seek land elsewhere. The British government considered the Bahamas and the West Indies to be the best location for resettlement because the climate resembled that of the southern colonies (Kozy 1991: 18). A fact finding expedition deemed the Caicos Islands and several islands in the Bahamas suitable for growing cotton and the Loyalists began taking up land grants in 1788.

Some 72 grants were made in the Caicos Islands from 1789–91 totaling 18,138 acres (Kozy 1991: 30). It is doubtful that any Loyalists would have settled on Grand Turk. Craton & Saunders (1992) claim that salinas on Grand Turk and Salt Cay were rarely included in grants of land to individual Loyalists (197) and there would have been little other reason for them to settle there since the land is not well-suited for agriculture. Kozy (1991) writes that "Grand Turk...attracted salt-rakers, but not planters" (29).

Records are available for 25 of the 72 Loyalist families who were granted land in the Caicos Islands. These families came primarily from Georgia (44%), South Carolina (32%), and East Florida (12%) (Kozy 1991: 32). Given the historical conditions of Georgia and South Carolina, many of the slaves brought to the Caicos Islands may have spoken a Caribbean Creole or an early form of Gullah, an English Creole that had been established in parts of South Carolina, Georgia, and on Sea islands between 1720 and 1750 (Mufwene 1995). With regard to Georgia, Hancock (1980) writes that the majority of the blacks in Georgia before 1770 were from the Caribbean (28). Based on this fact, Winford (1997) concludes that "many if not most of [the blacks in Georgia] probably spoke either a Creole variety or some kind of restructured English" (Winford 1997: 13). With regard to South Carolina, Winford (1997) notes that blacks remained a sizeable majority from 1730 up until the Revolution, conditions ideal for the emergence of Gullah.

The Caicos slaves would have been subject to a plantation regime similar to the one they left on the American mainland. However the tendency to plant the long staple Anguilla cotton, which grew all the year, with two crop peaks in February and early summer, also meant "more continuous seasons and a more difficult cleaning process than with the Persian type generally grown on the mainland" (Craton & Saunders 1992: 311).

The population in the Caicos Islands quickly increased along with the scale of the plantation economy from 1788–1800 although accurate population figures are not available.[4] The slave trade (but not slavery itself) was officially abolished in 1807 throughout the British Empire. Plantation owners, restricted by laws prohibiting the transfer or sale of slaves between colonies, began smuggling their slaves out of British territory before an efficient registration system could be put in place (Kozy 1991: 34; Craton & Saunders 1992: 224). In 1806, one plantation owner alone named Thomas Brown moved 643 slaves and 15 white overseers from the Caicos Islands to St. Vincent (Kozy 1991: 37). Table 3 shows the sudden rise in population between 1788 and 1807 followed by the beginning of the decline after 1807.

Cotton production in the Caicos Islands was initially promising but began declining rapidly in the early 1800s. As was true for the Bahamas, the cotton crop began to fail due to the thin soil, a particularly tenacious pest called the Chenille Worm, and the disastrous hurricane of 1813. According to Craton & Saunders (1992), most of the Loyalists in the Caicos Islands had abandoned their plantations and departed for other destinations in the British West Indies by 1820. In many cases, they left their slaves behind to fend for themselves and the islands were left so depopulated that all chances of sustaining a plantation economy were lost (Craton & Saunders 1992: 227).

Table 3. Caicos Islands Population 1788–1810[5]

	1788	1807	1810
Slaves	220	1,070	522
Freedmen	–	7	6
White Household Heads	6	20	32
Total	226	1,097	560

Over the course of the nineteenth century and well into the twentieth century, the remaining inhabitants in the Caicos Islands (virtually all descendants of American-born slaves) lived in relative isolation. There was only one notable influx of people from the outside. According to some historical accounts, the town of Bambarra on Middle Caicos was settled by a group of African slaves in 1842 who survived the shipwreck of a Spanish slave ship called the "Gambia."

From the early nineteenth century up until the very recent past, the main contact the Caicos Islanders had with the outside world was with people on Grand Turk whom the Caicos farmers supplied with fresh fruit and vegetables. The Caicos Islanders represent one of the few remaining unstudied "enclave" speech communities of persons descended from American-born slaves living outside the US.[6] According to one report, various customs and idiomatic expressions of southern United States origin still survive in the Caicos Islands (Great Britain Colonial Office 1966: 39).

Subsequent census data for the Caicos Islands indicate a small but stable black and colored population through the early twentieth century. As we see in Table 4, whites constituted a smaller proportion of the total population in the Caicos Islands than they did on Grand Turk. Historically, Caicos Islanders had much less contact with whites than Turks Islanders and the chances a Creole variety may have survived in the Caicos Islands would have been quite good. The population of the Caicos Islands dropped from 1950 onward to a low of 2,995 in 1970 (International Population Census). It began increasing slowly over the next two decades to its present level of about 11,000 people, most of whom live in Provo.

Table 4. Caicos Islands Population 1881–1943[7]

	1881	1891	1911	1921	1943
Blacks	1,812	1,712	2,480	2,865	2,946
Colored	271	508	676	681	1,075
Whites	49	69	81	39	27
Whites as % of total	2%	3%	3%	1%	1%
Total	2,132	2,289	3,237	3,585	4,048

4.   The sample

The data for this study were collected by the author over a six-week period during the summer of 1997.[8] All of the informants lived in Cockburn Town on the island of Grand Turk. The corpus consists of 13 hours of recorded interviews with 15 informants ranging in age from 18 to 104 (see Appendix 1). The informants had all lived most of their lives on Grand Turk although many had spent some time living or working abroad. Two of the informants were born on South Caicos but had spent nearly their entire lives on Grand Turk.

5.   Phonological features of TIE

Not surprisingly, some of the phonological features we see in TIE also appear
in Bermudian English. Discussing Bermudian English, Ayres (1933: 4) cites the
"interplay" of /æ/ and /ɛ/, as in *hat* (pronounced [hɛt]) or *ten* (pronounced
[tæn]), and the interchange of /w/ and /v/. Ayres (1933) observes that whites in
Bermuda pronounce *grass* as [græs], but that for blacks the vowel is [a]. Turks
Islanders were similar in this regard but did use /æ/ in words where many other
West Indians would use /a/. TIE speakers have little or no monophthongiza-
tion of diphthongs such as [aɪ]. Nor do they centralize the diphthong in words
like *oil* to [əɪ] as is common in other parts of the West Indies like Jamaica.
Unlike other Caribbean varieties of English, TIE speakers do not palatalize
velar stops. Nor does TIE have "h" dropping or epenthetic "h" as is common in
Jamaican English. TIE speakers invariably pronounce *ask* as [aks].

5.1   Vowels

[ɪ]	Words like *if* often sound like [ɛf]
[ɛ]	The mid front vowel /ɛ/ in words like *rest* and *Betty* is lowered to [æ] i.e., [ræst] and [bæri]. The second vowel in *again* is closer to [e] than [ɛ], i.e., [ə'gen].
[ʌ]	The vowel in *company* and *nothing* is closest to the low front vowel [a], i.e., ['kampəni] and ['naʔtən]. The vowel in *up* is close to [ɔ].
[ɔ]	Low mid back rounded vowels are slightly diphthongized before nasals as in *gone* [gɔan] and *haunted* ['hɔanɛd].
[ʊ]	The vowel in *could* is quite rounded, and is closer to [u].
[æ]	TIE vowels contrast with other varieties of English in the Caribbean, particularly with respect to the widespread use of [æ] in *back* and *man* where many other Caribbean varieties use [a] or [aː]. There was considerable variation among speakers, however: Some use [æ] in *master* but [a] in *after* and *can't*.[9]
[ou]	The diphthong in words like *go* and *boat* is fronted, sounding something like [öu].
[au]	The diphthong in *about* sounds something like [ə'bout].
[ə]	TIE has no rhotic vowels: Words like *birth* are pronounced [baf] or [bʌf]. This contrasts with Bahamian English and Gullah, both of which have the diphthong [ʌɪ] in words like *first* and *skirt* such that there is a merger of the vowels in *verse* and *voice* (Holm, 1989: 490; cf.

Wells 1982c). Turks Islanders identified the [ʌɪ] diphthong as some
thing that distinguishes Bahamian English from TIE.

5.2. Consonants

[ð]   The definite article *the* is categorically pronounced [di], but some
        speakers vary between stops and interdental dental fricatives for
        other words.

[θ]   Voiceless initial dental fricatives are variably realized as affricates.
        The TIE pronunciation of *thief* does not involve a full stop as it does
        in Jamaica and other parts of the Caribbean (i.e., ([tif]). Turks Is-
        landers say [tθif]. Medial dental fricatives are realized as labiodental
        fricatives, i.e., birthday ['bʌfdeɪ].

[ŋ]   The -ing suffix is replaced by [ɪn], e.g. *singing* "singin." In some
        words, the -ing suffix is syllabified, e.g. "meetin'" ['miʔtn̩].

[v, w] Initial /v/ and /w/ merge into a voiced bilabial approximant as in
        Bahamian and Gullah (cf. Turner 1949: 24), e.g. *well* [βɛl], *vex* [βɛks].

[t, k] Syllable final /t/ and /k/ are preceded by or replaced by glottal stops,
        e.g. *that* [dæʔt]. Other speakers do not have complete closure on final
        stops.

[ɾ]   Turks Islanders variably apply the American English flapping rule to
        medial alveolar stops. The name *Betty* is pronounced ['bæɾi].

5.3 Syllable structure

CC:C   Consonant cluster reduction in morpheme final consonant clusters
        of the same voicing, e.g. *last* [las], *stricter* ['strɪkə].

C:Ø   Medial consonants drop out in some words, e.g. *little* [lɪl]

VrC:VC Post-vocalic r-lessness, e.g. *Turks Island* [taks'ailən]. In other cases,
        Vr sequences are slightly diphthongized, e.g. *Lord's* [lɔadz]

VrV:Ø   Inter-vocalic r-lessness, e.g. *during* [da:n]

5.4 Prosody

Stress patterns differ in the pronunciation of certain words. The primary stress
in nouns of more than one syllable falls on the second syllable *grandma*
[granmá] and *ancestors* [ænsǽstəz].

6.   The noun phrase

6.1   Word order

In TIE, the basic sentence structure consists of a simple verb medial clause in which the subject or object need not be overtly expressed: ((S) V (O)). Occasionally, speakers start sentences without overt subjects when the subject has already been established as in (1) and (2) below.[10]

(1)   Miss D, 20: …they tell her they pray how long to put something on her leg, something they bring back from Haiti…Ø Say put this on her leg.

(2)   Miss D, 20: Ø Pullin' my auntie, she can't wake up, and I screamin' and cryin' 'til I sayin' the Lord's Prayer.

6.2   Nouns: Plurality and possession

Plurality is variably marked by the suffix -*s*, its allomorph -*z*, or Ø in the speech of Turks Islanders. Some speakers marked irregular plural nouns with -*s* (e.g. mens), as we see in (4). Consonant cluster simplification in words like *test* resulted in plural forms like *tesses*, shown in (5).

(3)   Miss G, 18: I mean Jesus, them [dɛm] **girls** [gʌlz] has got no shame! Man!

(4)   Miss D, 20: They call these two Haitian **mens** [mɛnz] and they come and they say to her, "Yeah, somethin in her leg…"

(5)   Miss D, 20: One minute she'll be good, walkin' around, next minute can't do nothin' for herself and they run all the **tesses** [tɛsəs] on her…

The post NP plural suffix [-dɛm], found in many Atlantic Creoles, as in [di boi dɛm] *the boys,* did not occur in the corpus.

Possession in TIE is variably expressed by possessive −*s* or Ø. Two examples of the Ø variant are shown in (6) and (7) below. There were not many tokens of this sort in the corpus so the extent of the variation was difficult to gauge. Possessive −*s* marking averaged about 50% for younger speakers. Some older speakers had a 100% rate of possessive −*s* marking. Genitive pronouns are marked for gender as in (8).

(6)   Mr. T, 94: You mean my ma__ family? Ten.

(7)   Miss D, 20: Then my granma__ leg started to heal….

(8)   Miss D, 20: Yeah, somethin in **her** leg eatin' **her** meat, eatin' **her** skin…

6.3 Determiners

An inventory of TIE determiners and demonstrative pronouns appears below in Table 5. The determiners found in TIE are similar to those found in other English varieties in the West Indies as well as in AAVE. TIE contains both definite and indefinite articles. All TIE determiners precede the noun.

Table 5. Determiners in TIE

	indefinite article	definite article	demonstrative determiner	pronoun
singular	[βʌn]	[di]	[dɪs]	[dɪs]
	[ə]		[dæt]	[dæt]
plural	–	[di]	[diz]	[diz]
			[dɛm]	[dɛm]
			[doz]	[doz]

The definite article is *di* [di] and the indefinite is *a* [ə].

(9)   Mr. T, 94: They had one [βʌn] in the [di] library some years ago…

(10)   Mr. T, 94: Oh yeah, when you get a rain you grow a [ə] good bit of food here.

Occasionally, nouns occurred with no accompanying indefinite article as shown in (11).

(11)   Mr. T, 94: One room over there [dɛə]. One room here [hiə]. Ø Room for (( )). Ø Rooms here. Ø Rooms outside. They got plenty rooms all about.

The plural demonstrative pronouns are [diz] (proximal) and [dɛm] or [doz] (distal).

(12)   Mr. T, 94: He say [diz] places are doomed from Hell.

(13)   Mr. T, 94: All of [diz] trees in my yard…I plant [dɛm] there.

(14)   Mr. T, 94: But you cannot take out of [dɛm] (the Haitians) [dɪs] black magic.

(15)   Mr. T, 94: …no, they never find [doz] (referring to some men lost at sea).

6.4 Personal pronouns

The inventory of TIE personal pronouns transcribed in IPA symbols appears in Table 6 below. Personal pronouns are marked for person, gender, number, and case in TIE.

Table 6. Personal pronouns in TIE

	nominative	accusative	possessive	reflexive
1 sg.	[ai]	[mi]	[maɪ]	[maɪsɛlf]
2 st.	[ju]	[ju]	[jɔ]	[jɔsɛlf]
3 sg. fem.	[ʃi]	[hə]	[hə]	[hasɛlf]
3 sg. masc.	[hi]	[hɪm]	[hɪz]	[hɪmsɛlf]
3 sg. neutral	[ɪt]	[ɪt]	*	*
1 pl.	[wi]	[ɑs]	[ɑwə]	[ɑwəsɛlf]
2 pl.	[ju]	[ju]	[jɔə]	*
3 pl.	[de]	[dɛm]	[dɛə]	*

* No examples

Unlike many English varieties in the West Indies that use *me* [mi] as the first singular nominative pronoun, TIE speakers exclusively use the acrolectal form *I* [ai] as shown in (16) and (17). In (18)–(20), we see the use of acrolectal reflexive pronouns.

(16)   Mr. H, 65: My mother was livin' with (( ))... and after she [ʃi]... I [ai] was about three months, **she** [ʃi] put me back over to Grand Turk and I [ai] came... I [ai] been here since then.

(17)   Mr. H, 65: I [ai] just give it to her [hə]!

(18)   Mr. M, 85: Well... (( )) I [ai] didn't burn **myself** ['maɪsɛlf] too ... big amount you see. I [ai] signed for three. **They** [de] have a workin' permit.

(19)   Miss D, 20: Um hum... somebody work obeah on **her** [hə]. **She** [ʃi] came and **she** [ʃi] was lingerin' ...lingerin' to die. One minute she'll be good, walkin' around. Next minute, can't do nothin' for **herself** [hasɛlf]...

(20)   Miss A, 75: Well if you're doing it **yourself** [jɔsɛlf] **you** [ju] can make it, yeah, but if somebody else (( )) for **you** [ju], **they** [de] will want more.

7.   Prepositions

Most prepositions in TIE such as *with, about, around, in*, etc., resemble usage in American and British English.

(21)   Mr. T, 94: ...before they had this last hurricane came from down (( )), it mess up all of my Yellow Ander. I had heavy Yellow Ander trees going right **around** the place.

Other prepositions seem to have a larger set of meanings. The preposition *by* [baɪ], for example, may mean "by," "at," or "next to" as in (22) and (23).

(22) Miss D, 20: How we celebrate it? They got like a…like if they have the wedding in the morning, the afternoon they'll have the reception **by** [baɪ] a hall or **by** [baɪ] their parent's house.

(23) Mr. T, 94: But for this year, this year (( )) has got…this place **by** [baɪ] Cable and Wireless, they got charts up there.

A similar range of meanings can accompany the preposition *on* [ɔn]. In (24), it means something like (at) (Waterloo is the name of the Governor's house).

(24) Mr. T, 94: This is up there by where [di] governor lives **on** [ɔn] Waterloo.

The preposition *for* [fɔ] has several functions in TIE. It can mean "for purpose of" as we see in (25), or "regarding" as in (26). In (27), it means something like "with regards to."

(25) Mr. M, 85: Oooh yeah. It's somethin' **for** [fɔ] the [di] man to do! (referring to a public works project to beautify the saltponds)

(26) Miss A, 75: They did but they … today you have trouble to – to – to you know…notice that because the children today have been away **for** [fɔ] educa- you know, **for** [fɔ] their learning, and you see, and — and one follow **the** [di] other.

(27) Miss A, 75: I don't want much **for** [fɔ] food.

In other cases, *for* functions as a complementizer, "meaning in order to" or "so that" (see Section 12 below).

The preposition *of* is frequently realized as [ə] as we see in (28) and (29). Its range of meaning seems quite consistent with English spoken in the U. S. or Britain.

(28) Miss D, 20: **They** [de] get out **the** [di] school yard, goin' home over to **their** [dɛ] boyfriend_ house, all **of** [ə] that.

(29) Mr. M, 85: 'Cause they was tryin' to keep **the** [di] young people from what do you call what — havin' plenty **of** [ɔ] bastard children!

From [frɔm] is a preposition that can have meanings other than those found in American or British English. In (30) it stands for a point in time, i.e., from the time the speaker was a baby. In (31) and (32) it forms part of a prepositional phrase (*from down to*) and refers to a geographical place or direction.

(30)   Miss A, 75: She did a little laundry to help herself but my father really supported me right throughout **from** [frɔm] a baby until the day I die…until the day HE died….

(31)   Mr. T, 94: The Ewings from Blue Hill… **from** [frɔm] down to Provo… Provo…denciales down here, they want…every family like had a boat..

(32)   Mr. T, 94: If they go? Oh yeah! Uhh from **from** [frɔm] down to Nassau right across (( )) Turks Island people. They (( )) **from** [frɔm] down there.

8.   The verb phrase

8.1   Verbal concord

TIE speakers generally use *is* with all persons and numbers as we see in (33).[11] Most speakers alternate *was* and *were* with third person plural subjects in past sentences as we see in (34)–(36).

(33)   Miss A, 75: (addressing interviewer) **Is** [əz] you be watchin' me?

(34)   Miss G, 18: Well, if your boyfriend die and they know you **was** goin' with him, and he call names, the doctor will call you in like that.

(35)   Miss D, 20: They **was** doin' it in school time.

(36)   Mr. T, 94: These lighters **were** made to carry salt on board the schooner and uhhh they went round the Caicos Cays.

8.2   Present tense

In TIE, the unmarked form of the verb alternates with the marked form for present tense verbs. The number of third person verbal –s/Ø tokens in the corpus was low since narratives tended to focus on past events, but all the speakers in the corpus used third person verbal –s variably as shown in the example below. A quantitative analysis of this variable for four individuals showed 37% third person verbal –s marking (n=70).

(37)   Mr. M, 85: Well, I have a son, he **goes** in the States side every year! You know what I mean. Every year! I have another one who **works** in the bank. He **go_** out there every year. Then my daughter only **come_** from out there Monday, Monday evening.

8.3 Past tense

Verbs with irregular past tense forms like *go/went, cling/clung, grow/grew* may retain their present tense forms in past tense sentences whereas regular verbs tend to be marked for the past. The verb *say* when employed as a quotative in narratives about the past invariably occurs with no past marking. The verb *go* is variable in this regard. The narrative below illustrates these patterns.

(38) Miss A, 75: (referring to her childhood) I never **go** about, you know. I **cling** to my mother. They was so that if a child **wanted** to play with me, they **had** to come to my mother's house to play with me. I **didn't** want to leave her to go to them (( )). I **was** afraid to go leave her, thinkin' that after she **used to** leave me to go to meetin.' I **was** 'fraid to leave her! When I **see** her dressin' I will…I **couldn't** say "Lucy," I'd say "Leedy, you goin' leave me t'night?" She **say**, "I only goin' round (( ))." I **say**, "You **say** that last week too." I say, "You **went** and you **buy** juice and peanuts and you **went** out the door a flyin'," I **say**, "and leave me there." But once I **followed** her! Yes! One night they had to bring me back! Yeah. And after that, my mother **left** (( )) because my daddy **told** her that havin' to bring ((me)) hot and sweaty from that place, I likely to stay cold and I **was** the only ((child)). They **wanted** a boy. After I **grow** up, he **get** to to like me as much as he would've liked the boy, I believe.

8.4 Past perfect

The use of past-perfect tense is a feature of AAVE narrative style. This feature appeared in the speech of Miss G, an 18 year-old, who had spent part of the previous year living in Miami. The fact that this feature did not appear in the speech of the other young informant (Miss D, age 20) suggests it may not be a feature of TIE and may have been something Miss G picked up from AAVE speakers in the U. S.

(39) Miss G, 18: Yeah. Yeah. We used to go one time ago but then he try to talk to my sister and and I **had** leaved him and I **had** ran back…

(40) Miss G, 18: Because the next day, I **had** called and I **had** [aks] ((…..)) and I know C had already told him something but I don't care because he couldn't say nothing bad about me…

8.5 Mood

Irrealis markers code future, conditional, and subjunctive utterances. Future events are coded by *gon* [gɔn] and *will* [βɪl] in TIE as we see in (41) and (42).

(41)   Mr. M, 85: I was about seven years and she told me, (( )), say, "See that boy there, he Ø [gɔn] build my house," and I was only seven years! That's right, she told all [di] children, say, "See that boy right there, he Ø [gɔn] build my house and I built her house…"

(42)   Miss A, 75: The man gave me this one you see … it [βɪl] ripe after a while. He went to look for a ripe one but he say all that he had was green.

Potentiality or ability is marked with *can* [kæn], shown in (43).

(43)   Miss A, 75: I say… yes, I say "skirt" [ska:t]. I **can** [kæn] say "skoit" [skoɪt] too (referring to the Bahamian pronunciation) but I *can't* [kan] go back Turks Island with that!

The conditional is either unmarked as in (44) or coded by *would* [βʊd] or *could* [kʊd] as in (45).

(44)   Mr. T, 94: If he (Henry the VIII) **see** the next woman that he wanted, he Ø **do** away with that woman. She gotta die.

(45)   Mr. T, 94: Wait. Now the food that come_ from Santo Domingo and Haiti … is better than what would come from the United States 'cause wait, **if** you buy something in the United States it **could** [kʊd] be on the ice before your grandfather was born…

The past tense form of conditionality is *woulda* [βʊdə].

(46)   Miss D, 20: Then [dɛn] my granma leg started to heal and (( )) man said if they didn't a leave it, centipede **woulda** [βʊdə] crawled right up and tried to go up her heart.

Necessity is indicated by *mus* [mʌs] as in (47). The past form is *musta* [mʌstə] followed by an unmarked verb as in (48).

(47)   Mr. M, 85: [di] lady, you **mus'** [mʌs] see that lady one day. She's got a house on the ridge.

(48)   Miss G, 18: Because he had called me and I say I showed him my middle finger and he **musta** [mʌstə] **get** upset.

8.6 Aspect

8.6.1 *Progressive aspect*

In TIE, progressive aspect is marked by an optional copula followed by an -*ing* verb. The copula is not overtly expressed in (49).

(49)   Mr. T, 94: I Ø **livin'** in a poor country like this and I send seven children to college.

8.6.2 *Past progressive*

Past Progressive is indicated by *was* or Ø followed by a continuative verb as in (50) and (51).

(50)   Mr. T, 94: No. I **wasn't living** in this house. Nineteen twenty-six, I **was livin'** I **was livin'** down in (( )) Street.

(51)   Miss D, 20:… Was on my back and when I say on my back jumpin' up and down and I Ø cryin' and screamin' and nobody Ø hearin' what I say.

8.6.3 *Habitual aspect*

So far, the data show that Turks Island English shares many morphosyntactic features with other Caribbean varieties of English such as variable copula absence, variable marking of past tense, and plurality. TIE also contains linguistic features not found in West Indian varieties such as third person verbal −*s* absence and habitual ([əz]) *be.*

Rickford (1986a: 261) claims that habitual *be* is not used in English-derived varieties in the West Indies which use [(d)a] or [(d)e] instead. He has proposed that habitual *be* in AAVE represents a decreolized form of [(d)a] and outlines a series of stages which explain its emergence in African American English (Rickford 1986a: 268–71).

(52)   Habitual marker for verbal non-continuatives from Sea Islands Gullah (Rickford 1986a: 268–71).

Stage 1	He **(d)a** work. (basilect)
Stage 2	But I **does** go to see people when they sick. ((d)a ~ does)
Stage 3	He **does be** up and cut wood sometimes. (de, Ø ~ be)
Stage 4	Sometimes you [**z**] **be** in the bed… (does ~ z)

Stage 1, according to Rickford, "probably represents convergence between English habitual *do* and similar West African forms" (1986a: 269). Stage 2 (unstressed habitual *does*) is modeled on English *does* rather than *do* and occurs as a mesolectal variant of [(d)a] in the Sea Islands and the Bahamas. Stage 3 involves the introduction of non-finite *be* after *does* and is attested in Caribbean mesolects (Alleyne 1980: 213 in Rickford 1986a: 270) and in the Sea Islands (See example (53)).

(53)   I'll miss C, cause she **does be** here and write letter for me sometimes (Rickford 1986a: 270).

Winford (1997) notes that similar constructions are found in "intermediate creoles" such as Barbadian Creole, urban Guyanese Creole and Trinidadian creole (See example (54)).

(54)   I/you/he/we etc. **does be** tired all the time (Winford 1997: 33).

In Stage 4, *does* is lost and habitual aspect is marked by *be* alone as we see in modern AAVE and Gullah. The initial stop of *does* is assimilated, and the remaining [əz] is subject to further contraction and deletion (Rickford 1986a: 271).

A form related to what we see in Stage 4 appears in the speech of Turks Islanders. TIE speakers mark habitual aspect by way of [əz] followed by *be*, a noun phrase, punctual verb, or locative as shown in (55)–(57) below. The distribution of [əz bi] and [əz] is slightly different: [əz bi] occurs with noun phrases, adjectives, locatives, and non-punctual verbs, whereas as [əz] by itself occurs exclusively with punctual verbs as we see in (57).

(55)   Miss D, 20: She [**əz bi**] home.

(56)   Miss G, 18: Some, certain things [**əz bi**] true.

(57)   Miss D, 20: ...the preacher, he Ø talkin'... he [**əz**] **talk** like... he ohhh... but he [**əz**] **drag** his voice and you [**əz**] **sit** there and you [**əz**] **go** sleep, wake up and he's still there talkin'.

One variant of habitual [əz bi] in TIE is [bi] by itself followed by an adjective, non-punctual verb or noun phrase as is found in AAVE. However it only appears in the speech of the two youngest informants Miss D, age 20 and Miss G, age 18 (see (58) and (59) below).

(58)   Miss G, 18: She **be** goin' there.

(59)   Miss D, 20: Rest [rɛs] of the [di] churches, establish churches **be** fun..."

Rickford (1986a) notes that in the Sea Islands, *does be* is used as a marker of habitual aspect among adults over sixty; but zero (before non-continuative

verbs) and *be* (before nominals, locatives, adjectives, and VERB + ing) are used
instead by the youngest generation (271). It could be that the variation we see
in TIE represents a change in progress (i.e., [əz bi] is giving way to [bi] among
younger speakers as has already happened in the Sea Islands).

When we examine the data more closely, we can see a pattern in the
distribution of these three variants according to the following grammatical
environment: [əz bi] and [bi] occur most commonly with NPs, adjectives,
locatives, and VERB + ing as shown in Table 7. This data set is very small
(n=40), but the distribution of these habitual forms suggests two things: (1) [əz
bi] and [bi] are to some degree in free variation with one another; (2) [əz bi]
and its variant [bi] appear to be in complementary distribution with [əz].

Table 7. Distribution of habitual markers in TIE by following environment

	___NP	___Adj	___Loc	___Verb	___Ving
[əz bi]___	29%	43%	21%	0%	7%
[bi]___	0%	50%	21%	0%	29%
[əz]___	0%	0%	0%	100%	0%

It is not clear that these habitual forms are necessarily the product of decreolization as Rickford (1986a) has proposed, but certainly the fact that forms
like [əz bi] have been documented in so many English-derived varieties suggests that these forms must be related (cf. Winford 1997).

8.6.4 *Past habitual*

Past habitual aspect is generally coded by *used to* [jʌstə] followed by an infiniti-
val verb (as in (60)), or by *been* [bɪn] followed by an *-ing* verb (as in (61)). The
use of *been* (unstressed) conveys a sense of a continuative perfect and appears
to be derived by contraction and deletion of *have* as is common in AAVE and
other dialects of American English (cf. Winford 1997).

(60) Miss A, 75: She had her but she [jʌstə] go close out the house and leave
      her so her grandmother took her so she only know the love of her
      grandmother.

(61) Mr. H, 65: Yeah. All my life I [bɪn] working hard.

Occasionally, TIE speakers alternate *will* [βɪl] and *would* [βʊd] in place of *used
to* [jʌstə]. Georgia (1940: 118) cited in Rickford (1986a: 266, fn 15) makes the
same observation for Gullah. The speaker in (62) uses both *will* [βɪl] and *would*

[βʊd] within a sentence. The speaker is describing things her father used to do for her when he was still alive.

(62)   Miss A, 75: Each week on a Tuesday he **will** [βɪl] send me grocery and he **would** [βʊd] send a few shillings to buy things, for he didn't send (( )) fish…

8.6.5   *Completive aspect*

No examples of completive forms such as *done* appeared in the corpus, although Miss G, an eighteen year-old female who had spent time in Miami used *did had* in what appears to be a completive sense. She also uses *had did* and *had talk* in the same utterance.

(63)   Miss G, 18: I dreamed she had a big brown-skinned girl and she **did had** a girl. But she was small. Her stomach was BIG. Her baby wasn't big. But I **had did** dream it and **had talk** it.

9.   Non-verbal predicates

Non-verbal predicates including nominal, adjectival, and locative predicates, are variably preceded by *is*, *'s*, *are*, *'re* or Ø. The sentences below are examples of Ø copula with nominal (64), adjectival (65), and locative predicates (66)–(67).

(64)   Mr. H, 65: I Ø the [di] small boy in the middle of 'em…

(65)   Miss D, 20: They [de] say the [di] lady next [nɛks] door Ø jealous [a] you…

(66)   Mr. T, 94: Oh yeah… and she Ø down there [de].

(67)   Miss A, 75: Sometimes they [de] Ø out in the tree, you don't know they [de] Ø up there gettin' tamarinds…

The absence of past copula forms occurs in certain frozen expressions such as (68). In most other cases, speakers alternate between *was* and *were* to code past events (see Section 8.1 above).

(68)   Mr. T, 94: Dala Ø born in this [dɪs] house and grow up in the north.

Some speakers used contracted forms of the past copula as in (69). The first person singular pronoun followed by the contracted copula can be glossed as "I was."

(69)   Mr. H, 65. But I's [a.ɪ] small! I's [a.ɪ] only fourteen years old and they
        give me six shillings a week!

Progressive sentences (past and non-past) were also commonly marked by Ø
(See examples (49) and (51) above).

Existential predicates took the form *it is/ it's/ it/ Ø* as well as *there is/ there
are*. The use of *it is* (as in (70)) where Standard forms of English use *there is* has
also been attested in AAVE (Wolfram 1974: 171).

(70)   Mr. T, 94: They said **it isn't** a watchman that didn't see Nelson goin' up
        forward or going down...

(71)   Mr. H, 65: **There's** more crime now in this island since [di] drug, since
        we had [di] drug...

9.1   Copula distribution

Table 8 shows copula distribution in the speech of five Turks Islanders.[12]
Excluding all cases of *it* and *that* as subjects (all of which occur almost categorically in contracted forms), habitual *be* ([əz bi] and [bi]), and first person
pronouns, we obtain the following frequencies and probabilities of copula
absence. Probability values less than .50 disfavor copula absence while values
above .50 favor it.

Table 8. Copula deletion excluding *it, that,* and 1st person singular

	__NP	__Loc.	__Ving	___Adj.	__Gonna
Freq.	7%	41%	43%	49%	69%
Prob.	.13	.61	.62	.64	.83
# tkn	n=84	n=57	n=32	n=47	n=16

The high rate of pre-adjective copula absence we see here is a pattern typically
found in mesolectal varieties such as AAVE, Barbadian, and Trinidadian
(Singler 1991b: 156). In fact, the probabilities reported by Rickford & Blake
(1990) for Barbadian are very comparable to the data from TIE as we can see in
Figure 2.

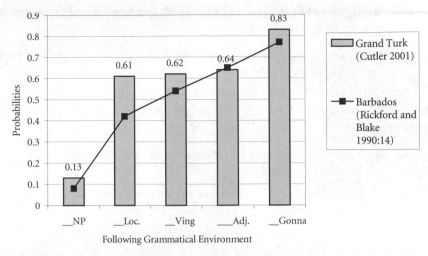

Figure 2. Copula absence in TIE and Barbados English

10. Negation

TIE speakers commonly alternate *ain't/isn't* and *don't/didn't* in negative constructions.

(72)   Miss D, 20: She say, "No, I **ain't** hear you."

(73)   Miss D, 20: I know Mick but I **didn't** know his face, 'cause Mick was the first white man I ever saw in my life.

Double negation is a common negation strategy in TIE and generally consists of a negated nominal, verbal, or adjectival predicate followed by a negative indefinite pronoun.

(74)   Mr. T, 94: That fellow, he **didn't have no** money to go to pay for any education that was a little bit better.

(75)   Mr. T, 94: And they **ain't got no** chemicals to put in the ground. They grow natural. And they taste different.

The inventory of negative modals found in TIE includes *can't, couldn't*. No instances of *musn't* occurred in the corpus. The negative indefinite pronouns in TIE are *nothin', nobody,* and *never*.

11. Interrogation

TIE speakers usually leave the order of words in interrogative sentences unchanged. Intonation and context make it clear that these are direct questions
rather than statements or echo questions. In (76), Mr. H is talking about
"wompers," the kind of shoes that people in the Caicos Islands used to wear.

(76)   Mr. H, 65: You know what is wompers? It's a car tire, cut and then a hole
       in it and a string down the back and tie around your feet.

Another feature of TIE interrogation is the absence of auxiliaries such as *do*,
did, etc. seen in examples (77) and (78).

(77)   Miss A, 75: Ø You have sisters?

(78)   Miss A, 75: Ø You think they will ever come down this way?

12.   Complement clause

Complement clauses in TIE are usually introduced by the acrolectal forms *to*
[tu] and *that* [dæt], although the more mesolectal *for* [fɔ] and Ø were occasional variants.

(79)   Miss A, 75: I was afraid **to** [tu] go leave her, thinkin' that after she used **to**
       [tu] leave me **to** [tu] go to meetin' I was 'fraid **to** [tu] leave her!

(80)   Miss A, 75: I never questioned him but I know **that** [dæt] his father was
       Portuguese… you know.

(81)   Miss A, 75: Oh yes. That one there used to …the children nighttime used
       to throw throw rocks up there **for** [fɔ] them to…**for** [fɔ] the guineps
       (fruit from guinep tree) to drop down because it was over the wall you
       know…

13.   Left dislocation

TIE allows left dislocation. This is a syntactic process by which a copy of one of
the noun phrases is made at the extreme left side of the sentence and the
ordinary rule of pronominalization converts the second of the two identical
noun phrases to the appropriate pronoun. This feature was quite common in
the speech of Turks Islanders.

(82)   Mr. T, 94: **John Wesley, he** ain't had no church.

(83)   Mr. H, 65: **The lady that live in this house right here,** this same house right here, **she** was a teacher, was a teacher…

14.   Relative clauses

There is some variation in the use of relative pronouns in relative clauses in TIE. Speakers tend to use *that* [dæt] in sentences where the noun referent is a person ((84) and (85)) and *what* [βʌt] in cases where the referent is an inanimate object ((86) and (87)). In some cases, *what* [βʌt] can also apply to human referents (as in (88)).

(84)   Mr. T, 94: I got some of my grandchildren **that** [dæt] I have is a master of science.

(85)   Mr. T, 94: He's a man **that** [dæt] took care of his children.

(86)   Mr. T, 94: Well, [di] school, [di] high school they had **what** [βʌt] Mr. Crawford, Mr. C. E. Crawford used to keep, he didn't take everybody. Only take people from certain families.

(87)   Mr. T, 94: Man, after they had all this rain and rough sea and all a that …they, [di] [di] food **what** [βʌt] they had would probably give out…

(88)   Miss A, 75: Yeah, I feel so. Not the young ones **what** [βʌt] just grow up because some of them, I can't call their names. They just have such heavy names.

15.   Lexis

My informal surveys on Grand Turk suggest that people are not familiar with Bahamian terms listed in Holm & Shilling (1982) like *hoecake* (cornmeal cake), *sperrit* (ghost), *hoppin' John* (beans and rice), or *ninny* (breast). The local terminology that I found of interest on Grand Turk were directional expressions like *norret* and *surret* meaning "northwards" and "southwards." The small open boats used to carry salt to the large ships are called *lighters*. I heard people refer to a child born out of wedlock as an *outside child* and a two-story dwelling as an *upstairs house*. People on Grand Turk say *reach* to mean to "arrive." I also heard people use the word *fix* to mean "to cast a spell on," or "put a curse on" someone (cf. Allsopp 1996). A man from North Caicos told me that expressions like *grabalicious*, *gutlin*, and *gutless* meaning "greedy," and *huff* or *grits* referring to "corn flour" are unique to the Caicos Islands. In the past, the Caicos Islanders were said to wear *wompers* or sandals made from old car tires.

16. Conclusion

The linguistic evidence given here suggests that Turks Island English is a mesolectal to acrolectal variety that may have more in common with AAVE, Gullah, and Bermudian English than other West Indian varieties of English. Roberts (1988) has noted that many people in the Caribbean do not even consider the Virgin Islands, the Bahamas (and by extension the TCI) to be West Indian and classify the inhabitants as "American" on the basis of their speech (3). A better understanding of the linguistic differences that prompt such attitudes is needed before we can categorize TIE as "American." There are some similarities between Turks Island English and Bermudian English, particularly the interchange between /æ/ and /ɛ/ and the merger of /v/ and /w/. TIE does differentiate /æ/ and /a/ where many other West Indian varieties have only /a/. In terms of its pronoun system and morphology, TIE is mesolectal to acrolectal. The fact that it has features like variable third person -*s* marking and habitual *be* which are not found in other parts of the Anglophone Caribbean is certainly worthy of note. The existence of habitual markers such as [əz bi] and [bi] in TIE has a great deal of potential for further cross-linguistic analysis given the fact that it appears in Gullah, Bahamian, Bajan, Trinidadian and other varieties (cf. Roberts 1988: 89).

   The sociohistorical and linguistic overview of the TCI provided here also suggests several directions for further research. It is likely that some linguistic differences exist between the Turks Islands and the Caicos Islands given the unique historical origins of their respective settlers, but these differences have yet to be investigated. It is also likely that such differences were more marked in the past than they are today following decades of migration from the Caicos Islands to Grand Turk. Examining the speech of the Caicos Islanders, most of whom are descended from American-born slaves, may also help to answer some pressing questions on the origins of AAVE (cf. Poplack & Sankoff 1987; Rickford 1987, 1998; Rickford & Blake 1990, Rickford et al. 1991; Singler 1990, 1991a, b, 1998; Tagliamonte & Poplack 1993; Winford 1997). Heretofore, speech data from the descendents of American born slaves outside the U. S.

(i.e., Liberia, Nova Scotia, and Samaná) has provided conflicting answers as to the character of earlier varieties of AAVE. Looking at the speech of people like the Caicos Islanders is one way we can gain a better understanding of what AAVE may have looked like at the time various groups left the United States.

Notes

* This research was partially funded by the Center for Latin and American Studies and the Linguistics Department at New York University. I am indebted to Barrie Dressel and Brian Riggs of the Turks and Caicos National Museum for allowing me use of the archives and office space at the museum and for copious information on Grand Turk. I would also like to thank Laura Hunter-Mitchell and Carl Been for help with data collection. I received tremendous encouragement and guidance from John Singler and Renée Blake throughout the course of my research and very helpful advice from Hubert Devonish of the University of the West Indies. The shortcomings in this paper are entirely my own.

1. To "fix" someone means to work obeah on a them or to put a curse on them (Allsopp 1996).

2. The most complete bibliography of historical sources on the Turks and Caicos Islands is found in the *World Bibliographical Series*, Vol. 137 "Turks and Caicos Islands," Paul G. Boultbee (compiler).

3. The figures for 1773–1810 come from Craton & Saunders (1992: 180). Data for 1807 are estimated. The figures for 1881–1943 come from the International Population Census for Latin America and the Caribbean under Jamaica. Data for 1980 comes from the International Population Census for Latin America and the Caribbean under Turks and Caicos.

4. Census data from the early settlement period of the Caicos Islands (1789–1807) is hard to come by since formal censuses were not conducted in the TCI until the 1840s (Travis 1990: 633). It would be very difficult to estimate the population of the Caicos Islands from land grants and quotas. Forty acres (and in some cases as much as one hundred acres) were given to every head of household and 20 acres for each white or black man, woman or child in a family (Kozy 1991: 23, 29, 30). However, Kozy (1991) notes that "it is doubtful that all seventy-two grantees established plantations [since] grants as small as 40 acres or 60 acres would not have been adequate for the plantation system of agriculture" (32). Furthermore, it seems that by 1800, the land became concentrated in the hands of a few owners. The Delancey, Brown, and Bell estates alone account for nearly 7,000 of the 18,000 acres of land in the Caicos Islands (Kozy 1991: 32, 36). Extrapolating from the limited data available, there may have been as many as 2,000–2,500 slaves living in the Caicos Islands at the height of the cotton industry around 1800.

5. Figures for the Caicos Islands come from Craton & Saunders (1992).

6. Three such speech communities have been studied thus far: The Liberian Settler community (John Singler 1984, 1991a, 1991b), the Nova Scotia African American community

(Poplack & Sankoff 1987 and Tagliamonte & Poplack 1993), and the Samaná speech community in the Dominican Republic (Poplack & Sankoff 1987, Hannah 1995).

7. The figures for 1881–1943 come from the *International Population Census for Latin America & The Caribbean* under Jamaica.

8. All but two of the interviews were conducted by the author. Miss E and Mr. K were interviewed in 1996 by Barrie Dressel, former director of the Turks and Caicos National Museum on Grand Turk.

9. As a general rule in Received Pronunciation, the low back vowel [a] alternates with [æ] according to the following phonological environment: [a] appears before voiceless fricatives (except [ʃ]) and before nasals followed by voiceless obstruents: e.g. *can* [kæn] vs. *can't* [kant] and *past* [past].

10. Speakers are identified by a gender specific title, followed by their age. The conventions used in the transcriptions are:

[ ]	IPA phonetic transcription
italics	gloss
Bold	item of central interest in discussion
(( ))	speech inaudible or questionable
( )	stage directions or clarification

11. The form [əz bi] in (33) marks habitual or durative aspect (see 8.6.3). The form [əz bi] is, I believe, derived from *does be* discussed by Rickford (1986a) and is not related to the plural second person *yous* found in other vernacular forms of English.

12. The five speakers in the sample were Mr. T, Miss D, Mr. M, Miss A, and Miss G. Invariant *be* forms are excluded by most researchers on the grounds that *be* is typically habitual while zero and conjugated forms are not. Rickford & Blake (1990) also note that Labov (1969) and others exclude full forms of *it's*, *that's* and *what's* in the count because they occur overwhelmingly as frozen, contracted forms.

Appendix 1

The Informant Pool

Informant	Occupation	Schooling
Miss A, age 75	n/a	high school
Miss B, age 20	Bartender	high school
Miss D, age 20	shop girl	high school
Miss E, age 102	Uncertain	?
Miss G, age 18	high school student	some high school
Miss H, age 40	Uncertain	?
Miss P, age 78	retired principal	college degree
Miss W, age 22	Waitress	high school
Mr. H, age 65	retired seaman	grammar school
Mr. K, age 104	retired seaman	high school
Mr. L, age 98	retired seaman	high school
Mr. M, age 85	retired plumber/builder	grammar school
Mr. P, age 60	retired postmaster	grammar school
Mr. S, age 80	retired truck driver	grammar school
Mr. T, age 96	stock manager	high school

Language variety in the Virgin Islands

Plural marking

Robin Sabino, Mary Diamond and Leah Cockcroft
Auburn University / University of Tennessee, Memphis

1. Introduction

Members of African Diaspora communities have long recognized that language choice is "tied to questions of intelligence, creativity, literacy, culture, politics, race, and representation" (Andrews, Smith, and Trudier 1997: 687). In the Caribbean, the 1970s witnessed growing public appreciation of the systematic nature and linguistic legitimacy of non-standard (including Creole) varieties of Caribbean English. Nevertheless, differences (and, more importantly, incompatibilities) between Western European and West African cultural orientations largely preserved the long standing symbolism of linguistic codes in Caribbean communities — a symbolism that is ultimately due to colonial misapprehensions of Creole language structures.[1] European colonization of the Caribbean archipelago successfully transmitted racist notions about language through a variety of means, especially religious training and formal education. However, even in communities, like the Danish West Indies (now the U. S. Virgin Islands), where standard varieties of English historically have been available, local network strength has insured the cross-generational transmission of non-standard Caribbean English grammatical patterns. Holm (1988: 144) discusses structures "that are found in a number of Atlantic creoles but not in the standard European languages from which they draw their vocabularies... [that] are so wide spread that their existence can hardly be explained by mere coincidence." For convenience, in this chapter we refer to such structures as *Caribbean Creole language patterns*.

For decades creolists have been aware of the methodological difficulties posed by data collection in Caribbean settings where standardized and nonstandardized varieties are in contact and, sometimes, in conflict. A number of postings on the CREOLIST list serve in February 1999 arguing the virtue of native versus nonnative field workers reflect current awareness of the degree to which "the conceptions that speakers hold about language ... affect and are implicated in the daily use of language in social situations that are laden with power dimensions and politics" (Mertz 1996: 150). This concern about the collection of data representative of Caribbean Creole language patterns is the theoretical focus of the present chapter. The descriptive focus of our discussion is noun pluralization, specifically the alternation of {-s}, {-dem}, and the noun stem, a Caribbean English language pattern that has received considerable attention (see Section 2 below). Our study is longitudinal: the data span 51 years from 1933 to 1984 and represent speakers from four of the Virgin Islands: St. Thomas, St. John, Anegada, and Tortola.[2] Our goal is to investigate the choices speakers of Virgin Islands English make when pluralizing nouns. Since, as in other Caribbean communities, Virgin Islands culture was forged largely by the descendants of Africans who survived the abuses of European colonialism, we hypothesize that the strategies Virgin Islanders use for plural marking will be consistent with the Atlantic creole pattern described by Holm (1988).

We approach the issue of representativeness with the following assumption firmly in mind: members of Caribbean communities, like speakers everywhere, have "multi-systemic repertoires" (Carrington 1992: 98) so that all frequently used varieties become stable and hence linguistically identifiable. We also assume that speakers' linguistic knowledge and the self-images they wish to project (Le Page and Tabouret-Keller 1985) combine with their beliefs about listeners' linguistic abilities to determine the selections speakers make from their available alternatives. We recognize that vernacular speech is demonstrably the most systematic variety in a speaker's repertoire (Labov 1972). Nevertheless, as Schilling-Estes (1998) argues, both on the basis of empirical evidence and by drawing on Goffman (1981) and Baktin (1981), vernacular speech is only one of several systematic varieties that speakers have available to them.

2.   Review of the literature on pluralization in Caribbean Englishes

Plural marking is morphologically straightforward in Standard English. In contrast, the number and nature of grammatical options open to speakers of

Caribbean Englishes is complicated. Creolists have tackled the description of plural marking both qualitatively and quantitatively.

Qualitative researchers agree that Creole nouns do not obligatorily encode number. Alleyne's (1980) analysis of African-American Englishes makes two fundamental points: pluralization operates on definite nouns and appears to be etymologically related to pluralization in West African languages such as Twi, Ewe, and Yoruba. In contrast, Janson (1984: 304), drawing on published accounts, rejects the notion of substrate influence. He instead attributes the development of pluralization in Caribbean creoles to "disruptive language change" during which "language learners who presumably have no wish to conform to the social norms embedded in that language" learn vocabulary and highly salient syntactic patterns. Nevertheless, he too observes that "creoles usually have no obligatory plural markers" (318). Mufwene (1986a) points out that in a number of English creoles, including Gullah, Jamaican, and Guyanese, there is no morphologically indefinite plural. Rather, he argues, indefinite nouns name kinds or classes. Holm (1988: 193) similarly recognizes that "[u]nlike nouns in their European lexical-source languages, creole nouns are not inflected to indicate number ...[but] can co-occur with a free morpheme which indicates plurality and is homophonous with the third person plural pronoun 'they.'" He further observes that this plural marker, which is generally more frequent with animate nouns, conveys the idea of definiteness. James's (2001: 10) detailed analysis of the Tobagonian Noun Phrase also provides a useful discussion of the association of definiteness and plurality. Like Mufwene, James describes Creole nouns as signaling only "class or category of referents" (7). Definite nouns can be further marked as countable, that is, for singularity or plurality.

Examples (1) and (2) demonstrate that these alternatives are also available to Virgin Islanders.

(1) [*bʌd* kya:n flʌi widʌut *wiŋ*]³   Indefinite
     "birds can't fly without wings"

(2) [lai dʌŋ wI dʌ *dag*,   Definite, Singular
     ju wʊ gɛt ʌp wid de *fliz*]   Definite, Plural
     "[if you] lie down with dogs,
     you will get up with fleas"

Also of interest are several quantitative studies, which identify statistically meaningful influences on the alternation of plural variants: Patrick 1994, Rickford 1986b, Schneider 1997 and Singler 1989. We summarize these studies in Table 1, below. As the table shows, three of the four studies address only the alternation of the bare noun and the Standard English morpheme. This is because the Creole variant either did not occur or occurred too infrequently for quantitative analysis. Patrick's data allow him to consider {-dem} as well as {-s}. Since he reports different conditioning factors for each of these morphemes, we present his results in separate rows in Table 1.

Interestingly none of these studies identifies semantic factors (e.g., definiteness, genericity) as key. However, all agree that the frequency and nature of plural marking is speaker dependent and that the alternation of {-s} and the noun stem is associated with phonological conditioning, especially on the segment preceding the plural morpheme. In these corpora, neither definiteness nor genericity was found to significantly influence plural marking.

As we show below, the resolution of this paradox lies in recognizing that bare nouns represent four very different types of conditioning: semantic content, morphological form, phonological form, and discourse (speaker/cultural) orientation.

Table 1. Quantitative studies of plural marking in varieties of Englishes in the African Diaspora

Study & Variety	Dep. Variable	+/-Def.	Pre- nominal Modifier	+/-Animate	Prec. Seg.	Fol. Seg.	Speaker	+/-Generic
Patrick 1994 Jamaican Patwa	{-s} bare noun		Def. Art. > Poss. > Unmarked>	Weight /measure > Time/day> Human > Thing > Inanimate> Animal > Crop/plant	Vowel > +Sib. > -Sib. Cons.	NS	8 spkrs. p. = .13–.87	NS
Patrick 1994 Jamaican Patwa	{-dem} bare noun		Def. Art. > Unmarked > Poss. > Quant. > Num. > Demonstrative	Human > Inanimate	NS	Cons. > Pause > Vowel	NS	NS
Rickford 1986b[4] Gullah	{-s} bare noun	NS[5]	NS		Vowel > +Sib. cons. > - Sib. Cons.	Vowel > Pause = Cons.[6]	1 spkr.	
Schneider 1997 AAE	{-s} bare noun		Other > Quant > Num.		Vowel > +Sib. cons.> - Sib. Cons.	Vowel > Cons. > Pause	10 spkrs. p. = .29 - 1.00	
Singler 1989 Liberian Settler English	{-s} bare noun				+Sib. cons. > Vowel > – Sib. Cons.	NS	3 spkrs. p. = .25–.64	+Generic > -Generic

3. Analysis

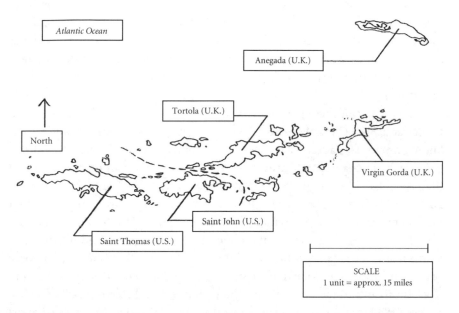

Map 1. Geographic proximity of British and U. S. Virgin Islands Saint Thomas, Saint John, Tortola, and Anegada

3.1 The corpora

St. Thomas, St. John, Tortola, and Anegada are geographically proximate. However, like much of the Caribbean, these islands have been partitioned by foreign interests. Today St. Thomas and St. John form one district of the U. S. Virgin Islands[7] whereas Tortola and Anegada are part of the British Virgin Islands (BVI). Nevertheless, the history, economy, and culture of these islands unite them. For example, the first sugar cane planted on St. Thomas came from slips grown in Tortola, and petty trade was conducted among these islands even before the colonial infrastructure was fully established (Dookhan 1994: 76, 93). Ties were strengthened among the four islands when, for a short time in 1801 and between 1807–1815, all of the Virgin Islands were under British control. Since what Virgin Islanders call "slavery time," kinship networks have extended across the four islands (e.g., Olwig 1985), and, even today, it is not uncommon to find Virgin Islanders with family on two or more of these islands. As we show below, this intra-island connectiveness has resulted in a degree of linguistic unity.

When a conversational frame is established (by speech act, participants, setting, etc.), Virgin Islanders, like speakers everywhere, respond with an appropriate language variety. In order to illustrate the role conversational frame plays in data collection, the present study draws on corpora from four settings, all of which represent performed speech. The settings differ crucially in terms of audience (local vs. non-local) and speech event (folktale vs. political forum).

The earliest of these corpora contains folk tales collected by Arthur Huff Fauset and Elsie Clews Parsons (Parsons (1969 [1936]). Parsons was a well-known folklorist; Fauset was a "public school teacher and principal, anthropologist, businessman and author [who] engaged in civic and race betterment undertakings" from a "prominent 'old line' Philadelphia family" (Andrews, Foster, and Harris, 1997: 268). The data we examine is from three of their informants: three adolescent males from St. Thomas, aged 11, 16, and 17.

The second corpus also contains folk tales. These were told by 16 informants from Anegada, St. John, and Tortola in the late 1930s[8] to J. C. Trevor, a British anthropologist known primarily for his research in physical anthropology.[9] In his introductory "Note on the Collection and Recording[10] of Tales" Trevor (1949, n. p.) indicates the transcriptions are "verbatim, a special effort having been made to reproduce variations in pronunciation, which often occur in the same tale " (Trevor 1949: 4).

We do not know to what extent Parsons, Fauset, and Trevor shared either their research agendas or their university affiliations with their informants. Nevertheless, the Virgin Islanders who told their folk tales to these researchers would have been well aware of the elitist assumptions formally educated people often hold about nonstandard language varieties. Moreover, it is not uncommon for outsiders (whatever they profess) to have difficulty comprehending conservative Virgin Islands English.[11] For these reasons, Parson-Faucet and Trevor's narrators are likely to have presented their tales in a language variety that would establish them as sophisticated and intelligent and that would have permitted easy and accurate documentation: they would have avoided their most conservative varieties.

The third set of folk tales was audio recorded by Sabino as she sat in the audience at the Enid M. Baa Library and Archives in St. Thomas during a Saturday morning program celebrating Virgin Islands culture in 1984. The program was radio broadcast live by a popular local station with a strong vernacular orientation. All of the storytellers are well known for their active participation in and their commitment to the preservation of Virgin Islands culture. We transcribed and coded the folktales, told by native Virgin Islanders, all of whom were from either St. Thomas or St. John.

The fourth corpus, a political forum broadcast by the same radio station that broadcast the folk tales, was audio-recorded by Sabino at her St. Thomas home in 1982. During this evening program, candidates campaigning for a seat in the U. S. Virgin Islands Legislature addressed a number of issues in response to questions put to them by the public. We transcribed and coded only candidates from St. Thomas and St. John.

3.2 Coding

There were several types of items excluded from the analysis. No tokens followed by a /s/ or /z/ in the oral texts or by an *s* in the written corpra were counted.[12] Additionally, we excluded tokens with two or more pre-nominal modifiers (e.g., *all his* frien's togeder [Trevor]) and doubly marked plurals (e.g., de girl*s dem* [Library]) since they could not be accommodated in a straightforward manner by the coding scheme required for the variable rule analysis. We also discounted strong plurals (e.g. children, men [Trevor]) since these were not subject to phonological conditioning.

4. Results

Previous studies have operationalized Creole plural marking as the occurrence of {-dem}. We think this is too narrow a definition and propose instead a more comprehensive analysis. Based on the findings of both the quantitative and qualitative studies, we suggest Figure 1 as a grammatical model for number marking that is shared by speakers from the islands under consideration, even those whose productions were invariant for particular speech acts. Crucially, in our view, these Virgin Islands English speakers control three morphological alternatives: the Creole plural marker {-dem}, the Standard English plural marker {-s}, and the noun stem, which, as shown in Figure 1, can represent either the deletion of {-dem}, the deletion of {-s}, or an indefinite noun that is undelimited for number. The validity of our proposal is born out by our analysis.

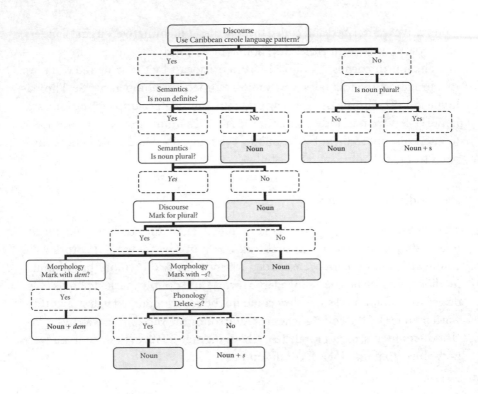

Figure 1. Pluralization within the multi-systemic Virgin Islands English repertoire

Departing substantially from previous quantitative analyses but consistent with the discussions in Alleyne (1980), Mufwene (1986a) and James (1994), our model recognizes, in addition to the conditions under which the plural morphemes {-s} and {-dem} appear, five distinct sources for a bare noun. Like Mufwene (1986a), we see the semantic factors as ontologically prior to the phonological factors within the Creole system. This raises substantial difficulties for analysis since, when a bare noun occurs, it is at times impossible to determine whether or not it replaces an underlying plural morpheme, and, if it does, whether the underlying form was {-dem} or {-s}.

We begin by examining all nouns that are semantically plural in the entire database. From this perspective, Virgin Islanders marked 451 (80%) of 562 plural nouns. Table 2 compares the rate of plural marking for the four corpora. As expected, given the formal nature of the event and the nature of the audience, the political forum shows the greatest proportion of marked nouns (91%).

Table 2. Number of variably marked plurals

	Parson-Fauset		Trevor		Lib. Tales		Pol Forum	
	N	%	N	%	N	%	N	%
Bare Noun	14	16	49	23	34	31	14	9
Marked	73	84	163	77	74	69	141	91
Total	87	100	212	100	108	100	155	100

Table 3 shows the rates at which definite and indefinite nouns are variably marked. Because, as we see in Figure 1, Standard English marking is embedded within the larger multi-systemic repertoire. Thus, we operationalize the Creole system as the first three rows of the table. The fourth row represents an alternative available only in Standard English (i.e., marked indefinite plurals).

Table 3. Variably marked plurals for definite and indefinite nouns

	Parson-Fauset		Trevor		Lib. Tales		Pol Forum	
	N	%	N	%	N	%	N	%
Def. Marked	33	38	106	50	64	59	119	77
Def. Unmarked	8	9	21	10	29	27	6	4
Indef. Unmarked	6	7	28	13	5	5	8	5
Indef. Marked	40	46	57	27	10	9	22	14
Total	87	100	212	100	108	100	155	100

As Table 4 demonstrates, it is only when we consider the role of audience (visitor vs. local) and genre (narrative vs. speech) that the Virgin Islands data are consistent with the published literature: we find the least marking of definite nouns (31%) occurs in the narrative discourse addressed to a Virgin Islands audience and that when marking of nouns is increased for a local audience, definite nouns are unmarked at a substantially lower rate (4%) than indefinite nouns (27%).

Table 4. A comparison of unmarked definite and indefinite nouns

	Parsons-Fauset (visitor/narrative)		Trevor (visitor/narrative)		Lib.Tales (Local/narrative)		Pol. Forum (Local/speech)	
	N	%	N	%	N	%	N	%
Unmarked Indefinites	6/46	13	28/85	33	5/15	33	8/30	27
Unmarked Definites	8/41	20	21/127	17	29/93	31	6/125	4

Even more revealing is the distribution of forms in the library folk tale corpus shown in Tables 5 and 6. Table 5 shows the frequency of plural forms by speaker. Three of the storytellers used {-s} less frequently than they did the Creole alternatives (i.e., -*dem* plus noun stem). The exception is Speaker C, a writer who frequently uses {-dem} in the dialog of her undereducated, working class characters.

Table 5. Frequency of plural forms by speaker

	N. Marked	N. Unmarked	% {-s}	% {-dem}	% Noun Stem
Speaker A	10	11	48	0	52
Speaker B	4	9	31	0	69
Speaker C	32	3	89	3	9
Speaker D	28	11	38	33	28

Table 6, which illustrates the distribution of only the marked forms in the library folk tale corpus, provides additional evidence of Atlantic Creole patterning (Holm 1988), and demonstrate the usefulness of the definite/indefinite matrix in revealing it. Indefinite nouns were never marked with {-dem} whereas definite nouns were.

Table 6. Distribution of marked forms in the library corpus

	N	%
Def.{-dem}	14	18
Def. {-s}	55	69
Indef. {-dem}	0	–
Indef. {-s}	10	13

Due to a happy coincidence, Speaker D participated in both the library folk tale program and the political forum. Thus, we are able to compare this speaker's plural marking across the two settings. Although Speaker D produced the greatest number of {-dem}s when telling a folk tale, during the political forum, Speaker D consistently (100%) marked nouns for plural according to the Standard English system

As shown in Figure 1, because it is impossible to determine whether a bare noun is unmarked because of discourse, semantic, or phonological constraints, it is not to be expected that Varbrul analysis will reveal the semantic patterning of the Creole system in a straightforward manner. We believe this is what motivates the lack of agreement among the studies in Table 1 (above) and Table 7 (below) regarding the significance of the semantic factors.

As shown in Table 7 below, [13] different semantic factors emerge as significant in three of the four Virgin Islands analyses: for the Parsons-Fauset and the
political forum corpora, the factor +/–GENERIC was significant with –GE-
NERIC nouns marked more frequently than +GENERIC nouns. Similar patterning was reported by (Singler 1989). In addition, the factor +/–DEFINITE
was significant for the political forum. For the library corpus, which contained
the only instances of {-dem}, the relevant semantic conditioning factor is
identified as pre-nominal modification as it was in Jamaican Patwa (Patrick
1994) and in African American Vernacular English (Schneider 1997).

The phonological patterning reported in the literature is revealed to a
degree in two of the analyses. The Trevor corpus shows evidence of deletion at
the level of the word formation: for Trevor's informants both noun stems that
end in vowels (and thus take the [-z] form of the plural) and those that require
the [-əz] plural form are marked significantly more frequently than those that
end in non-sibilant consonants. Thus it appears that Trevor's informants are
avoiding the creation of word-final clusters. The political forum corpus shows
evidence of the level of speech production. The variable rule analysis suggests
that the politicians (most of whom are professional people with advanced
degrees) pluralize Standard English noun stems regardless of the nature of the
final segment. However, like Rickford's informant, there is also a tendency to
subsequently delete the Standard English plural morpheme when its addition

Table 7. VARBUL results for four Virgin Islands English Corpora

Study-date	Dep. variable	+/–Def.	Pre-nominal Modifier	Prec. Seg.	Fol. Seg.	Speaker	+/–Generic	Age	Sex	Island
Parsons-Fauset 1937	-s bare noun	NS	NS	NS	NS	NS (N=3)	–Generic > +Generic			St. Thomas
Trevor 1949	-s bare noun		NS	Vowel = + Sib. Cons> –Sib. Cons.	NS	N = 16 (p. =.05 –.63)	NS	NS	NS	St. John> Tortola > Anegada
Political Forum 1982	-s bare noun	+Def[14] > –Def. > NS	NS		Vowel[15] > Pause > Cons.	N=4 > NS	–Generic[16] > +Generic		NS	
Library tales 1994	-dem -s bare noun	NS	Num. > Unmkt > Quant. > Dem.	NS	NS	N=4. (p.=.07–.26)				

results in a word-final cluster that cannot be eliminated through re-syllabification (e.g., bills of → bill sof).

In addition, our Varbrul analyses show the expected patterning across the islands, a patterning that reflects economic development, especially involvement with tourism: Anegada < Tortola < St. John (< St. Thomas). Finally, as with the other communities that have been analyzed, plural marking in Virgin Islands shows the significance of the factor group speaker.

5.   Conclusions

Bearing in mind that the four corpora differ in terms of the settings and decades in which the data were collected and the audience to whom the speech acts were directed, these analyses of plural marking in Virgin Islands English illustrate the degree to which different methods of data collection lead to quantitative differences at the level of the community (Poplack 1988) as well as for individual speakers (Poplack 1981). When only the total frequency of noun pluralization is considered, the corpora are ordered as follows: Political forum (91%), Parson-Faucet (86%), Trevor (77%), Library tales (69%). However, when we consider the forms and strategies speakers used to arrive at these frequencies, we find discourse addressed to a local audience, whether formal or informal, shows greater evidence of the predicted Caribbean Creole language pattern. In the narrative discourse addressed to a Virgin Island audience, speakers used both the most conservative plural morpheme {-dem} and had the highest percent of unmarked nouns over all. The data also demonstrate that as discourse aimed at a local audience becomes more formal, speakers preserved the Creole language pattern by increasing the plural marking of definite nouns at a substantially higher rate than for indefinite nouns. These data also demonstrate that for this community audience has a greater influence on speech than does speech act. Additionally, comparison of the Speaker D's performance during the political forum and the library folk tale program reveals Virgin Islanders' facility with style shifting. Finally, comparison of the four corpora demonstrates that in over four decades there has been no appreciable shift towards Standard English in the semantics of this grammatical subsystem. The most recent corpus of folk tales performed before a local audience represents the most conservative variety of Virgin Islands English among the four corpora. However, this may not be the case for phonotactic patterning since preceding phonological environment, the factor group that speaks to permissible syllable shape, is a significant conditioning factor for only the early, most rural (i.e., Trevor) corpus.

Notes

1. Although more sympathetic than some observers, Pontoppidan's misperception of Neger-holland, formerly the vernacular language on St. Thomas and St. John, reflects the pervasive racism of his time.

2. Two of the four corpora we analyzed did not contain data for St. Croix or Virgin Gorda. Therefore, we cannot demonstrate that our findings are generalizable to these islands. However, although the St. Croix dialect differs from that of St. Thomas/St. John phonologi-cally, we hypothesize that the association of definiteness and plural marking is so widespread in the Anglophone Caribbean that a similar pattern exists on these islands as well. This hypothesis is based on published research (see below) as well as Sabino's knowledge of the community gained from more than ten years residence in St. Thomas.

3. These versions of the proverbs are from Trevor (1949). The pronunciation is that of conservative St. Thomas/St. John speech.

4. Rickford (1989) provides probabilities for zero. We have transposed these to provide the probabilities for the marked plural.

5. Rickford's (1989: 49) categories are "existentially presupposed (typically associated with the occurrence of a definite article in Creole languages) ... existentially asserted (typically associated with an indefinite article)... or existentially hypothesized (typically associated with zero, the creole 'generic' and/or non-specific article)."

6. Rickford's (1989: 51) text reads "Sibilant Consonants." However, logic and his example ("acre divide") suggest this is an error.

7. The United States purchased these islands from Denmark in 1917.

8. We omitted invariant speakers from the analysis. One speaker used only zero. Eight of Trevor's informants used only Standard English plural marking. Four of these were from Tortola, three from St. John, and one from Anegada. Two were women, six were men. Four were teenagers, two were adults in their 20s, one was in his thirties, and one was in his 40s.

9. Although his interests in eugenics and craniology might suggest his interest in the Virgin Islands was a bigoted one, this was not the case. Trevor held that "fallacious ideas of deep-rooted differences between [racial] groups of men (sic) are seized upon to serve political ends by discriminatory legislation and appeals to uninformed prejudice on quite hypotheti-cal 'racial' grounds" (Trevor 1973: 420).

10. Commercial audio recorders were being produced as early as the 1930s. Thus, it is possible that tales were audio recorded rather than transcribed.

11. For example, there is the apocryphal story of a maid who carried a child of the family for whom she worked to be baptized. When the minister asked for the child's name, the woman replied incredulously /tɪzpɪnpanši/. The minister, taken aback, repeated his question. The

woman politely repeated her answer. The exchange continued for some time in this manner until the minister shrugged his shoulders and said, "I baptize you, /pɪnpanši/ in the name of the Father, Son, and Holy Ghost". The woman, hardly believing her ears, returned home and sadly informed the family that inexplicably the minister had refused to use the name that was pinned to the child's gown, substituting instead a foreign name of his choice.

12. There were no tokens followed by /z/.

13. The factor groups +/– ANIMATE and +/– SUBJECT were not significant for any of the corpora.

14. Selected by both step up and step down.

15. Selected by step-down only.

16. Selected by step-down only.

The establishment and perpetuation of Anglophone white enclave communities in the Eastern Caribbean

The case of Island Harbour, Anguilla

Jeffrey P. Williams
Cleveland State University

1. Introduction

Small, isolated communities of local whites are found scattered throughout the Eastern Caribbean.[1] The members of these communities are descended from the indentured servants, *engagés*, and small-scale planters who participated in the European colonization of the region that began in the early seventeenth century. The dialects of English spoken in these communities, termed Anglo-Caribbean English by Williams (1987, 1988), provide important information regarding the nature and structure of the varieties of English that were present and participatory in the social matrix of creolization as it occurred in the Caribbean.

Investigations into the diachronic and synchronic relationships that hold between 'white' and 'black' English-derived speech in the Caribbean have been hindered by a lack of detailed knowledge of the 'white' dialects (however, cf., Childs, Reaser and Wolfram, this volume). The work that has been done has generally suffered from a lack of understanding of the social and cultural dynamics of 'whiteness' in Anglophone West Indian contexts (cf. Blake 1997, Holm 1980).

In this paper I will examine the establishment and perpetuation of the white enclave community of Island Harbour, with a focus on how these social events and processes have contributed to the development of a distinct dialect of the 'whites' within the village.

2.   Anguilla in the Eastern Caribbean

Situated approximately five miles north of St. Martin, Anguilla is the most northerly of the Leeward Antilles. It has an area of ninety square kilometers, being twenty-six kilometers long and five kilometers in width at its widest point. Anguilla is a low-lying limestone island with a maximum elevation of only sixty-six meters above sea level (Carty and Petty 1997: 3). There are very few sources of fresh water on the island, and no rivers or streams. Rainfall is scant on the island, with an average yearly precipitation of eighty-eight centimeters (Carty and Petty 1997: 3). Historically, the lack of rainfall and scarcity of freshwater made Anguilla a difficult environment in which to establish extensive plantations based on the production of sugar.

The population of the island is dispersed primarily along the extensive coastline in a number of villages. The preliminary count of the most recent census of May 2001, gives a population for Anguilla of 11,300. The Valley, which functions as the administrative center of the island, is the only major settlement located inland. A good system of hardtop roads links all of the villages together. The island is connected to the larger world through air service to Puerto Rico, Antigua, and St. Martin as well as frequent ferry service to St. Martin.

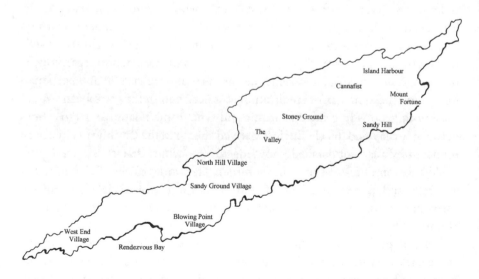

Map 1. Anguilla

3.   Early European settlement history

All of the existing colonial records indicate that the English undertook the first permanent European settlement on the island in 1650. The Dutch had attempted to establish a presence on the island as early as 1631, building a fort near the present-day village of Sandy Hill (see Map 1). The Dutch fort was destroyed by Spanish marauders long before the English arrived in the middle of the century.

Anguilla was somewhat unusual in the history of its settlement in that the island was settled without any commission from the King or the Governor-in-Chief of one of the other islands, and this left Anguilla out of the purview of most colonial administrators. Anguilla did not receive protection from the English Crown until 1660. The Crown's action to bring the island under its direct rule and protection was due in large part to a massive raid that took place in 1656. The raid dispersed much of the original English settler population, and the population that came after the 1656 raid was mostly freed and runaway indentured servants from nearby St. Kitts, Nevis, and Antigua (Anguilla Archives). The archival records also indicate that a percentage of the settlers were also made up of small holders, debtors, and criminals. Anguilla underwent another large-scale raid in 1666 at the hands of the French, and once again, a large portion of the settler population was forced to leave the island. William Willoughby sailed with a group of settlers — mostly "time out," a colonial term that refers to settlers who had only recently been released from servitude — from Barbados in 1667 to resettle the northern Leeward Islands of Montserrat, Saba, Antigua, and Anguilla (Anguilla Archives). Archival sources indicate that another shipment of settlers from Barbados reached Anguilla in 1668.

Late in the seventeenth century (circa 1688–89), there are references to a group called the "Wild Irish" coming to Anguilla from the French portion of St. Kitts (Anguilla Archives). The "Wild Irish" ravaged the settlements of Anguilla after their arrival, forcing the existing settlers to take refuge in the bush. Some Anguillians were also removed and resettled on Antigua in 1689 (Jones 1936: 16). The present-day Harrigans of the village of Island Harbour are in part descended from the "Wild Irish" of seventeenth century Anguilla.[2]

3.1   The eighteenth century and slavery on Anguilla

From all accounts, it appears that the island was often plundered by the French from nearby islands during the eighteenth century. The culmination of the hostilities between English Anguilla and French St. Martin came in 1796 when 400 French soldiers landed at Rendezvous Bay and advanced eastwards, destroying major settlements at South Hill and The Valley (Carty and Petty 1997: 59). The Anguillian militia was forced to retreat as far as Sandy Hill in the east. British reinforcements arrived from St. Kitts and the French retreated to St. Martin (Carty and Petty 1997: 60). The destruction caused by the French incursion did further damage to the already unstable socio-economic conditions on the island. The sugar industry on Anguilla had suffered throughout the seventeenth and eighteenth centuries due to a lack of dependable rainfall and a lack of investment capital by local planters. The Anguillian cash crop enterprise was not able to entice large-scale planters with capital to invest in large tracts of land, or in amassing a large labor pool comprised primarily of slaves. Instead, Anguillian settlers owned small plots of land, and typically only a few slaves who worked with them and their family members in the fields and pastures.

Slavery did not become fully established on Anguilla until late in the eighteenth century, and even then, the ratio of slaves to whites and free coloreds did not ever match the proportions that we find typical in most of the Eastern Caribbean during the height of slavery. Slave mortality on Anguilla was reportedly lower than that in many of the other English islands in the region (Knight 1997: 92). The 1750 population information for Anguilla, albeit incomplete, shows 350 whites, 38 free coloreds, and 1,962 blacks (Knight 1997: 48).

3.2   Pre-emancipation in nineteenth century Anguilla

Table 1 below gives the demography of the three Anguillian settlement regions in 1819.

Table 1. Census of 1819

	Whites	Free Coloreds & Blacks	Slaves
The Valley (center)	85	64	570
Spring (east)	183	109	901
Road (west)	97	144	917

This census demonstrates that by the early nineteenth century, the eastern end of the island was the most populous region. It is also the region that had the greatest number and percentage of whites vis-à-vis the total population of both the region and the community. The eastern end of the island would continue to be the stronghold of white settlement throughout the Emancipation and post-Emancipation history of the island and carry on into the present-day spatial demographics of Anguilla.

The Leeward Islands Administration that had included Anguilla was disbanded in 1816 and the various islands were then grouped into two large political and administrative units. The one that included Anguilla also was comprised of St. Kitts, Nevis, and the Virgin Islands (Carty and Petty 1997: 60). Despite actions on the part of the local Anguillian population and the local commissioners, Anguilla's permanent union with St. Kitts was established in 1825. Anguilla was permitted to send only one representative to the House of Assembly, and a local governing body known as Vestry was established in 1827 (Carty and Petty 1997: 61). The Vestry system divided the island into three large electoral divisions: Road, Valley, and Spring. The Spring included the entire eastern end of the island, while the other two divisions comprised the western end and the center respectively. This division had also been in place in describing the locations of various populations on the island prior to its official adoption through the Vestry system (Anguilla Archives).

By 1830, the white population of the island of Anguilla had diminished by nearly 30 percent. The census of that year breaks down the overall population into groups of 200 whites, 399 free coloreds, and 2600 blacks, without differentiating the data according to administrative region (Knight 1997: 51). A partial reason for the decline in the white population is the growing discontent among the Anguillian population with living conditions on the island. The weak political representation that the islanders endured prompted those who could emigrate to do so.

The 1830s on Anguilla saw a period of prolonged droughts that destroyed food crops, animals, and caused human famine. Slaves who had become idle as a result of adverse conditions were permitted by their masters to leave the island and earn a living on other islands. Some of these slaves were able to acquire enough money to buy their own or their family members' freedom. A remittance-type economy developed during this time that became the model for economic life on the island for decades to come.

Slavery on Anguilla came to end in 1838 when the St. Kitts Legislature abolished the apprenticeship system that had been provided for by the Emancipation Act of 1833 (Carty and Petty 1997: 61). By this time, the already fragile sugar industry had all but disappeared from the landscape.

3.3   Post-emancipation Anguilla

After emancipation, a number of white colonists left the island to settle in North America and other parts of the Caribbean. Their estates were sold piecemeal to the descendants of the slaves who had worked them, or acquired through the practice of quiet possession (Jones 1936: 22). Other ex-slaves were able to rent land through a system of in-kind payments, since cash in the poverty-stricken economy was scarce. Anguilla developed into a society of independent peasants who settled on any cultivatable piece of land that they could find.

Living conditions on the island did not improve during the 1840s, and the Governor of the Union established a plan to evacuate the entire population of the island to the Demerara colony of British Guiana (present-day Guyana) (Carty and Petty 1997: 62). Although three vessels arrived to transport the Anguillians to British Guiana, only a handful of Anguillians accepted the offer. Furthermore, most of the other islands in the Eastern Caribbean offered support to the devastated island by providing offers of free transportation, and guarantees of employment; still, few Anguillians were amenable to the offer of emigration. Anguillian society began to be referred to as an "assemblage of paupers" (Carty and Petty 1997: 62).

The general distressed conditions of Anguillian life prompted some Anguillians to work as indentured laborers on the sugar plantations in St. Croix during the 1870s (Jones 1936: 24). The 1880 census of the island shows 202 whites and 3,017 free coloreds and blacks (Knight 1997: 53). Figure 1 shows the relative stability of the overall population of the island during the eighteenth and nineteenth centuries, with a gradual decline in the white population. Although the status of blacks and coloreds changed after emancipation, their numbers did not fluctuate dramatically at any point during this time. Overall, the population

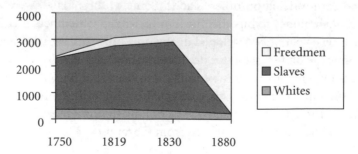

Figure 1.   Population trends on Anguilla

of the island has been stable, which has promoted a degree of linguistic stability that many other Eastern Caribbean islands have not experienced due to drastic influxes of new slaves and the large-scale exodus of whites.

The nineteenth century on Anguilla came to a close with a devastating famine in 1890 that was caused by an extended period of drought. According to colonial records, the drought obliterated all of the food crops of the island, and destroyed most of the cattle, sheep, and pigs. Nearly 90% of the total population of 4,400 was provided with government assistance to prevent starvation. This event prompted those that could to immigrate to the United States, and an Anguillian colony was established at Perth Amboy, New Jersey. During World War I, Anguillian men worked at the munitions factories in the region.

4. Present-day settlement patterns on Anguilla

Many settlements on Anguilla have their origins in the early colonization of the island. A few villages are situated in areas very near to pre-Columbian settlement sites on the island — most near sources of fresh water. Map 1 shows that the majority of settlements are found along the shore of the island, with the major exception being the capital of The Valley. There is a social and linguistic divide between East and West-enders. The polar extremes along this continuum are the villages of Island Harbour and West End respectively.

Development has come to Anguilla slowly, but its growth has been rapid. Phone service was not available on the island until the middle 1960s. Communication between communities before this was minimal. Individuals might only rarely leave their natal village. Electricity was not brought to the far eastern end of the island, to the villages of Island Harbour, East End, and Mount Fortune until the 1980s. Concrete-block houses did not become the common sights that they are nowadays until after Hurricane Luis devastated the island in 1995. Before that, many poorer Anguillians lived in wattle-and-daub houses; only one of which remains standing as of August 2001.

5. Color, class, and language choice in Anguilla

Not unlike other societies in the Eastern Caribbean, color and class on Anguilla serve to stratify society into several fluid classes. This system of social classification has its origins in the colonial history of the island, and differs from what is typically described regarding color and class in the United States. Anguillians recognize the differences implicitly as demonstrated by the fact that Americans, both "white" and "black," are classified using terms outside the local system.

The local system has three basic terms: clear or clear-skinned, brown or brown-skinned, and black. There is no corresponding term "black-skinned." While these terms are ostensibly based on phenotypic differences in skin color, they refer to a host of social variables that create a constellation of identity features, which can be negotiated in the course of social interaction and movement. One of the most salient variables in the constellation of identity features is the texture, or type of hair that an individual possesses. One consultant told me that you could always tell when someone is really a clear-skinned person by his/her hair. "Good" hair is straight, or slightly wavy hair. Kinky, curly, or otherwise marked hair is the outward sign of a person who cannot claim to be truly "clear" (J. O. Webster, p.c.).

Color and class are negotiable variables within the social discourse of Anguillian society. On many occasions, I have witnessed individuals asserting and negotiating their color/class identity. I was talking with a very dark skinned resident of the village, who, in the span of a twenty-minute conversation, self-identified as being black, brown-skinned, and clear-skinned. In each instance of color identification, this individual was seeking to establish membership in one group or another, while simultaneously erecting a social barrier to all other possible group identification. Clearly, the role of color and class is significant in the analysis of sociolinguistic variation in the varieties of Anguillian English.

For the remainder of this paper, I will present information on the varieties of English spoken in the village of Island Harbour, focusing primarily on the dialect of the "clear-skinned" individuals of the Webster family. The data for the description that follows were collected by the author during approximately three months of field research in the village spread over three different trips to the island. The corpus of tape-recorded data consists of thirty hours of spontaneous discourse, conversation about the history of the village, formal elicitation, and life history narrative.[3] All of the consultants for this study had been born in the village. Many of the men had spent considerable time working abroad, while the women had remained on the island for the majority of their lives. The consultants ranged in age from 43 to 82 years in 1999. There are no clear-skinned Websters younger than my youngest consultant who was 43 in 1999. The oldest clear-skinned female Webster died in late 2000, at the age of 83.

6. Background to the dialect of Island Harbour Village

The village of Island Harbour is located along a natural harbor with a protective cay on the northeastern coast of the island (see Map 1). The village has grown considerably over the past several decades, attracting residents from other West Indian territories including Guyana, St. Martin, and St. Kitts. However, the village still retains a parochial, isolationist attitude and the opinions of Anguillians from other parts of the island are that the residents of Island Harbour are haughty, aloof, and "in-bred."[4] Island Harbour is also one of the traditional communities of the local white population of the island. Other white populations can be found within the village of Stoney Ground, while the now abandoned village of Canafist once was home to a small white group.[5] (see Map 2).

The origins of Island Harbour Village are not indicated in any of the colonial records; however, the community's ethnohistory provides some details on the settlement history of the community. Utilizing genealogical reckoning, ethnohistory, and the record of shipwrecks on the island (cf. Berglund 1995), it is apparent that a group of Scottish-born settlers bound from Grenada to England shipwrecked on Scrub Island, a relatively small island just off the northern tip of Anguilla and visible from Island Harbour. The ship was the English brigantine "Antelope" which had left Grenada for England in 1771 (Berglund 1995: 5). Ethnohistorical accounts state that there were only three

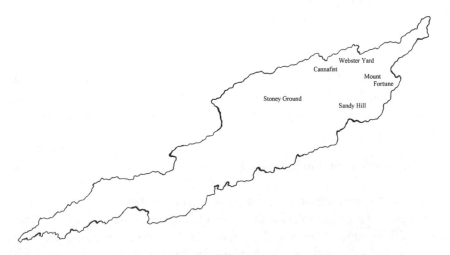

Map 2. Historic and Contemporary White Enclave Communities on Anguilla

survivors of the shipwreck — all brothers sharing the surname Webster. They are thought to have made their way to the main island of Anguilla shortly after the wreck, in search of a source of fresh water. Two of the brothers settled somewhere near the center of the present-day village near a site of fresh water called "The Fountain," which had also been a religious pilgrimage site for pre-Columbian peoples in the region. The local accounts go on to provide information that these two brothers found wives from the local white population that lived in the area south of Island Harbour, in the historical village of Canafist. The third brother is thought to have settled at a location called Sandy Point; however, no further information is known about him or any of his descendants.[6] The ethnohistorical account of the coming of Websters to Anguilla is reinforced by the archival records of settler lists, wills, and other legal documents, where the surname Webster does not appear in any transactions or records until 1832.

Within living memory of the older members of the village, Island Harbour was referred to as "Webster Yard." This toponym was used because everyone who lived there was a Webster, either by birth or marriage. The following is a quote from an 83-year-old clear-skinned resident of Island Harbour regarding the use of the name "Webster Yard."

> That part of Island Harbour was always called the Big Webster Yard [pause]
> because they were all like one big family [pause]
> and the children came up [pause]
> but the Island Harbour folk now are mixed up [pause]
> they have the darker sets [pause]
> and my color now, so still there [pause]
> and they all change up.

Being a Webster in Anguillian social classification is synonymous with being clear-skinned. One of my consultants who is of mixed parentage told me, "my mother was a Smith, but my father was 100% Webster" (B. Webster, p.c.).

7.   Linguistic variation in Island Harbour

According to Anguillians, each village had its own distinctive dialect in the past. Again, the social isolation that prevailed between villages was the likely cause of this pattern. However, these distinctions have been eroding steadily as communication between villages has become quick and simple with an extensive telephone service provided through Cable and Wireless, and a system of hard-surfaced roads that connects all of the major settlements on the island. In spite of the role that increased intra-island communication has played in dialect leveling across the island, the Websters of Island Harbour are noted by all Anguillians as possessing distinct accentual and dialectal features.

8.   Island Harbour as a Homestead Society

Island Harbour represents, in microcosm, a version of Chaudenson's Phase I Homestead Society (2001). Homestead societies in Chaudenson's theory of creolization are represented by a constellation of cultural and linguistic traits that establish patterns of cultural behavior, including languages that typically change in the social evolution of a society. Chaudenson applies his theoretical model to the early stages of European colonization and the developmental phases of cultural and linguistic creolization.

Island Harbour can be seen to fit this model with minor modifications. Island Harbour was not founded until sometime late in the eighteenth century. It grew from an isolated, white-dominated community to an integrated, primarily black-dominated community, in the same way that the majority of societal configurations did in the entirety of the non-Hispanic Caribbean. The linguistic effects of the historical shift in demographic proportions of whites and blacks throughout the Anglophone Caribbean can only be speculated upon now since there was no *in situ* chronicling of the events that took place. However, examining the settlement and linguistic history of a community such as Island Harbour, even though it lacks a plantation focus, can be illustrative of the process of linguistic change that gave rise to creole genesis and development (see remarks by Aceto, this volume).

In Phase I, Chaudenson states that there is a spatial and social proximity of blacks and whites, with few distinctions in terms of cultural traits between the two. Chaudenson uses the term "whites" here to refer to social classification, not a phenotypic or biological one (2001: 121). He states that the white class would also contain individuals of mixed parentage, and describes the relationship that held between whites and black slaves in the colonial homestead society as complementary and asymmetrical.

The social universe of Island Harbour both confirms and contradicts some of Chaudenson's assertions. While there was likely a spatial proximity of whites and blacks in Homestead Societies from a diachronic perspective, there was also as likely a spatial symbolism that served to maintain the social boundary between the two groups. Symbolically, the official decrees against racial mixing were examples of boundary maintenance devices. If there were no persons of mixed color, then everything would be as simple as white and black, free and slave. Mixed color individuals challenged the system and created fuzziness in the boundary that had sharply separated white and black previously. Whites maintained the social distance between whites and blacks in a rigorous manner. The "basilectalization" of black speech in Mathews' nineteenth century Kittian Creole English texts is one such example (cf. Baker and Bruyn 1998). By exaggerating the marked features of the black speakers he portrayed in his texts, he could further distance himself, a white creole, from the black creoles with whom he shared a territorial parentage.

Asymmetry in the social interactions refers to the differential treatment that each group gives to each other. The same pattern holds in Island Harbour. Clear-skinned individuals and brown-skinned individuals are treated differently by blacks and vice-versa. Chaudenson characterizes this asymmetry in terms of three binary oppositions: domination and submission, assistance and dependence, and model and imitation. Only one of these oppositions holds for the post-emancipation homestead society of Island Harbour and that is assistance and dependence. Clear-skinned peoples are characterized, often mistakenly, as having wealth. They are seen as being in a position to assist blacks, who are likewise characterized as being poor.

9.   The social development of the Webster dialect

In the analysis of the social differentiation of language, social factors such as class, style, sex, color, ethnicity and social networks are used to describe the patterns of linguistic variation that are present within a linguistic variety (cf. Chambers and Trudgill 1998). None of these social factors, nor any other that has appeared in the sociolinguistic literature, can adequately describe the convergence of social structure and language use that characterizes one segment of the Island Harbour population.

As I outlined earlier in this paper, three brothers of Scottish descent, sharing the surname Webster, founded the current village of Island Harbour late in the eighteenth century. It appears from oral history that the brothers took wives from the small pool of local whites that lived in the eastern end of the island. It is also evident from oral history that soon after, a pattern of endogamy developed that would characterize the community up until the present day.

Community is not the correct term to use here, instead, the term *deme* coined by the anthropologist George Murdock in the late 1940s probably best characterizes the social structure found in white enclave communities. The deme is a local group that is endogamous that does not possess any unilinear descent principles. The social unit is a kin group and not a community, in the sociological sense of the term. According to Murdock (1949), exogamous demes are one of the principal origins of clans. Clans, in the strict anthropological sense, are not found in the enclave white populations, although that form of social structure would have been common to some of the founding ancestor populations.

The local Websters chose their marriage partners from their relatives that lived in "The Yard" (R. Webster, p.c.). The village was isolated from other villages on the island, and as is typical in most West Indian communities, the territory of the village typically defines the social universe of interaction. However, in most typical West Indian villages, there is available to any individual a selection of marriageable partners, delimited by class and color constraints. Webster's Yard was a white enclave community that created a social barrier to exogamous marriage through isolationism and an elementary structure with a positive marriage rule of strict color endogamy.

Positive marriage rules define whom a person should marry as opposed to negative marriage rules that define whom a person should not marry, and are found in complex kinship structures (cf. Levis-Strauss 1969). I have consulted many Websters about the marriage rules that existed in the community, since in the present-day these are no longer in force. It is clear from their explications that the rule was of the prescriptive type: essentially, marry a clear-skinned person. Although there were a number of liaisons between Webster men and brown-skinned women, they were not marriages in the social sense.

The "Wild Irish," who are represented in the contemporary population by individuals with the surname Harrigan, had also settled in the eastern end of the island, and their kin members would have formed a potential pool of spouses for Island Harbour Websters. However, since many of the males of the Harrigan line had already mixed with non-whites, further increasing the brown-skinned population, the Websters chose, for the most part, not to seek them out as possible marriage partners. Instead, most Websters chose their marriage partners from their Webster relatives, who they could be sure were clear-skinned by local definition. The marriage of first and second cousins was common in Webster's Yard.[7]

Increased contact with the larger world, often through the mechanism of males pursuing employment "off island," and the stigma that is frequently attached to the practice of cousin marriage by outsiders, has lead to the discontinuation of the practice. The last potential pairing of clear-skinned Websters was aborted, and both found partners external to the Webster social group. Several of the middle-aged Websters who were married to their first cousins when they were in their late teens, have divorced due to social embarrassment.

Marriage in most West Indian societies has correlated with a mating pattern that conjoins individuals of equal status based on color and class (Smith 1996: 87). In the social universe that was Webster's Yard, the only individuals within reasonable proximity who were of equal status were consanguines, or blood relatives. Maintaining color and class, although the Webster group existed outside the larger social sphere of nineteenth century Anguillian society, made it necessary to rely on a system of endogamy that was based on the *deme*, as discussed previously. This social strategy has been employed in every white enclave community that I have encountered, in both the Anglophone and Francophone West Indies.

9.1 Grammatical description of the Webster dialect of Island Harbour

In what follows, I will present an overview of some of the features of the Webster dialect of Island Harbour Village. The Webster dialect of Island Harbour is only one variety of English within the Anguillian linguistic landscape. The linguistic situation on Anguilla has yet to be documented, and in the only mention that has appeared in print, Cooper (1980: 42) designates Anguilla with Barbados as special linguistic cases that lie outside the overall British West Indian Creole linguistic system. In spite of Cooper's proposed alignment, Anguilla does have a variety of English-derived creole spoken widely on the island. A detailed examination of its features is beyond the purview of the present paper; however, comparison to this variety will be made in the sections that follow whenever possible.

9.2 Sound system

The Webster dialect of Island Harbour shows some phonological features that are clearly derived from Scots or Scottish English sources, while there are other feⱥtuⱥes thⱥt are clearly missing from those same sources. This patterning is consistent with the variety's koiné status.[8]

The consonantal system of the Webster dialect of English exhibits features that both link and separate it from other white enclave dialects of English in the Eastern Caribbean. As opposed to some other dialects of English spoken in West Indian white enclave communities such as Cherokee Sound in the Bahamas, the Webster variety does not exhibit a significant degree of h- dropping. This pattern is in agreement with the fact that there is no h- dropping in Scotland (Wells 1982b: 412).

The Webster dialect is primarily non-rhotic, although [r] is variably pronounced in some contexts by some speakers. The rhoticity of the Webster dialect is not a product of its Scottish ethnic origins; instead, non-rhoticity is likely a product of the koinéization process that took place in the Caribbean, since many of the dialects of English spoken in white enclave communities are also non-rhotic.

(1) [gʸanʔfaðər]
     "grandfather"   IH, CS, f, 83

(2) [wamz]
     "worms"   IH, CS, m, 81

(3) [kar]
     "car"   IH, CS, f, 83

The Webster dialect exhibits the /w/ and /v/ alternation that is found in many of the lesser-known English dialects of the post-colonial world (cf. Trudgill et al., in press; see Cutler, this volume). Typically, in the Webster dialect, the realization is with the intermediate value of [ß̞] — the voiced bilabial approximant.[9] The Webster dialect differs in this regard from the Bahamian white dialect of Cherokee Sound where only the use of v in place of w was recorded by Childs, Reaser, and Wolfram (this volume). The replacement in the Webster dialect involves both v and w with forms such as [ß̞ɔmɪt] "vomit" and [ß̞ɛbstər] "Webster."

Webster dialect as well as Anguillian Creole English and other English-derived dialects of the island replace the interdental fricatives /θ/ and /ð/ with /t/ and /d/ respectively; Wells (1982c) refers to the process as TH stopping. There is a degree of variation in the replacement of the fricatives with the corresponding stops, especially in careful speech. Context and the effect of vernacular language loyalty are the factors that affect whether pronunciation /θ/ and /ð/ will occur.

(4)   [dæt enʔ fo mi nau]   IH, CS, f, 83
       "That ain't for me now"

(5)   [diz]
       "these"   IH, CS, m, 80

(6)   [doz]
       "those"   IH, CS, m, 80

The Webster dialect also exhibits a slight degree of palatalization of velar stops
before the vowels /a/ and /i/ as in examples (7) through (11) below.

(7)   [gʸanʔfaðər]
       "grandfather"   IH, CS, f. 83

(8)   [gʸɪlz]
       "girls"   IH, CS, m, 43

(9)   [kʸarɪdʒ]
       "carriage"   IH, CS, f, 83

(10) [golʔ]
       "gold"

(11) [kolor]
       "color"

Example (7) is noteworthy since it shows the palatalization of the initial velar
obstruent in a lexical item where it is not typically reported for any dialect of
English, due to the fact that the /r/ is normally present and blocks the secondary palatalization process.

      In the Webster dialect, some words that would be expected to exhibit this
pattern, such as 'car,' do not demonstrate it. The palatalized version of the
word is the typical pronunciation in the creolized English of the island. The
non-palatalized pronunciation is very salient in terms of the folk dialectology
of the island, and it is one of the features that is diagnostic of the "clear-
skinned" speech.[10] I have yet to fully investigate this variability in usage, but it
appears to me that the pronunciation of this word is a marker of "whiteness" in
terms of social class distinctions.

      Other features of the dialect include the voicing of intervocalic /f/ as in
[nevuz] "nephews," and the lenition of final /t/ and /d/ when preceded by
another consonant as in [golʔ] "gold" and [ainʔ] "ain't." Lexical items in the
MOUTH set are typically realized with the Scots pronunciation /u/, a well-
known Scotticism outside of Scotland.

The connotation of these features is what often tricks North Americans who believe that clear-skinned Anguillians, especially Websters, from Island Harbour are either Scottish or Irish. Some Anguillians use this general North American misidentification to their advantage when attempting to establish new identities outside the West Indies.

9.3   Word order

The Webster dialect of Island Harbour as well as all other varieties of English spoken on Anguilla has a typical English-derived creole word order of Subject-Verb-Object. Arguments both in subject and object position may not be overtly expressed in a clause, depending on the amount of common knowledge between the speaker/s and interlocutor/s.

9.4   Noun phrases and nominals

Plurality is variably marked in all dialects of Anguillian English. Nouns that undergo suppletive changes for plurality are often doubly marked in forms such as "womens," while zero marked forms such as "fish" are often rendered as "fishes."

The Island Harbour dialect does not evidence any use of the postposed plural marker /dɛm/ that is part of the grammars of many English-derived Caribbean creoles. This form is not part of the grammar of Anguillian English Creole as it is spoken in parts of Island Harbour village or in other villages on the island.

9.5   Determiners

The determiners found in the Webster dialect are similar to those found in other varieties of English in the Eastern Caribbean. There is a variable realization of the initial interdental fricatives as stops in all forms, determined primarily by context and the pressures of vernacular language loyalty. The indefinite article alternates between the more vernacular form "one" [wan ~ an] and the more formal form "a" [e ~ ə].

9.6. Possession

The Webster dialect of Island Harbour employs two means to indicate possessor/possessed relations: juxtaposition and suffixation. Simple juxtaposition of two nominals in the order possessor-possessed occurs frequently in the speech of both males and females.

(12)   my mother father... my daddy father were brothers   IH, CS, f, 83

(13)   the big Webster yard   IH, CS, f, 83

(14)   my mother race from St. Martin   IH, CS, m, 82

There are also occurrences of the Standard English possessive suffix attached to the possessor as shown in examples (15) below.

(15)   in my father's time   IH, CS, f, 83

9.7   Pronouns

The pronominal system of the Webster dialect is very similar to those of other dialects of English spoken by members of white enclave communities in other parts of the Eastern Caribbean such as Barbados, Bequia, Saba, and St. Martin. In the jargon of creolistics, the pronominal system is very acrolectal in nature: it uses "I" [ai ~ ə] for first person singular, and "he/she" [hi]/[ʃi] for third person singular human males and females respectively. Speakers of the Webster dialect also use [awi] "all we" as the first person plural pronoun; this form is also used by Anguillian Creole English speakers as well.

(16)   I takes she to her patient   IH, CS, m, 43

(17)   I go take he Scrub tomorrow   IH, CS, m, 43

The Webster dialect does not make use of some forms that are part of the grammar of Anguillian English Creole such as the second person plural form [aju] "all you."

9.8   The verb phrase

The verb phrase in the Webster dialect of English spoken in Island Harbour typically consists of a predicate and its direct and indirect arguments. Indirect arguments that would typically be headed by a preposition in Standard English are often bare in the Webster dialect. Prepositions in the Webster dialect are used very infrequently. Example (17) above is just one such case.

9.8.1 *Tense and aspect*
Verbs in the Webster dialect are usually marked for both tense and aspect. Many of these categories are marked by preverbal articles, or auxiliaries, as is typically found in the English-derived Atlantic creoles.

9.8.1.1 *Present and part tense*
As in most dialects and varieties of English in the Eastern Caribbean, the present tense in the Webster dialect of Anguilla is often overtly indistinguishable from the past tense. In vernacular usage, neither is marked in any significant manner. As will be discussed below, the third person present -s is often used with all persons in the Webster dialect; however, the usage does not reflect an extension of the number and person system in the present tense but instead is used to mark the habitual aspect (cf. Williams, ms.).

9.8.1.2 *Verbal -s*
The extension of third person -s to all persons in the paradigm is a feature of the Webster dialect of Island Harbour. It is also a feature of the speech of other members of the village, and can be found as well in the speech of brown-skinned individuals and blacks in other villages on the island. Examples (18) through (21) provide only a few examples of the usage.

(18)   I goes there every Sunday   IH, CS, f, 83

(19)   I works here every night   IH, CS, m, 43

(20)   I goes to the Village everyday   IH, BS, m, 26

(21)   I goes there   IH, CS, m, 43

Another analysis of "does" in mesolectal varieties of the Eastern Caribbean English-derived creoles as well as the Webster dialect of Island Harbour is to see it simply as an example of the verbal -s habitual extended to all persons in the paradigm. This feature is common in many of the English dialects of the British Isles, including Scotland. In the southwestern counties of England, Elworthy (1879) provides information that the present habitual can be formed either with preverbal "do" [d?] or with the use of the third-person singular present tense form (verbal -s).

9.8.1.3 *Past perfect*
In the Webster dialect as in most other varieties of Anguillian English, the past perfect is commonly used in a variety of contexts. This form has been widely associated with the structure of African American Vernacular English (AAVE)

narrative style. In Anguillian Englishes, the form is common both in black and white varieties on the island, and is associated, to some degree, with formality and level of education. Its use is not restricted to the narrative style as has been reported in AAVE. Little work has been done regarding the provenance of this feature, and when it is reported in West Indian varieties, it is sometimes attributed to influence from AAVE (see Cutler, this volume). However, its presence in the Webster dialect provides preliminary evidence that the form does not likely derive from a North American source, and instead, likely has a source, or sources, in English dialects.

(22)	my friend, Eddie, he had call	IH, CS, m, 43
(23)	had buy/ had bought	IH, CS, m, 43
(24)	had gone/ had went/ had go	IH, CS, m, 83

9.8.1.4 *Future tense*
The future is marked with the preverbal particle /gɔn/ in Webster dialect. Similar forms are found in other varieties of Anguillian English and Creole.

(25)	Someday I /gɔn/ call you too, you know	IH, CS, f, 83

9.8.1.5.0 *Habitual/continuative*
The habitual/continuative aspect in Anguillian Englishes is a very salient feature. There is a continuum of marking for this category in the present tense that ranges from [də] to [də bi] to [dʌz]. The form [dʌz] is the only form that is not stigmatized within Anguillian social networks. The use of [də] or [də bi] is seen as being a mark of a person who would have not had a chance to participate in formal education. Color and class seem not to be salient variables that have an explanatory adequacy regarding the distribution of the forms, since all dialects make use of all forms (see examples (34) through (39) below). The Webster dialect of Island Harbour seems also to have variably had all three forms, as shown in examples (26) through (33).

(26)	It [də] leak	IH, CS, m, 43
(27)	Every night she [dʌz] come for you	IH, CS, m, 43
(28)	Those rooms [də] come hot	IH, CS, m, 43
(29)	When you goin down, the wind [dʌz] come up.	IH, CS, m, 81
(30)	From noon 'til three o'clock, it [də bi] hot	IH, CS, f, 83
(31)	We [dʌz] like the small ones	IH, CS, m, 83

(32)   It [dʌz] cause a fight   III, CS, f, 80

(33)   I [dʌz] send it always   IH, CS, f, 80

(34)   Shallow water [dʌz] feather the sea funny   IH, BS, m, 62

(35)   [mi hanʔ də hɔtʔ]   IH, BS, m, 27

(36)   If I [də] work six days, what day I /gɔn/ rest?   IH, BS, m, 62

(37)   I [dʌz] construction   IH, BS, m, 62

(38)   They [dʌzbi] big and big.   IH, B, m, 6

(39)   See why we [də] check um   BP, B, f, 40

9.8.1.5.1 *Past habitual*

The past habitual is typically marked with the preverbal "used to" with the verb in the unmarked, or infinitive form as in example (40) below. Anguillian Creole English uses the same construction to signal past habitual.

(40)   I ... I does ... I used to ... now I takes too long   IH, BS, m, 27

9.8.1.6 *Progressive aspect*

The Webster dialect exhibits significant variation in the forms that are used to mark the progressive aspect. This formal variation is typical of many of the dialects of English spoken by members of white enclave communities, again likely a product of the koinéization that gave rise to the ancestral dialects. In the speech of Websters in Island Harbour, the following constructions are heard.

(41)   Prefixed/suffixed progressive
       . . . and the new ones did now start [ə-] comin in   IH, CS, f, 83

(42)   Suffixed progressive
       she is goin' college in Maryland   IH, CS, m, 43

(43)   "do be"/suffixed progressive
       February, March corn do be comin'   IH, CS, m, 81

The suffixed progressive forms are the most common forms heard in public contexts, or when the dialect is being used with outsiders (i.e., non-Websters). However, in vernacular conversation especially among the oldest Websters, the prefixed/suffixed construction is common. This construction, along with the *do be*/suffixed one are considered to be archaic, and examples of the way that the older Websters spoke, especially in the times when there was no formal education.

9.8.1.7 *Completive aspect*

The completive aspect is not frequently used in any variety of Anguillian English due in part to its association with less-educated speech. On those occasions that I heard the form used and would ask another consultant about it, the response was typically that older people who hadn't been to school would use the construction. The use of completive "done" can be found in all speech varieties on the island.

(44)   He die done   IH, CS, m, 83

(45)   I done fire already   WE, B, m, 35

(46)   I done gone   IH, B, f, 45

9.8.2 *Copula*

The presence/absence of the copula has been a focus of discussion and debate for many contact varieties of English, including those spoken in the Eastern Caribbean. In the Webster dialect of Island Harbour, the copula is variably realized. I have not engaged in an exhaustive study of the variables that may affect its usage, and the examples that follow simply provide raw data.

(47)   That how the Island Harbour folk get so close one to another

(48)   The telephone is another something

(49)   That why my mother and father are in that way

10.   Questions

Varieties of Anguillian English follow the general Anglophone West Indian pattern of not inverting subjects and auxiliary verbs in question forms. Interrogatives are indicated through intonational cues and not through syntactic constructions.

(50)   you did go?   IH, CS, m, 43

11.   Negation

Speakers of the Webster dialect frequently mark negation with preverbal "ain't"/"t'aint"/"tisn't." Doubly marked forms are also typically of the Webster dialect of Island Harbour.

12. Lexicon

The lexicon of the Webster dialect differs from those of the other varieties of English spoken on Anguilla. In particular, there are some archaic forms and regionalisms that are not present in other varieties.

(51) gi
       "to give"   Scots

(52) lass
       "girl or woman"   Scots

(53) holt
       "to stop, or halt"   Scots

(54) [sɪmprɪs]
       "seamstress"   unknown

(55) corn on the hub
       "corn on the cob"   unknown

(56) latitude
       used as a directional indicator for land coordinates

(57) strangled up
       "tangled up"   unknown

(58) [fʌgairi]
       "an annoyance accompanied by excessive noise and lewd behavior"

This last form is possibly from the Scots form *feegarie* ~ *fleegarie* that has the following meanings:

(i)   a vagary, whim, (ii) finery, (iii) a 'jaw harp', (iv) a fastidious person, one fond of trifles (Scots Dialect Dictionary, 187).

While the form in the Webster dialect of Anguillian English is very similar phonetically to the Scots form, the semantic relationship between the two forms is obscure at best.

(59) stone sack
       "scrotum"   unknown

(60) jig
       "to dance vigorously"   Scots

13. Conclusion

The dialect of English spoken by members of the Webster *deme* functions as a marker of social identity. It provides the linguistic delineation of clear-skinned individuals in a broad color spectrum of modern-day Island Harbour village. In the times prior to present, when residential integration was not a social practice on Anguilla, the Webster dialect would have been the regional variety spoken within the territorial confines of "Webster's yard." However, with the disappearance of the yard as a bounded, spatial, and social space, the dialect of the family group — those who can bilaterally trace their ancestry to Websters — has become the boundary maintenance mechanism. In the speech of Websters of my generation — mid forties in age — the forms are changing, and shifting towards the Anguillian Creole English variety. I am certain with the passing of the last of the elder Websters, this enclave dialect of English, which developed within the social contexts of isolationism and endogamy, will disappear from the Anguillian linguistic landscape.

Abbreviations

CS	=	white, "clear skinned"
BS	=	brown skinned, "colored"
B	=	black, "dark skinned"
m	=	male
f	=	female
IH	=	Island Harbour
V	=	The Valley
WE	=	West End Village
BP	=	Blowing Point Village

Notes

* Funding for the research presented in this paper was provided by grants from The College of Graduate Studies, EFFRD program and The College of Arts and Sciences, Cleveland State University. I want to thank my friends and consultants in the village of Island Harbour, Anguilla, who have been so accommodating to me and my family during our stays in the community. I also wish to thank the Anguilla Archives and the Anguilla Public Library for access to unpublished materials relating to the history of the island. Any errors or discrepancies in this paper are solely my responsibility.

I would like to dedicate this paper to the memory of Miss Ruth Webster and Mr. Elbert Webster, both of who provided me with a window on life as it used to be in "Webster Yard," and who passed away in August of 2000 and January of 2001 and respectively.

1. A partial listing of these communities can be found in Williams 1985, 1987, 1988.

2. Although this group is partly Irish in ethnicity, they are typically classified as "brown-skinned" in the local color classification scheme. Historically, this group mixed with members of the African-descended population more readily than did the other European-descended groups on the island. This information, albeit in need of further investigation, may be further evidence of the alliances that were created between the Irish servants and the African slaves in the colonial Caribbean (cf. Beckles 1990).

3. All recordings were made using a Sony TC-D5M with Maxell Normal Bias cassette tapes. I obtained permission from all consultants before taping, with each participant completing an Informed Consent Statement.

4. This outsider view of white enclave communities in the West Indies replicates itself throughout the various islands — both Anglophone and Francophone — where a white minority is found.

5. Canafist village is no longer occupied. There are only a couple of houses still standing on the site. An older, clear-skinned female of the Webster family who now resides off-island owns one of these.

6. The Anguilla Archives provide information regarding the descendents of the original Websters with genealogical reckoning charts that ascend to two male individuals, one of whose name was Peter Webster. If there was a third brother who did survive and settled at Sandy Point, he most likely died before he and his spouse created any offspring.

7. Saunders (1994) reports similar patterns of marriage in the white communities of Spanish Wells, Cherokee Sound, Man-O-War Cay, and Hope Town in the Bahamas. For information on the linguistic situation in the white community of Cherokee Sound, see Childs, Reaser, and Wolfram, this volume.

8. Following suit with other varieties of English spoken in white enclave communities in the Anglophone Caribbean, the Webster dialect can be classified as a koiné (cf. Williams 1988).

9. A detailed set of arguments is presented in Trudgill et al. (2002) for this phonetic realization. The use of the subscript diacritic [¢] with the bilabial fricative symbol indicates a more open stricture, with no audible friction, no lip rounding (except before round vowels), and without approximation of the tongue towards the velum as in [w].

10. This pronunciation is found beyond the Webster dialect among other individuals in Island Harbour who are not Websters.

What are Creole languages?

An alternative approach to the Anglophone Atlantic world with special emphasis on Barbudan Creole English

Michael Aceto
East Carolina University

1. Introduction

My own recent fieldwork on the island of Barbuda, just to the north of Antigua, has raised questions regarding the social context and geographical location of creole language emergence. In many ways, questions about the nexus of creoles sharing the same lexifier language are among the most contentious in the field, stimulating no end of debate (e.g. see Huber & Parkvall 1999 as one example). Barbudan Creole English (BCE), as can be seen from the data presented below, represents a so-called "basilectal" creole, if one subscribes to the terms of the purported creole continuum and the associated decreolization model. Whether one views creole language varieties in a specific location within that theoretical model or not, the question of where the features of BCE emerged, locally or at some other location, either in the Caribbean or West Africa, may shed light on intra-lexifier relations throughout the Western Hemisphere.

For other languages called creoles by linguists, the question of where a specific variety emerged is less controversial. For example, the English-derived varieties in St. Lucia, Dominica, Carriacou (and presumably Grenada, which shares a similar joint Francophone/Anglophone history as the previous three cases) seem to have emerged considerably in situ on their respective islands (however, see Kephart 2000 for a view which suggests that the emergence of Carriacou English Creole as an importation even while acknowledging the influence of the island's earlier French Creole). How ever these language varieties emerged (e.g. significantly via relexification or calquing processes) and how to classify them are questions that still remain to be answered fully, though the contributions in this volume certainly illuminate these questions and suggest possible answers (see Garrett's contribution). However, in other cases of English-derived language emergence it is not entirely clear where the variety in question emerged. If it could be demonstrated, for example, that BCE had emerged on the island of Barbuda itself, then this would be a finding of great theoretical importance since BCE emerged within the time frame of slavery and colonization and yet Barbuda was not a plantation society but one in which the locals (i.e. African slaves and their descendents) lived their lives in some independence often with only a single Anglophone European as supervisor. The goal for the slaves on Barbuda was to provide goods (e.g. making leather and rope, raising livestock and limited crops) for consumption on the plantations on nearby Antigua (even today Antigua and Barbuda have maintained their association through a political confederation). In fact, during slavery, Barbudans were often threatened with transfer to Antiguan plantations as a punishment for what Europeans defined as unacceptable behavior.

This chapter examines some core features of BCE and then attempts to place BCE as well as other creoles within a typology of Creole languages that does not rely on the alleged creole continuum or related concepts such as decreolization as the means by which to differentiate creoles sharing a general geographical space (i.e. in this case, the Western Hemisphere or, on a smaller scale, the Caribbean) and the same lexifier language. This alternative system of classifications is an attempt to move away from viewing creoles only as more or less like their lexifiers. Nevertheless, one of these categories does in fact present some creoles as, more or less, dialects of the lexifier language.

2.   Some features of Barbudan Creole English

Grammatical features derived from data collected via fieldwork on Barbuda and the history of that location are discussed in more detail in Aceto (2002b), but the following is a short presentation of some of its core grammatical features. Barbuda is an island of approximately 1,500 residents, yet the breadth of variation heard on the ground is startling.

2.1 Progressive aspect

The following data illustrate no fewer than four different present progressive aspectual constructions in BCE: *a* + V(erb), *de* + V, V-*in*, and *a* + V-*in*. Clearly, the emergence of the *a* + V and *de* + V constructions on Barbuda cannot be viewed as the result of so-called "decreolization" by even the staunchest defender of the creole continuum concept since they are both assumed to be so-called "basilectal" constructions. Both constructions are heard in Barbuda, though there does seem to be a strong local preference for *a* + *V* constructions. The *V-in* construction exhibiting bound inflectional morphology is typically associated with so-called "mesolectal" varieties, though that characterization is only relevant if one subscribes to the assumptions built into the creole continuum perspective and the related concept of "decreolization" (see Aceto 1999 for a treatment of these concepts and their failure to capture some variation data collected in English-derived creole-speaking Caribbean locations). Perhaps what is most interesting about the aspectual data below is the use of *a* + *V-in* constructions, combining features of two of the previously listed grammatical strategies. The same pattern is described by McPhee (this volume) in her Bahamian data, though she labels it as "rare instances." Williams (p.c., September 2001) informs me that *a* + *V-in* constructions are widely used in Saba, also an island of the Eastern Caribbean (see also his contribution on Anguilla, this volume). The same construction is also heard in St. Croix (Arnold Highfield, p.c., September 1997). I assume that subscribers to the continuum model would possibly suggest that *a* + *V-in* results from a knowledge of both the basilectal and mesolectal forms or is a conflation of two segments of the purported continuum. However, I would describe this anticipated explanation as weak since it merely attempts to justify the existence of the continuum model rather than handle the data in a theoretically unbiased manner. Besides, this construction is extremely similar to what is found in archaic regional varieties of English as exemplified in the well known constructions "Ten Lords a-leapin," "She'll be a-comin round the mountain" or "The times they are a-changin" (see Wolfram & Christian 1976 and their discussion of this construction in Appalachian English). The topic of progressive aspectual constructions in Afro-Caribbean varieties of English and their relationship to dialect varieties of the lexifier will be treated in detail in Aceto (fc.a). Furthermore, notions associated with the creole continuum are not generally applied or expected to be found in such small and geographically precise locations as an island like Barbuda with a population of only

1,500 persons. Generally, communities even larger than the one found in Barbuda are designated as either "basilectal," "mesolectal" or "acrolectal," and if one moves across the territory in question, say, Jamaica or Guyana, one finds other communities that would be designated with one of the three terms. That is, one does not typically expect to find such as small community as that in Barbuda to reveal features typically associated with two or more of the lects in question.

(1)   yu mami a kaal yu ~ yu mada de kaal yu
      "Your mother is calling you."

(2)   ma mami a kaalin yu
      "My mother is calling you."

(3)   so waa mi a traiin fu se?
      "So what am I trying to say?"

(4)   wi a taak
      "we are talking."

2.2   Habitual aspect

A range of variation is also exhibited by several strategies for illustrating habituality in BCE. Data with preverbal *does* /doz/ are often associated with the Eastern Caribbean, though I have also documented this construction in use among speakers of a variety of Panamanian Creole English, which is typically grouped with the Western Caribbean Creoles (or Jamaican group) that is often assumed not to have this feature. Note also that many of the above constructions associated with progressive aspect may also indicate habituality as well (see Winford 1993 for a discussion of these two grammatical categories and their semantic overlap). Furthermore, an unmarked option is available when used with adverbials like /aal taim/ "all the time" or /aalwez/ "always."

(5)   wi doz traiin fi get di haus finiš nau
      "We have been trying to finish the house (for some time)."

(6)   ši du om aal taim ~ i doz aalweiz a du om
      "She does that all the time/she's always doing it."

(7)   buot a kam in bai nait
      "Boats often arrive at night."

2.3 Future markers

Winford (1993: 58–59) states that the semantic difference between the preverbal future markers "go" and "a go" is generally that the former indicates
"volition" and the latter "intention." However, I was unable to elicit these
purportedly different meanings explicitly through interviews with informants
on Barbuda. That is, all informants maintained that "go" and "a go" were the
same as was the rare instance of "gwan," which one consultant insisted was a
contraction of "go + on" or /go/ + /an/. It is possible that the meanings
Winford assigns to these two related markers "go" and "a go" were diachronically accurate and that they have subsequently collapsed into one semantic
range in a manner similar to the process documented for "will" and "be +
going + infinitive" future markers in more standard varieties of English (see
Scheffer 1975 and Wekker 1976). Few instances of /gwain/ were found in
Barbuda, and all suggestions by this researcher that /gwain/ was possibly a local
future tense marker were rejected by informants. In several instances, "gan"
arose, as did "wil."

(8) ya ga du dat tumaro?
     "Are you going to do that tomorrow?"

(9) mo go du dat tumaro
     "I'm going to do that tomorrow."

(10) mo go du am tumara
     "I'm going to do it tomorrow."

(11) yu šut wan dir an de go briŋ yu in
     "You shoot a deer and they're going to bring you in."

(12) ma sisa a go antiga tumara
     "My sister is going to Antigua tomorrow."

(13) ma sisa a go swiip di flor tumaro
     "My sister is going to sweep the floor tomorrow."

(14) mi a go du dat tumaro
     "I'm going to do that tomorrow."

(15) dem a ga kaal di šat; wa dem se keiri
     "They're going to call the shots. What they say must be listened to."

2.4 Past tense markers

The simple past tense marker /min/ is also realized as [mɪŋ] (with a velarized nasal) or as the reduced form /mi/. The form /di(d)/ is widespread in the Caribbean and is often associated with so-called "mesolectal" forms, but that characterization overlooks the highly likely fact that the past tense marker /di(d)/ may have always been a feature of many Caribbean Englishes since their emergence in the seventeenth through nineteenth centuries. That is, there is no historical reason not to assume that a variety of grammatical options were not always present in a range of Caribbean English-derived creoles in specific locations (see Alleyne 1971, Winford 2000).

(16)   an de mi hab plenti gol
       "And they had a lot of gold."

(17)   an a mi get op in pajama an go aut said
       "And I got up in my pajamas and went out side."

(18)   Luk mɪŋ go a skul
       "Luke went to school / Luke has gone to school."

(19)   de min a inglišman (a inglišman dem bi)
       "They were Englishmen."

(20)   so dem diez britania mi rul di wiev
       "In those days, Britain ruled the sea."

(21)   inglišman min a ruom di sii wid aal kaina buot, rait?
       "Englishmen were roaming the sea in many boats, right?"

(22)   las yir wan inglišman miŋ doŋ der investiget di polisman an dem
       "Last year an Englishman was down there to investigate the policemen."

(23)   an dem di luz dir laif den…
       "And they lost their lives then."

(24)   dem disaid dem aks Britan fu indipendent an Britan di gi am
       "Over here, they decided to ask Britain for independence and Britain gave it."

(25)   a inglišman di bi čif a polis; da kamišina a polis woz a inglišman
       "An Englishman was the chief of police; the commissioner of police was an Englishman."

3   Classifiying the English derived languages of the Caribbean

Many scholars (e.g. Thomason & Kaufman 1988) insist that creoles represent a case of broken transmission between the language providing the source of basic lexical material and the speakers creating the subsequent emerging creole language. However, this perspective may be most (and perhaps, in the Western Hemisphere, only) appropriate, when considering the English-derived cases, for the Surinamese creoles Sranan, Ndyuka, and Saramaccan in which English, as a possible source of on-going lexical and grammatical influence, was withdrawn from the emerging linguistic matrix as the British exchanged the colony with the Dutch for what was then in the seventeeth century "New Amsterdam" (later renamed "New York"). This description is clearly less accurate and appropriate for the vast majority of English-derived languages that also bear the name "creole" (e.g. Jamaican, Gullah, Belizean, et al.). That is, English persisted as an ambient language of power (and thus as one potential source of linguistic contact and influence) in these former colonies and territories before and well after the emergence of local Creole varieties, even if the intensity of contact with English dialect speakers varied from location to location over time. In fact, in Creole studies, rather than considering the Surinamese Creoles as exceptional cases of language emergence (i.e. in terms of external social circumstances which would have provided a crucible for the emergence of the subsequent languages), the field instead often considers these languages as the baseline against which all English-derived creoles in the Atlantic region are measured. Not surprisingly, all other English-derived Atlantic creole languages appear lacking regarding assumed "creole" features in this comparison despite the fact that no satisfactory typological inventory of so-called creole features has been established within the field (Plag 2001;[1] cf. McWhorter 1998). The circularity of calling these languages "creoles" and discussing them in terms of shared features without a satisfactory typological definition of what constitutes a creole language is a problematic reality of the field. In recent publications (e.g. Kautzsch and Schneider 2000), this conclusion is acknowledged and then inevitably, if one is to pursue study of these languages, pushed to the side. The distorted assumption that all English-derived creoles once "looked" more like one of the Surinamese creoles in terms of features thus ensures that all other English-derived creoles in the Atlantic region will appear less "creole-like" in comparison, despite the fact that the specific sociohistorical factors that gave rise to the Surinamese creoles are uncontroversially unique in the Americas. That is, the historical and social circumstances surrounding the genesis of the

Surinamese creoles only superficially resemble the emergence of most other English-derived varieties of the Atlantic region in which the diachronic source of many of the morphemes/lexemes (i.e. the superstrate) in the subsequent "creole" language has remained in contact with most of these languages (albeit in varying degrees of intensity) since their emergence (see similar remarks in Winford 2000: 242).

It is likely that comparing the Surinamese creoles to other English-derived creoles in the Atlantic region has encouraged researchers to perceive "decreolization" as an all-pervasive force moving English lexifier creoles in a unidirectional manner towards features associated with metropolitan or more standard varieties of English. Any language, creole or otherwise, has options for variation and change unrelated to the pressures of lexically related (even politically and socially prestigious) metropolitan languages (see Aceto 1999). Even if the purported effects of so-called "decreolization" could rigorously be distinguished from what is regular and normal diachronic change through language contact, which all languages (whether they be called "creole" or otherwise) exhibit everywhere, this concept has a tendency to obscure diachronic change that is not derived from contact with metropolitan varieties of English and to discourage research on Creole varieties which are assumed, from this perspective, to be less "creole-like" or "decreolized" variants of an earlier more "pure," "real," or "radical" Creole. These observations are discussed in more detail in Aceto (2002a).

The slave plantation is often considered the proto-typical environment for the emergence of Creole languages since this colonial context brought together components of a social matrix that seem especially conducive for the emergence and restructuring of colonial language varieties. That is, out of a demographic matrix formed in terms of a disproportionate ratio between the socially subordinate (i.e. often slaves in the Atlantic scenario) and the numerically smaller but politically more powerful superordinate group who were the original sources of most European language forms (i.e. colonial Europeans, in the Atlantic region), emerged a variety (creole or otherwise) that began to be used by African slaves at least initially as a lingua franca (see Baker [2000: 48] for what he terms "a medium for interethnic communication") and then later as a first language by children born into this context as well as a primary language of communication by adults (see Baker [2000: 54] for what he terms "a medium for community solidarity"; see McWhorter [2000] for a view of creole language emergence in which demographics plays little or no role). This general scenario accounts for many of the Creole Englishes spoken in the Atlantic

region such as Sranan in Suriname and some varieties of Jamaican, but it often
obscures the likely fact that a range of English-derived varieties may have
emerged in any geographical and cultural space where English was spoken as a
colonial language of power (see Alleyne 1971, Mufwene 2000). Furthermore,
though most of the participants on the dominated side of the equation were in
fact originally slaves in the Americas, not all the languages called creoles by
linguists, and not even all those varieties with an English-derived lexical base,
historically emerged within the context of the slave plantation.

There are several cases of language emergence that sit awkwardly within the
classification of the plantation experience, even if some of them are outgrowths
and extensions of the same general experience of European colonialization. For
example, Barbuda was populated with slaves for the explicit function to raise
food crops and manufacture goods to supply plantations on nearby islands such
as Antigua. In fact, Barbuda was not a colony but the private property of the
Codrington family, who used the island to offset the expenses of their plantations on Antigua, which was a British colony. These Barbudan slaves often came
in contact with no more than a handful of Anglophone Europeans and often
only a single individual (Aceto 2002b). Furthermore, several of the English-
derived varieties spoken in the Caribbean are significantly the result of
intra-Caribbean migration. Winer (1993) demonstrates that the emergence of
Trinidadian Creole English in the nineteenth century is largely the result of
immigration by a variety of ethnic groups who already spoke pre-existing and
wholly formed Creoles and Englishes while many locals in Trinidad were still
speaking a French-derived creole (see the more recent cases of language emergence in which English-derived languages were significantly influenced by
earlier Francophone languages described below). Winford (2000) insists that
Bajan immigrants provided one significant target for speakers in Trinidad as an
English-derived variety began to emerge strongly on that island. Nonetheless,
out of this matrix of Englishes derived largely from the Eastern Caribbean, a
new English-derived language variety emerged.

Non-Afro-American Anglo-Caribbean varieties, i.e. those English varieties
spoken among the descendants of Irish, Scots, and English settlers, have largely
been ignored within research paradigms except for the work of Williams
(1985, 1987). These English-derived language varieties spoken largely by Euro-
Caribbeans on Saba, Bequia, the Cayman Islands, and Barbados (see Williams,
this volume, for the case of Anguilla) may shed light on the Anglophone
component heard by Africans or Afro-Caribbeans working alongside many
of these European immigrants. These white indentured servants were often

treated socially no differently than African slaves; some of them even joined African-derived Maroon communities (see below).

At least two Surinamese creoles (Ndyuka and Saramaccan) are Maroon creoles that emerged as runaway slaves and rebels formed independent societies in the interior of the country. Maroon languages also emerged in remote mountainous areas of Jamaica (for the Surinamese Maroon creoles, see Smith 1987; for Jamaican Maroon language, see Bilby 1983). These creoles may still be considered related to (albeit crucially different from) the plantation creole phenomenon since in the Americas many of the new recruits to these independent societies were speakers of or at least familiar with the language emerging on plantations closer to population centers near the coast. In some locations in the Caribbean, Maroon groups even received some recruits from Irish servants who presumably spoke some form of English in addition to any familiarity with Irish (Beckles 1986).[2] However, what makes Maroon creoles truly unique (other than the specific matrix of contributing languages in any individual case of language emergence) is that they developed in greater isolation from European influences than languages emerging on plantations. Thus, not only are the Surinamese creoles extraordinary in that the original source of lexemes in those languages was removed as the colony transitioned from an English to a Dutch colony, but the Maroon creoles were further isolated from the major cultural developments (whether they be linguistic or otherwise) in population centers on the coast. These historical circumstances (and their linguistic repercussions) involving separation from the lexifier are qualitatively different from most if not nearly all other cases of creole emergence in the Anglophone Caribbean. That is, the social contexts for creole language emergence in Suriname are in fact not typical but unique to the extreme.

The emergence of other Creoles or Englishes are the result of transference of property from one colonial power to another (again, similar yet crucially different from the Suriname case discussed above). Several former French-held colonial territories in the Eastern Caribbean such as St. Lucia, Grenada, Dominica, and Carriacou, where a French-derived creole had earlier emerged, were subsequently transferred to British colonial control in the late eighteenth and early nineteenth centuries (there had been several exchanges of the same territories between these two European powers throughout the colonial period).[3] British dominion over these French creole-speaking islands for the last two centuries or so has resulted in the emergence of local varieties of English that seem to have been significantly calqued from or influenced by the earlier French-derived creole as the functional usage of English expanded more strongly into social domains (e.g. education, government) previously reserved for French or the French-derived creole (see Garrett, this volume, for the case of St. Lucia). These fascinating cases of language emergence have largely been ignored by researchers and are only now beginning to be studied (as many cases of non-plantation creoles have similarly been neglected; see Aceto [2002a] for a detailed description of Englishes and Creoles in the Western Hemisphere that have received little or no attention from linguists).

To sum up: in the Americas, there are English-derived varieties that have emerged due to the general colonial plantation experience and its influence, marronage, patterns in immigration, and/or the result of colonial transference in which the ambient European language of power has been switched. The fact of the matter is that even in the straightforward cases of plantation creoles such as Sranan in Suriname and some varieties of Jamaican, the results of all three scenarios have made themselves felt diachronically in a specific geographical location. That is, it would be difficult to find a location in the Anglophone Caribbean that has not been affected by the languages spoken by immigrants since emancipation in the nineteenth century and/or by varieties of the colo-nial language heard in local metropolitan population centers.

Aceto (1999) pointed out that a reliance on the concepts associated with the creole continuum/decreolization model has a tendency to view all changes in, at least, English-derived creole-speaking Caribbean societies only in terms of whether the feature in question was similar to or different from more standard varieties of English in form and function. I also provided examples from my data drawn from work on the English-derived creole of Bastimentos, a Panamanian island in the Caribbean Sea, which did not require externally based language contact explanations such as "decreolization" in order to ac-count for the variation and change exhibited in Bastimentos Creole English. The creole continuum terms "acrolect," "mesolect," and "basilect" reveal little about linguistic or sociohistorical processes invoked by speakers involved in the creation, distribution and maintenance of their language, except for the assumption (which is undoubtedly true in some specific well-defined cases) that some speakers are consciously or unconsciously shifting their language to-wards norms associated with metropolitan English. These terms "acrolect," "mesolect," and "basilect" only measure whether a given feature (or bundle of features) appears more like its lexifier language or not. From this perspective, the common assumption in the use of these terms is that so-called "mesolec-tal" varieties have simply "decreolized" under pressure from more standard varieties of English and that "basilectal" creoles have not undergone this same unidirectional change toward features associated with the lexifier. It must be remembered that the variety of Jamaican found in Bailey (1966) represented an abstract bundle of features (i.e. the bundle is abstract, not any individual feature) associated with the so-called "basilect," and DeCamp (1971) considered this type of abstraction to be a necessary first step in understanding variation in creole-speaking communities (the idea of the so-called [post-creole] continuum originated with DeCamp 1961). This abstraction suggests very strongly that, both from a diachronic and synchronic perspective, there have always been few if any speakers of the purported "basilect" revealing all of its associated features; in other words, relatively few individual English-derived creole speakers can be said to have ever exclusively displayed all the features of the largely abstract notion of "basilect." The reification "basilect" is simply a compilation of features that are considered typologically the furthest or most different from varieties of metropolitan English. Furthermore, any language, including Creole languages, can change in ways left unexplored by the assumptions of the creole continuum. For example, the effects of internally induced change have been left largely unexplored by researchers studying creole-speaking societies (Aceto 1999). In addition, some types of change, whether they are externally or internally motivated, may occur that do not resemble metropolitan varieties of English. In other words, I agree with researchers like Michaelis (2000: 163): "there are restructuring processes in creole languages that do not differ in principle from diachronic changes in non-creole languages." "Decreolization" undoubtedly occurs in some creole-speaking communities (and similar effects undoubtedly occur in what would be labeled non-creole-speaking communities; after all, it is one kind of language shift), but it is only one type of externally-motivated change, and does not simply represent change in and of itself in creole-speaking communities (see Mufwene [2000: 77] as well).

Agreement among creolists about terminology and definitions needed to discuss these languages has always been conspicuously lacking. Recently, the issue of whether creoles can be considered a linguistically distinct typological class has been reinitiated by McWhorter (1998), though many creolists would probably agree with Mufwene (2000) that creolization is a social process and not a structurally defined one. Many of the contributions found within Neumann-Holzschuh & Schneider (2000) also suggest strongly that there is not even an agreed upon definition of what precisely constitutes "restructuring" within the context of creolization and language change or whether the concept is related to the effects of second language acquisition, first language acquisition or contact-induced phenomena such as "decreolization." Winford

(2000: 242) notes, "we have some way to go in understanding the creative adaptation of substrate and superstrate inputs which shaped the grammar of the languages called creoles."

4. One alternative approach

Several researchers suggest that creolistics is best viewed as one of the branches contained within the discipline of contact linguistics (e.g. Thomason 1997, Neumann-Holzschuh & Schneider 2000). Though undoubtedly scholars more interested in language universals and cognitive issues might wish to nudge that characterization a bit towards a more inclusive definition, it is surely the case that contact between cultures and languages in the broadest possible sense is responsible for the emergence of so-called "creole" languages even if one believes the features of these languages are the result of first language acquisition processes displayed by children or second language acquisition phenomena produced by adults. The latter case appears more squarely grounded within language contact phenomena than the former even if principles of Universal Grammar are undoubtedly invoked by children born into a speech community in which all members grappled with and tried to make sense of previously unfamiliar language data (thus, considered here as broadly the result of language contact). The three labels presented below for Anglophone Caribbean language emergence focus on the results of the sociolinguistic factors (in terms of the speakers and the languages) involved (even if the terms are somewhat provisional) but not in terms of the specific resultant language contact effects (i.e. lexical, phonological, syntactic, etc.) à la Thomason and Kaufman (1988). Furthermore, there is no reason to assume that only one of each category (contrary to the assumptions of the continuum/decreolization model) may have emerged early in the history of a geographical space such as, for example, Jamaica. In fact, the distribution of each case type described below in a given area would also account for the range of varieties so often viewed as evidence or a reification of the so-called creole continuum.

The terms suggested below are born out of a need to clarify and distinguish major sociolinguistic and historical differences between so-called "creole genesis" and local language or dialect emergence. Few English-derived restructured languages in the Western Hemisphere seem to represent varieties "radically" different from the original input forms of the lexifier (e.g. the exceptional cases of the Surinamese creoles, some of the "deep(er)" varieties found in Jamaica and

Barbuda); other restructured languages appear to resemble more closely dialect emergence. For example, should all English-derived varieties in the Americas be considered as individual cases of actual creole genesis? For those who argue for up-dated variants of the monogenetic theory in regard to the Anglophone Atlantic world (e.g. Hancock 1986; McWhorter 1997a, 1998), the answer might be a qualified no. For these theorists, pidgin/creole genesis is largely assumed to have been a sui generis event in which many of the most significant grammatical features were later dispersed throughout the Atlantic region. Nevertheless, there is no doubt that every language has its own unique history in terms of language varieties involved in the local contact situation, the specific demographics present during crucial periods of formation and change, and the specific results of language contact and diachronic change in general. The present discussion is motivated by the theoretical orientation that most English-derived languages in the Caribbean never resembled one of the Surinamese creoles nor "deep" or so-called "basilectal" Jamaican or Guyanese, although, of course, every language called "creole" by linguists, in fact every dialect everywhere, will naturally exhibit the effects of common diachronic change since the earliest period of its local emergence. However, only certain creoles will exhibit actual creole genesis depending on the circumstances of their particular origins. For example, it seems appropriate to discuss the restricted list below of "Autonomous Creole Varieties" in terms of creole genesis but perhaps less appropriate when discussing "Immigrant Creole Varieties," in which wholly formed English-derived varieties already existing in the minds of immigrants deriving from various points of origin were in contact with speakers of other non-lexically-related languages (e.g. varieties of Spanish, decreasing African language usage, or French-derived creoles in some cultural and geographical spaces). In these cases, subsequent waves of Anglophone immigrants "swamped" whatever languages were spoken in situ whether these varieties be lexically-related or not in the specific area under consideration. For the group designated as "Dialect Creole Varieties" (at first glance this term may seem an oxymoron, but certainly not if one considers the term "creole" only to be representative of a social process) it also seems less appropriate to consider these as actual cases of creole genesis, though this designation does not contradict the fact that a new language variety has emerged. This category is significantly different from other cases in terms of specific demographic factors involved in language contact and the linguistic features that subsequently emerged. These distinctions are explained in more detail below.

The cases discussed below are an attempt to provide designations that reflect the different historical, demographic, and sociolinguistic factors involved in English-derived language emergence in the Caribbean. It is not intended in any way to imply that the different scenarios described below entail different cognitive processes on the parts of the human beings involved since it should be intuitive, to linguists at least, that the same species-specific brains are processing linguistic data in any and every case of language emergence in the world.

4.1 Immigrant Creole Varieties

In the Anglophone Caribbean, these languages are the result of pre-existing English-derived varieties "mixing" together to produce new varieties that are subsequently different in their totality from any single one of the input variet-ies. This category is transparently tied to the phenomenon of immigration and the leveling or koineization that may occur among related varieties (largely English-derived in this case) brought together in a new location.[4] That is, immigrants arrive, of course, speaking wholly formed native languages, and what defines these cases crucially is that at least one significant segment of the immigrant population arrives natively speaking English-derived varieties.[5] In this scenario, these Anglophone immigrants provided possible targets in their new host location for the emergence of local varieties based upon features heard among the immigrants but also influenced by the languages spoken by the locals in situ and by whatever non-English-derived languages were also spoken by some immigrant groups. The locals present earlier in the host location (see Mufwene 1996 and his concept of the Founder Principle) and the immigrants form an original linguistic matrix out of which new locally defined varieties (with also some of their own unique features) emerge. From a dia-chronic perspective, the language processes involved are similar to any human language (i.e., all languages exhibit the effects of language contact). English-derived creole languages in the Caribbean that fit this description would be those heard in Panama, Costa Rica, Trinidad, and perhaps any of the other former Francophone territories that are now transitioning towards an English-derived variety or Anglophone/Francophone bilingualism (see below). Immi-grant varieties are often overlooked, since their emergence is not directly tied to creolization during the period of slavery but are instead the result of more current (i.e. in the last 100–150 years) post-emancipation social circum-stances, due to the largely ignored fact and impact of intra-Caribbean migra-tion, but they may constitute a larger class than is typically considered.

The category of "Immigrant Creole Varieties" illustrates well (though not exclusively) the point that a range of English-derived creoles can emerge and be maintained in one location without each one converging towards a lexically related metropolitan variety. Among the English-derived varieties of Central America, the absence of a consistent model of spoken metropolitan English (i.e. in officially Spanish-speaking countries) excludes the concept of "decreolization" as a likely source in explaining the range of variation that can be found in these areas. The data from Aceto (1995, 1996, 1998, 1999) illustrate the range of variation that is possible in Bastimentos Creole English, suggesting that several related creole varieties — some with more creole features (how ever those are ultimately defined), others with more dialectal features — have always existed on Bastimentos (and perhaps in the larger province of Bocas del Toro in Panama as well) since they emerged from the matrix of fully-formed English-derived varieties spoken by West Indian immigrants in the late nineteenth and early twentieth centuries. Thus, present-day variation need not be considered only the result of "decreolization." This general conclusion regarding a range of English-derived creole varieties originally spoken by immigrants as well as the general time frame in question is similar to that presented by Winer (1984), who argues that Trinidadian Creole English is the result of contact between pre-existing Creoles and Englishes imported into Trinidad due to intra-Caribbean migration largely in the nineteenth century. Furthermore, the conclusion that a range of Creoles can co-exist within the same community without resorting to "decreolization" as the explanatory factor agrees with Alleyne (1971, 1980), who suggests that, due to what he calls a varied "acculturative process" (1971: 181), a spectrum of lexically-related varieties emerged from the earliest contact between Africans and Europeans.

Former Francophone areas that are shifting to English-derived varieties over the last century or more (e.g. St. Lucia, Grenada, Carriacou, and Dominica) are a bit problematic to handle. Garrett (this volume) argues that Anglophone linguistic targets and models in St. Lucia had been historically limited to institutional educational settings, and thus instruction in English and second-language learning is largely responsible for the emergence of vernacular English there. In St. Lucia, it appears the role for Anglophone immigrants or models originally was limited largely to the minds and mouths of English-speaking educators, though there does seem to be some Anglophone immigration from other points in the Caribbean mainly to the urban Castries area. The matrix of input varieties in other locations such as Carriacou, Grenada, and Dominica needs to be researched further and may indicate that some of the former

Francophone areas belong to the Dialect type below or as a combination between both the Immigrant and Dialect types. More research for these varieties is needed before these issues can be resolved satisfactorily.

4.2 Dialect Creole Varieties

Often "dialect" and "creole" are seen as mutually exclusive terms. Clearly some of the languages linguists call "creoles" due to social processes may appropriately be viewed as dialects of the superstrate (see Mufwene 2000). However, that does not mean that varieties labeled as "dialects" display no substrate effects. There is absolutely no principled reason why the term "dialect" should denote a priori no effects from the first languages (African or otherwise) spoken by persons originally present during various stages of local language emergence. These varieties are called "Dialect Creole Varieties" because access to dialect varieties of the lexifier was relatively more sustained throughout their respective histories than in the cases of "Autonomous Creole Varieties" discussed below. However, this does not imply in any way that "decreolization" must have shaped these creoles, but only that "decreolization" may be considered as one possible factor in accounting for the synchronic "shape" of a given language if it can be conclusively demonstrated that only one "Autonomous" or "Deep" variety emerged in a specific location and that that variety has shifted diachronically towards features associated with metropolitan varieties of the lexifier. It is assumed here that in some well-defined areas of geographical space, contact with the lexifier varied in intensity and accessibility, leading to varieties with relatively more autonomous features (i.e. what might be called "basilectal" creoles from the continuum/decreolization perspective; see below) and others with a greater number of dialect and even metropolitan-like features. "Dialect Creole Varieties" are more like dialect varieties of the superstrate because the "sea" of first language or substrate speakers (of, in this case, West African languages) was never as "deep," substantial or sustained as with other cases described below. Furthermore, access to the superstrate in terms of contact with speakers of European dialect varieties was more consistent and available (although varied from region to region of a given geographical space), and thus the dialect nature of the locally emerging language was able to maintain its superstrate "look," even if one would expect there to be differences between the superstrate or contributing varieties spoken by Europeans and whatever new variety that has emerged as spoken by locals. Examples of this type of language variety may be found in any area of the Anglophone

Americas (except Suriname most likely) and some examples of the more likely candidates would be varieties heard in the Bahamas, Cayman Islands, African American Vernacular English, Saba, Anguilla, St. Martin, and possibly St. Eustatius. We would predict "Dialect Creole Varieties" to contain a higher percentage of grammatical forms that can be traced directly to input colonial varieties present during the years crucial to that language's emergence than other varieties discussed here. The crucial difference between "Immigrant Creole Varieties" and "Dialect Creole Varieties" is that the former category is a post-emancipation phenomenon created in the Americas mostly by Afro-Caribbeans while the latter often has its roots in the pre-emancipation colonial history of an area.

The case of St. Eustatius Creole English or Statian probably represents a dialect variety. Statian is an English-derived variety spoken in a territory that has been controlled by the Dutch since the seventeenth century. How did this restructured English variety originate in a Dutch-controlled colony? The answer to this one question for Statia may fill in our understanding for many different matrices in specific locations around the Atlantic region. Is it possibly similar to the immigrant type in which a variety of wholly formed Englishes were brought by slaves who had been exposed to these forms earlier in other locations at perhaps some slave entrepot in the Caribbean such as St. Kitts or Barbados? Aceto (fc.b) presents possible solutions to these questions.

4.3   Autonomous or Deep Creole Varieties

In these cases, access to lexifier sources was historically more restricted than in the above two cases but never withdrawn in the Anglophone Americas as a source of on-going linguistic influence in a language's history except in the Surinamese case. These "Autonomous" or "Deep Creole Varieties" are the creoles that are largely considered to have emerged on or been influenced by large-scale plantations when scholars discuss so-called "creole genesis." That is, historically the Anglophone component was proportionally smaller vis-à-vis other language components present within a specific linguistic matrix (Hancock 1986) or was present and eventually withdrawn in a relatively short period of time (e.g. more or less after 15 years) as in the case of the Surinamese situation, even if at some earlier stage in a creole's history, a variety with fewer so-called "creole" features was possibly heard (see Mufwene 1996). The cases that would fit this description are restricted in number in the Western Hemisphere to largely the Surinamese creoles Sranan, Ndyuka, and Sarmaccan, but more than likely also include the so-called "basilectal" creole varieties heard in some locations (e.g. Jamaica, Antigua, Barbuda, some varieties of Gullah on the Sea Coast Islands; note that I assume a range of varieties may have emerged in any given location, *not* just a single variety that was subsequently affected by the purported effects of "decreolization"). I suggest the term "Deep" creole in the sense that the "superstrate" or European component often becomes submerged within a significant "sea" of speakers of other first language varieties (e.g. African languages in the Americas); this relative proportion is the inverse perspective from the case of "Dialect Creole Varieties" above in which the first languages of non-Anglophones become over time demographically "swamped" by a range of English speakers. However, the term "Autonomous" is preferred here because these creoles are largely unintelligible to speakers who only know dialect varieties of the lexically-related European language (while acknowledging that "mutual intelligibility" is a problematic criterion) but more importantly because these varieties have a critical mass of features that are distinct in either form or function (or both) from any of the contributing English-derived dialects spoken by colonists and settlers in a specific location.

Often the Eastern Caribbean is considered a mesolectal or "intermediate" area, and thus, from this perspective, often, aside from the cases of Barbados and Guyana, uninteresting to Creole studies. This perspective considers only "Autonomous" or "Deep Creole Varieties" (or "basilectal" creoles from the traditional continuum/decreolization perspective) as the most revealing for study. This perspective is flawed on many levels as is discussed above. In Barbuda, there are varieties that belong to the "Autonomous" type and others that may be more appropriately considered part of the "Dialect" type. In fact, in every location I have carried out fieldwork (in Bastimentos, Panama; Barbuda; and St. Eustatius), many speakers consider and call their native languages simply "English" regardless of whether the features present in their languages would be labeled as "basilectal" or "mesolectal" by some creolists. Ratios in which a substantially higher proportion of West Africans vis-à-vis Europeans figure largely in the work of many researchers trying to understand the sociohistorical matrices under which Creole languages emerged in the Atlantic region (e.g. Bickerton 1981, Mufwene 1996, Parkval 2000). Barbuda is an important case of a non-plantation creole in which "Autonomous" varieties (among others) emerged: During the period of slavery, one European often lived among 500 West African slaves. This fact of an extremely low European presence (often one at most four) within the island's matrix seems to confirm the idea that Creole Englishes developed in Anglophone colonies for use primarily as a type of lingua franca among slaves themselves, and not primarily for communication with Europeans (see Baker 2000). Whether some slaves arrived in Barbuda with only a familiarity with West African languages and others with some exposure to varieties of restructured English acquired on the West African coast or at other Anglophone locations in the West Indies is an important point that needs to be researched further. Furthermore, did Barbudan slaves derive from another location in the Caribbean (i.e. from a slave entrepot such as St. Kitts or St. Eustatius perhaps)? The Barbudan case is presented in more detail in Aceto (2002b).

Trying to define different English-derived varieties of the Caribbean in terms of linguistic features, social factors, separate histories, and/or demographics is becoming clearer as more fieldwork on neglected varieties comes to light. It is hoped that this chapter and this volume in general will provide an impetus to continue expanding our base of knowledge in these areas and moving the discussion forward a step or two.

Notes

1. Many of the ideas presented in Plag (2001) were anticipated by the detailed written comments of Michel DeGraff on CREOLIST, a now defunct internet subscriber service for those interested in pidgin and creole languages.

2. Beckles (1986) describes how slaves and white indentured servants in Barbados joined forces to engage in resistance and even marronage to escape the island for other locations in the Eastern Caribbean. I am indebted to Jeff Williams for pointing this source out to me.

3. Other locations in the Eastern Caribbean such as St. Kitts also reveal a joint Franco-Anglo history. However, the French were expelled from St. Kitts in 1713, somewhat earlier than in other Eastern Caribbean Francophone locations that are significantly Anglophone today.

4. See Mufwene (1997), who concludes, "Koine is a term/concept which may as well be abandoned" (53). The reference to the term here indicates that the historical matrix of this type of English-derived language is largely formed by pre-existing English-derived varieties already spoken in the Caribbean, out of which a new variety emerges.

5. Of course, in other contexts, non-English-derived languages may be crucial to understanding different features found in local language emergence.

Language variation and language use among teachers in Dominica

Beverley Bryan and Rosalind Burnette
Department of Educational Studies, University of the West Indies,
Mona, Jamaica / Faculty of Education, Dominica State College, Roseau,
Dominica.

1. Introduction

This paper is an investigation of the language varieties used by a group of teachers in Dominica and their knowledge of and attitude towards these varieties. The rationale for such work is the fact that the school has been recognized as an arena of language contact (Edwards 1994) and therefore a variable in language maintenance. Language maintenance can be defined as continued use and proficiency in a non-prestigious language, while changes in language use can be labeled language shift (Fase et al. 1992). Central to that process of language shift within the school setting must be the role of the teacher. Information about the language background of teachers in speech communities with dynamic variation needs to be made available to those concerned with bi- and multilingual issues. Such data would be useful in indicating the variety of languages in the possession of teachers who are usually called on to inculcate a target language, and their role in the maintenance of other varieties. The data in this paper is certainly one source of information about language shift, the impetus behind the changes in use, and the norms of language behavior operating at a given time. The language situation in Dominica, especially with respect to teachers and schooling, is one such source of study. However, it is necessary to preface this investigation with some description of the territory's language history.

2.   Background to Dominica as a language contact situation

Political history and geography have been important in the formation of Dominica's linguistic varieties and have affected the type of language contact situation that now exists on the island. The island was originally occupied by Caribs and, like many of those around it, was for many years part of the English and French struggle for domination in the Eastern Caribbean. In the earliest years of its European occupation it was the French language that held sway. From the seventeenth century, small groups of Frenchmen and their slaves lived among the Caribs in scattered settlements carrying out small-scale tobacco and coffee farming. The evidence of this early French occupation is reflected in such as the place-names of villages (Dublanc, Massacre, Soufriere, etc.). When the British finally achieved ascendancy over their French rivals in 1763, English rather than French became the official language of Dominica, but this did not conclude the political struggle or settle the language question. In 1778 French control of Dominica was instituted for five years, the only period of official exclusive French control. Nevertheless, even under British governance the strong numerical and economic presence of the French planters meant that the influence of the French language remained strong well into the nineteenth century.

The nature of the type of contact mentioned above, over a relatively long period, is highly significant in accounting for the establishment and early spread of a French-lexicon Creole in Dominica. Added to this, the slaves of French planters had brought the French Creole of neighboring Martinique and Guadeloupe to the island, in the 17th and 18th centuries (Christie 1982). The influence of these slaves would seem to have been critical as their presence helped to secure the hold of that creole on slaves in Dominica who had little inclination or opportunity to acquire English. The influence of the French colonies, with regard to language, continues to this day. As Honychurch (1984: 76) notes, "The movement of people and the business and family connections which were maintained between the islands defied the state of war, peace, or treaties between the colonial powers." Additional language contacts, significant to other varieties existing on the island, came in the form of Dominica's federation with the English-based Leeward Islands of Antigua, St Kitts, and Montserrat from 1871 to 1939.

Generally, the conquest of this rugged island was not a totally profitable venture for the British. It is only in the last few decades that travel within and to the island has become less problematic. In the period of slavery, the mountainous terrain meant that securing the island for commerce and full economic exploitation was difficult. Resistance to European incursion led to Caribs retreating to the northeast of the island as the African slaves turned to the hills, thus depleting labor stocks and undermining the plantation economy. In the post-emancipation period, communication remained generally difficult with poor roads further depressing development. Within that period, the Caribs have largely been reduced to a tiny minority of the population mostly living on or near the Carib Reserve. Their language, Island-Carib, is no longer spoken, although there has been some local resurgence of interest in their linguistic and cultural antecedents.

2.1   The education system in Dominica; the source of its teachers

Dominica's educational situation is similar to many Caribbean nations. It is a young country where education is highly regarded as an avenue of social mobility. The church has had some influence on the system that began early in the life of the British regime. The first missionaries sent out to Dominica from England, set up schools in the areas in the north, which were strongly dominated by the British. Well into the latter part of the nineteenth century, French continued to be used in public life and the African-descended population used the French-lexicon Creole. Thus, the English-based education initiative developed slowly even into the twentieth century. Up until the late 1960s, the only recognized secondary schools were the Catholic Boys' School, the Convent for Girls, Wesley High School, and the non-church Dominica Grammar School. All are in the capital, Roseau, but the government has since increased spending for all kinds of secondary education with a move to universal secondary education and a common curriculum for the first three years.

In the primary sector, the government controls 54 schools and assists a further 10; three are independent. At the tertiary level, the institutions are even more recent, with a government-funded sixth form college, a teachers' training college and a center for distance education operated by the University of the West Indies.

2.2   Past inquiry into Dominica's language situation

Research into the language situation in Dominica has been relatively limited. Taylor (1977) and Christie (1982, 1983, 1987) have carried out most of the significant work characterizing the language situation in Dominica. Christie

(1982) concentrated on the two dominant languages: the French-lexicon Creole and English. For the French-lexicon Creole, Christie used the term "Patwa" as the label available at the time. However, increasingly some local speakers and culturally aware activists are using the term "Kwéyòl" to denote a more appropriate orthography that is without reference to its colonial antecedents (Fontaine & Roberts 1991). The movement to promote Kwéyòl can be seen as part of a wider movement throughout the Eastern Caribbean to encourage the French-based vernaculars of St Lucia, Martinique, and Guadeloupe. The orthography promoted in the Fontaine and Roberts' text will be that used for the purposes of this paper wherever Kwéyòl is discussed.

Christie (1982) points to evidence from historical sources and official reports showing that teachers used Kwéyòl to aid understanding on the part of their students. She also reported on a census carried out in 1946, the results of which are still significant as they represent the only available official record of language use in Dominica. The census revealed that a quarter of the population was made up of monolingual Creole speakers, while sixty-nine percent (69%) were said to be bilingual speakers of Creole and English. The remaining six percent (6%) claimed to be monolingual speakers of English. Christie questioned these assertions, suggesting that respondents' competence in Dominican Standard English (DSE) might not be as high as imagined because notions of what constitutes "English" remain broad. She indicated that, at the time of writing, bilingualism was growing with parents using what they considered to be English with young children, even though they might use Kwéyòl with each other. She gives a geographical distribution of the spread of Kwéyòl and English. There were Kwéyòl monolinguals in Vielle Case; Kwéyòl-dominant bilingual speakers in Grand Bay; Kwéyòl or English-dominant young bilinguals in villages such as Pointe Michel; equal numbers of young Kwéyòl and English dominant bilinguals in the capital, Roseau; and finally, English-dominant bilinguals in Marigot. Evidence of code switching was also noted, as both English and Kwéyòl expanded in the domains in which each was used. English was more widely used in the home and in songs, for example, and Kwéyòl more widely used in the media.

Christie (1987) offers a sociolinguistic profile of Dominica, which describes a more complex picture. Four language varieties are discussed as being available to Dominicans: Dominican Standard English (DSE), the French-based Creole (Kwéyòl), Dominican Creolised English (DCE), and an English-based Creole called Kokoy (Cocoy). Although English is the official language, Kwéyòl remains the first language for most of the population. Christie offers a number of explanations for the continued dominance of Kwéyòl. The arguments include: the gradual adoption of Kwéyòl by Caribs, which led to the loss of their own language; the retention of metropolitan French by a segment of the planter class until the late nineteenth century; the close links between Dominica and the French West Indian islands; and, most significantly for this paper, the slow progress of education, which would inevitably use English as the medium of instruction. Christie's assumption seems to be that the development of the education system will lead to a decline in the number of monolingual Kwéyòl speakers. Christie also notes the relative stability of Kwéyòl syntax in comparison to its morphophonemic variation, e.g. *we/vwe* for the verb "see." Other examples that might be added are *layvyé/wivyé* "river" and *déja/ja* "already." In terms of lexicon, there are significant examples of loanwords from English, such as *braf* "broth" or *fwenn* "friend," words that, however, rely on the phonological structure of Kwéyòl. Other examples would be *twafik* "traffic" and *bokit* "bucket." A driving force for these borrowings has been the need to communicate concepts for which Kwéyòl has no adequate expression, e.g. *taypraita* "typewriter," *titja* "teacher." Other features of Kwéyòl include the use of *te* as anterior marker and *ka* as nonpunctual marker within the verb system and the reliance on tone rather than subject-auxiliary inversion to denote questions, e.g. *Ou ka apwann Kwéyòl?* (You NONPUNCT learning Kwéyòl.) "Are you learning Kwéyòl?"

Dominican Creolised English (DCE) has been presented as a language initially acquired through schooling (Christie 1983; see Garrett, this volume, for the similar case of vernacular English emergence in St. Lucia) and "arguably" a creole (Christie 1987). Taylor (1977) raised this discussion in relation to Kwéyòl suggesting that an examination of the structural differences would determine whether the variety be classified as a deviation of a European superstrate or an entirely new natural language, a Creole. Christie (1983) presents DCE as an English lexicon variety sharing some features with other recognized Caribbean creoles such as *did* as an anterior marker; *be+ V-ing* used to indicate habitual action; and the frequent lack of inflection for number, possession or tense. DCE's relationship to English is evident in the pronominal forms *I* and *my*. Christie (1987) also notes some similarities between DCE and Kwéyòl. The similarities appear in such loanwords from Kwéyòl as *vep* "a free ride," *timoun* "child" used at the beginning of an exclamatory utterance, and in tags such as utterance-final *wi*. Transfers from Kweyol to DCE include syntactic structures such as *did* as an anterior marker and phonological similarities such as the absence of interdental fricatives that allows *thin* to become *tin*.

In her discussion of the Creole characteristics of DCE, Christie (1983) considers its origin as a language acquired through teaching, facilitated by English as the medium of instruction in the state-controlled schools, which began in the post-Emancipation period of 1838. She likens DCE to "so-called mesolectal varieties, identified in other islands and Guyana" (20). She is, however, careful to reject the continuum notion, emphasizing the highly evolutionary nature of DCE: it is a language that "is still being acquired as a second language" (19) with the concomitant tendency towards variability.

The third language variety to be considered is the English-lexicon Creole, Kokoy, a type of speech resembling Jamaican and Antiguan conservative forms, sometimes referred to as basilects. It is a regional variety most closely associated with the villages of Marigot and Wesley in the north, which were areas of the first British settlement and also areas with strong ties to the long held British islands of Antigua and Montserrat. Like the conservative creoles of the aforementioned islands, Kokoy is not, for example, characterised by inflections; it uses the unmarked verb extensively; and front focussing is a notable feature of its grammar. Other features of Kokoy include pronominal *im*, "third person singular subject and object," and *fu* "for;" *om* "third person singular object," and *mi* as anterior marker. The lexicon too reveals its connection with English-derived creoles. Below are some examples of these:

[bɔtʌm fʊt]	bottom + foot	=	sole of foot
[bʌn pan]	burnt + pan	=	saucepan
[haɪs]	hoist	=	lift up
[ʃeɪkɪ ʃeɪkɪ]	shaky + shaky	=	weak, feeble

Because of the relationship of both Kokoy and DCE to English, Christie (1987) believes that all Kokoy speakers control some variety of DCE.

2.3   The varieties in use

This brief description of the language contact situation and the varieties in use provides a context to discuss language behavior. Edwards (1994) confirms that code-switching behavior occurs in most communities where there is language variation. In Dominica, intrasentential mixing is common, e.g. *I did want to vole it, gason* (I did want to steal it, boy) "Boy, I wanted to steal it!" In fact, Christie states that code switching is the norm as Dominicans move from one variety to the next, unconsciously responding to the context in which they are operating. English is often reserved not only for more formal situations but also for domains of business and those locations requiring urbanized interactions because English carries with it a veneer of sophistication. Code switching is a skill used as a conversational strategy to enrich a communicative event. The choice of strategy is dependent on extralinguistic as much as linguistic factors.

The difficulties described by Craig (1976) of Jamaican Creole speakers attempting to reach the target of Standard Jamaican English are also recognized here by Christie (1987) in Dominica. Some of these problems are attributed to the status of English as the official language. At the present time, Kwéyòl is being fostered in the media through radio programs, religious services, cultural presentations, and today all such events are supported by a new accessible Kwéyòl dictionary. In schools, Kwéyòl Day is celebrated on the last Friday in October. Yet the language is not accepted as fully able to express all levels of cognition and, significantly, not recognized as being suitable as a language of instruction. In fact, Christie asserts that because of its low status, Kwéyòl is regarded as a barrier to educational success, even though so many Dominicans use it on a regular basis. It would seem that the ambivalence evident in other territories towards the mother tongue, although not as pernicious, is also present in Dominica (Winford 1994).

3. The survey of teachers

The foregoing explains the existence of a distinct number of language varieties in Dominica. Attitudes to these varieties and their use are affected by schooling and these attitudes, in turn, have an effect on schooling. With respect to the struggle between French and English, early official Dominican sources have pointed to the role of teachers in language maintenance and in promoting linguistic success in the classroom. Recent developments in the secondary curriculum in Dominica underscore the role of teachers in relation to not only English and Kwéyòl but also the other two vernaculars in use. There is a move towards universal secondary education with a common curriculum and approach to language teaching. It is important, therefore, to get some sense of the perceptions of teachers in this dynamic language situation. How aware are Dominican teachers of the language environment in which they live and work? What do they see as their mother tongue? What language do they use at home? What are their attitudes to these varieties and how do they treat them in the classroom?

The purpose of the study was to investigate teachers' knowledge and use of the language varieties in Dominica. The sample consisted of 80 teachers from different parts of the island who were pursuing certification at the local teachers' college. Twenty-two of the teachers came from secondary schools, 51 from the primary sector, and seven from the junior secondary schools. They were young people, mainly in their twenties. It is also relevant to note that some fifteen percent (15%) of the teachers took a course *Introduction to Language* that included a brief overview of the Dominican language situation. The whole cohort completed 80 questionnaires that included the following questions:

- What languages are spoken in Dominica?
- Which one do you consider to be your mother tongue?
- What language(s) do you use at home?
- What language(s) do you use in the classroom?

It was hoped that the responses would give a broad picture of the language behavior of a defined and important sample, namely teachers, and, at the same time, confirm or deny some of Christie's (1987) findings, made 12 years earlier. The specific findings of Christie that this paper would want to focus on are: the trend towards bilingualism in English and Kwéyòl, with the concomitant result of fewer monolinguals in Kwéyòl, and the presence of Kokoy speakers who control some variety of DCE.

The survey produced some interesting results:

Table 1. Teachers' level of recognition of languages used in Dominica

Language	Recognition level
English	80 (100%)
Kwéyòl	78 (97%)
Kokoy	60 (75%)
Dominican Creolised English (DCE)	49 (61%)

In response to questions about the languages available to Dominicans, there was high recognition of the four varieties available. The recognition of English by all 80 teachers and Kwéyòl by 78 was expected; the increasing recognition of the French-based Creole, through the media, has been a feature of Dominica's growing cultural self-assurance. There was also a high level of recognition of the other two languages by the teachers. Sixty of the teachers named Kokoy as a Dominican language. Some gave a precise description of the English-based Creole suggesting that they understood its linguistic relationship to Kwéyòl and wanted to differentiate between Kokoy and the French-lexicon Creole. Forty-nine of the teachers named DCE as a language. It is likely that they would have been influenced by their linguistics course but it is relevant that Kokoy's existence was noted, even if one person's reference to "sub-standard English" did suggest a pejorative definition. Such a definition is in line with what is seen as influential voices in the mainstream of Dominican society, including in education circles, which still resist the recognition of any variety except what they perceive as an internationally recognized version of Standard English. It is interesting to note that two respondents believed that Island-Carib was still spoken in Dominica even after the last speaker reportedly died in 1920 (Taylor 1977).

When asked about the language the teachers recognized as their first language (i.e. the language they felt was closest to them) the responses were revealing and worth setting out in full:

Table 2. The acknowledged mother tongue of a group of Dominican teachers in training

Language	Speakers	
English	(19%)	15
Kwéyòl	(57%)	46
Kokoy	(9%)	7
Dominican Creolised English (DCE)	(15%)	12

The fact that eighty-one percent acknowledged that English was not their mother tongue showed a positive attitude towards Kwéyòl and other local varieties. It has been indicated before (Holm 1988, Craig 1976) that creoles which do not have the official language as their "superstrate" usually find easier acceptance. This is the case with Kwéyòl, and its acceptance might have had a beneficial effect on attitudes toward other varieties. With respect to the nineteen percent who acknowledged English, we might note again that a question remains about what the teachers were identifying as English. It is the case that the use of English increases with education but the definition of what constitutes English is wide. Similar observations have been made about other groups of teachers in other islands (Robertson 1996, Shields-Brodber 1989). The number who acknowledges Kwéyòl is not as surprising as the recognition of DCE as a distinct variety. This is a departure from Christie (1983) where DCE was discussed as a second language; in this instance, at least, it is also acknowledged as a mother tongue. What the findings point to is the inevitability of multilingualism in an environment where four varieties are in operation. The findings suggest the significance of mother tongue ownership and reveal an important success in diminishing negative attitudes towards vernacular languages.

The responses to a question about languages used at home confirmed that many teachers are at least bilingual, if not multilingual. These responses are important also because as teachers interact in their homes with families they provide a window to what is happening in the wider community. The responses showed ten permutations for the languages used in the home:

Table 3. Languages used at home by a group of Dominican teachers

Combination	Number of speakers
Kokoy and English	4
English and Kokoy and DCE	3
Kokoy	1
Kokoy and DCE	1
Kwéyòl and English	30
English	18
DCE	6
English and DCE	4
English, DCE and Kwéyòl	7
Kwéyòl and DCE	5

The first point to note among these teachers is that on the evidence of language use at home, monolingualism is rare: these are mainly bilingual speakers. The table indicates that English retains a dominant place: only 13 teachers said that they used no English at home while 18 said they used English exclusively. Kwéyòl is also well used with 42; over fifty percent use it at home, but it is concentrated in three of the 10 combinations. It is also worth noting that there is a reverse discrepancy to the one noted with English: four teachers who claimed Kwéyòl as the mother tongue did not use it at home. It is possible that different members of a household might have different varieties available to them and these varieties are now being acknowledged even when not actively in use. For example, Kokoy is now acknowledged in use in nine homes in conjunction with either English or DCE. Christie (1987) noted that Kokoy speakers are likely to control DCE, and by extension English, rather than Kwéyòl. There were no Kokoy and Kwéyòl combinations, suggesting the regional nature of language use in Dominica. The use of DCE in 26 homes is significant, as only half of that number had identified it as a mother tongue. Such usage would suggest that this variety rather than Kwéyòl is likely to be in competition with

English, especially as it is used in combination with several other languages. DCE seems, like English, to be the additional language to have.

One other useful collection of responses relates to the language varieties these teachers use in the classrooms. It is an important question because the teachers come from across the island and work in schools where all varieties would be represented. Which languages they use with their students gives us some idea of the language use in these communities.

Table 4. The distribution of language(s) among teachers in 80 Dominican classrooms

Language	Distribution
English	80 (100%)
Dominican Creolised English (DCE)	26 (33%)
Kwéyòl/Patois/Patwa	52 (65%)
Kokoy/Cocoy/English dialect	9 (11%)

All the teachers asserted that they used English in the classroom. A comment has already been made as to the nature of the precise English variety being used. It is certainly the case that teachers would have wanted to be on the side of virtue and would see themselves using English extensively in the classroom. Not surprisingly, Kwéyòl is the next most widely used language with sixty-five percent usage. These teachers are using the language to aid understanding among children in the primary and secondary sector and so in the schools, at least, the use of Kwéyòl is still widespread. This is significant because the fact that schoolchildren use Kwéyòl suggests that it is also well used in the home.

DCE was not as widely used as Kwéyòl, but a distribution of thirty-three percent reveals that it is available in the teachers' repertoire. The distribution of Kokoy, on the other hand, confirms that it is a localized language of the northeast region, owned and spoken by approximately ten percent of the teaching and general population. The significant finding from these figures is that *all* teachers use more than one language. Bilingual and multilingual teachers are working with children who are, at least, bilingual.

4.   Concluding remarks

What can we conclude from this survey of teachers in Dominica? There are a number of points of caution. First, this study involved a highly stratified sample of young beginning teachers, who may or may not even be representative of Dominica's teachers. Second, the investigation took the form of self-reporting and is, therefore, subject to the usual qualifications with regard to the interpretation of wording and the understanding of some of the distinctions between varieties. However, such caveats notwithstanding, we can make a number of observations about the nature of the language situation among the teaching population in Dominica. All the languages used in Dominica are well recognised and positive attitudes are displayed towards them. English is used by nearly twenty percent of this population. The other two lesser-used English-derived varieties, Kokoy and DCE, are also significant, especially DCE, which is gaining ground as an additional language of communication. Both English and DCE are the two additional languages of communication.

We can also consider what is likely to be the fate of Kwéyòl. The fact is, Kwéyòl is not as dominant as it was reported in the general survey of 1946; half of this population of young teachers say they do not use it at home. This is not really so surprising after more than fifty years and considering the spread of English-based education. Instead, English and English-related varieties are now much more in evidence. Yet the lack of Kwéyòl use by some of these teachers belies its continued use in some schools. The progress of Kwéyòl confirms that we should not look at this variety as a "minority language" in the way it might be viewed in some discussions on language shift. Kwéyòl is still the language most owned and used in informal settings. It would seem that teachers report that they use it less often than their young students and the influence of education may be a significant factor. However, there are also external factors affecting Kwéyòl's survival. The political and community thrust is towards Kwéyòl with an assertion of pride and interest in the language, evident in the publication of an accessible, populist dictionary for visitors to Dominica. Teachers in the survey spoke proudly of the celebration of the language and culture on Creole Day and of its inclusion in a range of other informal and cultural settings. Such occasions also free the Kokoy speaker to promote his or her own variety.

The survey shows Dominica's diverse multilingual environment that teachers operate in on a daily basis. It also shows that the teachers' own background reflects much of that variation and positive attitudes towards vernacular languages. These attitudes are important in developing linguistically aware teachers who can formulate a conscious program for bi- and multilingualism. Such a program would acknowledge the use of the mother tongue but would also emphasize the use of bilingual strategies that allow children to hear, practice, and use the target language for real communication.

Appendix

Teacher's Questionnaire:

1. What languages are spoken in Dominica?
2. Which one do you consider to be your mother tongue?
3. What language(s) do you use at home?
4. What language(s) do you use in the classroom?
    - How often do you use the language(s) in the classroom?
    - In what context or situation do you use the language(s)
5. What language(s) do you use with co-workers?
    - How often do you use the language(s)?
    - In what context or situation do you use the language(s) with them?
6. What language(s) do you use with friends?
    - How often do you use the language(s) with them?
    - In what context or situation do you use the language(s) with them?

An "English Creole" that isn't

On the sociohistorical origins and linguistic classification of the vernacular English of St. Lucia*

Paul B. Garrett
Temple University

1. Introduction

Although the present-day official language of St. Lucia is English, relatively few St. Lucians are proficient speakers of standard English.[1] Most St. Lucians today speak Kwéyòl, a French-lexified creole that dates back to the island's French colonial period (1642–1803), as well as a significantly restructured English-lexified vernacular. This latter language variety exhibits numerous non-standard features commonly associated with the Caribbean English Creoles (CECs), and has often been characterized as a CEC variety itself in the literature on language in St. Lucia. It is proposed here, however, that this variety should *not* be regarded as a CEC, and for that matter should not be regarded as a "creole" at all. The present chapter considers this vernacular's origins, its ongoing emergence as a distinct language variety, and the question of how it should be classified as a variety that is clearly related to, yet also quite distinct from, both Kwéyòl and standard English.

The language variety in question will be referred to here as VESL, an acronym for "Vernacular English of St. Lucia." This designation is used as an alternative to "St. Lucian English Creole" and similar labels that have elsewhere been applied to this variety;[2] it is intended to distinguish it from the CECs and to emphasize (if only in shorthand fashion) the fact that it differs from them in important ways, especially in terms of its sociohistorical origins. VESL is of quite recent vintage, even among the numerous contact-induced language varieties spoken in the Caribbean region (few if any of which began to take form more than about four centuries ago). Available historical evidence suggests that VESL first began to emerge no earlier than the mid-nineteenth century, and it has come to be spoken widely in St. Lucia only over the course of the past few decades. For this and other reasons that will be considered below, VESL stands apart from the various contact-induced restructured language varieties, spoken throughout the Caribbean region and elsewhere, that are commonly referred to as creoles.

The term *creole* has proven notoriously difficult to define, especially in recent years as linguists and others have revisited the fundamental question of whether or not "creoles" as a group differ (structurally, sociohistorically, or otherwise) from the rest of the world's languages — and if so, precisely how (see e.g. Mufwene 1986b; Thomason and Kaufman 1988; Thomason 1997; McWhorter 1997b, 1998; DeGraff 1999). Mufwene (1997) provides an insightful discussion of *creole* and other terms that have commonly been used in referring to contact-induced restructured language varieties (and of the potential pitfalls associated with the continued use of these terms), pointing out that such terminology has been applied to a sociohistorically particular set of languages in ways that have not been (and indeed cannot be) rigorously based on structural criteria alone (cf. McWhorter 1998 for a contrasting perspective).

Putting aside, for present purposes, the as yet unresolved problem of establishing a working definition for the term *creole* that is both meaningfully specific and widely applicable (or of deciding whether or not it is worthwhile to continue trying to do so), it should be noted from the outset that VESL does resemble, in various respects, the language varieties that have often been referred to collectively as the Caribbean English Creoles. Apparently due to this outward resemblance, various scholars who have acknowledged the existence of this St. Lucian vernacular have assumed it to be a CEC variety that must have been introduced into St. Lucia from elsewhere.[3] Those who have suggested a particular geographic source (most have not) have pointed to Barbados (Le Page 1977, Le Page and Tabouret-Keller 1985).[4] But as will be explained here, there is little in the way of demographic or sociohistorical evidence to support the supposition that VESL is a transplant. More important, these cursory explanations of VESL's origins ignore the fact that it has taken form and has become established in St. Lucia, by and large, in a quite different fashion.

VESL, it is proposed here, therefore should not be lumped together with Jamaican, Guyanese, Antiguan, Bajan (Barbadian), and related varieties as another Caribbean English Creole. The language varieties that are generally grouped together in this category came into being in an earlier historical era and under a particular set of sociohistorical circumstances, namely those associated with the Atlantic slave trade and the development of colonial plantation societies (as in Jamaica and Guyana), or else the diffusion of varieties that initially took form under these circumstances to other geographic locations (e.g. parts of Panama and Costa Rica) in later years.[5] In contrast to these varieties, VESL has emerged much more recently and under quite different circumstances: primarily through the acquisition of English as a second language by monolingual speakers of Kwéyòl whose access to English was limited to exposure gained during a few years (at most) of attending primary school. These learners subsequently passed their heavily Kwéyòl-influenced English-as-second-language on to their children, whose access to English was otherwise almost as limited, in many cases, as it had been for their parents. VESL thus began as an interlanguage, one that has subsequently stabilized and is now being reproduced across the generations. Many of the characteristic features of this restructured variety, not surprisingly, reflect the influence — phonological, semantic, and above all syntactic — of Kwéyòl. As a historically quite recent product of second language acquisition processes operating within a French-creolophone context, VESL differs in significant ways from those language varieties generally regarded as Caribbean English Creoles, notwithstanding the fact that some of these varieties have doubtless influenced it to some extent and are probably a source of at least some of its characteristic features (as will be considered below).

While Kwéyòl has been an object of intensive study (most notably in Carrington 1984), VESL has not yet been comprehensively described, although certain of its non-standard features have been examined in some depth (e.g. Isaac 1986; Simmons-McDonald 1988, 1994). Studies concerning language in St. Lucia have typically noted the fact that English is spoken along with Kwéyòl; some have also noted, if only in passing, that the English spoken by most St. Lucians is not necessarily standard English. But those studies that have acknowledged this latter fact have rarely investigated the matter much further. The non-standard variety in question has often been referred to (again, in passing) as an "English Creole" or "creolized English." Explicitly or implicitly, VESL has thus been assumed to belong to the great extended family of Caribbean English Creoles that are spoken in more than two dozen island and mainland territories throughout the region (Winford 1993) — a family that includes such luminaries of Caribbean language studies as Jamaica and Guyana, numerous steadfast (if less well known) core members such as Antigua and St.

Vincent, and some marginal cousins such as the Bahamas and the Bay Islands of Honduras.

It is proposed here that VESL is only a rather distant relative of these others. Its closest relative, furthermore, is not English (its predominantly English lexicon notwithstanding); nor is it the English-lexified creole of Barbados or any other nearby territory (although these elders have doubtless had, and continue to have, a hand in its upbringing). VESL's closest relative is Kwéyòl, St. Lucia's own French-lexified creole.

The question of VESL's origins and status will be approached from two angles: through an overview of VESL's characteristic non-standard linguistic features, and through a consideration of demographic and sociohistorical evidence. The overview of VESL's non-standard features will show that VESL shares numerous features with Bajan and other CEC varieties. These similarities do not constitute proof of CEC influence, however, since the CECs in turn share many features with Kwéyòl and other Caribbean French Creoles. The fact that VESL has doubtless been influenced by Kwéyòl, and probably by one or more CEC varieties as well (if to a lesser extent), makes it difficult if not impossible to say with certainty which source of influence accounts for these features. Furthermore, other distinctive features of VESL that will be examined below are not characteristic of CEC varieties; these seem to derive quite directly, and exclusively, from Kwéyòl.

When these various points are taken into consideration, three main possibilities present themselves with regard to VESL's origins. One is that VESL is a CEC variety that took form outside St. Lucia, presumably in Barbados or some other CEC-speaking Caribbean territory, and subsequently entered St. Lucia by some means. This potential explanation requires, first and foremost, that the historical fact of that "foreign" CEC variety's introduction into St. Lucia be established; and second, that some vector of transmission or diffusion be identified, such as a significant influx of CEC-speaking immigrants or the arrival in St. Lucia of some smaller group of CEC-speakers whose prestige and social influence were great enough to motivate much of the "native" population of St. Lucia to adopt their ways of speaking and to regard their language variety as the "target" of second language acquisition. As will be explained in a later section, there is very little evidence to suggest that such a large influx of immigrants, or any comparable demographic phenomenon that could account for the introduction and subsequent establishment of a foreign CEC variety in St. Lucia, has ever occurred in the island's history. As for the Kwéyòl-like but non-CEC-like features that VESL exhibits, in this scenario these presumably would have

to be attributed to gradual processes of language change, resulting from sustained contact with Kwéyòl, that have affected this CEC variety since its
introduction into St. Lucia.

A second possibility is that VESL's non-standard features are primarily or
exclusively attributable to the influence of Kwéyòl, i.e. the outcome of sustained contact between Kwéyòl and English in the St. Lucian context. In this
explanation, the primary mechanism of this Kwéyòl influence would presumably be the second language acquisition process, whereby monolingual
Kwéyòl-speakers acquired English in large numbers (especially through primary education) but with limited access to models of standard English outside
of school settings. Such a situation of limited access to the "target language"
(including a lack of reinforcement of pedagogical norms of English usage in
homes and communities that remained largely Kwéyòl-monolingual) can reasonably be expected to have given rise to a non-standard variety of English that
is substantially influenced by Kwéyòl. Considering that until quite recently all
speakers of VESL were native speakers of Kwéyòl who had acquired their
"English" as a second language, the appearance of these features in VESL can
be attributed more readily and more reasonably to Kwéyòl than to any foreign
(i.e. non-St. Lucian) source. This potential explanation is strengthened by the
fact that some of VESL's distinctive features are not characteristic of CEC
varieties and appear to derive directly from Kwéyòl. An important weakness of
this explanation, however, is that it tends to treat St. Lucia as an island in a
sociolinguistic sense as well as in the geographic sense, ignoring or minimizing
the fact that St. Lucians have in fact had various kinds of contact with CEC-
speakers over the years (although the nature and extent of these contacts is
difficult to ascertain from available historical evidence).

A third approach, which combines the strongest elements of the previous
two while also minimizing their weaknesses, starts from the assumption that
both Kwéyòl and CEC varieties have influenced VESL, though not necessarily
to the same extent. This approach takes into account the possibility that
similarities between VESL and CEC varieties may reflect either CEC influence
(like the first approach) or Kwéyòl influence (like the second); but it also
considers the possibility, to be considered further below, that some of the
features that VESL shares with the CECs may reflect broader pan-creole similarities, i.e. features that occur in both English-lexified and French-lexified
Caribbean creoles. Following on this, it is assumed that those features that exist
in Kwéyòl as well as in CEC varieties would have been mutually reinforcing,
and hence would have been especially likely to be selected into VESL. Although

it takes both Kwéyòl and CEC influences into account — along with the possibility that Kwéyòl and CEC influences may sometimes have operated in tandem, effectively reinforcing one another during the course of VESL's emergence — this scenario ultimately leaves open-ended the question of the extent to which Kwéyòl and CEC varieties may have influenced VESL independently of one another.

This last potential explanation of VESL's origins is the one that will be developed here, guided by the assumption that in the absence of evidence to the contrary, Kwéyòl — by reason of its ubiquitous presence and its sustained, uninterrupted, intimate contact with English in St. Lucia over the years — has had greater influence on VESL (probably much greater) than any CEC variety. In order to bolster this last assertion, demographic and sociohistorical evidence will be considered, including census data, colonial school inspectors' reports, and statistics on population movements among West Indian territories. Evidence from these sources reveals, among other things, that there has been relatively little population movement from CEC-speaking territories to St. Lucia over the years, and that Kwéyòl "interference" in the English spoken by St. Lucians is well attested and has been remarked upon by various observers over the last century (roughly the same period of time during which VESL has emerged). It will be concluded that although Bajan and/or other CEC varieties probably played some part in VESL's origins, it is the sustained influence of Kwéyòl that has been the predominant factor in VESL's emergence. By and large, VESL is thus a uniquely St. Lucian language variety that has followed its own distinct sociohistorical and sociolinguistic trajectory, largely independent of the Caribbean English Creoles.

2.   VESL as a "contact language"

The preceding section proposes that although VESL exhibits features that are commonly found in Caribbean English Creoles, it should not be regarded as another CEC variety on this basis alone. Furthermore, although VESL, like other Caribbean language varieties, does not exist in isolation and has doubtless been influenced by these other varieties, its emergence in St. Lucia cannot be attributed solely, or even largely, to transmission or diffusion from some other location.[6] Demographic and sociohistorical evidence that will be examined in later sections suggests that VESL is not merely a transplanted CEC variety· nor is it a composite or amalgam of multiple such varieties (such as the English-lexified creole, or vernacular English, of Trinidad seems to be).

What *is* VESL, then? VESL is the outcome of a case of sustained language contact crucially involving the acquisition, within a particular sociohistorical and sociolinguistic context, of English as a second language by native speakers of Kwéyòl. As such, it is essentially no different from numerous other contact-induced restructured language varieties, of varying degrees of stability, that have taken shape in situations of language contact and second language acquisition all over the world. The fact that this particular case of language contact happens to have occurred on a Caribbean island does not make VESL any more a "creole" (or variety of Caribbean English Creole) than is, for example, "Singlish" or Singapore English (Kuiper and Tan Gek Lin 1989), "indigenized" Indian English (Kachru 1983a, b; Mesthrie 1992),[7] or Gastarbeiterdeutsch (Blackshire-Belay 1993), for that matter. Sustained contact between a "creole" language and a non-creole language, or between two creole languages, may reasonably be expected to give rise to a contact variety that exhibits numerous "creole" features. But that fact alone does not make the resultant contact variety a creole, unless that term is being defined strictly in terms of the presence or absence of particular structural features and without regard to the circumstances of the new variety's origins (in which case it might become necessary to include in this category Khmer and other languages that exhibit various typical "creole" features, but that are not ordinarily regarded as creoles). Rather, VESL is among those non-pidgin, non-creole "contact languages" that have attracted increased scholarly attention in recent years: language varieties such as those examined in Thomason (1997: 1), which she characterizes as "a third type of contact language — bilingual mixtures that (unlike pidgins and creoles) must have been created by bilinguals."[8]

While Thomason's characterization is an apt one for this category of language varieties overall, VESL in particular is not so much a *creation* of bilinguals as it is *a product of the process of becoming bilingual,* that is, a product of the second language acquisition process in the St. Lucian context. There is substantial evidence to suggest that VESL has emerged largely, if not primarily, through the acquisition of English as a second language by native speakers of Kwéyòl who had limited access to any variety of English (standard or non-standard, "creolized" or not). For practical and ideological reasons having to do with English's status as the language of officialdom and power, socioeconomic advancement, etc., these learners then passed their far-from-standard, heavily Kwéyòl-influenced English-as-a-second-language on to their children, whose access to any other model of English was in some cases almost as limited as it had been for their elders. Many (possibly most) St. Lucian children today are acquiring VESL as a first language, in some cases to the partial or even total exclusion of Kwéyòl. (Garrett 2000 examines some aspects of this ongoing process of language shift, primarily with regard to related processes of language change that are currently affecting Kwéyòl; see also Frank 1993.)

VESL as spoken in the rural village where I conducted field research, Morne Carré (as well as other rural areas of St. Lucia), has its roots in today's generation of young adults. This group consists largely of persons who grew up in Kwéyòl-speaking households, acquired Kwéyòl as their first language, and subsequently learned their "English" (very partially and imperfectly in most cases) in school as members of the first local generation to have access to primary education.[9] Historically, access to education in St. Lucia has been rather unevenly distributed across the island's population; it became available to some residents of Castries (St. Lucia's capital city) and a few other large towns in the mid-nineteenth century, a century or more before schools were established to serve those living in relatively remote rural areas of this ruggedly mountainous island, as recently as the mid-1970s, in the case of Morne Carré. Access to formal education is limited even today for families who can ill afford the books, uniforms, and other necessities for sending their children to school.

As a result, different sectors of the St. Lucian population have gained access to English as a second language at different times, and there is a significant urban-rural divide to be taken into consideration. As might be expected, social class differences (which partially map onto the urban-rural divide) have also been an important factor in the population's uneven access to formal education. Some elderly persons of today who grew up in Castries and had relatively privileged family backgrounds acquired English (standard English or a near-standard variety, in some cases) as children, both at home and in school. In Morne Carré, in contrast, most of today's young adults did not begin learning English until they entered primary school, and even then they did not speak English at home (except with school-age siblings, perhaps) since their parents and other elders were monolingual Kwéyòl-speakers. Although formal education may not have been the only source of St. Lucians' exposure to English (standard or otherwise), it has been the primary source for many; even today in rural areas, children in some predominantly Kwéyòl-speaking households acquire little English (or VESL) before entering primary school.

For many if not most St. Lucians, then, VESL was, in the early stages of its emergence at the local level, a sort of interlanguage — the outcome of their efforts to learn English in primary school with little or no reinforcement from their Kwéyòl-dominant households and communities, and with very limited access to models of English outside of school. While they were typically successful in acquiring English vocabularies, many aspects of English grammar (e.g. the relatively complex and irregular verb morphology) undoubtedly presented considerably greater difficulties. Of necessity they fell back on Kwéyòl grammar to help fill in the gaps in their English proficiency; hence the many examples of calquing that are typically evident in their VESL.[10] These bilingual (or semi-bilingual) adults, then, have been largely responsible for the emergence of VESL as it is spoken today in Morne Carré and other rural areas. Many members of this generation, furthermore, now make conscious efforts to speak only "English" (i.e. VESL) to their own children; this may be having a stabilizing effect on VESL as it becomes "nativized" and as it replaces (or at least displaces) Kwéyòl as the primary vernacular of the next generation. Although this process of nativization[11] has gotten underway only fairly recently in Morne Carré and other rural areas, it has probably been well underway for at least two to three generations in Castries, where it is not uncommon to encounter youth and some young adults who have only minimal command of Kwéyòl and are virtually monolingual speakers of VESL.

3. A brief overview of VESL's characteristic non-standard features

In order to provide some sense of VESL's non-standard characteristics, various examples of VESL sentences, phrases, and other constructions are presented below. It should be borne in mind that VESL currently comprises a fairly wide range of variation, ranging from the most non-standard (or most creole-like) lects to those that most closely approximate standard English (hereafter SE). This variation has both geographic (especially urban-rural) and social class dimensions, as well as a historical dimension having to do with the time period in which the shift from Kwéyòl monolingualism to Kwéyòl-VESL bilingualism (and then to VESL monolingualism, in some areas) got underway in different parts of the island. The particular form of VESL likely to be used by a particular speaker, then, typically has much to do with various aspects of the speaker's background such as age, place of birth and/or upbringing, level of formal education, and occupation. The examples under examination here can be taken as broadly representative of the most heavily restructured VESL, typically heard in rural areas where Kwéyòl is still spoken among adults on an everyday basis and where access to formal education and other models of SE remains limited.

This section in no way pretends to be a comprehensive description of VESL or any of its subsystems; such a task is clearly beyond the scope of this chapter. The examples in this section are intended only to provide a brief (and necessarily selective) overview of VESL's more salient non-standard characteristics, with a view to demonstrating some of its many structural similarities to Kwéyòl and, in many cases, to CEC varieties. In addition to providing some sense of the degree to which VESL diverges from SE, the sample utterances highlight some of the features that VESL shares with Kwéyòl, with CEC varieties, and with *both* Kwéyòl and CECs. The main purpose of this two-way comparison is to help ascertain, on structural grounds, the extent to which Kwéyòl and CEC varieties have influenced VESL, as well as the extent to which structural parallels between Kwéyòl and CEC varieties may have caused these two potential sources of influence to be mutually reinforcing.

The fact that many of VESL's non-standard features are also characteristic of Bajan and other CEC varieties may make it tempting to interpret those features as evidence that VESL has been significantly influenced by one or more of these varieties. But the fact that VESL shares numerous features with the CECs is hardly surprising when it is considered that Caribbean creole languages in general, regardless of their lexifiers, have many features in common. (The Caribbean French Creoles, to take the most relevant example, bear numerous structural similarities to their CEC counterparts.) This being the case, those non-standard features that occur in Kwéyòl as well as in CEC varieties (e.g. absence of present-tense equative copula, reduplication, left-dislocation, predicate clefting) will not be taken as conclusive evidence for either CEC influence or Kwéyòl influence on VESL. (There remains the possibility or the likelihood, however, that these features show up in VESL precisely because they occur *both* in CECs and in Kwéyòl, about which more below.) Features that occur in Kwéyòl but are not known to occur in CEC varieties, on the other hand, will be identified as such and will be taken as evidence for Kwéyòl influence on VESL.

It is perhaps an understatement to say that the difficulties associated with tracing a particular feature to a particular source language are well known to creolists. It is likewise difficult (perhaps impossible) to demonstrate conclusively that VESL's non-standard features are primarily attributable to Kwéyòl, ᴀꜱ ʜᴀꜱ ʙᴇᴇɴ ꜱᴜɢɢᴇꜱᴛᴇᴅ ʜᴇʀᴇ, **rather than to** ᴏɴᴇ ᴏʀ ᴍᴏʀᴇ ᴏf ᴛʜᴇ CECs. Singler (1993: 236) asserts that "the best case for substratal influence is made when a particular phenomenon cannot be accounted for in any other way." But aside from the complications caused by structural parallels between Caribbean French Creoles and Caribbean English Creoles, it is not even clear in the case of VESL whether Kwéyòl, one or more CEC varieties, or some combination of these should be regarded as VESL's "substrate" language(s). For similar reasons it is difficult to identify a "superstrate" for VESL. Was it SE (i.e. an "acrolectal" variety of English such as children might have been exposed to in school), one or more CEC varieties (such as St. Lucians might have been exposed to, to varying degrees, through contact with CEC-speakers in a variety of vernacular contexts), or some combination of these? Is VESL the outcome of partially successful acquisition of an SE "target" to which learners had only limited access, or of successful acquisition of a CEC target that was more readily accessible? Whatever the case, it is clear that the proposal being advanced here — that the influence of Kwéyòl, not Bajan and/or other CEC varieties, accounts for the bulk of VESL's non-standard features — ultimately cannot be adequately substantiated by formal-structural evidence alone. Moreover, as Singler (1996) remarks elsewhere with regard to the origins of Haitian Creole, any explanation of creole genesis must be compatible with the relevant sociohistorical evidence (186, 218, 221). Despite his focus on Haitian (which has often been regarded as a "classic" or "prototypical" creole, something that VESL clearly is not), Singler's concerns are relevant to any case of language contact and restructuring in which one is attempting to ascertain the relative degree of influence that a particular pre-existing language or language variety has had (or has not had) on the resultant contact variety. The basic account of VESL's origins that has been proposed here will therefore be buttressed in later sections by means of demographic and sociohistorical evidence from a variety of sources.

The VESL utterances given as examples below are shown in phonemic transcription;[12] for purposes of comparison, they are followed by their Kwéyòl equivalents[13] (which in many cases can be seen to correspond to the VESL examples morpheme by morpheme), and then by SE glosses. The first subsection below deals with non-standard features that VESL has in common with Kwéyòl as well as with CEC varieties. The second subsection focuses on those features that are not characteristic of CECs and are more clearly attributable to Kwéyòl influence.

§1. *Features attributable to CEC, Kwéyòl, or both*

In VESL, as in Kwéyòl and in various CEC varieties, verbs are not inflected for person, number, tense, etc. The basic verb form (which in most cases corresponds to the SE infinitive) remains invariant, as in these examples:

> hii goo in toun
> i alé an vil
> 'He went to town.'

> dee teek it
> yo pwan'y
> 'They took it.'

In the case of certain verbs, some VESL speakers may use a form derived from a "fossilized" inflected SE verb form rather than from the infinitive, e.g. *lost* rather than *lose*; but these forms also remain invariant, yielding utterances such as the following:

> shii doo waan tuu lohst it
> i pa vlé pèd li
> 'She does not want to lose it.'

The unmarked verb in VESL indicates either the simple present, in the case of statives:

> hii hav inof monii
> i ni asé lajan
> 'He has enough money.'

or the simple past, in the case of non-statives:

> hii goo tuu skuul yestedee
> i alé lékol iyè
> 'He went to school yesterday.'

The verb is modified for tense, mood, and aspect by means of a small set of preverbal particles. Anteriority is indicated by means of the particle *had*.[14] It is important to realize that VESL *had* is not an inflected form of the SE auxiliary *to have*; rather, it functions as an invariant preverbal marker, and seems to be directly equivalent to the anterior marker *té* in Kwéyòl. Thus *had* + V yields not the VESL equivalent of a past participial construction in SE, but an anterior construction, the equivalent of *té* + V in Kwéyòl:

hii had iit do brod biifeh **hii goo tuu** skuul
i té manhé pen-an avan i alé lékol
'He ate the bread before he went to school.'

Irrealis is variously marked by the particles *wud*, *goo*, and *wil*. (The forms *wud* and *wil* are not contracted to -'*d* and -'*l*(*l*), as they often are in colloquial American English.) The first of these three markers, *wud*, indicates conditionality:

> ai wud giv yuu bonano, but dee naat yet raip
> mwen té kay ba'w fig, mé yo pòkò mi
> 'I would give you bananas, but they are not yet ripe.'

Goo and *wil* both indicate the future:

> ai goo giv yuu/ai wil giv yuu raip bonano tuumaaroo
> mwen kay ba'w fig mi denmen
> 'I am going to/I will give you ripe bananas tomorrow.'

The two forms seem to be interchangeable, although *wil* is perhaps more likely to be used by speakers with some command of SE (or speakers of more "acrolectal" VESL).

In addition to these preverbal markers, the suffix -*ing* is used just as the nonpunctual aspect marker *ka* is used in Kwéyòl. (Unlike -*ing*, however, *ka* in Kwéyòl occurs as a preverbal particle; more on this below.) As a result, -*ing* occurs even in contexts where it normally does not occur in SE:

> yuu luking laik hiz brodo
> ou ka sanm fwè'y
> 'You look like his brother.'

This suffix is the sole morphological modification to a verb that regularly occurs in VESL.[15] V + -*ing*, like *ka* + V in Kwéyòl, can express either a progressive-durative meaning:[16]

> hii naat in toun, hii woking in gaadn
> i pa an vil, i ka twavay an haden
> 'He is not in town, he is working in (the) garden.'

or a habitual-iterative meaning:

> dee gooing in toun evrii sondee
> yo ka alé an vil chak dimanch
> 'They go to town every Sunday.'

In addition to preposed *goo* and *wil*, another means of expressing the immediate or prospective future (as in colloquial American English) is by means of the *-ing* suffix:

> do bredfruut kuk oredii, ai teeking piis in it
> bwapen-an ja bouwi, mwen ka pwan tjò andan'y
> 'The breadfruit is cooked, I am taking a piece of it.'

VESL's preposed TMA particles do not combine in the various ways that such particles combine in Kwéyòl and in the "basilects" of various CECs (including Bajan; see Roy 1986). In Kwéyòl, for example, two basic combinations are possible: *té ka*, indicating anterior nonpunctual, and *té kay*, indicating conditionality. In VESL, anterior nonpunctual, in either the progressive-durative or habitual-iterative sense, is expressed by *woz* V + *-ing* (never by **had* V + *-ing*):

> dee woz woking wen ai paas
> yo té ka twavay lè mwen pasé
> 'They were working when I passed [by].'

The conditional, as already noted above, is formed by preposing *wud* to the verb.

The auxiliary verb *to do* is not used in the formation of interrogatives as it is in SE. An interrogative that does not involve a WH word is generally distinguishable from a declarative only by a rising terminal intonational contour. Interrogatives involving WH words that would take auxiliary *to do* in SE do not do so in VESL:

> waat shii tel yuu?
> sa i di'w?
> 'What did she tell you?'
>
> foh waat yuu breek it?[17]
> pou ki (sa) ou kasé'y?
> 'Why did you break it?'
>
> yuu noo we shii goo?[18]
> ou sav ki koté i alé?
> 'Do you know where she went?'

Passive and anticausative constructions are effected by using the transitive verb intransitively:

yoh kloos woting
had ou ka mouyé
'Your clothes are getting wet.'

Verb focusing is effected by means of predicate clefting:

bai yuu bai dat?
achté ou achté sa?
'Did you buy that?' (verb emphasized, i.e., 'You didn't make it yourself?')

Emphasis of adjectives may be achieved by means of reduplication, e.g.,

dat fing haat haat haat!
bagay sa-a cho cho cho!
'That thing is very hot!'

Reduplication of verbs to convey iterativity is also possible, though somewhat less common:

dee de waashing, waashing, sins do taim
yo la ka lavé, lavé, dépi lè-a
'They have been there washing for a long time/for all this time.'

Nominals can be topicalized by left dislocation:

piinot hii iiting
pistach i ka manhé
'He is eating peanuts/Peanuts are what he is eating.'

A noun may also be emphasized or intensified by preposing the word *waan*,[19] which yields a construction similar in meaning to colloquial American English *such a* N:

yuu dotii mai klooz, ai giving yuu waan slap!
ou sali had mwen, mwen kay ba'w yonn kou!
'[If] you dirty my clothes, I will give you such a slap!'

The plural form of nouns is unmarked; no -*s* or other pluralizing form is used, other than numerals and expressions indicating quantity such as *soo menii*:

hii hav soo menii peel, en hii doo waan tuu bohroo mii waan
i ni kanté bonm, èk i pa vlé pwété mwen yonn
'He has so many pails, and [yet] he does not want to lend me one.'

The possessive is not marked by -'s, as in SE; simple juxtaposition indicates possession:

> huu teek do man monii?
> ki moun ki pwan lajan nonm-lan?
> 'Who took the man's money?'

Negation is in some contexts marked by *naat*:

> naat mii dat see it
> pa mwen ki di'y
> 'I did not say it/It was not I who said it.'

and in others by *doo*:

> ai doo hav noo fuud fo yuu
> mwen pa ni pyès manhé ba'w
> 'I do not have any food for you.'

The SE auxiliary *to do* is not used in VESL, and many VESL-speakers apparently do not analyze *doo* as a contraction of *do not*, i.e. as the equivalent of SE *don't*. Double negatives are common, as in the last example. The negative imperative is formed by preposing *naat tuu* to the verb:

> naat tuu toch dat!
> pa manyen sa!
> 'Do not touch that!'

Comparisons are often expressed by means of the construction ADJ *moh den:*

> hii taal moh den yuu
> i pli ho pasé ou
> 'He is taller than you.'

This may well be a calque on the equivalent Kwéyòl construction (*pli*) ADJ *pasé: I pli ho pasé ou.*[20] (The *pli* may be omitted from such constructions.) Comparative constructions may also be formed with verbs (V *moh den*), which yields the meaning 'better than':

> hii kan sing moh den yuu
> i sa chanté pasé ou
> 'He can sing better than you.'

Rather than SE *there is/are*, VESL uses the existential constructions *it hav* or *de hav*, which are probably calques on Kwéyòl *i ni* or *la ni*. (The two Kwéyòl constructions are equivalent in meaning, but *i ni* is probably the older of the two; *la ni* may be a partial back-translation of SE *there are*.)

In some cases, the semantic fields of English words have been expanded in VESL, apparently to match those of their Kwéyòl equivalents. Examples of this include *bohroo* 'borrow', which also means 'to lend':

> bohroo mii yoh koom
> pwété mwen penng ou
> 'Lend me your comb.'

skrach 'scratch', which also means 'to itch':[21]

> maisef skraching mii
> kò mwen ka gwaté mwen
> 'I itch/I feel itchy' (literally 'Myself/my body scratching me').

kom 'come', which like Kwéyòl *vini* also means 'to become':

> yuu naat iiting flesh, yuu koming moh slim
> ou pa ka manhé salézon, ou ka vini pli még
> '[If] you do not eat meat, you become slimmer.'

ool 'old', which like Kwéyòl *vyé* also means 'unpleasant, repulsive':

> ai heet dat ool gol
> mwen hayi vyé tifi sa-la
> 'I hate that ugly/disagreeable girl.'

The semantic field of the English adverb *again* has been broadened in VESL, quite probably on the semantic pattern of Kwéyòl *ankò*, to include the additional meanings 'still', 'anymore', and 'else':

> yuu hav moh klooz tuu waash ogen?
> ou ni pli had pou lavé ankò?
> '[Do] you still have more clothes to wash?'

> hii naat koming hiir ogen
> i pa ka vini isi-a ankò
> 'He doesn't come here anymore.'

> yuu bai bred en waat ogen?
> ou achté pen èk ki sa ankò?
> 'You bought bread and what else?'

Locatives can act as nominals. This includes deictic locatives such as *hiir* 'here' and *de* 'there':

> de hav mod
> la ni labou
> 'It is muddy there' (literally 'There [the specific place indicated] has mud'; not an existential construction).
>
> doun de nais
> anba-a la bèl
> 'It is nice/pleasant down there.'

Other locative phrases such as *at hiz hoom* 'at his house/home' and *bai do biich* 'at the beach' are also heard:

> at hiz hoom hav frii che
> lakay li ni twa chèz
> 'There are three chairs in his house.'
>
> bai do biich hav krab
> bò lanmè ni kwab
> 'There are crabs at the beach.'

§2   *Features attributable to Kwéyòl influence only*

The features described in the preceding subsection are among those that VESL shares with Kwéyòl as well as at least some CEC varieties. This is not to say that any or all of the features described above are attributable to CEC influence, but merely to acknowledge that some of them may be; there remains the possibility that many (perhaps most) of them are attributable to the influence of Kwéyòl, or else to a mutually reinforcing combination of both CEC and Kwéyòl influences. Those described in the present subsection, in contrast, are features that VESL shares with Kwéyòl but that are *not* known to be characteristic of CEC varieties.

The deictic distinction afforded by the two SE demonstratives *this* and *that* is not made (lexically) in VESL. Kwéyòl has a single demonstrative, *sa-(l)a*, and VESL likewise employs only *dat*.

Certain verbs that are always transitive in SE, such as *to have* and *to want*, can be used intransitively in the negative, like their Kwéyòl counterparts. For example, if a shopper finds that a store does not sell a specific thing that he wants to buy, he may comment,

dee doo hav
yo pa ni
'They do not have [it].'

Similarly, if a child is offered food but refuses it, an observer may comment,

shii doo waan
i pa vlé
'She does not want [any].'

Prepositions of English origin are used (or not used) in various non-standard ways. Many of the differences in preposition usage between VESL and SE are attributable to calquing on Kwéyòl verbs and prepositions that function differently from their SE counterparts, as in these examples:

muuv *in* do reen
sòti *an* lapli-a
'Get out of the rain.'

hii sending stoon *biihain* piipl
i ka voyé woch *dèyè* moun
'He is throwing stones *at/after* people.'

ai bai bred *in hiz han*
mwen achté pen *an lenmen'y*
'I bought bread from him.'

The verb *to laugh*, which in SE must be followed by the preposition *at* in order to be made transitive, does not require a preposition in VESL:

hii lafing mii
i ka wi mwen
'He is laughing at me.'

Likewise, no preposition is used in utterances such as

wai yuu duu mii dat?
pou ki sa ou fè mwen sa?
'Why did you do that to me?'

In other cases a preposition is used, but not the one that would be used in SE; instead, the direct equivalent of the one that would be used in Kwéyòl[22] is used, e.g.:

ai naat laiying *foh* yuu
mwen pa ka manti *ba*'w
'I am not lying *to* you.'

These various examples can be at least partially explained by the fact that the meanings contained in English prepositions are often contained in the Kwéyòl verb, especially in verbs of directional movement such as *sòti* 'to go out from' and *tiyé* 'to pull or draw away from.' (Various "two-part" verbs such as *faal doun* 'fall down' do occur in VESL, however, as they do in SE, notwithstanding the fact that their Kwéyòl equivalents — *tonbé*, in this case — are monomor-phemic verbs.) Prepositional meanings can also inhere in a nominal, as in the case of *lakay* '(at) home':

wen skuul jraap ai goo *at mai hoom*
lè lékol ladjé mwen alé *lakay mwen*
'When school was dismissed I went *home*.'

The prepositional meaning inherent in this form is made most apparent when it is combined with a possessive marker (which is generally the case, as in the example above); the typical response to a question such as *Ki koté Judy?* 'Where is Judy?', if Judy is known to be at home, is simply *Lakay li* '(At) her home'.[23]

Completive aspect is marked by *oredii* (reflex of SE *already*), which usually occurs clause-finally.[24] The following examples illustrate its use:

luk at evriifing yoh modo duu fo yuu oredii
gadé tout bagay manman'w ja fè ba'w
'Look at everything your mother has done for you [in your lifetime].'

yoh modo riich oredii
manman'w ja wivé
'Your mother has arrived.'[25]

It is important to note that *oredii* in VESL often does not function as an adverbial, as it does in SE; it functions instead like the completive marker *ja* in Kwéyòl (as will be explained further below). In SE, the adverbial of aspect *already* generally lends a sense of emphasis; that is, it is used to reinforce or call special attention to the completiveness or perfectness of a given verb relative to other discursively proximate verbs. For example, in the SE equivalent of the first example above, an SE-speaker would only use *already* if this sentence were followed by something like *And now you expect her to make the down payment on your house?!*; or if it were preceded by something like *You're going to ask your mother to do that for you too?!* In the VESL example in question, neither was the case; the addressee was simply being asked to consider the many sacrifices that his mother had made for him over the years, and was being urged not to do something now that would break her heart. Regarding the second example, an SE-speaker would only use *already* if, for example, it were known that the child was expected to be home to meet his mother at a certain designated time, and is now late. But this was not the case when the example was recorded; prior to this utterance, it had not been known just when the mother would return, nor had it been expected that the child would go home prior to her return.

So in neither of the VESL examples above is *oredii* being used in an SE-style emphatic sense. Rather, it is being used as a completive marker, in a manner analogous to that in which auxiliary *to have* is used to form the perfect in SE (or in which *don* is used in many CECs).[26] The two examples in question are therefore probably best glossed in SE as perfects (as they are glossed above). The SE perfect is not always the best gloss, however; for example, the VESL utterance *Hii dai oredii* can mean 'He has died', but it can also mean simply 'He is dead'. It is important to note, furthermore, that there is no perfect in VESL; SE-type perfects occur only in relatively "acrolectal" forms of St. Lucian English.

In order to help demonstrate that this particular example of one of VESL's non-standard features derives directly from Kwéyòl, it is worthwhile to consider here how the form equivalent to VESL *oredii* is used in Kwéyòl. There are actually two Kwéyòl forms that need to be taken into account: *déja* and *ja*. The former conveys approximately the same meaning as the French word of which it is clearly a reflex; it likewise seems to be semantically equivalent to *already* in SE, functioning as an adverbial of aspect. The latter form, *ja*, seems to be a reduced form of *déja* that has become at least partially grammaticalized. It can function proclitically, i.e. as a preverbal particle that is structurally dependent on the presence of the verb. It also seems to be somewhat semantically bleached, at least as used in some contexts; that is, it is not always a full semantic equivalent of *déja*, although it can be. This distinction between bleached and unbleached has to do with the context in which the form is being used. For example, the sentence *Yo ja annonsé lanmò'y* can convey either of two meanings: 'They have announced his death (so it's true, he's dead!)', or 'They have already announced his death (haven't you heard?)'. In either case, *ja* marks the morphologically invariant verb as completive; the difference seems to lie in whether or not the completiveness of the verb is being emphasized. VESL *oredii* thus functions in much the same way as Kwéyòl *ja*: it generally marks the completive. Its sometime function as an adverbial of aspect, somewhat less common, is dependent on context.

Overall, the examples in this section suggest that while some of VESL's non-standard features (those examined in §2) are attributable to Kwéyòl, some others (those examined in §1) may just as well be attributable to CEC influence, or else to some combination of Kwéyòl and CEC influences. Clearly, then, the proposal that VESL's non-standard features are primarily attributable to Kwéyòl influence cannot be substantiated on formal grounds alone; indeed, the preceding examples might even lead one to the conclusion that CEC influence has been of greater importance. In the sections that follow, however, various other kinds of evidence will be examined which strongly suggest that Kwéyòl has had the greater influence on VESL.

4.   Earlier characterizations of VESL

Although VESL has never been comprehensively examined and described, its existence has been acknowledged at various times in the literature on language in St. Lucia — a small literature, but one that now spans four decades. This section considers the various ways in which VESL has been characterized in that literature, starting with the earliest studies and working forward in chronological order to the most recent.

The earliest relevant published work is Alleyne (1961), who noted that at that time, English was spoken by very few St. Lucians, mainly by the most highly educated and privileged, and that it tended to be restricted to the most official and formal domains:

> English as spoken in St. Lucia is very conservative and particularly among people who have no opportunity of speaking it with Standard English speakers and whose contact with English has been exclusively through the school, it is very literary. Among many people in St. Lucia, a conversational Standard English style has not yet developed....[T]he class in which linguistic innovations are born does not possess English as a spontaneous means of self-expression; it has no facility in the familiar, colloquial use of English (9).

So far, this hardly sounds like VESL. Even so, Alleyne's brief description provides an important glimpse of the sociolinguistic situation in St. Lucia four decades ago. He indicates that Kwéyòl monolingualism was common and widespread in St. Lucia at this time; that English (of any kind) was not yet being used widely as a medium of vernacular communication; that those St. Lucians who did speak English had learned it primarily (if not "exclusively") in school; that those who had learned it in school had few if any opportunities to speak it

outside of schools and that the English that they spoke was very conservative"
and "very literary," i.e., it clearly was not a CEC variety. Elsewhere in this same
article, moreover, Alleyne writes of a large sector of St. Lucian society that has
"only the rudiments of primary education" and is "developing a distinctive
English vernacular which is strongly influenced by [French] Creole phonetic,
semantic, and syntactical patterns" (6).

Carrington (1969) is another relevant early work. Carrington does not
apply any label to VESL, and for that matter does not regard it here as a discrete
language variety; but he does note that the "Deviations from Standard English
in the Speech of Primary School Children" that he examines are produced
systematically by schoolchildren, and that they "fall into readily recognisable
patterns" (166). This clearly suggests that a distinct non-standard English
vernacular had taken form by this point in time, and that primary schools were
an important (possibly crucial) context in which it was emerging. This early
study by Carrington can be regarded as a foundational work in the now
sizeable body of education-oriented research, much of it produced locally in St.
Lucia over the past three decades or so by teacher trainees and other educators,
that has been concerned with the "influence," "transfer," or "interference" of
Kwéyòl in St. Lucian schoolchildren's English — a phenomenon that has been
regarded locally as a perennial problem (see Simmons-McDonald 1996).

Writing only nine years after Alleyne (1961), Midgett (1970) remarks on a
St. Lucian "colloquial English." Significantly, he characterizes this colloquial
English as a variety that is intermediate between Kwéyòl and English, i.e. an
English-lexified variety that demonstrates strong syntactic similarities to
Kwéyòl. He provides two examples, along with their Kwéyòl and SE equivalents,
to show the type of "transitions" that are giving rise to this distinct variety:

> pu ki u ka kwiyé shê u?
> for what you are calling your dog?
> 'Why are you calling your dog?'
>
> mwê ka kuri vit pasé u
> I am running fast more than you
> 'I run faster than you.'

For Midgett, these examples make clear that "loan translation," or the use of
English-lexified calques on Kwéyòl, is the single most important process by
which this "colloquial English" has taken form; and he observes that this
emergent variety has "certain grammatical correlations with Patois, which is in
many cases its functional equivalent" (166). Crucially, he also notes, "This

colloquial style is interesting in that it approximates dialectical [sic] variations found on most other British islands although *there is nothing approaching an English Creole spoken on St. Lucia"* (165; emphasis added).

The three descriptions reviewed thus far suggest that VESL is the outcome of fairly recent contact, particularly in pedagogical contexts, between Kwéyòl and English in St. Lucia. A somewhat more nuanced approach is taken by Le Page (1977), who refers to both "a local creolised English vernacular" and "creolised varieties of English" (109). Le Page's use of the term "creolised" here goes unspecified and is therefore rather vague, but it presumably refers to certain creole-like structural features of the variety in question (as opposed to the demographic and sociohistorical context of its emergence). He indicates that this variety exhibits Kwéyòl influences as well as Caribbean English Creole influences, but no specific evidence of CEC influence is adduced other than the occasional use of *does* and *did* as tense-aspect markers in samples of schoolchildren's speech. Considering the circumstances under which the samples were collected — tape-recorded interviews conducted by a standard English-speaking adult researcher who questioned the children about "more formal" topics "such as school work," and subsequently about "more informal topics such as games and black magic and witches" (Le Page and Tabouret-Keller 1985: 139–140) — the children's use of these forms may well have been hypercorrections (albeit hypercorrections that presumably reflect an aware-ness of certain norms of "English" usage, but any such norms surely would have had less salience for the children in their everyday colloquial interactions than they did in these semi-structured interviews).[27]

Robertson (1982) does not deal directly with St. Lucia, but makes some important observations of a general nature concerning cases in which a creole differs lexically from the standard language with which it co-exists, and con-cerning the course of second language acquisition in such cases. (Note that Robertson seems pointedly to avoid the use of "English creole" or any similar term in the following passage.)

> [I]n countries such as Trinidad it has always been assumed — perhaps errone-ously — that there is no *English-based structural equivalent* of the French-based creole. It is further assumed that there is a gap in the transition to an English target….This [assumption] seems to make nonsense of the notions of negative transfer especially in untutored second language learning. More recent work in Trinidad (Carrington et al. 1976) and the work of Christie (1968) in Dominica clearly point to the very real possibility that some of these basilectal features have existed, and indeed still do exist in Trinidadian and St. Lucian *English-based speech* (68–69; emphases added).

Le Page and Tabouret Keller (1905), which draws its St. Lucian data from the same study that Le Page (1977) is based on, attribute the characteristic features of the language variety in question[28] to several factors, including Barbadian influence, the influence of Kwéyòl, and the staffing of schools with teachers who do not have full command of standard English. At times the authors make a broad distinction (supported by quantitative analyses of their interview data) between a "vernacular" of local, primarily rural origin (the distinctive features of which they attribute to Kwéyòl influence) and a "Creole English" (which they suggest has come to St. Lucia primarily from Barbados and has had the most influence in Castries). As in Le Page (1977), this distinction is based in part on the occasional use of *does* as a marker of habitual aspect (and as an alternative to the *-ing* suffix, which they attribute to Kwéyòl influence):

> *-ing* forms are associated with a quite widespread regional English vernacular with its roots in former Patois-speaking territories and *does* forms with another widespread regional English vernacular with its roots in Barbados and influencing St. Lucia via the urban vernacular of Castries (164).

Elsewhere Le Page and Tabouret-Keller (1985) emphasize the second language acquisition process (but still refer to a "creolized English") when they mention "the gradual shift of a population from a French-patois-like vernacular to a creolized English as their native language, via an intermediate stage of 'Standard English as a second language in the classroom'" (155; quotation marks in original). Still elsewhere they suggest that "re-creolization" has been a factor, but nowhere do they specify what this term might mean (and it is not made at all clear by the context in which it is used). Here again they cite both Barbadian influence and Kwéyòl influence, which they see as coming together in pedagogical contexts: "That school English, however, has been to some extent re-creolized according to a pattern partly due to Barbados, and partly to interference from Creole French itself" (79).

Dalphinis (1985) writes in passing of a "relexified Kwéyòl" (49), and elsewhere of an "English Creole of Kwéyòl structure" (201). He states unequivocally that relexification of Kwéyòl is the process by which this variety has arisen.[29] Elsewhere Dalphinis seems explicitly to dismiss the possibility of Bajan influence when he notes that this relexified Kwéyòl is "different from, though convergent with, Barbadian/English Creole" (49). (Unfortunately, he offers no further explanation of what he means here by "different from, though convergent with.")

Isaac (1986), writing on the topic "French Creole Interference in the Written English of St. Lucia Secondary School Students," sets forth a continuum-like model of language in St. Lucia that posits an uninterrupted cline between Kwéyòl and standard English. In between the two, she identifies a mesolectal "St. Lucian Creolized English" as well as an English-lexified "St. Lucian Basilect." Of the latter she writes, "The St. Lucian basilectal variety is generally a calqued form of the French Creole…and may be referred to as an anglicized equivalent of French Creole from which there is a gradual decreolization towards Standard English" (29). Much like Midgett and Dalphinis, Isaac identifies calquing, relexification, and related phenomena arising from sustained contact between Kwéyòl and English as the central processes that have given rise to the variety (or varieties) in question.

Various other observers of language in St. Lucia refer in passing to an "English Creole" or "creolized English." Christie (1989), for example, refers to a "creolized English" when she states that "there is a growing proportion of speakers whose first language is creolized English" (247). Pollard (1990: 83–84) refers to an "English Creole:" "In Castries, the English Creole is without a doubt heard more frequently than the French Creole" (83–84). It is also worth noting here that Winford (1993) classifies St. Lucia's English-lexified vernacular language variety, along with those of Trinidad, Dominica, and Barbados, as an "intermediate" (as opposed to "conservative") variety within the "Eastern" group of Caribbean English Creole lects.

Le Page (1998), which was first published in 1992, revisits the St. Lucian study on which Le Page (1977) and Le Page and Tabouret-Keller (1985) are based. Here Le Page states, "Our survey showed that the English used by the schoolchildren, supposedly the English they had been taught at school, reflected in a number of morphological features (the level of analysis on which we concentrated) differing patterns of influence from both indigenous and external contacts, today and in the past" (84). Le Page does not specify what the nature of these "external contacts" might have been, however. He continues, in the next paragraph: "Among the external influences however were: the geographical proximity of Martinique to the north, a Department of France still using Creole French and French; of St. Vincent to the south, using Creole English and English; and of Barbados to the east, using what can best be labelled 'Bajan' and English." Le Page's geography is of course correct, but the mere fact of St. Lucia's geographic proximity to other islands does not constitute evidence of actual sociolinguistic influence from these (potential) sources. One might ask, for example, what influence the French spoken in Martinique (which is four times closer to St. Lucia than Barbados and is clearly visible on the horizon from the northern end of the island) has had in St. Lucia. Aside from the fact that French has not been maintained among any group of speakers in St. Lucia, the influence of contemporary French on Kwéyòl seems to be exceedingly minimal despite the fact that movement of persons and goods between the two islands is by no means uncommon.[30] But Le Page does not elaborate on the potential importance of the geographic proximity of other islands except by noting in passing that St. Lucia's links to Barbados have been "particularly important in and around the capital, Castries, in the past for reasons of the colonial administration and of trade;" he also notes that unspecified numbers of laborers and teachers went to St. Lucia ("schools...were staffed to some extent by expatriate Englishmen or Barbadians"). Le Page summarily concludes that "St. Lucia is probably on the same road towards the use of some variety of Creolized Eastern Caribbean English as Grenada and Dominica" (85). Here again, the precise meaning of the term "creolized" in this context is left unspecified.

This characterization of the St. Lucian situation as the outcome of multiple sociolinguistic "inputs" reflects the thought-provoking (if sometimes frustratingly vague) "multidimensional" approach to creole sociolinguistic settings developed in Le Page and Tabouret-Keller (1985). Le Page (1998: 85) acknowledges that this approach, which is based in part on the assumption that multilingual communities tend to exhibit varying degrees of relative "diffuseness" and "focus" due to a wide range of social and historical factors, "is anathema to some creolists, who dismiss it pejoratively with the term 'the cafeteria principle.'" For Le Page, the fact that some of the St. Lucian schoolchildren in his study used three distinct ways of expressing habituality in their "English" (each of which is attested for one or more CEC varieties: Ø, does, -ing) is a reflection of the fact that at that particular point in St. Lucia's history, "[a]ll three forms were available to them;" the sociolinguistic setting was still relatively "diffuse" in the sense that sociolinguistic norms within St. Lucia as a whole were not yet "focused" with regard to the relative "prestige" (and other social meanings, presumably) of each form (86). Although there is much that is of value in this approach, one of its major weaknesses, at least as it is applied in this particular study, is that it does not rigorously pursue and substantiate the source of each of the linguistic forms in question; rather, it merely assumes that certain forms are attributable to Bajan influence, others to Kwéyòl influence, etc.

Finally, and most recently, Simmons-McDonald (1996) writes of an "English vernacular" which she otherwise refers to by the abbreviation "SLCE" (for "St. Lucian Creole English"). She does not go into much detail concerning its origins, but seems to find it safe to assume that it has arisen due to the fact that many Kwéyòl-speaking children acquire English as a second language in school (from teachers whose own command of standard English is less than perfect), while other children acquire the English vernacular as a first language (presumably from elders who learned their "English" as a second language). "If this is the case," she observes, "we must admit that the formal education system, particularly at the elementary level, is fostering the development of an English vernacular when its aim is ostensibly to help learners acquire the official language, St. Lucian Standard English" (123–124). Like Alleyne, Carrington, Isaac, and others before her, Simmons-McDonald thus sees St. Lucian primary schools as a driving force in VESL's ongoing emergence.

What emerges from these varied characterizations of VESL, spanning four decades, are two main points of view. In one, by far the less developed and less substantiated of the two, VESL is regarded as an "English Creole" or "creolized English," the origin of which is either left completely unspecified and unaccounted for, or is assumed to lie somewhere outside of St. Lucia. Le Page (1977) and Le Page and Tabouret-Keller (1985) are the only proponents of this view who venture to specify a possible source: they point to Barbados. But very little evidence (demographic, historical, or otherwise) of actual Bajan influence is adduced; they merely assume that the route of transmission must be there (by reason of geographic proximity and administrative ties, among other factors that are named but not explored), and that it has been an important one historically. It is important to note, however, that Le Page and Tabouret-Keller do not subscribe fully or exclusively to the view that VESL is an English creole of foreign origin that was imported more or less intact into St. Lucia. They also take into account the other major viewpoint that emerges in the literature, which is that VESL has emerged in St. Lucia itself, through contact between Kwéyòl and English, primarily through the acquisition of English as a second language by speakers of Kwéyòl, largely in the schools. (Much to their credit, Le Page and Tabouret-Keller are the only researchers who take both of these potential sources of influence into account and attempt to show how they may have worked in tandem.)

It seems worth noting that the latter viewpoint outlined above, which attributes VESL's emergence largely if not exclusively to the influence of Kwéyòl, is the one that is espoused by all of those researchers who have done in-depth, field-based research on language in St. Lucia and have strong (in some cases native) familiarity with Kwéyòl: namely Carrington, Midgett, Isaac, and Simmons-McDonald. Then again, it is perhaps to be expected that those researchers who are most familiar with Kwéyòl are likely to be especially attentive to (and to find especially striking) VESL's numerous and extensive similarities to Kwéyòl. Furthermore, it is possible that such detailed knowledge of Kwéyòl might predispose these researchers to overlook, or at least to give short shrift to, the potential importance of those similarities that do exist between VESL and varieties of Caribbean English Creole. For these reasons as well as others alluded to previously (concerning the numerous syntactic and other similarities between Kwéyòl and CECs), it is important to look beyond comparisons of the formal-structural features of Kwéyòl and VESL and to consider other kinds of evidence, namely demographic and sociohistorical evidence.

5.   Demographic and sociohistorical evidence

Although there is no evidence that anything resembling VESL was spoken in St. Lucia prior to the mid to late nineteenth century, it is worthwhile to begin by looking well back in St. Lucia's history, to the pre-Emancipation era. In order to be certain that the origins of VESL do not date back farther than might be suspected, it is necessary to establish that the British, following their take-over of the island in 1803[31] (or during any previous period of British control, of which there were several), did not bring slaves into St. Lucia who might have been speakers of an English creole. Some of the available evidence that this was not the case comes from Le Page and Tabouret-Keller's (1985) work. They begin, "We have been able to discover very little about the direct slave-trade to St. Lucia;" but, they continue, "It is likely that it was mostly in French hands" (59). They go on to say:

> [I]t seems likely that Martinique would have been able to supply St. Lucia's slave needs to a large extent and that established slave merchants in Martinique would have tried to keep the St. Lucian trade in their [own] hands…But during this period [the latter part of the eighteenth century] neither Barbados nor Jamaica exported [slaves] to St. Lucia. We find ourselves still with no very satisfactory picture of the origins of St. Lucian slaves beyond this: the majority reached the island after spending some time in Martinique (60).

Le Page and Tabouret-Keller thus find nothing to suggest that there was ever an influx of slaves from Barbados or any other British West Indian island who might have brought an English creole with them; on the contrary, virtually all of St. Lucia's slaves came via the French slave trade, based locally in Martinique. This is not surprising when it is considered that French landowners were allowed, even encouraged, to stay on in St. Lucia after the British takeover; the island had been coveted by the British due to its strategic location, but they subsequently showed little interest in settling it and otherwise developing it as a British colony. Furthermore, strong ties to Martinique continued long after the British decisively seized control of St. Lucia from the French in 1803. Le Page and Tabouret-Keller continue:

> The population link with Martinique was to continue long after the administrative link had been severed [i.e. during the subsequent British colonial period], as a source of maintained family connections and influences, as a source of both open and surreptitious immigration, and as an entrepôt for slaves and trade (61).

So for quite a few years, the British takeover of St. Lucia had little impact on the local cultural and sociolinguistic milieu. Le Page and Tabouret-Keller note elsewhere that St. Lucia's white population during the British colonial period had ties to Barbados as the regional administrative center, as well as to Britain (59); but it is certainly unlikely that this tiny (and doubtless quite insular) administrative class would have introduced into St. Lucia a vernacular that in any way resembled VESL.[32]

Regarding education in St. Lucia in later years, Le Page and Tabouret-Keller note,

> Primary school teachers were recruited mainly through the pupil-teacher system, taking bright adolescents out of the sixth grade of the primary school and setting them to work simultaneously teaching and learning to teach under the Head-teacher's supervision. Such teachers had themselves very little direct access, except in books, to the Standard British English they were supposed both to teach and to teach in (67–68).

Strangely, they do not take into consideration that this significantly hampered process of learning English as a second language is very likely to have been a crucial means by which English in St. Lucia came to be restructured, just as has been the case in other situations that they themselves mention, such as Singapore, where local English-as-a-second-language has been greatly influenced by Chinese (176). Still elsewhere in this same volume, however, Le Page and Tabouret-Keller do make passing mention of "the gradual shift of a population from a French-patois-like vernacular to a creolized English as their native language, via an intermediate stage of 'Standard English as a second language in the classroom'" (155; quotation marks in original). But no explicit link of any kind is made between this process of second-language acquisition and the origins of the so-called "creolized English" in question.

Evidence adduced by Dalphinis (1985) reinforces that offered by Le Page and Tabouret-Keller. Dalphinis notes that most if not all St. Lucian slaves entered the island via the French trade and Martinique (45). He further notes that St. Lucia with its rugged terrain was a haven of almost mythical proportions for escaped Martinican slaves; this would have assured a continuing influx of French creole-speakers (34). Dalphinis also remarks, "The development of St. Lucian Kwéyòl could only have benefitted from the ingress of Trinidadian slaves some of whom also spoke a French Creole" (and none of whom, presumably, would have spoken an English creole during this period in Trinidad's history, i.e. the pre-Emancipation era).

Moving forward into the post-Emancipation era, Dalphinis makes passing mention of an unspecified number of Barbadians who came to St. Lucia during the period 1901–1905. He says that they settled mainly in the capital, Castries, and "featured as dockworkers, teachers, and criminals" (46–47). If he is correct about their occupations, this group must have been quite a mix of basilectal and acrolectal Bajan speakers. Jesse (1994 [1956]) also mentions the arrival of an unspecified number of Barbadians in the south of St. Lucia in 1939, under the auspices of the Vieux Fort Land Settlement Scheme (65); but this settlement project was (according to Proudfoot 1950: 21) "from the beginning, fraught with difficulties, mainly owing to the St. Lucia sugar quota." The settlement was liquidated after only three years, in 1942, due to the fact that the land in question was taken over by the United States government for a World War II defense installation.

Table 1. Statistics on St. Lucia from the 1946 British West Indian census

Source: Proudfoot (1950)
Excerpt from Table 27, "Place of birth of all persons enumerated at the British West Indian Census of 1946" (85):

Total population of St. Lucia:	70,855
# of persons born in	
Trinidad and Tobago:	1,347 (1.9% of total)
Barbados:	825 (1.2% of total)
British Guiana:	788 (1.1% of total)
Leeward Islands	
Antigua:	64
Montserrat:	14
St. Kitts:	32
Virgin Islands:	–
Leewards total:	110

Neither Dalphinis nor Jesse specifies the number of Barbadians who went to St. Lucia during these two periods. But Proudfoot's (1950) statistical analyses based on the British West Indian Census of 1946 can help fill in the missing information. The figures in Table 1 show that in 1946, only about 1.2% of persons living in St. Lucia had been born in Barbados. Note also that the numbers of persons born in other CEC-speaking territories, such as Guyana and the Leeward Islands, were also very small (almost vanishingly small in the case of the Leewards). The single largest group of immigrants were from Trinidad and Tobago (unfortunately for present purposes, the two islands are treated as a single administrative unit), but even they amounted to only 1.9% of the total population, and it should be borne in mind that Trinidad still had its own French creole. Although Trinidadian French Creole was already in decline by this time, it was still in use as a vernacular (if only in restricted contexts, e.g. in certain households and communities) by some sectors of the Trinidadian population. This being the case, Kwéyòl's close similarity to Trinidadian French Creole may have been a factor in at least some of these Trinidadian migrants' choice of St. Lucia as a destination. Furthermore, any emergent English-lexified vernacular that Trinidadians may have been speaking at this point in time may well have been influenced, to at least some extent, by Trinidadian French Creole (in much the same way that it is being suggested here that Kwéyòl has influenced VESL in St. Lucia; more on this topic below). Whatever the case, there is little to suggest that Barbadians and/or other English creole-speakers, at 2.4–4.3% of the St. Lucian population (the former figure excludes Trinidadians, the latter includes them), formed a large enough or influential enough group to have had a major impact on VESL.

Looking farther back in time, one finds that earlier census figures on potentially English creole-speaking foreign-born persons in the St. Lucian population are not significantly higher (despite a higher overall number of foreign-born

Table 2. Statistics from the 1921 St. Lucian census

Source: *Report on the Census of the Colony of St. Lucia, 1921.*
Excerpts from Table 22, "Birth places of the Population" (34–35):

Total population of St. Lucia: 51,505
Total foreign-born: 3,629 (7% of total)

# of persons born in the three Caribbean territories most heavily represented:
      Barbados: 1,045 (2% of total)
      St. Vincent: 551 (1.1% of total)
      Antigua: 211 (0.4% of total)

Table 3. Statistics from the 1980–81 St. Lucian census[33]

Source: *1980–81 Population Census of the Commonwealth Caribbean; St. Lucia, Vol. 1.*
Excerpts from Table 3.1, "Foreign-born population by sex, age group, and country of birth"
(68–69):

Total population of St. Lucia:	113,409
Total foreign-born:	3,515 (3.1% of total)

# of persons born in the three Caribbean countries most heavily represented:

Guyana:	489 (0.4% of total)
Barbados:	326 (0.3% of total)
Trinidad and Tobago:	141 (0.1% of total)

persons). The 1921 census, for example, shows that out of the total population of 51,505, persons born outside St. Lucia numbered as shown in Table 2. Figures representing migrants from all of the other British-administered Caribbean territories listed in this census — Anguilla, the Bahamas, Grenada, Guyana, Jamaica, Montserrat, Nevis, St. Kitts, Tobago, Tortola, Trinidad, and Turks Island (Dominica, where the sociolinguistic situation at this time was presumably comparable in most respects to that in St. Lucia, is excluded for present purposes) — add up to only another 472 persons, or 0.9% of the total population. So the grand total of persons born in what may be regarded as English-creole-speaking territories — applying the most liberal definition, i.e. including Trinidad and Grenada, where local varieties of French creole closely related to Kwéyòl were still spoken at this time — amounted to no more than 4.4% of St. Lucia's population.

As shown in Table 3, figures from a more recent (post-Independence) census, that of 1980–81, show that the numbers of immigrants from other parts of the Caribbean for more recent years are significantly lower than in these earlier years.

As these and all of the preceding figures suggest, immigration from English creole-speaking territories has never been a significant factor in the makeup of the St. Lucian population. The overwhelming majority of the St. Lucian population is, and has always been, made up of native-born St. Lucians, a fact that is not surprising when one considers that St. Lucia has never had much to offer to outsiders in the way of economic opportunity and social advancement (unlike, for example, Trinidad, or to a lesser extent Barbados).

6.   VESL and Bajan: A brief comparison

A broad overview of VESL's similarities to CEC varieties (taken collectively) was provided in Section 3, but the extent to which VESL actually resembles Bajan or other specific varieties of Caribbean English Creole has not been addressed thus far. A comparison of VESL to all of the CECs, or even a handful of them, is beyond the scope of this article. But since there is no historical evidence to suggest that Jamaican, to take one example, has ever been an important source of influence on VESL, such a broad-based comparison would not be particularly relevant or instructive anyway. Le Page (1977) and Le Page and Tabouret-Keller (1985) are the only proponents of the CEC-influence argument to specify a geographic source of that influence, and they point unequivocally to Barbados. As shown in the last section, there is in fact solid evidence that Barbadians have been well represented in the relatively small overall numbers of immigrants to, and/or sojourners in, St. Lucia. The administrative link between Barbados and St. Lucia is also a matter of historical fact (although its relevance to the sociolinguistic issues at hand is unclear and poorly substantiated). It therefore seems worthwhile to focus here on Bajan rather than any of the numerous other CEC varieties.

Even a cursory comparison suggests that the extent of VESL's resemblance to Bajan is less than remarkable. A perusal of Collymore's (1955) glossary of Bajan, for example, reveals that even names for local flora and fauna that are shared between Bajan and VESL are relatively few and far between. As for grammar, VESL exhibits few of the structural features that are said to be characteristic of contemporary and historical Bajan by Burrowes (1983); and not surprisingly, VESL bears even less resemblance to the samples of early Barbadian speech examined by Rickford and Handler (1994).

Of the twenty-four "creole grammatical features" identified in contemporary Bajan by Rickford (1992), nine are tense-aspect features (187). Of these nine, VESL shares with Bajan only four at most: unmarked past tense, absence of third-person -s, use of *doz* to mark habituality, and use of *had* to mark anteriority. (VESL shares these same four features with other CECs besides Bajan, however, so their presence in VESL cannot necessarily be taken as specifically indicative of Bajan influence.) The first two of these features, unmarked past tense and absence of third-person -s, are hardly surprising or meaningful; they are by no means unusual in English as a second language, regardless of the linguistic background of the learner and regardless of the variety or dialect of English being acquired. As for the use of *doz* to mark habituality, its use in VESL is by no means universal, or even common. Use of *doz* is more characteristic of urban speakers than rural speakers, and urban speakers are more likely to be influenced by "foreign" language varieties (including Bajan, to be sure). Few Morne Carré residents or other rural dwellers use *doz* on a consistent basis, and most use it far less frequently than they use *-ing* forms. Use of the *-ing* suffix to mark habituality (e.g. *ai gooing tuu skuul evrii dee* 'I go to school every day'), as noted previously, seems to be a direct equivalent of the Kwéyòl *ka* + verb pattern. It is interesting in this regard that most VESL speakers do *not* use *doz*, since in purely formal terms *doz* + V corresponds to the *ka* + V pattern much more closely than does V + *-ing*. (One possible explanation for this is that *doz* was not available as a candidate, whereas *-ing* forms were available, perhaps via formal education).[34] When *doz* is used by rural speakers, furthermore, it often seems to be a hypercorrection of sorts, a feature that crops up only when the speaker is in a situation that calls for his or her "best" English (e.g. a conversation with a tourist or other Anglophone foreigner).

The use of *had* to mark anteriority in Bajan may be of some significance with regard to VESL, but it must also be considered that Rickford (1992: 187) lists two other anterior markers for Bajan besides *had*: *bin* and *did*. In VESL, furthermore, *had* can reasonably be regarded as a direct translation of the Kwéyòl anterior marker *té*; it is not difficult to imagine that schoolchildren learning English as a second language and being drilled on the "proper" use of auxiliary *to have* in English (e.g. to form past participles) might have generalized its use to other contexts, namely anteriority. Still, where two or more inputs into a restructured variety are possible, any feature that they share is more likely to turn up in the restructured variety than one that is not shared. So a measure of Bajan (or possibly other CEC) influence cannot be ruled out here; it may be, for example, that St. Lucians learning English selected *had* from Bajan as a better candidate for marking anteriority than either *bin* or *did*.

VESL does not share with Bajan any of the other five tense-aspect features identified by Rickford: anterior *bin*, continuative *da*, habitual *(d)a*, anterior *did*, or completive *don*. (Another important respect in which VESL differs from Bajan is that VESL's TMA particles cannot be combined in the various ways that Roy [1986] attests for basilectal Bajan.) Nor does VESL exhibit various other features mentioned by Rickford, such as absence of pronominal case,[35] use of *en*, *na*, and *no* as negative preverbal markers, or pluralizing/deictic *dem*.

As for those non-standard features shared by VESL and Bajan that *can* be identified — and there are some, to be sure, such as reduplication and absence of -*s* as nominal pluralizer — it can be argued that these are relatively un-marked as "Bajan" compared to those mentioned in the preceding paragraph. That is, they are not peculiar to Bajan, and therefore their presence in VESL cannot be traced reliably or conclusively to Barbados. Furthermore, most can readily be attributed to *pan-creole* similarities: that is, features common to *both* English-lexified and French-lexified Caribbean creoles. Caribbean English Cre-oles do have numerous structural parallels to Caribbean French Creoles, as is well known. So when these same features turn up in VESL, or in the English-lexified vernaculars of other islands like Dominica and Trinidad and Carriacou (all of which also have French creoles in their background), how are we to decide where the feature in question comes from? For a start, it seems reason-able to unsheathe Occam's razor and look to the most proximate, most consis-tently and readily available potential source, which in the St. Lucian case, given the lack of compelling demographic and sociohistorical evidence to the con-trary, is unquestionably Kwéyòl. As an example, let us return to the example of *ogen* 'again', which in VESL can have any of four different meanings. One is the same as the standard English sense, denoting repetition, while the other three correspond to the SE words *still, anymore,* and *else* (as in the examples given previously):

> yuu hav moh klooz tuu waash ogen?
> ou ni had pou lavé ankò?
> '[Do] you still have more clothes to wash?'

> hii naat koming hiir ogen
> i pa ka vinn isi-a ankò
> 'He doesn't come here anymore.'

> yuu bai bred en waat ogen?
> ou achté pen èk ki sa ankò?
> 'You bought bread and what else?'

On one hand, it can perhaps be argued that the word *ogen* is used in some or all of these same ways in Barbados and in various other parts of the Caribbean, not to mention in parts of West Africa. But why look to influence from any of these far-flung places when the Kwéyòl word *ankò*, which any St. Lucian schoolchild will readily translate into "English" as 'again,' also expresses all four meanings? The intent here is not to make a strong case for relexification, as Dalphinis (1985) does; although it has doubtless been one important factor, relexification alone cannot adequately account for VESL's emergence. The basic point to be made here, rather, is that many aspects of VESL's grammatical structure do appear to derive quite directly from Kwéyòl; and even in those cases where there is a possibility that they may reflect influence from a foreign CEC variety, one is left with the task of deciding whether the feature in question derives from Kwéyòl, from the CEC, or from some mutually reinforcing combination of the two.

7.   English in the classroom

The basic observation that English in St. Lucia has been influenced by Kwéyòl has certainly been made many times before; as was mentioned previously, "transference" and "interference" phenomena have long been regarded as vexing problems by educators in St. Lucia. One can get a sense of just how long by considering reports filed by British colonial school inspectors. The earliest such reports available in the St. Lucia National Archives, dating from the early years of the twentieth century, give some indication not only of the nature and origins of VESL, but also of how long ago it began to emerge as a distinctly St. Lucian language variety. Excerpts from these reports will be considered below. But first, it is helpful to consider the general state of education in colonial St. Lucia, in order to determine what role formal schooling might have had in the emergence of VESL.

According to Alleyne (1961: 5),

> Education in St. Lucia really starts with the Mico Schools in 1838. Until 1842 these were the only public schools in existence. They continued until 1891 when the schools were handed over to religious denominations which, however, retained the majority of Mico-trained teachers. The interest for us is that Mico-trained educationalists were protestant English-speakers. They were trained in the Mico Training Colleges in Jamaica and Antigua where French Creole was never spoken.

"The influence of these Mico teachers," Alleyne asserts, "and of others who came from Jamaica, Antigua, and other English-speaking islands (i.e. Barbados and St. Vincent), affected the language situation immensely." And doubtless it did, in that the schools staffed by these teachers made it possible for more St. Lucian children to learn English than ever before. But it is also important to establish that the presence of these Mico-trained teachers, even in large numbers, would not have resulted in the introduction of a foreign English creole into St. Lucia. In the first place, the number of persons concerned was quite small. Alleyne states, "In 1904, of the 43 Head Teachers throughout St. Lucia, 30 were born and had grown up in exclusively English-speaking islands; 7 of the others were Irish." Based on the number of head teachers given here (assuming one head teacher per school), there were apparently forty-three Mico schools by 1904. Even if the faculty of each school had numbered ten teachers (and it is very likely that most of the schools had fewer teachers than that),[36] and even if each of those teachers had come from an "English-speaking" island (and it is quite certain that this was not the case, since only thirty out of the forty-three head teachers were from the British West Indies, and surely most of the non-head teachers were St. Lucians who had been, or were being, trained by these head teachers),[37] this would have meant that there was a total of 430 foreign teachers resident in St. Lucia at a time when the island's total population was approximately 45,000.[38] This means that these foreign teachers would have made up less than one percent of the population; it is likely that they in fact made up significantly less than one-half of one percent. To be sure, these teachers would have been prominent members of their communities, and would have had far more social and linguistic influence than an equal number of foreign stevedores or agricultural laborers. Although no direct evidence is available, it is unlikely that these schoolteachers, specially trained abroad and specially recruited by the British colonial administration in order to make primary education and the English language more widely accessible in St. Lucia, would have been using in the classroom a CEC variety with such decidedly non-standard features as those that VESL exhibits; nor, presumably, would they have been speaking such a variety in their dealings with St. Lucians outside the classroom.[39]

Moving on now to the British colonial school inspectors' observations: in 1918 (about the time that today's oldest living St. Lucians would have been in primary school, if they attended) the inspector commented, "The greatest obstacle to the progress of the children is the continued use of 'patois' coupled with irregular attendance. It was painfully evident during the examinations that English was only a *school* language for the children [emphasis in original], being neither heard nor spoken anywhere else. Even when the children are just leaving the school to go to their homes, they chatter in patois."

When English *was* spoken, the Inspector of Schools reported in 1919, "Present and Past Tenses were hopelessly confused and the Active Voice was commonly used for the Passive Voice." In 1922, the inspector commented on "errors in syntax, which are common, e.g. use of wrong tenses, wrong use of prepositions, disagreement of subject and verb both in person and number, etc." It seems that the children's English did not improve as they progressed through school; in fact, the opposite seems to have been true, perhaps because these early non-standard features of usage became established and reinforced outside the classroom, e.g. as "English" came to be used by schoolchildren within their peer groups. In 1920, it was observed: "Grammatical errors were common in Standard IV, which was invariably the weakest class. Among these errors [in English Composition] were: indiscriminate use of present and past tenses; non-agreement of verb with its nominative; confusion of past participle and present infinitive, of direct and indirect speech, and of active and passive voices." These "errors" cited by the colonial school inspectors (with the possible exception of "confusion of … direct and indirect speech") are all characteristics of VESL as spoken today, of course.

The inspectors were chagrined to find that local teachers (i.e. St. Lucian teacher trainees) as well as students were speaking English like this. The 1922 report notes, "Unfortunately many Pupil Teachers make use of faulty English in addressing their classes, such as 'How you call this?' — 'A dog, what it is?'" Most if not all of these examples of errors in English indicated by the school inspectors seem to be direct calques on their Kwéyòl equivalents. For example, "A dog, what it is?" follows the Kwéyòl pattern of focusing: *An chyen, (ki) sa sa yé?*; and "How you call this?" is most likely a calque on *Kouman ou ka kwiyé sa?* (Speakers in Morne Carré and other rural areas today generally calque even more directly: *hou yuu kohling dat?*) The inspector for 1931 brings up examples that he readily attributes to outright ignorance: "Lack of knowledge on the part of the Teachers is another source of failure. 'The bee stings with its mouth' — 'Another name for the chest is the stomach' are but two of the many interesting pieces of information collected by the Inspector of Schools." While the former is a factual error, the latter statement, "Another name for the chest is the stomach," is only apparently a factual error. It can be attributed to an instance of non-correspondence between Kwéyòl and English semantic fields: the Kwéyòl lexeme *lèstonmak* (evidently a reflex of the French *l'éstomac,* and thus a formal cognate of English *stomach,* which is doubtless what misled the teacher) does indeed mean 'chest', not 'stomach' (cf. Kwéyòl *bouden* 'stomach, belly').

All of this suggests that VESL has taken shape over the course of the last century, and especially over the last few decades as public primary education has become near-universally accessible to ordinary St. Lucians. There is much to suggest that VESL has taken shape largely as a result of the efforts of Kwéyòl-monolinguals to acquire English as a second language. It is then necessary to ask what the actual target language of these learners was, i.e. what model of English they had access to. By and large, those St. Lucians who were learning any English at all in the first few decades of the twentieth century were learning it in the classroom, a context in which one might expect to find a fairly acrolectal model. The school inspectors' reports make clear that this was often not the case; the English-as-a-second-language of many of the local student-teachers was far from standard, and showed heavy Kwéyòl influence. But those student-teachers in turn had presumably learned their English in school from more qualified (in many cases foreign-born and foreign-trained) senior teachers and head teachers, who would have been speaking and teaching something approximating the "very conservative" and "very literary" English mentioned by Alleyne (1961: 9) — not, at any rate, any variety of Caribbean English Creole.

8.   Out-migration and other possible sources of "foreign" CEC influence

The emphasis on the teaching and learning of English in schools, in the above section and elsewhere, is not meant to gloss over the possibility that some St. Lucians may have learned "English" in other, less formal, vernacular contexts — for example, while working as migrant laborers in CEC-speaking territories.[40] Nor is it meant to deny the possibility that returned migrants have brought back to St. Lucia certain linguistic features that may then have been taken up by other St. Lucians. But it seems unlikely that this can account for more than a small few of VESL's distinctive features. Those Morne Carré residents who have worked abroad or otherwise spent some time in other Caribbean territories take delight in imitating (for the sake of amusement) the peculiar colloquial expressions, vocabularies, and accents of other islands. Some even complain of not being able to understand persons from these other islands, which suggests that they recognize major differences between the CEC varieties that these others speak and what they think of as their own St. Lucian "English" (which may be nearly as important a marker of their identity as St. Lucians in these foreign contexts as is Kwéyòl). Furthermore, most migrant workers of today have not learned their English from scratch in these foreign contexts. However little formal education they may have, they have learned their "English" (i.e. VESL) while growing up and attending school in St. Lucia.

As for members of older generations who may have learned all or most of their "English" in such foreign contexts, there is little to suggest that St. Lucians have ever emigrated in sufficient numbers to make this a potentially significant factor. Reubens (1961; 21) provides some relevant data. In 1959, St. Lucia's total population was 86,194; the net population movement for that year was only −1,145 (or 1.3%). The net movement of St. Lucians to other territories within the Federation of the West Indies (i.e. all of the major CEC-speaking territories combined), furthermore, was only −97. (Net migration to the United Kingdom, meanwhile, totaled −1,012.) Taking a broader view, Reubens's (1961: 22) overall net migration figures for St. Lucia for the years 1954–1959 are as follows:

1954:	−655	1957:	−1,414
1955:	−584	1958:	−1,429
1956:	−732	1959:	−1,145

Unfortunately, there are no data on how many of these migrants eventually returned to St. Lucia; but here again, the figures are too small to be regarded as significant anyway.

Some other potentially relevant data appear elsewhere in Reubens's (1961: 39) study. One hundred persons departing from St. Lucia to other West Indian territories were interviewed. Of these, the majority, sixty-five, were bound for Barbados. But of these sixty-five, only eight stated that they were going there to reside, and only ten for employment. The other forty-seven queried offered shorter-term motivations for their travel abroad: twenty-seven for vacation, six for business, five for trading, seven to seek medical attention, and two for study. Of these one hundred persons, furthermore, seventy-three were residents of urban areas in St. Lucia; only twenty-seven were from rural areas. The preceding data suggest, not surprisingly, that an important sector of the St. Lucian population in which VESL has taken form, namely rural dwellers with limited financial resources and limited access to education and other social services, are not a highly mobile sector of the population.

9.   Other cases of contact between French creoles and English

Cases of contact between French-lexified creoles and English are fairly numerous. Parkvall (1997) examines seven cases besides St. Lucia in the Lesser Antilles alone: Dominica, St. Vincent, Carriacou, Petite Martinique, Grenada, Trinidad, and Tobago. (He notes that two of these cases, St. Vincent and Tobago, are not well attested, however.) Looking beyond the Caribbean, three additional cases can be added to the list: Louisiana, Mauritius, and the Seychelles. Each has its sociohistorical particularities and vagaries, and although only a few of these cases have been examined in any depth, they provide interesting and potentially instructive points of comparison to the St. Lucian case.

Vernacular English in southern Louisiana has recently begun to be studied in detail (e.g. Dubois and Horvath [1998]). Neumann (1985: 22fn) notes that this variety "would not be a standard English, of course, but rather a non-standard English characterized by numerous interferences from French-lexified vernaculars [i.e. Cajun French and Louisiana Creole]."[41] Given the similarities between Louisiana Creole and Kwéyòl, it would not be surprising if there were similarities between this vernacular English and VESL as well. Marshall (1982: 308) states that "English and French influenc[e] each other in varying degrees. Cases of integration, code-switching, and interference are found in all codes spoken" in the rural southern Louisiana community that was the site of her study. Marshall shows that local vernacular English is affected on various levels, and specifically identifies phenomena such as "syntactic borrowings," omission of the present-tense copula, "leveling" of inflection in verb paradigms as well as in noun phrases (e.g. non-use or over-use of third-person singular -s, and non-use of pluralizing -s), and calques of various kinds (314–16). Most of these features are very similar if not identical to those observable in VESL.

A case that has recently been examined in greater depth is that of Carriacou's "Broken English," described in Kephart (2000). Though it is called "broken English" by its speakers, Kephart refers to this variety as "Carriacou Creole English." The designation "Creole English" is considerably more fitting here than in the St. Lucian case, since it is clear that this language variety, unlike VESL, became established in Carriacou following a significant influx, in the latter half of the eighteenth century, of speakers of what Kephart characterizes as "Old Creole English:" "The Creole English which arrived at that time appears to have resembled, to some degree, the more conservative varieties still existing in Jamaica and other parts of the Caribbean, as well as parts of West Africa" (27). Kephart does not offer further information as to the numbers or origins of the CEC speakers who arrived in Carriacou, or the circumstances of their arrival. According to Parkvall (1997), however, "Much of today's population is descended from slaves brought by British immigrants from Barbados, St. Vincent and other islands after the British conquest [in 1763 of Carriacou and nearby islands controlled by France]." Parkvall cites Redhead's (1970: 61) division of the island into three distinct zones: one in which the population is "of Scottish descent," a second consisting of "those of African descent who speak English only," and a third comprising "those who are of African descent, but are bilingual in English and French Patois." Based on this and information concerning the religious affiliations of Carriacouans provided in Smith (1962), Parkvall extrapolates that "almost 70% of the population of Redhead's two 'African' sectors are Protestant, leaving less than a third as plausible descendants of the pre-1763 (natively FC-speaking) population."[42]

It thus seems clear that the numbers of CEC-speakers who arrived in Carriacou were very large relative to the "native" French creole-speaking population, and that the sociolinguistic influence of the former must have been significant. Based on Kephart's (2000) description, Carriacou Creole English exhibits various features typical of "basilectal" CEC varieties that are not found in VESL, including *di(d)* as past-tense marker (92), stressed *bin* used in combination with both stative and non-stative verbs (92–93), nominal clitic *-andem* as plural marker (79), and serial verbs such as *bring... + kom* (101–102).

Kephart also notes, however, that Patwa (Carriacou's French creole, a Lesser Antillean variety closely related to Kwéyòl but now very much in decline) "apparently influenced the phonological and morphosyntactic patterns of Carriacou Creole English from the time Creole English was introduced into Carriacou. Many syntactic constructions of CCE are morpheme-for-morpheme replacements from *Patwa*" (25). This statement is followed by only a few examples (26), but other examples turn up elsewhere in Kephart's study, e.g. *na tu* + V as negative imperative (100) and prepositional use of a form derived from English *give* (as in the example *Dei no spikin Patwa gi yu* 'They wouldn't speak Patwa for you') (102).[43] It thus seems likely that although Carriacou's "Creole English" has been far more heavily influenced by CEC varieties than has VESL — indeed, it is probably accurate to characterize it outright as a transplanted CEC variety — it has also been influenced by a French creole in much the same way that VESL has, though doubtless to a lesser extent (due in part to the fact that Carriacou's French creole began to go into decline several decades ago).

Probably the best-documented case of contact between a French-lexified creole and English, but perhaps also the most complex one, is the case of Trinidad. In Trinidad, a variety of Lesser Antillean French Creole closely related to that of St. Lucia became established during the latter part of the eighteenth century, while the island was under Spanish control. According to Parkvall (1997), the Spanish had begun encouraging Catholic French colonists to settle in Trinidad in 1776. The British captured the island in 1797, and subsequently made English the official language in 1823. Holm (1989: 377), citing Winer (1981: 11, 14), notes that "within a century the majority of the population spoke English and creole English." Holm continues, "Since education in English was not available to most of the population during this period, the cause for the shift would seem to lie in the considerable immigration of laborers from Barbados and other English-speaking islands during the nineteenth century." Elsewhere (460) Holm notes in this same regard that during the period 1810–20,

> several groups of English speakers immigrated to Trinidad. The first were the British landowners and overseers who came to grow sugar and cacao, as well as to administer the island's government. The second were black veterans of the British army, including demobilized West India Regiment soldiers and escaped slaves from the United States who had fought on the British side in the War of 1812 (Winer 1984). In 1823 English was made the official language, but it was clearly spoken only by a minority at that time. However, the census of 1831 already indicates that approximately half of the total population was born in Barbados (Le Page and Tabouret-Keller 1985: 54).

It is thus clear that the vernacular English of Trinidad is the outcome of a complex constellation of influences, largely "foreign" influences. Foremost among these influences was the introduction into Trinidad of multiple varieties of English creole. Most of these varieties were introduced via immigration from other parts of the British West Indies, with Barbados most heavily represented among them.

Whether or not Trinidad's present-day English-lexified vernacular should be regarded as an "English creole" has been a matter of some debate. Holm (1989: 460), citing Goodman (p.c.), suggests that it should not be so regarded, and Winer (1993: 11) acknowledges the possible validity of this position. Holm comments that if the language variety in question is not an English creole, "it is because the varieties that contributed to it in the nineteenth century were themselves post-creoles (e.g. Leeward Islands CE [Creole English]) if not semi-creoles (i.e. Bajan)." Winer (1984: 181) proposes that it may be "a dialect-levelled composite English Creole," which formed after "several varieties of Atlantic EC were brought to Trinidad and underwent subsequent merging and modification there" (188).

However varied the inputs to this Trinidadian English-lexified vernacular may have been, the fact that a French creole became the most widely and most commonly spoken language in Trinidad in the late eighteenth century, remained such for much of the nineteenth, and continued to be spoken well into the twentieth century demands attention.[44] Winer gives relatively little consideration, in her various publications, to the possible influence of this French creole on the vernacular varieties of English that emerged in Trinidad. Winer (1995: 145) makes mention, on one hand, of "the shared French Creole linguistic component in TEC [Trinidadian English Creole] and the English Creoles of Grenada and St. Vincent" as a potentially important factor in the emergence and consolidation of what she calls "more conservative" forms of "Trinidadian English Creole." She also cites, on the other hand, "the lack of French Creole features in Bajan and some other CECs" as a factor that would have had the opposite effect, i.e. would have presented an alternative and perhaps competing set of linguistic norms. Winer (1984: 190) elsewhere suggests in passing that "the development of second language interlanguage" (presumably she is referring here primarily, if not exclusively, to the acquisition of English by native speakers of French creole) may have played a part. Elsewhere in the same article she notes, "At least some of the early 19th-century Trinidad-born and immigrant population were bilingual in FC and EC, and could have served as valuable cultural and linguistic brokers" (189). But these various potentially crucial facts are not explored, and their implications are not examined.

Although she broaches the topic here and there (as in the above-cited examples), Winer gives little consideration overall to the role of Trinidadian French Creole in the emergence of the distinctive vernacular forms of English spoken in Trinidad today. She states, for example,

> It does…seem reasonable to distinguish…two broad streams or types of TEC: (a) a "basilectal" variety, or group of varieties, brought by basilectal English Creole speakers from other countries, predominantly rural and uneducated urban; and (b) a "mesolectal" variety, or group of varieties, predominantly urban and often literate. In addition, until the early 1900s, French Creole was widespread amongst Afro-Creoles and many whites, particularly in rural areas (1995: 128–129).

Here the potential influence of French creole is acknowledged, but almost as an afterthought; evidently Winer considers the various English creoles that immigrants brought to Trinidad to be the primary source of the distinctive features of contemporary "TEC." Holm (1989: 460) notes,

> Winer (1984) concludes that the shift of the dominant language from Creole French to (Creole) English that occurred between the early nineteenth and early twentieth century took place not through formal education, which was seldom available, but through informal contact with the black immigrants. Thus Trinidadian (Creole) English did not originate in Trinidad but resulted from the modification of several varieties of (creolized) English brought by immigrants.

Here is described another potentially crucial difference between the

Trinidadian case and the St. Lucian case: many, probably most St. Lucians of the first widely bilingual generations (especially in rural areas) acquired their English largely through formal education, whereas Trinidadians, it seems, learned their "English" primarily in vernacular contexts, through interaction with speakers of various CEC varieties. "As the Protector of Immigrants, C. W. Mitchell, pointed out in 1888," Winer (1995: 142) notes in describing one example of this phenomenon, "the concentration of Bajans in the main towns led to more Trinidadians in these areas learning to speak English than did the education system." The differing historical periods in question must also be borne in mind. Significant numbers of Trinidadians were acquiring English as far back as the early 1800s, at which time English was virtually non-existent in St. Lucia outside British colonial circles. Even a full century later, i.e. in the early 1900s, the great majority of St. Lucians were still monolingual speakers of Kwéyòl (Alleyne 1961: 4); and in rural villages like Morne Carré, most adults were monolingual Kwéyòl-speakers as recently as a generation ago. Furthermore, the shift to Kwéyòl-VESL bilingualism in Morne Carré and many other rural villages like it, when it occurred, was due primarily to the introduction of schools and primary education (i.e. English-speaking teachers and formal instruction in English).

In her accounts of the evolution of Trinidadian English Creole, Winer thus assigns considerably more importance to the influence of imported English creoles and the presence of large numbers of West Indian immigrants than to the influence of Trinidad's French creole. The numbers are indeed significant. Winer (1995: 140–141) notes that there were "massive population influxes into Trinidad throughout the 19th century, again during the Great Depression, and then during the war years of the 1940s." By 1901, "Barbadians constituted a sizable proportion (40.26%) of the West Indian immigrant population," and "the total number of West Indian immigrants was 46,748, or 18.3% of the total Trinidadian population of 255,148." Winer notes that "during this period French Creole was still the lingua franca," but she regards this as important less for linguistic reasons than for cultural reasons; use of the French creole at this time by persons born in Trinidad was an important component of their Trinidadian identity, an important factor distinguishing them from Bajans and other immigrants. The French creole was thus one aspect of what Winer identifies as a sort of nascent nationalism, or at least a heightened sense of Trinidadian identity, that was taking form among native Trinidadians at this time. She regards this as a crucial reason why they wished to distinguish themselves linguistically from Bajans (who tended to be successful and occupied relatively prestigious social positions, and were therefore resented by locals):

> Trinidadians did not want to sound like Bajans...The fact that so many Bajans were resident in Trinidad, and were in such influential positions, but that virtually no specifically Bajan elements are apparent in TEC (unless one wishes to posit the use of TEC *does* as originally Bajan) can surely be at least partially attributed to acts of nationalist identity and rejection on the part of TEC speakers (145).

Although Winer does not explicitly state that the acquisition of English or English creole as a second language by native speakers of French creole was unimportant, she gives surprisingly little consideration to its potentially major role in the emergence of the distinctively Trinidadian variety (or varieties) of vernacular English that eventually took form. This is somewhat odd since one of Winer's (1995) major points is that Trinidadians explicitly and actively rejected certain "foreign" norms of English (and/or English creole) usage, particularly those characteristic of Bajan speech. If one accepts this, one is led to wonder what norms of usage took the place of those rejected. Winer gives little consideration to this question, but it seems reasonable to hypothesize that if native speakers of Trinidadian French Creole were feeling beleaguered by the influx of English creole-speaking immigrants, and wanted, as she suggests, to advance and maintain a sense of their own Trinidadian identity vis-à-vis these others (even while faced with the socioeconomically driven need to learn and use English), they would have emphasized their own distinctively "Trinidadian" ways of speaking English. In effect, this is just what Winer (1995) hypothesizes, although she does not address in much depth the question of just what those distinctively Trinidadian ways of speaking English might have been and where they might have come from. A significant hint at the answer, it seems, is to be found in some of the vernacular-language newspaper texts she is working with. One of the texts that she examines contains French Creole code-switches, and another contains an entire poem "written in French Creole, an act of national linguistic identity against Bajans, who would not be able to understand this anti-Bajan poem without help" (144). It seems clear that "native" Trinidadians in the late nineteenth and early twentieth centuries were clinging to their French creole as a marker of identity. If they were motivated, as Winer proposes, to keep their "English" distinct from that of Bajans (and from those of other recent West Indian immigrants, if to a lesser extent), might they not also have clung to, perhaps even emphasized and elaborated, their own French creole-influenced ways of speaking English as a second language?

These questions aside, one point that emerges is that there is good reason to question (on sociohistorical grounds if not linguistic grounds) the notion that Trinidad's English-lexified vernacular is an "English creole," as Winer and others generally regard it. But in any case, the preceding suggests that "English creole" more accurately describes the language variety spoken in Trinidad (much like that spoken in Carriacou) than it does VESL. Whatever the extent of French creole influence on Trinidad's English-lexified vernacular, there is more than enough historical evidence to suggest that this vernacular may in fact have been significantly influenced by English creoles of foreign origin. Trinidad had massive immigration from various parts of the British West Indies, and it is difficult to imagine that this would not have had significant impact on the vernacular English(es) that emerged there, even if they were also strongly influenced by the local French creole. Furthermore, Trinidad with its powerful economy and relatively highly developed industrial and commercial base has continued to attract significant numbers of English creole-speaking immigrants (as well as short-term migrants) from elsewhere in the region. So even if the case can be made that Trinidad's French creole did not significantly contribute to its "English creole" in the way that it is being proposed here that Kwéyòl has influenced VESL in St. Lucia, the fact remains that St. Lucia has never drawn large numbers of speakers of foreign English creoles. Although some such "foreign" influences have doubtless contributed to its emergence, VESL, by and large, is not an import or a transplant; its origins must be accounted for in some other way.

10.   Conclusion

The evidence of various kinds examined here suggests that it is Kwéyòl influence that is responsible for most (though doubtless not all) of VESL's non-standard characteristics; and that for the most part, VESL has arisen on St. Lucian soil through quite ordinary processes of language contact and second language acquisition. Doubtless some "foreign" influences have had a part in shaping this still-emergent vernacular, in decades past as well as in more recent times, via immigration of CEC-speakers to St. Lucia, returned St. Lucian migrants, Jamaican and Trinidadian popular music, and various other sources. Perhaps the clearest evidence of influence from foreign English creoles is the fact (as noted by Le Page 1977 and Le Page and Tabouret-Keller 1985) that some St. Lucians sometimes use *doz* as a marker of habituality, e.g. *ai doz pree evrii dee* 'I pray every day' instead of the more typical V + -*ing* form *(ai preeying evrii dee),* (However, those who use *doz* in this fashion do not necessarily use it consistently and to the exclusion of the V + *-ing* form, an observation made by Le Page [1998: 86] as well as in his earlier work.) But certainly these influences alone have not made VESL what it is.

Garrett (2000) describes an ongoing process of convergence between Kwéyòl and English in St. Lucia whereby a continuum-like array of language varieties is emerging between these two linguistic poles despite their lexical and typological differences. During my fieldwork I often found that I could figure out how to say something "correctly" in VESL (i.e. in accordance with local norms) by thinking of how it would be said in Kwéyòl, and vice-versa. This brought to mind the classic article by Gumperz and Wilson (1971) on language convergence in Kupwar, a village on the Indo-Aryan-Dravidian border in India. Three codes spoken in this village (Marathi, Urdu, and Kannada), though grammatically and typologically (as well as lexically) distinct when defined in normative terms, were found to exhibit "an extraordinary degree of translatability from one local utterance to the other" and "a single syntactic surface structure" in Kupwar (154–155). The result of sustained language contact in this setting had been what Gumperz and Wilson describe as "the creation of three parallel creole-like local varieties" (164). Note that Gumperz and Wilson refer here to "creole-like varieties," not "creoles."

Similar reservations about applying the latter term to VESL would seem to be in order. But ultimately the question of whether VESL is best regarded as a creole or as something else is surely not the most important or productive question to ask. Like all creoles, and like the various non-creole contact lan- guage varieties that have come under scrutiny in recent years, VESL is the outcome of a specific confluence of factors and influences — linguistic, social, demographic, economic, political, and otherwise. Despite VESL's historically quite recent emergence, some of the potentially important vectors in this confluence are difficult to discern. It is difficult to estimate, for example, the degree of influence that Caribbean English Creole varieties may have had in VESL's emergence based on simple demographic data. Much is left to specula- tion: for example, the extent to which monolingual Kwéyòl-speakers might have been interacting with the relatively few immigrants within the St. Lucian population half a century ago, the specific nature and social contexts of those interactions, and the degree to which St. Lucians may have been motivated to learn the language varieties spoken by these immigrants (or for that matter, the degree to which some of these immigrants might have been motivated to learn Kwéyòl). At present it seems important not to exclude any potentially relevant factors. The major task that remains is to weigh and sort these various factors, with a view to producing the most accurate and detailed account possible of VESL's origins and of its still-ongoing emergence.

Concerning other potential directions for future research, it seems likely that those English-lexified vernaculars (usually referred to, aptly or not, as "English creoles") that have French-lexified creoles in their pedigrees — and there are several of these in the Lesser Antilles besides St. Lucia, namely in Dominica, Carriacou, Petite Martinique, Grenada, Trinidad, and possibly St. Vincent and Tobago (Parkvall 1997)[45] — may have some subset of characteristics in common that are attributable to French creole influence, and that distinguish them as a group from those English creoles (Jamaican, Guyanese, Bajan, etc.) that have no such French creole heritage. To be sure, it will be no simple matter to estimate the extent to which this is the case, and research efforts will be confounded by the demographic and sociohistorical vagaries of each island — for example, in the case of Trinidad, the fact that the demographic profile changed drastically after the British takeover of the island, with large numbers of immigrants and indentured laborers arriving from all over the British West Indies and indeed the world. But the hints of French creole influence that one frequently encounters in samples of speech from these various islands is intriguing: for example, the fact that Carriacouans commenting on the weather say *meikin hat* '[It (the weather)] is hot', evidently on the pattern of the local French creole *ka fè cho* (Kephart 2000: 26). Such an expression is likewise commonly heard in Trinidad (Winer 1993: 52). The data presented in Hancock (1987) might serve as a useful point of departure for a broad-based comparative analysis; the data on nine Atlantic English Creoles presented in Baker (1998) are likewise well worthy of consideration in this regard. Anything approaching a resolution to this issue, of course, can only come with still more data, drawn from throughout the region.

Notes

* Field research in St. Lucia (January 1996-April 1997) was funded by a Fulbright Fellowship (and an extension thereof), a National Science Foundation Dissertation Research Grant (#SBR-9522567), and a Wenner-Gren Foundation for Anthropological Research Predoctoral Grant (for the final phase of fieldwork). The Spencer Foundation provided postfieldwork support in the form of a Spencer Dissertation Fellowship for Research Related to Education. I am grateful to Hazel Simmons-McDonald and Lawrence Carrington for brief but encouraging comments on early oral and written versions (respectively) of this paper.

Thanks are also due to John Singler for his comments both oral and written, on later versions; I wish to acknowledge that his interpretations of much of the material presented herein differ from my own, and that I alone am responsible for any and all of this paper's shortcomings. Finally, thanks to Michael Aceto for his detailed written comments (and for his encouragements and patience) as one of the two editors of this volume.

1. The term "standard English" is always a somewhat imprecise and potentially problematic one (Lippi-Green 1997). For present purposes, it refers to spoken English that corresponds broadly to "standard" literate/print usage, and that would generally be deemed fitting for use in pedagogy, broadcast news, and other "official" domains in St. Lucia and elsewhere.

2. As explained in Garrett (2000: 73–74), St. Lucians themselves generally think of themselves as "bilingual" in Kwéyòl (more commonly called "Patwa") and "English." The local metalinguistic label "English" encompasses a wide range of variation, however. Although St. Lucians are in many ways keenly attentive to that variation (readily recognizing, for example, that one person speaks more in accordance with pedagogical standards than another), the non-standard vernacular that is referred to here as VESL does not have a local name, and it is rarely spoken of by St. Lucians as being distinct from any other type of "English."

3. These characterizations (some explicit, others less so) of VESL as a transplanted language variety pre-date the recent proliferation of scholarship concerning diffusion as a crucial factor in the development of the Atlantic creoles (see e.g. Huber and Parkvall 1999), and are not based on the kinds of evidence and research reflected in these more recent studies.

4. Le Page (1977) and Le Page and Tabouret-Keller (1985) do not treat VESL as a single discrete variety that is of exclusively Barbadian origin, but they do posit strong Barbadian influence.

5. It is not my intent here to ignore or gloss over the evidence and arguments for diffusion from a common source (namely the West African coast or St. Kitts) that have been made in Huber and Parkvall (1999), Baker and Bruyn (1998), and elsewhere by scholars concerned with the origins of, and interrelationships among, the Atlantic creoles. I do not delve into those issues here since there is no reason to believe that VESL followed the same routes of transmission, or that it emerged during the same historical era, as the language varieties examined in these studies.

6. As Derek Bickerton has commented (albeit not in specific regard to VESL or St. Lucia), "The whole problem with this transmission thing is that there were no carriers. It's assumed! Something crops up in A, something similar crops up in B, and immediately people jump to conclusions: 'It must have been transmitted'" (from "A Debate on Creole Origins," the transcript of an oral debate held at the Third Westminster Creolistics Workshop in 1996, published in Huber and Parkvall 1999: 305–318). It cannot be said that there were "no carriers" in the St. Lucian case; the relevant question that remains is whether or not there were sufficient numbers of "carriers" to account for VESL's emergence in St. Lucia. This question will be considered in a later section.

7. See e.g. García and Otheguy (1989), Mufwene (1994), Smith and Forman (1997), and the journal *English World-Wide* as representative of the growing literature on "indigenized" Englishes.

8. Cf. Bakker and Mous (1994) and Bakker and Muysken (1995) on "mixed" or "intertwined" languages, a particular type of contact language in which the inflectional morphology and grammar of one language combine with the lexicon of a second. Among the best-documented examples are Media Lengua (from contact between Spanish and Quechua) and Michif (French and Cree). Bakker and Muysken (1995: 51) note that speakers of such varieties typically "do not identify themselves as belonging to either of the groups whose languages they speak;" use of the intertwined language thus expresses a distinct, culturally intermediate social identity on the part of persons who in many cases are fully proficient in both of the contributing languages as well. (This is clearly not the case in St. Lucia, and it is not claimed here that VESL belongs in this category.) Cf. also McWhorter's (1999: 24) argument that these "intertwined" languages need not (and therefore should not) be regarded as "a discrete phenomenon, taxonomically and ontogenetically distinct from Creole languages."

9. Kwéyòl has never been officially sanctioned as a medium of instruction in St. Lucian schools, but teachers in rural primary schools have been known to resort to Kwéyòl occasionally in order to get a point across. This is becoming much less common, however, as most St. Lucian children are now acquiring more VESL (and less Kwéyòl, in many cases) before entering school.

10. Thomason (1993: 284–285) makes a distinction (if a fairly subtle one) between "PC [pidgin/creole] genesis" and "a specific type of change that occurs within a single language — namely, change that results from imperfect group learning of a target language during a process of language shift." This type of language change, she notes, can be characterized as "substrate interference." Later she remarks that in any such case of language contact and/or language shift, "what is going on is a process of second-language learning: learners are making guesses about the structure of whatever they are learning, and 'right' guesses are those that are accepted by the people they are talking to." In the St. Lucian case, "the people they [were] talking to," aside from teachers, would have been other learners of English as a second language whose first language was Kwéyòl.

11. This is not to suggest that nativization has been a necessary or crucial factor in VESL's emergence as a distinct language variety. It remains to be seen, however, whether or not its increasingly widespread acquisition as a first language — to the exclusion of Kwéyòl, in more and more instances — will have significant effects on VESL.

12. The system of phonemic transcription used here is that used by Rickford (1987) for Guyanese; Rickford's system, in turn, is based on that devised by Cassidy (1961) for Jamaican. The phonological particularities of VESL will not be addressed here, and I am not aware of any work that has been done on this topic. One feature that is particularly noteworthy, in that it is not to my knowledge shared with any CEC variety, is that the unvoiced interdental fricative [θ] of standard English systematically becomes the unvoiced labiodental fricative [f] in VESL (e.g. [wIθ] → [wIf] 'with'). (Cf. Baker 1998: 317, who states that [θ] becomes [t] — not [f] — in all nine of the Atlantic English Creoles that he examines.) The same is true in Dominica's vernacular English (Amy Paugh, p.c.), which like VESL is typically characterized as an English creole. Amastae (1979) and to a lesser extent Taylor (1955) examine the phonological characteristics of this variety, providing a useful

basis for comparison to VESL. Due to their parallel histories as French colonies that later became British colonies and then independent states (all within the same general timeframe), Dominica and St. Lucia have many strong sociohistorical and sociolinguistic similarities. However, there is also at least one crucial difference: the fact that large numbers of CEC-speakers (from Antigua and elsewhere) have settled in Dominica at various times (Parkvall 1997).

13. The orthographic system used for representing Kwéyòl is the now widely accepted system set forth in Louisy and Turmel-John (1983).

14. Anterior markers in Jamaican, Guyanese, and other CEC varieties typically derive from *been* (i.e. the past tense or past participle form of the verb *to be*). According to Holm (1988: 152), however, "Decreolizing varieties of CE [Creole English] often have alternate forms derived from *did, had,* or *was;* these are frequently less deviant from standard usage and thus less stigmatized."

15. VESL *-ing* is generally not reduced to *-in,* as is typical in CEC varieties; the velar is distinctly pronounced.

16. Preposed progressive markers such as *a, da,* and *de* are widely attested for the CECs; according to Baker (1998: 318), the latter two forms are attested for all nine of the nine Atlantic English Creoles that he examines (including Bajan, for which *da* is attested; Rickford 1992 also attests it for contemporary Bajan). Since *da* + V clearly corresponds directly to the Kwéyòl *ka* + V pattern, it is interesting that VESL uses the *-ing* suffix. One possible explanation is that *da* (or *a,* or *de*) simply was not available to St. Lucians as a candidate form, whereas V + *-ing* was available (probably via formal education).

17. According to Baker (1998: 324), the form *what for* 'why' is attested for eight of the nine Atlantic English Creoles that he examines. The fact that the word order is reversed in the VESL form (*foh waat*) suggests that this is a calque on the equivalent Kwéyòl form (*pou ki* [*sa*]) rather than a CEC form of foreign origin.

18. According to Baker (1998), the form WH *side* is attested for seven of the nine Atlantic English Creoles that he examines (325); WH *part* is attested for five of the nine (331); and WH *place* is attested for three of the nine (335). The first two of these three forms are both attested for Bajan. It is therefore interesting and perhaps somewhat puzzling that VESL uses the monomorphemic *we,* since any of these three Bajan/AEC forms would more transparently correspond to the equivalent Kwéyòl form (*ki koté*) and would thus be highly likely to be selected into VESL. One possible explanation for their absence in VESL is that they simply were not available to St. Lucians as candidate forms. Consider also in this regard the case of WH *fashion,* which is attested for four of Baker's nine English creoles, including Bajan (333); the equivalent Kwéyòl form is *ki mannyè,* yet the form used in VESL is *hou.*

19. According to Baker (1998: 320), use of a form based on English *one* as the indefinite article "is one of the most widespread characteristics of English lexicon contact languages throughout the world;" it is attested for all nine of the Atlantic English Creoles that he examines. VESL *waan* is never used as an indefinite article, however.

20. According to Baker (1998: 330), comparative constructions using *pass* are attested for five of the nine Atlantic English Creoles that he examines. *Pass* would seem to correspond

far more transparently to the Kwéyòl verb *pasé* than does the bimorphemic form that is actually used in VESL (*moh den*). One possible explanation for the absence in VESL of the widely attested English creole form is that it was not available to St. Lucians as a candidate form.

21. John Singler (p.c.) notes that a reflex of the English verb *itch* (rather than *scratch*) expresses both of these meanings in many Atlantic English Creoles.

22. The Kwéyòl words in question should not necessarily be regarded in the same light as English prepositions. Kwéyòl *ba*, for example, functions like the English prepositions *to* and *for*, as in the example shown; but this prepositional use may well be secondary to the word's status as the verb meaning 'to give'. This prepositional use of the verb may be of African substratal origin, as was discussed as long ago as 1936 by Sylvain (in regard to Haitian).

23. Kwéyòl has two related forms, *kay* 'house' and *lakay* 'home', which provide for a semantic distinction much like that between SE *house* and *home*. (Kwéyòl *lakay* does not have the extended semantic range of contemporary French *chez*, nor is its semantic range as restricted as that of *foyer*.) VESL uses the cognate forms *hous* and *hoom*, but it is rare to hear a VESL speaker combine *hous* with a possessive (unlike in many dialects of American English, for example, in which an utterance such as *I'm going to Judy's house* is more typical than *I'm going to Judy's home*); in VESL, possessives generally combine with *hoom*, just as in Kwéyòl they generally combine with *lakay*.

24. The preverbal completive marker *don* is found in most CECs, but is not used in VESL. (See also note #26 below.)

25. Some contextual detail may be necessary to clarify this example. This utterance is an announcement to a child that his mother has returned, and that it is now time for him to leave the person who has been babysitting him and go home. There has been no prior mention of his mother's impending return.

26. In a consideration of fourteen English-lexified creole (and creole-like) varieties, Schneider (1990: 89) remarks, "The existence of preverbal aspect markers is the structural phenomenon most closely associated with creoleness and most typically taken to be indicative of a language's status as a creole. Of these, completive *don* is clearly the most widespread form, being attested for all the varieties under consideration." Baker (1998: 322) reports attestations of the same form for eight of the nine Atlantic English Creoles that he examines (the sole exception being Sranan).

27. Le Page (1998: 84) describes the same study as follows: "In St. Lucia we were concerned to discover what kinds of English or Creole English would be used by the schoolchildren *when they were spoken to in English...*" (emphasis added). Le Page and Tabouret-Keller (1985: 164) address the broader issue of hypercorrection as follows: "We hypothesize...that hypercorrection is associated with a desire to be identified as a Standard English speaker...or perhaps as an urban Castries speaker."

28. In keeping with the broader theoretical approach developed in this work, which is concerned in part with "the problem of defining 'a language'" (8), the authors generally avoid labeling (and thereby reifying) the language variety (or varieties) in question. They do occasionally apply labels in passing, however, as when they refer to "the urban Creole English

of Castries" (61) and to an "English vernacular" (135). They eventually sum up the situation by asserting, "There are a variety of repertoires of various kinds of English in use among the children of St. Lucia." Although their quantitative analyses indicate that "[t]he children can be grouped according to their use [of particular forms] in formal and informal contexts," the authors conclude that "[t]he groups cannot be placed on a linear continuum between one particular model language and the Patois" (147). This rejection of the continuum model reflects their guiding theoretical concern with devising a multidimensional model of socio-linguistic "space." (Cf. Carrington 1992 and 1993 on the notion of "creole space.")

29. Schneider (1990: 79) remarks, "One of the issues that is not clear is whether a language that appears to be characterized more by relexification than by structural mixture and modification satisfies the conditions for inclusion in the category ['creole']."

30. It is my retrospective impression that slightly more of the people I knew in Morne Carré mentioned having family connections with Martinique than with Barbados.

31. British control of the island was subsequently formalized by treaty in 1814.

32. The possibility that members of this colonial elite may have brought with them to St. Lucia some servants from Barbados (or elsewhere) must not be overlooked. I have thus far come across no mention of such an occurrence, however; and even if it were the case, the numbers involved are unlikely to have been significant.

33. A note from the Director of Statistics appended to this publication reads as follows: "Users of this publication are advised to note that the total population of 113,409 as reported in this document has inadvertently been under-enumerated by 8,855. Considering the adjustment for this under-count, the total population of St. Lucia as at May 12th, 1980 (Census Date) is 122,264. Consequent to this adjustment, all tables in this publication are affected. Therefore, users are kindly requested to use the data with caution and to take particular account of the limitations of this document if any meaningful analysis is to be made."

34. On the other hand, it is possible that there is a direct connection between -ing forms and the presence of Caribbean French Creoles (as opposed to CECs). Le Page and Tabouret-Keller note that "habitual -ing forms...are common in Grenada, co-exist with does forms in Trinidad, and do not seem to occur in Barbados;" they then hypothesize that "-ing forms are associated with a quite widespread regional English vernacular with its roots in former Patois [i.e. French creole]-speaking territories" (164).

35. But Kwéyòl has no pronominal case either, it should be noted.

36. It is fairly certain that this was in fact the case, since in 1957, by which time St. Lucia had 52 primary schools, there was a combined total of only 431 teachers in the island (St. Lucia Annual Statistical Digest 1966: 63).

37. Of the 431 teachers mentioned in note #36 above, only 24 are in the category "trained"; the rest are classified as "untrained."

38. According to Jesse (1994: 48–53), the population in 1891 was 42,220, and had risen to 48,637 in 1911.

39. That the propagation of English (and the eradication of Kwéyòl) was the essence of these teachers' mandate can hardly be doubted. Alleyne (1961: 5) notes, "St. Lucians relate that the Mico Head Teacher in the village of Mon Repos would walk the village by night and flog any child whom he heard speaking patois...Notices were displayed prominently in schools to the effect that school children were forbidden to speak Creole at school or in the playground."

40. I have thus far been unable to find information concerning St. Lucians' movements to and from other Caribbean territories. Brana-Shute's (1983) bibliography on Caribbean migration lists no sources of information on St. Lucia in either Appendix D, "Origin of Migrants," or Appendix E, "Destinations of Migrants." The St. Lucian government's *Annual Statistical Digest* records only the annual numbers of "Arrivals and Departures by Countries of Embarkation and Destination," which shed little if any light on the matter in question.

41. "Il ne s'agit pas, bien entendu, d'un anglais standard, mais plutôt d'un anglais non-standard, caractérisé par un grand nombre d'interférences avec les vernaculaires à base de français."

42. Parkvall (1997) also notes, "Emigration has traditionally been significant on Carriacou" — another potentially important factor in that it may have been another vector of CEC influence.

43. Although Kephart presents this example under the category "Serial Verbs," he notes that it is "almost certainly a loan calque from CF, which uses the verb *ba* 'to give' in the same way" (102), i.e. like the benefactive prepositions *to* and *for* in SE. *Ba* likewise functions this way in Kwéyòl (see note #22 above), and although the corresponding verb *giv* is sometimes used as a preposition in VESL, its use seems to be limited to two main groups of speakers: young children who also have some command of Kwéyòl, and adults who are Kwéyòl-dominant and have only minimal command of VESL. During my fieldwork I occasionally heard *giv* being used in this way by young children (at home as well as in classroom settings), but they would without fail be corrected (i.e. would be told to use the preposition *foh* or *tuu* instead, as appropriate) if overheard by adults. (Teachers are especially keen to break their young charges of this habit as quickly as possible.) The fact that young children from Kwéyòl-speaking households and Kwéyòl-dominant adults with minimal knowledge of (any variety of) English show the strongest tendency to use *giv* in this fashion would seem to lend support to important aspects of the account of VESL's origins being proposed here: namely, that Kwéyòl has exerted strong influence on VESL, even as that influence has been countered in certain ways by normative/pedagogical pressures from more standard forms of English (especially English as taught in local schools to children from largely Kwéyòl-speaking homes and communities).

44. Although moribund, Trinidadian French Creole is still spoken today by a small minority of Trinidadians, mostly elderly persons. There are probably no monolingual speakers left, however, and very few if any children are acquiring proficiency in the language today.

45. Thus far only the varieties spoken in Trinidad and Carriacou have been described in detail by Winer (1993) and Kephart (2000) respectively.

The Carriacou Shakespeare *Mas'*

Linguistic creativity in a Creole community*

Joan M. Fayer
University of Puerto Rico, Rio Piedras

In the 1960s, Roger Abrahams began a series of studies of folk performances in the Anglophone Caribbean some of which were included in the important work, *The Man-of-Words in the West Indies* (1983). The concept of the man-of-words described not just the types of men-of-words and their performances but also what Abrahams called "the cultural conditions of creativity" (1983: xix). In his research, Abrahams found that the folk performances "were tied to certain times of the year and to community occasions for fun-making"(1983: xix). On islands such as Nevis and St. Kitts, the seasonal folk performances were at Christmas. On other islands such as Grenada and Carriacou, which were under French control for various periods of time, the performances were pre-Lenten carnival celebrations. Some of these performances were based on British texts, for example *St. George and the Turk*, a mummers' play, and John Bunyan's *Pilgrim's Progress*. Portions of Shakespearean plays were also incorporated in the holiday folk performances. Like the British mummers, the performers in the Caribbean were working class males. This continues to be true for most of the Caribbean folk performances.

Other performances which did not have literary or religious sources include Neagar Business, which were original satiric skits based on local gossip, and Tea Meetings which generally combined both literary texts and original flamboyant speeches. The folk performances were not just opportunities for fun making, although that certainly was an important function. They all provided the performers with occasions to demonstrate that they were men-of-words who could demonstrate their linguistic creativity.

The earliest references to these holiday folk performances are found in accounts written in the eighteenth century, not in the Eastern Caribbean, but in Jamaica (Long 1774). During the pre-emancipation period throughout the Anglophone Caribbean, slaves were given several days off from work at Christmas and New Year's when they received clothing allotments and were permitted to have their own holiday celebrations and to join their masters in special meals and holiday celebrations. In addition to singing, dancing, and masquerades, the festivities could include brief skits based on historical events or Shakespeare's plays. The earliest reference to the inclusion of parts of Shakespeare's plays in holiday folk performances in Jamaica is found in Alexander Barclay's account (1826: 13) of Christmas celebrations in 1823 in which parts of *Richard III* were used. In 1825 Henry T. De La Beche described a group of musicians and masqueraders dressed as kings and warriors who went to his house in Jamaica at Christmas and performed a very brief part of *Richard III* including the line "A horse, a horse, my kingdom for a horse" (1825: 42–43). The two references, several years apart, suggest the use of Shakespeare (in both cases *Richard III*) was not unique. However, in Jamaica these Christmas performances that evolved into what today is known as Jonkonnu do not have any attested recitations from Shakespeare (Bettelheim 1979).

In the Anglophone Caribbean, both before and after emancipation, similar holiday folk celebrations developed that combined European and West African folk traditions. Some of these continue today in the well-known Trinidad carnival celebrations that emphasize music and masquerading. On other islands there are still performances based on literary and/or religious texts that provide evidence of the eighteenth and nineteenth celebrations that were once common in the Eastern Caribbean.

One of these is a folk performance in Carriacou, the largest of the Grenadine islands. This island of 13 square miles which has a population of approximately 6,000 has what Antonio Benitez-Rojo (1996: 307) described as the "Caribbean's tiniest carnival" that is a pre-Lenten festival, the traditional time for carnival. Despite or perhaps because of its small size, Carriacou has a unique carnival folk performance, a masquerade or masque called the Shakespeare *Mas'*, which consists of performances of speeches from Shakespeare's *Julius Caesar* at the crossroads of villages and in the main street of the largest town, Hillsborough.[1] The Shakespeare *Mas'*, is a type of verbal and physical warfare between pairs of costumed male *mas'* players to determine who can recite the most speeches from *Julius Caesar* in a competitive exchange.

Early on Shrove Tuesday morning (the day before the beginning of Lent on Ash Wednesday) the Shakespeare *Mas'* players wearing pierrot-like costumes "jump out" to join others in the first of several competitive recitations of passages from Shakespeare's *Julius Caesar*. Their costumes consist of a head-piece or crown made from colorful fabric pasted on paper cement bags that covers the head and extends down the back of the players. Under the crown, a cotta woven from the air roots of a ficus tree is tied to the head supporting the crown and giving protection. A white screen wire mask over the face also gives some protection. The players wear a loose-fitting, bright-multicolored shirt that has overlapping rows of fabric cut in triangles. A large black heart and mirrors adorn the front of the shirt. They also wear a white petticoat trimmed with ruffles of lace or eyelet; baggy trousers tucked in tennis shoes or leather boots and carry a whip, called a bull, made from telephone cable or wire covered with tape. Some players wear white gloves and carry a bell. The clashing patterns and colors of the fabric of the shirt and crown differ for each player enabling the spectators to recognize the individual players from the different villages of Mt. Royal, Brunswick, Bogles, etc.

The Shakespeare *Mas'* performance revolves around a challenge and a response. One player challenges another to recite a specific speech from Shakespeare's *Julius Caesar*, but if the recitation is poorly delivered or inaccurate, he is hit by the whip his opponent carries. The "lashes" on the top and down the back of the cape-like crown make loud whacking sounds. The "loser" may strike back before challenging his opponent to recite another speech. After several verbal and physical interchanges, another player challenges the "victor." Rhythmic dance-like movements, foot stamping and even rolling on the ground can accentuate the recitations.

The speeches do not occur in any particular order and are not related thematically. No two interchanges between the players are the same. Further-more, some performers do not restrict themselves to the speeches of a single character but may take over lines assigned to two or more characters in *Julius Caesar*. One player might recite Antony's soliloquy over Caesar's body, "O pardon me, thou bleeding piece of earth…", and his opponent might respond with Cassius' speech begging for Brutus' forgiveness, "Cassius is aweary of the world…" Thus the performance is not a summary of Shakespeare's play, but rather a competitive interchange of both well known as well as lesser known speeches, some as long as 52 lines. There are common passages that many players have learned, but there are no set passages that must be memorized. An experienced player may know up to 30 speeches while a younger inexperienced player as few as three.

Many passages in performances fit in the category of famous speeches from Shakespeare suggesting that the players memorize only well known speeches such as those found in *The Royal Readers*, former school texts. However, the speeches by Cassius and Calphurnia which were recorded in several performances are relatively obscure and do not fit in this category. Some of the famous *mas'* men of the past were said to have memorized the entire "book," the term used to describe the whole play. This may have been true, but there is no evidence that this is true today.

In each village people gather to cheer the players on, and follow the players to the crossroads of the next village where there are more "opponents," more challenges and more fighting. The speeches get louder and the whipping can lead to fights that "peacemakers" have to break up. Abrahams found that masculine power is symbolized by the whip and "Nothing is enjoyed by the participants and audiences so much as a fight, and if the fight is physical, interest and hilarity are highest" (1967: 475). However, today in Carriacou several young men said that though they would like to participate in the *mas'*, they dislike the fighting. Most of the spectators and the current players do not share this feeling.

The Shakespeare *Mas'* players are truly men-of-words as Abrahams has described them. He noted that there were two kinds of men-of-words, those who were good talking/talking sweet and those who were broad talking/talking bad (1983: 3). The broad talkers are masters of wit and repartee in conversation. The *mas'* players are the former — the good talking/talking sweet men. "Talking sweet [good] refers to speech that exhibits elevated formal diction and patterns that are believed to approximate Standard English" (1983: 90). According to Abrahams (1983: 3), a good talker needs an audience in a structured situation such as religious services or carnival festivities. "The good talker usually represses himself in toasts, speeches, or recitations" (xv). In Carriacou, the pre-Lenten carnival celebrations provide the settings for the recitations from *Julius Caesar*.

As in many carnival events, there is a hierarchical structure in the *mas'* groups similar to that in British courts or military. The best or most experienced *mas'* performer in each village is the king of the village players. At the final competition in Hillsborough, the best player from all the villages is then recognized as king. This courtly hierarchy is also found in other carnival events such as the beauty contest, the Queen Show, and the calypso contest in which a king is named.

The king of each group of *mas'* players calls the members of his group "his men" whom he helps to select and train. A peacemaker, an experienced player, is chosen because he knows the rules of the combat. He may stop fighting that becomes too violent.[2] In the past the island was divided into two general groups of *mas'* players — the Heroes in the north and the Banroys in the south (David 1985: 45). The fighting between these two groups became violent in the 1950s resulting in serious injuries. In one famous "battle" in the Hillsborough market square, the women joined the final fight by providing stones and boiling water. Brass knuckles and knives were also used in the fighting in the past. While the fighting now is between players at the village crossroads and not in Hillsborough and is less violent, nevertheless, it continues to be one of the more popular parts of the *mas'* and can lead to injuries, usually face cuts when the mask is not in place.

The coming together of village groups has the appearance of preparation for battle. Led by the king, the players walk down the hills and roads in loosely formed lines waving their whips and shouting. When they reach a wide cross-road, they engage in "warfare," whipping and fighting with players from a different village.

The *mas'* is truly a community celebration with an audience made up of infants in arms to "old heads." The spectators get more excited as the players "get their blood up." For some in the crowd the excitement is caused by the verbal interchanges and for others it is the fighting. Spectators take active roles in the performances cheering their village players and shouting "Brave," "Bull, bull," "Tell him," "Go on," "That's right." As the amount of Jack Iron, a strong rum, and beer consumed increases so does the audience participation.

In spite of the general noise of the increasing crowd, spectators pay remark-ably close attention to the speeches, and may correct mistakes made, for example shouting, "He got the <u>will</u> wrong." At one exciting moment in a recent performance, a player inserted an obscenity in his recitation. Someone in the crowd shouted, "Ain't no F words in Shakespeare!" No variation in the speeches is permitted, and many in the audience who know the speeches as well as the players shout corrections.

The spectators follow the *mas'* players to Hillsborough where less struc-tured recitations occur. At mid-day before other carnival events occur, a king, the best performer, is informally declared. There is no cash prize for the best performer, although sometimes a collection is taken up "for the *mas'* men." In the Shakespeare *Mas'* there is no musical accompaniment as there is in the *Giant Despair* and *Pilgrim's Progress* performances in Nevis and St. Kitts; in Carriacou the focus is entirely on verbal eloquence, challenges and fighting.

The spectators take great pride in these recitations from Shakespeare. During one performance in the early stages of the fieldwork on which this study is based, a woman turned to another member of the audience, who was not a native Carriacouan and said, "That's Shakespeare you know." She wanted to make sure that the importance of the text that served as the basis of the performance was known. While most Carriacouans do not realize the uniqueness of the *mas'* they do share the woman's pride and love of the *mas'*.

Although, as noted above, there were once similar folk performances of Shakespeare throughout the Anglophone Caribbean, today the Carriacou Shakespeare *Mas'* is the last surviving performance of this type. Little documentation of the *mas'* exists before the 1950s. Older people tell of fathers and grandfathers who participated year after year in this carnival event; the oldest island resident who was born at the end of the nineteenth century remembers *mas'* performances when he was a boy. Since then changes have taken place in the texts used and the type of fighting.

Today Shakespeare's *Julius Caesar* is the only text used in the *mas'*, but in the past other Shakespearean plays such as *Henry V* were utilized as well as portions of the biography of Queen Victoria and descriptions of historical events such as the Battle of Waterloo. The historical source of Shakespeare in this creative form is probably to be found in *The Royal Readers*, books used in the educational system in the British West Indies from the late nineteenth century through the 1950s. Selections from Shakespeare appeared regularly beginning with Book IV.[3]

However, portions from *Julius Caesar* are just one of the literary texts found in *The Royal Readers*. When the former and current *mas'* performers were asked why this play is the only source for the recitations today, the answers varied. One reason was given by a former player who said that Shakespeare plays were "sweeter" than the histories of Queen Victoria and famous battles in the readers. The histories and battles were accounts of facts, but the speeches of Shakespeare were full of beautiful or "sweet" language. He then went on to recite one of his favorite "sweet" speeches from *Julius Caesar*, Marullus' speech in the opening scene, which begins "Wherefore rejoice? What conquest brings he home?"

Although not mentioned by any of the players, another reason for the utilization of a Shakespearean play is probably that iambic pentameter aids in the memorization of long speeches and adds rhythmical beauty. Moreover, *Julius Caesar*, in particular, is appropriate for the type of verbal combat that takes place in the carnival performance in that it is built around rhetorical structures that allow characters to exchange passages of debate in set speeches. A dialectic text written in dialogue is a "natural" vehicle for competitive verbal activity in which players "throw one speech against another," a phrase that was used by a former player who took part in the Shakespeare *Mas'* as a young man.

It might seem that the political uncertainties, cycles, and philosophies developed by Shakespeare in *Julius Caesar* have relevant parallels in Carriacou's history and therefore contribute to the use of this text for the *mas'*. Political and economic events of the nineteenth and twentieth centuries in both Grenada and Carriacou do in fact have many analogues in *Julius Caesar* and for that matter in all of Shakespeare's plays which deal with Roman or English history, but research has not as yet uncovered any information which indicates that the play is popular because of its political philosophy and/or relevance. As noted above, another history play, *Henry V*, was once used in the *mas'*, but for reasons that cannot be determined, it no longer is. Whatever the reasons for *Julius Caesar* being the only text for the *mas'*, it is unlikely that another will be used for as long as the *mas'* continues. *The Royal Readers* are no longer used, more emphasis is given to contemporary literature, and memorization is not stressed in schools.

Although school texts seem to be a primary way for *mas'* players to learn *Julius Caesar*, not all the *mas'* players had extensive schooling. Some did indeed go on to higher education off the island, but many have had very limited education. Sir Nicholas Brathwaite, a native of Carriacou and former Prime Minister of Grenada who was a *mas'* player, commented on this in a recent interview.[4] He said that many of the *mas'* performers that he knew as a boy and a young man in Carriacou were students who did not do well in school. He recalled that they did not excel in subjects such as geography or math and some were not good readers. Yet somehow, they memorized long passages from Shakespeare and came to love these selections.

While some of the performers learned their speeches from *The Royal Readers* and from other texts in higher education, many with limited reading skills learned from other *mas'* men. This was especially true in the past. Older players recounted gathering at village crossroads in the evenings months before carnival to practice or learn speeches. Boys and young men learned by listening to the experienced players. Often these were members of their families — a father, an uncle, a cousin. Participating in the *mas'* seems to "run in families." Some families have been participating for years; other families may be avid spectators but not participants. Still today not every *mas'* player has a copy of *Julius Caesar*, they continue to learn by listening to others, and there are *mas'* men who can read and write very little but who can recite many long speeches from *Julius Caesar* with feeling.

Many years after former *mas'* men stopped participating they still can recite their favorite speeches. Shakespeare remains part of their lives. Recently one of the best performers who had participated in the *mas'* for approximately 50 years died. Although he migrated to England and worked there for many years, he often returned at carnival time to visit family and to play *mas'*; eventually he retired to Carriacou and was a star performer. He was buried with his *mas'* costume, which was one of the most beautiful. At his funeral, other *mas'* men reciting their companion's favorite passages followed the procession to the burial. In life and in death, Shakespeare was one of the important parts of this *mas'* man's life. Although this may not be the common pattern, it serves to illustrate the profound love that these *mas'* players have for Shakespeare and the *mas'* performance.

While it is only in Carriacou that the recitations from *Julius Caesar* are still part of a holiday folk performance, Abrahams (1973: 123–125; 1983: 14–15) found selections from *Julius Caesar* were performed in Nevis until the 1950s by the Shakespeare Lesson group which went from house to house during the Christmas season.[5] The performers were men who wore "beautiful costumes and acted out in stentorian tones and stately movements … in the most elevated sort of oratorical English" that is the language of Shakespeare (1983: 14). Musicians accompanied the Shakespeare Lesson group, "and the divisions of the scenes are punctuated by them and by the dancing of the players" (1973: 125) which causes the performers to change the order of the speeches.

The captain of the Pond Hill Shakespeare Lesson group wrote out a text that Abrahams found not to be typical of the performances he observed. "Most are considerably longer, and make more verbal and dramatic sense" (1983: 125). However, no other text has been recorded. Analysis of the text indicates that it differs in significant ways from the performances in Carriacou. Though it seems to be an attempt to follow the action in *Julius Caesar*, it does not. Some speeches are out of order and others condensed. Names of the characters are not accurate (Cinner for Cinna). Words are changed thus distorting the meaning. For example "Bindarius lead your charges and commanders upon the ground" for "Bid our commanders lead their charges off" and "Directly I am going to seize a funeral" for "Directly I am going to Caesar's funeral." Some of the speeches are accurate, but many are not: speeches attributed to one character are from another character (Caesar instead of Cassius). These deviations from the standard text of *Julius Caesar* may be due to the writing skills of the Lesson Group performer. They also may have been due to lack of texts from which to learn and practice the speeches. Learning by listening to other players could explain the changes found.

The Shakespeare Lesson group performances differ from the Shakespeare *Mas'* in Carriacou in significant ways. In Nevis, they were part of Christmas Sports and the Shakespeare *Mas'* is part of carnival. In Carriacou, the performances are not in yards of houses but at village crossroads so there are larger audiences. In Carriacou, there is no attempt to follow the order of the speeches; the format is verbal and physical challenges. The speeches are recited with more accuracy, and errors are often corrected by spectators. There is no musical accompaniment or dancing in Carriacou although the movement of the players can be described as dance-like. However, these movements are to accentuate the speeches. Both types of performances are alike in that they provide opportunities to display verbal eloquence and creativity. Today although there are still folk performances in Nevis, they are no longer at Christmas but as part of Culturama in July, and they do not utilize selections from Shakespeare (McMurray 1999).

Many of the holiday folk performances in the Anglophone Caribbean that provided opportunities for verbal eloquence based on Shakespeare and other literary texts were once common (Abrahams 1967, 1973, 1983; Bettelheim 1979; Carr 1956; Crowley 1956; Mills, Jones-Hendrickson and Eugene 1984; Nunley 1988; Payne 1990). However, today only in Carriacou does this creative performance, the Shakespeare *Mas'*, continue as part of carnival. Other folk performances featuring music and dance such as the Big Drum and Nation Dances are still performed in Carriacou, but not on other islands. (Hill n.d., 1973, 1977; McDaniels 1998). These retentions may also be attributed to several sociocultural factors. The performers in the eighteenth and pre-emancipation nineteenth century holiday performances in the Anglophone Caribbean were slaves, and in Carriacou, slaves constituted a very high percentage of the total population. In 1833 just before emancipation, there were 3,200 slaves in the total population of about 4,000 (*St. George's Chronicle and Grenada Gazette* 1833: 273). After emancipation European planters departed, and the ex-slaves were able to develop "their society and culture in splendid isolation [while] new racial and cultural elements were being introduced to larger possessions nearby" (Smith 1962: 2).

Another factor that made it possible for an event such as the Shakespeare *Mas'* to survive is the small size of the island that even today remains relatively isolated. A daily ferry goes to Grenada; only very small planes can land at the airport. There are no large tourist resorts. While development of the island may be restricted, this may be a significant factor in the preservation of the Shakespeare *Mas'* as well as other aspects of the strong folk culture.

The Shakespeare *Mas'* is derived from an English literary text and British mumming traditions and combines these with European carnival traditions, European pierrot costumes and West African costumes, West African whip/stick fighting and masquerading creating an example of what Antonio Benitez-Rojo called a syncretic artifact, "a signifier made of differences" (1996: 21). The British mumming plays were Christmas folk plays that were common in rural areas in the sixteenth century and continued in Ireland until the mid-twentieth century (Glassie 1975). The mummers who were groups of working class males performed traditional plays such as *St. George and the Dragon* at farmhouses where they would be given food, drinks, and money. "Sometimes the mummers from one village would encroach on the traditional sphere of another village and there would be a battle in earnest" (Archer 1904: 35).

Although just how the Carriacou *mas'* began has not yet been determined, British mumming traditions may have been brought to the island in the pre-emancipation period by British planters or their slaves in a form that already included portions of Shakespearean plays. Windward, a village on the northern coast of Carriacou was settled by Scots (Smith 1962: 16), but there are no written or oral accounts that make any reference to the *mas'* originating in this village.

Throughout the Caribbean, planters and slaves at times moved from one island to another for various reasons. Thus, the *mas'* may have come to Carriacou by way of Jamaica.[6] Seafaring and boat building have been important in Carriacou throughout its history, and men engaged in these occupations may have been a part of the development of this celebration.

While at this point it is difficult to ascertain just how the mumming tradition and recitations of Shakespearean plays first came to Carriacou, the West African traditions were brought by the slaves. Strong African influences are seen in the culture of the island, for example, the Big Drum and Nation Dances (McDaniel 1998). To determine the West African influences on the Shakespeare *Mas'*, the early census data, limited though they are, provide information as to just how many West Africans came to Carriacou and from what areas they were purchased. The earliest data are in the 1750 census that has been analyzed by Brinkley (1978). At that time, Carriacou was a French possession and there were 202 people on the island. Of these, 90 were blacks. This census also identified some of the language areas in West Africa that these slaves came from: Congo, Bambara, Ibo, Arada, and Anan. For several slaves, although an area is noted, it is difficult to determine the location. After the island was ceded to the British, the population grew. By 1773, there were 2,700 blacks and 100 whites; in 1778, there were 3,046 slaves and 107 whites. In 1829 just before emancipation there were 3,452 slaves, 45 whites and 303 described as "colored" (McDaniel 1998: 33–34). While in Grenada after emancipation in 1834, there were over 6,000 "late-arriving" indentured Yorubas, who displaced other West African traditions, there is no evidence that Yorubas came to Carriacou. This means that the strong Yoruba influences found in the culture of other Anglophone Caribbean islands such as Trinidad may not be present in Carriacou. The high number of slaves in proportion to the white population is one of the factors influencing the West African contribution to the folk performances in Carriacou. As noted above, after emancipation, the Europeans left.

Census data do not describe the complete history. In Carriacou, as in other Caribbean islands, the concept of nation is important. McDaniel (1998: 36) in her study of the Big Drum Ritual still performed in Carriacou said: "[N]ation denotes not only a geographic region but also a linguistic/ethnic group as well. ... owners of enslaved people often categorized their imprisoned servants by nation in order to manage them in reference to the cultural behaviors ascribed to each group." The Big Drum dances and songs have been categorized by McDaniel as Cromanti, Igbo, Manding, Kongo, Banda, Moko, Temne, and Chamba.[7] According to McDaniel (1998: 51), "[T]he Kongo group was the most evident within the early Carriacou population. Their musical and political prowess was probably overtaken by the militant Cromanti upon their later arrival [after 1763 when the island became a British possession] into the society."

Although the identification of Big Drum music and dances provide valuable insights into the areas of West Africa from which the Carriacouans have come, they present some problems. Names of countries and areas have changed over time. Moreover, a nation can consist of several linguistic and cultural groups. For these and other reasons it is difficult to determine with certainty the exact areas the slaves came from and to attribute one pattern or practice exclusively to one group (Fayer 2000).

West African influences did not determine the time of the year of the Caribbean folk celebrations since in West Africa they were often a part of agricultural activities. For example, the yam festivals were held in September or October. On some Caribbean islands there are "crop over" ("crop done") celebrations that originated with the end of the sugar harvest (Nicholls 1998: 71), but these no longer occur in Carriacou (Hill 1977: 379). Since the slaves were not the ones who chose the time for their free time and celebrations, public merry making had to be at times determined by those in control.

More direct influences are probably found in the festivities held by secret societies in West Africa. These were primarily all male societies which had "religious, social and recreational functions [which were] involved in rites of passage such as initiation, and in the representations of dead ancestors" (Barnett 1978–9: 25). The secret societies could also sponsor yam festivals as was done by the Mmo Secret Society of the Ibo.

As noted above, the Yoruba influence was non-existent or minimal; therefore, the Egungun celebrations in which there were processions and plays that included pantomime seem to be unlikely influences for the Shakespeare *Mas'*. Of course, it is possible that this influence came with the workers from Carriacou who went to islands such as Trinidad where there are strong Yoruba influences.

The costumes that the *mas'* men wear with their strong contrasting colors, the wire mask, and the fringed shirt seem to be a hybridization of both European and West African masquerade costumes. However, the whip that each player carries and the way that it is used can be traced to West African stick fighting. The black heart with mirrors on the front of the shirt is similar to that on the costumes of the stick fighters in Trinidad (Burton 1997: 210). Early references in print and representations in art attest to stick fighting in the pre-emancipation Caribbean.

The whip is not the same as the wooden sticks used in kalinda, stick fighting, which is part of Big Drum celebrations that are still part of carnival canboulay barbecues late on Monday evening in villages in Carriacou. However, the movements of both are similar. Hill described stick fighting as a "dance like fight accompanied by kalinda drums. Two fighters, each holding a two or three foot stick, perform a series of stylized moves until one is knocked down or draws blood" (1977: 384). A player holds the stick before the face. The other player tries to give good blows, and the fighting continues with offense and defense reversing. Hill said the players' objective is "to artistically 'dance' into various positions while making the opponent look foolish, and to sing well… Playing stick, however, is considered a serious art: 'It is beautiful as well as serious'" (322). Warner-Lewis (1991: 151–2) noted the famous stickmen and the popularity of stickyards in Trinidad and the "emotional involvement with stick fight culture of Congo descendants interviewed in the 1970s in contrast with the attachment of Yoruba, Rada, and Hausa descendants to religious ceremonies." (Slaves identified as Congo were listed in the 1750 Carriacou census.) Unlike kalinda in Trinidad, in the Shakespeare *Mas'* the players recite, not sing and there is no drumming or any other type of music.

In the Shakespeare *Mas'* the older players are the ones who incorporate the kalinda movements. They hold the whip in front of the face or over the head at the beginning of the challenges and are more adept at both the foot movements and the giving of lashes. Unlike the early stick fighters, the *mas'* players are protected by their costumes. However, if the wire mask is not in place, the face can be cut. If the fighting becomes too intense and the peacemakers do not separate the players, injuries can still occur. For many, but not all, *mas'* players and spectators, the whipping and the fighting are the favorite parts of the *mas'*.

West African influences can also be seen in the body and foot movements utilized by the *mas'* men. These seem to be similar to those used by Jonkonnu players in Jamaica which Bettelheim (1979) analyzed in detail. She said, "Jonkonnu dancing is a version of West African dancing. ... The dancers are not afraid to make contact with the earth. Many steps are executed in a low, deep knee position, seen in similar steps in West African dance" (173). The *mas'* men use these movements as well.

Benitez-Rojo noted another West African influence, the importance of memory in the *mas'* as "proof of competence" which is similar to the "high esteem that the *griot* enjoys in African villages" (309). Griots, men who are storytellers, preserve the oral history of a family or West African village. For the Carriacou *Mas'* player the ability to memorize long speeches accurately is necessary.[8] If mistakes are made in the speeches, the spectators may shout out "He got the <u>will</u> wrong." When the speech is good, there may be shouts of praise such as "That's right."

Ethel M. Albert (1964) also described the importance of speech in West African life saying:

> speech is explicitly recognized as an important instrument of social life; eloquence is one of the central values of cultural world-view, and the way of life affords frequent opportunities for its exercise (Quoted in Abrahams 1983: 22).

Abrahams did not include the Carriacou Shakespeare *Mas'* in his studies but noted the influence of West Africa on other creole performances and found that "the African elements seem dominant, in spite of the forms... [and] the base patterns of performance are more characteristic of African modes than European ones" (1967: 33). This can also be said of the Shakespeare *Mas'*.

The whipping in the Shakespeare *Mas'* is an example of syncretism in that it can be traced to both the sword fighting in the British mummers' Sword Plays as well as West African stick fighting. But it is not just this feature of the *mas'* that is an example of syncretism; the *mas'* as a whole is a syncretic artifact (Fayer and McMurray 1999).

In the Shakespeare *Mas'* each component — the recitations, the verbal challenge-response format, the body movements, and the whipping/fighting — is related but nonetheless different from British mummers' folk performances and West African folk performances. Verbal performance is dominant in the *mas'*, but it is mixed with rhythmic dance motions before and during the recitations, actions, and gestures with the whip, and movements that call attention to the elaborate costumes. These components are in fact the details that make the Shakespeare *Mas'* an example of Benitez-Rojo's syncretic artifact that he said was "not a synthesis, but rather a signifier made of differences." (1996: 21). These differences are the European and African supersyncretic signifiers of the Shakespeare *Mas'* (21).

In describing the syncretism of traditions that produced Caribbean folk performances, Abrahams said:

> In bringing together these two vital traditions in a world alien to both, each was drawn upon at those places where it came closest to the other: the process of "syncretism." European forms and subjects were adopted in which African patterns of performance and technique could be practiced, African forms and subjects persisted where they were enjoyed by the masters. Out of the newly-created world of the plantation grew the traditions and aesthetic which drew upon major Old World cultural expressions and adapted them to their new situation (1967: 460–461).

The Shakespeare *Mas'* players are truly men-of-words, good talkers. They utilize their skills by the eloquent recitations of selections of *Julius Caesar*. The skill with which the performers recite the speeches, while different from those of stage performances, is certainly moving. The use of one of the great works of British literature in a creole carnival celebration not only demonstrates creativity but it also empowers both the performers and the spectators. The spectators are proud of the men in their villages who can recite passages from an important English writer. In describing the working class men who performed in Christmas Sports in Nevis and St. Kitts, Mills et al. (1984) described them as artists. They added that the performance "imbues the players with a sense of personal importance and worth which they are never able to acquire in other ways at any other time of the year or in their entire lives" (11). This description is also true of the *mas'* players. In a recent study, Richard Burton's comments about carnival in Trinidad can also be applied to carnival in Carriacou. He noted that carnival is "an attempt by the low to raise, enhance, and aestheticize themselves to the level of the high …" (1997: 157). In Carriacou, as noted above, many *mas'* players did not do well in school; as adults, many do manual work. Yet during carnival, they are kings and peacemakers dressed in colorful costumes who are able to recite long passages from Shakespeare. From early morning until mid-day on Shrove Tuesday, they perform for large audiences in the "sweet talk" of Shakespeare. Abrahams found that the eloquent language used in seasonal celebrations such as carnival is "judged by the community as good and beautiful and is in contrast to everyday creole talk" (1983: 34).

In Carriacou, according to Kephart (2000: 31), Carriacou Creole English is the variety spoken and understood by everyone. The term used by the people themselves to describe their everyday language is Broken English. It contrasts with the more standard variety, which Kephart (11) called Metropolitan English and defined as "the variety of English generally considered 'standard' in Great Britain, the United States and Canada." In his analysis of Carriacou Creole English, he found that it "is as far from Metropolitan English as any other variety of Creole English" (16). In their daily lives, the *mas'* players are creole speakers, but during carnival, they become speakers of a prestigious archaic variety. They not only recite Shakespeare by memory but become performers of selections from Shakespeare with eloquence and emotion.

The Shakespeare *Mas'* demonstrates not just linguistic proficiency and creativity of the players but also enables the men-of words to be men-of-action as they physically compete with other players. Abrahams described a man-of-action as a man who has talent for competing with other performers (Abrahams 1967: 470–471). "The man-of-words or the man-of-action exhibits his talents best in contest with other performers. Many West Indian entertainments are simply traditional occasions for these battles" (1967: 471). The players in the Carriacou Shakespeare *Mas'* compete both verbally and physically. The performer who recites the most speeches accurately is the king, but the king also has to know how to defend himself with his whip. In short, he is a good talker and a brave fighter.

The *mas'* performances can be placed in the tradition of West Indian verbal dueling meant in fun and play that is popular in other Anglophone Caribbean folk performances. The Carriacou Shakespeare *Mas'* enables the players to be both men-of-words and men-of-action who demonstrate their verbal and physical skills. Over the years there have been some changes in both the texts and the fighting techniques, but the same structure of challenges and combat produce brave, sweet-talking kings and their men. The hybridization of West African celebrations, a British literary text, and British holiday mumming traditions has created a unique carnival performance.

Notes

* Fieldwork for research on the Carriacou Shakespeare *Mas'* was funded by Proyecto Atlantea, Oficina de Asuntos Académicos, and Administración Central of the University of Puerto Rico. Joan F. McMurray collaborated in fieldwork conducted on five trips to the island from 1995 to 1999. Each trip was approximately one week long. Some were during carnival time. Other trips were not at holiday times thus permitting more time to interview current and former *mas'* players, spectators, costume makers, carnival organizers, local historians, staff at the Carriacou Museum, Big Drum performers, etc. Dr. McMurray assisted with the revision of this study.

1. For a more complete description of the Shakespeare *Mas'* see Fayer and McMurray 1994 and 1999.

2. Today choosing both the king and the peacemaker seems to be more informal than it was in the past. Interviews with current and former players state that there is a king and peacemaker for each village group, but this seems to be the ideal rather than the practice. Violent fighting at the crossroads may be stopped not just by peacemakers but also by men in the crowd who pull the players apart.

3. As yet, it has not been possible to determine how the Shakespearean plays that were included in the *Royal Readers* were selected. All of the plays in the books were well known plays. It does not seem that they had any particular political relevance.

4. An interview with Sir Nicholas Brathwaite was video taped by the Grenada Broadcasting Network in April 1999. Selections of the interview are included in a video of the Shakespeare *Mas'* produced by the author and Joan McMurray. For availability, contact the author directly.

5. On several field trips to Nevis from 1996 to 2001 with Joan McMurray, interviews were conducted with current and former folk performers. No written or oral data about the Shakespeare Lesson Groups were found to supplement that in Abrahams (1973, 1983). Just what caused the Shakespeare Lesson Groups to stop their performances has not been determined. The factors that caused another Christmas Sport in Nevis, Neagar Business, to be discontinued are discussed in Fayer 1999.

6. The eighteenth and nineteenth century accounts of holiday performances in Jamaica provide data not available for other islands. While early performances may have existed on other islands, there are no extensive descriptions of these.

7. McDaniel makes a distinction between "Kongo" the name of the nation and "Congo" the name of the region in Africa (38).

8. However, there is also a tradition of female "griottes," especially in Mali (Hoffman 2001).

Creole English on Carriacou

A sketch and some implications

Ronald Kephart
University of North Florida

1. Introduction

The purpose of this paper is to describe and illustrate some selected structural highlights of the variety of Creole English spoken on Carriacou, Grenada, in the Eastern Caribbean (hereafter CCE).[1] This variety of language is sometimes classified, along with Barbadian and some others, as an "intermediate" form of African-American English, i.e. one that is not as "deep" as the Suriname Creoles or Jamaican Creole (see, for example, Alleyne 1980). In this paper I wish to propose that, despite the presence of several features which might make CCE appear to be less like these "deeper" creoles, the morpho-syntactic system within which these features occur does indeed bring CCE closer to these other Caribbean Creoles, and farther from its lexical source language, Metropolitan English.[2] In addition, I wish to suggest that it is precisely these "deep" features of the language that create barriers to the learning of Metropolitan English which are the most difficult to overcome for children seeking to acquire proficiency (oral or written) in the standard language.

This paper looks at those areas of grammar in which CCE is least like metropolitan forms of English: nouns and their marking for number and specificity; verbs and their marking for tense, aspect, and mode; basic patterns of predication; question formation; and negative marking. Some aspects of phonology are also described. The paper argues that these areas of difference link CCE more closely to other varieties of Creole English than to "standard" English, and that this fact has implications: When children speak a variety of creole that has surface grammatical forms that appear equivalent to forms of the standard language, it is easy to believe that they have a deeper knowledge of the standard language than they actually do. I suggest that teachers and educational planners need to take this into account in the design of language arts curricula.

2.   Background

Carriacou is the largest island of the Grenadines, an archipelago of small islands and cays that connects Grenada to the south with St. Vincent to the north. The island is about 13 square miles in area, and has a population of about 6,000 people. Most Carriacouans are the descendants of people brought from West Africa, first by the French and later by the British, to work as slaves on plantations producing tropical export crops such as cotton, tobacco, indigo, and, ultimately, sugar. There is also a small population descended from indentured laborers brought from the British Isles; in this century especially, these people have mixed with the population of African descent.[3]

It was sugar, introduced on a large scale by the British after 1763, that had the greatest impact on this little island. Under the French in 1750 Carriacou supported only about 200 people, half free and half slaves, scattered around the island on a number of small farms (Brinkley 1978). By 1776, the British had introduced a large-scale sugar operation, with some 3,000 slaves working for a couple of hundred Europeans. Carriacou has never recovered ecologically from this deliberate overdevelopment (Richardson 1974).[4] Linguistically, the largely Creole French-speaking society of 1750 was transformed into a mostly Creole English-speaking one in about a quarter century. A local variety of Creole French (CCF) is still present, however; there are still some people who learned it during their childhood, but, more importantly, the presence of CCF continues to be felt in the lexicon and grammar of CCE, as well as in the culture of Carriacouans (Kephart 1991).

The language spoken at present by most people on Carriacou in most unmarked situations is the language variety that I call Carriacou Creole English (CCE). As in most situations where a Creole English is in intensive contact with Metropolitan English (ME), there is variation in the speech of Carriacouans. As an illustration, note the sequence in (1), taken from a conversation among some Carriacouan schoolchildren. The children were given a tape recorder and asked to talk about anything they wished, and then left on their own. The boy who began the story with the first sentence was one who was successful in school and who had obviously learned quite a bit about standard English. The other children, however, knew that I was interested in "their" language, and guided him through several stages until they reached what seemed to them to be a satisfying utterance, the third one. *Tochin* (torching) refers to hunting land crabs at night with a light made, traditionally, from a beer bottle filled with kerosene and fitted with a cloth wick; or, more recently, with a flashlight.[5]

(1) may broda an ay went tochin.
     mi an mi broda went tochin.
     mi an mi broda di gouin an toch.
     'My brother and I went crab-hunting.'

The first form is essentially ME, the third is least like ME, and the middle form is in between; note however that the pronunciation, for example, of 'brother' as *broda* is consistent throughout. Note too that the major split is between *di gouin* where *di* is the past tense marker, and the other two that use ME *went*.

Data like that in (1) is frequently found in situations where the creole language exists alongside the standard language from which most of its lexicon is taken (though language variation also exists in all speech communities). The terms *acrolect, mesolect,* and *basilect* are sometimes used in describing these situations as examples of *decreolization,* the presumed diachronic process of shift toward the standard or acrolect which the basilectal creole is presumably undergoing, and which (again, presumably) gave rise to the observed mesolectal phenomena. However, it is no longer clear that this process is the source of the so-called mesolectal forms in all cases (see, e.g., Mufwene 1999a). In other words, the instances of *went* in (1) may not reflect a process of decreolization, or any attempt by speakers who at one point had only CCE *di gouin* to get closer to ME; it may be that *went* was present from the beginning as an available alternative, as it seems to be in most people's speech today. In any case, this paper does not take a stand on this issue. Rather, it recognizes the presence of variation in the speech of Carriacouans, but attempts to show that these forms overlay an apparently stable system of categories and contrasts that align CCE more closely to other varieties of creole than to ME (for Jamaican Creole see Bailey 1966; for Antiguan Creole see Farquhar 1974; for a more general descriptive statement Holm 1988). The *di*+verb+*in* structure is part of this system, and it is this that constitutes the focus of this paper (for a more complete description of Carriacou Creole English, see Kephart 2000).

3.   Nouns

Nouns are forms that can be marked for number and specificity. In CCE, as in most Atlantic creoles, the unmarked noun is generic, i.e. non-specific, and ambiguous with regard to number. Nouns are marked specific by the definite article *di*, the indefinite article *a*, a personal specifier (e.g. *mi, yu,* etc.) or a demonstrative, as in (2):

(2)   hows 'house(s)'; maniku 'opossum(s)'; di hows 'the house'; a maniku 'an opossum'; alyu hows 'your house'; dis maniku 'this opossum'

The CCE plural marker is -*andem,* Only specific nouns can be marked plural; since proper names are inherently specific, they too can be marked with -*andem*; with the sense of the person named and their family or others associated with them. Some examples are given in (3). Note that the ME plural and CCE plural can occur together, as in the last example.

(3)   wi ting-andem 'our things'; mi kan-andem 'my corn, etc.'; Pitaz-andem 'Peters and others'; shi frenz-andem 'her friends'

However, in CCE it is important to distinguish forms with the ME plural from forms that appear to be unanalyzable into a contrasting singular form, such as those in (4).

(4)   a ans 'an ant'; a pans 'a pair of pants'; a sizaz 'a pair of scissors'; stichiz 'stitches (i.e. surgical)'

An important difference between ME and CCE is that in CCE plural is not over-marked; a plural element in the noun phrase, such as a plural determiner or a number, is sufficient to mark the noun plural, while ME requires marking on the noun as well:

(5)   som maniku 'some opossums'; dem maniku 'those opossums'; fayv maniku 'five opossums'

Briefly, then, CCE nouns, although for the most part drawn from the lexicon of English, are embedded in a system which distributes specificity and number differently.

4.   Verbs

Verbs are forms that can be marked for tense, aspect, and mode. CCE verbs fall into two categories, dynamic and stative; which of these classes a verb belongs to determine what kind of aspect marking it can take. Dynamic (action) verbs such as *gou* "go" and *kom* "come" can take the suffix -*in* which signals progressive aspect, as in (6). In the past, a progressive marker *da-* or *a-* was apparently more frequent, as in the third example which is from a folk tale about the mythical *Lajables*.

(6)   dei gouin in tong
'They are going to town.'

rein komin
'It's going to rain.'

we yu a-gou?
'Where are you going?'

Stative verbs, such as *dei* (to be located), cannot take the progressive suffix because they already inherently represent a state "in progress." Note that I have included *reivn* `(to be) greedy' and similar attributives as stative verbs, since they take all the other TMA (Tense-Mood-Aspect) markers.

(7)   shi dei in skul
'She is at school.'

yu reivn
'You are greedy.'

Unmarked verbs normally signal a tense which best corresponds to ME present perfect; note the glosses for the unmarked verbs in the sentences in (8):

(8)   shi gou in skul
'She went (has gone) to school.'

Yu reivn
'You are (in the state of being) greedy.'

All verbs can be marked for past and future tense. Both the past (*di*) and future (*gou*) markers are unstressed (but see below for more on the *gou* future). Note that the past marker *di* conveys the sense that the action or state has not carried through to the present; with verbs of motion, this translates into a round trip.

(9)   shi di gou in skul
'She went to school (and came back).'

shi di dei in skul
'She was (no longer is) at school.'

yu gou reivn
'You will be greedy.'

yu di reivn
'You were (no longer are) greedy.'

CCE has a special past tense structure with stressed *bín*; this form occurs alone, with stative verbs, and with dynamic verbs marked for the progressive. *Bín* also occurs with unmarked dynamic verbs in the *bín an* structure, which may be a serial verb structure (see below).

(10)   we yu bín?
'Where were you?'

wi bín gouin houm
'We were going home.'

a bín an pik mangou
'I was mango-picking.'

Verbs can also be marked for habitual or iterative aspect with *doz*, as in (11). Note that the stative *reivn* can take either *doz* or *dozbi*.

(11)   a doz dei al di taym.
'I am present regularly.'

yu doz(bi) reivn
'You're habitually greedy.'

Finally, verbs can be marked for modes such as potential and inferential, among others, as in (12); the accent mark over *kyán* calls attention to the fact that this form, unlike the other TMA markers, is stressed.

(12)   shi kyán gou in skul
'She can't go to school.'

shi mosbi gou in skul   '
Evidently she has gone to school.'

Other CCE modals include *kud, mos, shud,* and *da.* These forms, as well as the tense and aspect markers, cannot occur alone; they are clitics and they must have the support of a verb.

CCE verbs can be combined in a single verb phrase, as in other Creole languages and some West African languages. Such structures are called serial verbs. In these cases, the subject is the same for all the verbs in the series, as illustrated by the examples in (13); the second example is from a folk song. There is good reason, having to do with the process of negation, to consider the future as a serial verb construction; see the section on negation for more explanation of this.

(13)   i liv gouin an bring di chayl in dakta
'He left to take the child to the doctor.'

hari dou bring no moni kom
'Harry doesn't bring any money.'

a en gou dans wit yu
'I won't dance with you.'

As can be seen from the examples in (6–13), verbs represent a portion of CCE grammar that is strikingly different from ME. For one thing, in CCE adjectives function as stative verbs with no need for support from an auxiliary verb. For another, the categories of tense and aspect are distributed differently, with marking required for dynamic verbs to be interpreted as something other than "present perfect." Furthermore, all TMA marking other than [+progressive] is realized by preverbal clitic forms that resemble, but do not function quite like, English auxiliary verbs. In particular, these forms cannot stand alone as the predicate as they can in ME.

5.   Predication

CCE has two kinds of sentences; first, there are sentences in which the predicate consists of a noun or noun phrase. Usually, the predicated NP is marked by *iz*, the CCE copula. These sentences are not marked for tense or aspect, except by replacement of *iz* by the past tense form *waz*. Some examples are given in (14):

(14)   dat iz fud-stof
'That is foodstuff (provisions).'

dem iz enemi
'They are enemies.'

An interesting fact about CCE *iz* is that, unlike ME *is*, which loses its vowel in rapid speech (*that is* > *that's*), CCE *iz* may lose its consonant (*dat iz* > *da i*). This is a result of the fact that CCE is syllable-timed, like Spanish, rather than stress-timed like North American ME. So the first example in (14) would likely be pronounced as in (15):

   (15) [da i fudstɔf]

Next are those sentences whose predicate is formed around a verb. Here "verb" includes the progressive form of dynamic verbs, which need no supporting auxiliary, and also of course forms that are isomorphic with ME adjectives but which function here like stative verbs.

   (16) dei gou in skul
        'They went to school.'

        dei gouin in skul
        'They are going to school.'

        dei kôkosâ
        'They are biased.'

CCE sentence structure allows for sentences in which some element of the predicate is topicalized, i.e. emphasized by either moving it to the front of the sentence or by placing a copy of it at the front of the sentence. The copula *iz* may be used to mark these fronted constituents. Note that both the verb and its complement can be fronted for emphasis, but only the verb must be copied.

   (17) iz gou dei gouin
        'They're really going.'

        iz kôkosâ dei kôkosâ
        'They are really biased.'

        jouk a meikin
        'I'm only joking.' (< a meikin jouk)

6.   Questions

In CCE, yes-no questions are formed by a change in intonation, and also by optional fronting of the topic, but note that there is no auxiliary movement rule as in ME (in any case, there is no auxiliary to move):

(18) dei gouin in skul?
      'Are they going to school?'

      iz in skul dei gouin?
      'Are they going to school?'

      dei kôkosâ?
      'Are they biased?'

CCE Wh-questions, as in ME, front the interrogative pronoun (Wh-form); however, as mentioned before, the rest of the sentence remains in place.

(19) we dei gouin?
      'Where are they going?'

      wat yu sei?
      'What did you say?'

7. Negation

There are two patterns of negation in CCE, one of which resembles more closely that of other creoles, including those of French lexicon (see DeGraff 1993), and one which seems to be more like the ME negation pattern. The "creole" pattern involves placing a negative form, either *no*, *dou*, or *en*, before the entire predicate, including any TMA markers, as in (20).

(20) i en mosbi filin eniting
      'It must not have been feeling anything.'

      dei no spikin Patwa gi yu
      'They wouldn't speak Patwa for you.'

      i dou gyetin mangou
      'He wasn't finding any mangoes.'

The more ME-like pattern places the negative, universally *en*, between any TMA markers and the verb. The *en* cliticizes to the TMA marker when one is present. The negative marker (*en* or *no*) always precedes the future marker *gou*; and, unlike the other TMA forms *gou* itself is a verb that occurs alone. Therefore, it seems that future *gou* is not in fact a TMA preclitic, but rather a part of a serial verb construction.

(21) dei mosbi en bat
      'They must not have batted.'

alyu di'n si mi?
'Didn't you (pl.) see me?'

a en gou dans wit yu
'I won't dance with you.'

8.   Phonology

CCE phonology contrasts sharply with most ME phonologies in several ways. First, CCE has a basic seven-vowel system, which marks it as quite different from both ME and also some other creoles, especially Jamaican. To find a similar system in the Caribbean we have to go to Dominica, which coincidentally also harbors a variety of Creole French similar to CCF (Amastae 1979); among the Atlantic CEs generally, the Suriname creoles probably come closest (see Holm 1988). In both systems, the only tense/lax contrast is in the mid vowels. Second, as mentioned previously, CCE is syllable-timed: the length of an utterance depends on the number of syllables, rather than on the number of stresses, and stressed and unstressed syllables receive approximately equal time.

Another phonological feature that sets CCE apart from both ME and other CEs is the presence of nasal vowels. These occur in words which CCE shares with CCF, as illustrated in (22).

(22)   sukuyâ 'vampire'; tetshê 'boa constrictor'; kôkosâ 'biased';
       gwâgozhei 'brown pelican'

CCE speakers pronounce these words with the nasalization intact; they don't convert a nasal vowel to a vowel plus nasal consonant, even in word-final position.

At the word level, stress in CCE tends to occur on the last syllable. Noun and verb roots carry relative stress in a sentence, as do all negative markers and the lexical past *bin*. The other TMA markers, including future *gou*, are unstressed relative to their verbs. Finally, CCE, like CF and other CEs, is syllable-timed, rather than stress-timed as are some varieties of ME, especially North American.

9.   Contributions from *Patwa*

In addition to its contribution to CCE phonology and vocabulary, especially place names and names for local plants and animals (*Piti Matinik* 'Little

Martinique'; *kaka-kabwit* 'goat-mess plant'; *soley* 'big-eye fish'), Creole French has apparently provided the base for a number of loan-calques, illustrated in (23). The CF equivalents are spelled in the system used officially in Haitian for writing Kreyòl (Valdman 1988).

(23)   i av (CF: i tini)
       'there is/are'

       how yu neim? (CF: kouman non-ou?)
       'What is your name?'

       meikin hat, wi? (CF: ka-fè cho, wi?)
       'It sure is hot!'

       luk im ye. (CF: mi i isi-a)
       'Here he is' (answer to 'where is he?')

       du dat gi mi. (CF: fè sa ba mwen.)
       'Do that for me.'

10. Conclusion

We have seen that CCE contrasts with ME in a number of ways, including: marking of nouns for specificity and number; marking of verbs for tense, mode, and aspect; patterns of predication; and movement rules. In addition, CCE allows processes that are not typically a part of ME grammars, especially fronting and serial verb constructions. We see, furthermore, that these differences are masked by a lexicon that seems "English." For example, consider the sentence in (24).

(24)   They go in the shop.

This sentence was presented to a group of high school students on Carriacou, who were asked what it means in Carriacou speech, i.e. CCE. They immediately provided the paraphrase "they went into the shop and they haven't come out yet." Their teacher, who happened to be from Great Britain, was stunned, since for her the sentence had a habitual meaning: "they go into the shop regularly." Here, it is not any difference in lexicon that hampers communication, but rather *the way tense and aspect are organized into a system and marked on verbs.*

This is not a question of merely academic significance; there are implications for local educators and others involved in language policy decision-making. Some of these implications involve basic attitudes toward and treatment of people. For example, in 1979 a Grenadian physician, after listening to me describe my goal of discovering the grammar rules for Carriacou Speech, asked if I had thought about the political ramifications: according to him, if I was able to show that CCE had its own grammar, then I would have proven that those who speak it are real human beings, and should be treated accordingly.

Other implications involve education: What does the fact that children on Carriacou and other parts of the Caribbean arrive at school speaking a human language imply for their language arts education? How can they best acquire literacy, and in what language should they acquire literacy first? Given that they might find mastery of ME useful, how best to provide them with that mastery? There is a wealth of research in similar linguistic contexts that suggests that children's introduction to formal education, including literacy, is best carried out in their first language. Although public attitudes toward the use of varieties of Creole English are changing gradually (Devonish 1986), residual negative ideologies about the scope and use of these creoles continues to impede the application of this research to this problem. My own research on Carriacou challenged some of the mythology surrounding creole literacy and hinted that learning to read CCE might assist students' learning of ME (Kephart 1992; and see the other essays in Siegel 1992).

I end with the fervent hope that this essay might help CCE and its sister languages of the Eastern Caribbean gain the respect and attention they deserve, not only from linguists (which they already have to a large extent), but from their speakers and those who find themselves in the position of dealing with them, in education and elsewhere.

Notes

1. The fieldwork that formed the base for this research was carried out on Carriacou in April-August, 1979, and in 1982–84, with funding from the Inter-American Foundation, the Florida Foundation, and the University of Florida Graduate School. I want to thank, as always, the good people of Carriacou for their assistance and tolerance, and for sharing their language and culture with me all these years. The present paper is a revised version of a presentation titled "Creole English on Carriacou: A linguist's perspective," given at a conference on "The Islands in Between: Language, Literature, and History of the Eastern Caribbean," held November 18–20, 1999, on Carriacou, Grenada. Of course, I must claim full credit for any errors in data or analysis.

2. I am using *Metropolitan English* as a very imprecise cover term for the variety of English considered "standard" in the United States and Great Britain. In this usage, I am focusing on morphology, lexicon, and syntax, and I am ignoring for the sake of argument the

differences that certainly exist among these "standard" varieties, which are trivial compared to the differences between them and the Caribbean Creoles.

3. Smith (1962) is an early ethnographic account of Carriacou, focusing especially on kinship. For the most thorough ethnographic description of Carriacou, see Hill (1977). For more discussion of the African traditions, especially in the Big Drum music and ceremonies, see McDaniel (1998).

4. Richardson (1974) considers overdevelopment in both ecological and human terms: destruction of the ecosystem is accompanied by the introduction of a population larger than the ecosystem can support.

5. The CCE examples offered here come from my own data and are written in a slightly modified version of a phonemic spelling system designed for a literacy project carried out on Carriacou in 1982–84. This system represents the sounds of the language in a regular way, usually with one but sometimes with a combination of two letters for each distinctive sound. Briefly, the consonants have approximately their usual English values, with the following exceptions:

ch	[tʃ];	*bachak* 'leaf-cutter ant'
g	[g];	*gwana* 'iguana'
s	[s];	*siks* 'six'
t	[t];	*tatu* 'armadillo'
sh	[ʃ];	*kyalabash* 'gourd'
zh	[ʒ];	*Boseizhu* 'Beausejour (place name)'
y	[y];	*yam* 'yam'
w	[w];	*wom* 'caterpillar'

The vowels represent a more difficult adjustment, the result of English having inherited only five vowel symbols from the Latin alphabet. The seven basic vowels and three diphthongs of CCE are represented as follows:

i	[i];	*biti* 'cassava skin'
ei	[e];	*keik* 'cake'
e	[ɛ];	*fet* 'party'
a	[a];	*wata* 'water'
o	[ɔ];	*fo* 'for'
ou	[o];	*bout* 'boat'
u	[u];	*fut* 'leg'
ay	[ay];	*spayda* 'spider'
ow	[ɔw];	*kow* 'cow'
oy	[ɔy];	*morokoy* 'tortoise'

In addition, a spelling system for CCE has to accommodate the diphthong *ey* and nasal vowels from Creole French:

ê	[ɛ̃];	*tetshê* 'boa constrictor'
â	[ã];	*sukuyâ* 'vampire'
ô	[ɔ̃];	*kôkosâ* 'biased'
ey	[ɛy];	*soley* 'big-eye fish'

Barbadian lects

Beyond meso

Gerard Van Herk
University of Ottawa

Introduction

Bajan, the vernacular language of Barbados, occupies a middle position among Caribbean language varieties, less studied than "full creoles" like Jamaican Creole English, Saramaccan, or Guyanese, but considerably better-known than, say, Barbudan. Unlike its linguistically high-profile neighbors, however, Bajan is not universally accepted as a full creole. Hancock (1980: 22) says "then, as now, it was a local metropolitan, rather than creolized variety of English that was spoken by both Blacks and whites," and cites the description of Bajan in Le Page (1957) as "grammatically closer to standard English." Reinecke et al. (1975: 376) describe Bajan as a "less creolized dialect than most islands," and Alleyne (1980: 186) lists it as decreolized. On the other hand, Cassidy (1986) describes the present creole features of Bajan as relics of a former full creole. Burrowes (1983), Roy (1984, 1986), Fields (1995) and Rickford (1992) describe many creole features in conservative Bajan, and Schneider (1990: 104) says it is "clear beyond any doubt that Barbadian deserves to be called a creole."[1]

For many creolists, a resolution to this debate is most important in terms of what Bajan *was*, rather than what it is today, because Barbados supplied slaves, and, potentially, linguistic raw material to the creolophone areas of Jamaica, Guyana, and South Carolina. Although I will touch briefly on some of the sociohistorical evidence relevant to this issue, my main interest in this paper is the current linguistic situation, in which many creolists (and most Barbadians) see Bajan as mesolectal,[2] while others (myself included) are able to find clearly basilectal creole features. After describing such features, I will suggest that the current Barbadian continuum may be wider, especially at the basilectal end, than generally accepted, and that both mesolectal and near-basilectal interpretations are tenable, depending on one's view of methodology and the nature of evidence.

In Barbados, of course, popular discourse is not concerned with acrolect, mesolect, or basilect, but with *dialect*, the generally-accepted term for the widespread vernacular. For the purposes of this paper, I appropriate the term "dialect" to refer to the constructed lect, or perception of lect, that is best known to Barbadians. Cassidy (1986: 195) refers to "a longstanding Barbadian tradition" that holds that Bajan is not a creole, and adds that he has "tried without success to trace this belief to its source but there is no doubt that it exists — that it is generally accepted without challenge." Bajans I have inter-viewed ascribe "creoleness" to faraway, generally French-based varieties.

The unchallenged, or mutually-agreed-upon, features of dialect include subject pronoun forms in object position, non-inverted questions, habitual *does*, copula deletion, and the second-person-plural pronoun *(w)unna*. All Barbadians seem to control these features for use in intimate conversation, proverbs, humor, scolding children, and what Feagin (1979) calls "downward quotation." These are also the features that show up in cartoons, dialect literature, and Bajan e-mail postings, as in example (1).

(1) a. Ya know ya is a bajan when
        …jug is somethin ya eat and not somethin ya *does* put ya food in
        …yuh constantly explaining dat de dolphin you *does* eat is a fish and not a mammal!
     b. De smell from de oven *did* fillin my head —
        My Mudda was mekin some coconut bread (from e-mail).

Compare the above examples with the more basilectal "constructed" Jamaican Creole English in a newspaper column:

(2) So it nuh spell sense smady else a go tan up oneside an feel seh a next man crass lighter dan fe him   (Keane-Dawes 2000).

When I suggest that a language can be "constructed," I do not mean to imply that it is a fiction. In fact, mesolectal Bajan, involving most or all of these features, is the most widespread non-standard language of the island. This is the mesolectal Bajan described in Blake (1997) and, I would suggest, is the

variety that both real people and linguists are thinking of when they describe
Bajan as less creole or semi-creole. I am concerned, however, that the widespread acceptance of this construct obscures the existence of basilectal features.

In recent years, these features have come under some scrutiny. Like Blake,
Rickford (1992) applies quantitative methods to a frequently-occurring feature of Bajan (copula deletion), but he has also compiled a list of creole features
found in the speech of his most basilectal speakers, Mrs. Thankyou and Mrs.
Grateful, from the northern parish of St. Lucy. This list includes several features not elsewhere described for Bajan. Burrowes (1983: 40) also features such
a list, derived from "her own knowledge and from conversations overheard,
but also from the media and from some historical texts." Fields (1995) describes basilectal features in representations of Barbadian speech in written
documents of past centuries. Collymore (1955) is largely concerned with
lexicon, but makes several observations on grammatical features, based on
personal observation. Blake (1997) focuses on copula deletion and past tense
marking in an east-coast village, though several other features (especially
phonological) are mentioned. Schneider (1990) lists features of a range of
Caribbean creoles, including Bajan, based on Hancock's elicitations of "most
conservative" forms. Roy (1984, 1986) describes rather basilectal forms, based
largely on grammaticality judgments, also from an east-coast village. The
thorough reader will want to consult all these sources.

It should be noted that in most work on Bajan the term "creole" is often
used to describe all non-standard forms that appear to be part of the system of
the vernacular. This is a natural choice in a Caribbean context, where a continuum between a creole and Standard English (StdE) is assumed by many
linguists (e.g. DeCamp 1971, Bickerton 1975). It means, however, that forms
found in non-standard Englishes around the world (*ain't*, negative concord,
them for *those*) are described in much of this work as "creole." A reader seeking
a more complete investigation of the possible English roots of some Bajan
features is directed to Niles (1980). Some other "creole" features described in
the literature may result from the interface of non-creole forms and Bajan
phonology, so that *da* (that) and *dere* (there), among others, may not be
basilectal grammatical features. My task here is not to trace the pre-creole
origins of all features of Bajan, but simply to describe and document such
features. First, though, I consider the sociohistorical contexts that led to the
current linguistic situation.

Geography and history

Barbados is the easternmost island in the Caribbean. It is one of the world's most densely-populated nations, with over 250,000 people on just over 200 square miles (Handler & Lange 1978: 13). Unlike most Caribbean islands, Barbados is non-volcanic and relatively flat. As a result of all these features, it has never had wild areas that would support communities of runaway slaves, nor physical barriers to movement within the island.

Barbados appears to have had no remaining indigenous population by the time of the first British settlement in 1627. Although African slaves were part of the population mix from the very beginning, their numbers in the early years of settlement appear to have been quite small. The great majority of the population was indentured servants and small landholders from Scotland, Ireland, and England's West Country. One early settlement was known as "Little Bristol." Tobacco and cotton were the main cash crops. A rapid switch to large-scale sugar planting began in the early 1640s, with the introduction of sugar technology and the settlement of competing land claims. The sugar industry grew quickly, partly due to lack of control from England during a period of political uncertainty. By the early 1650s, Barbados was described as the richest spot in the New World.

The requirements of an expanding sugar plantation system led to a rapid expansion of the slave population. Estimates of the total Barbadian slave population in the 1630s range from 50 to 800, a very small African input to a "founder population" (Mufwene 1996). Large numbers of both African slaves and British indentured servants were imported during the 1640s and 1650s, but by the early 1650s slaves had become much cheaper and thus the slave population grew. By 1655, Dunn (1972: 87) estimates the population at 20,000 blacks and 23,000 whites. However, Ligon (1657), who lived in Barbados from 1647 to 1650, puts the number of black slaves at double the "Christian" (white) population. This disparity may be due to regional settlement patterns, with black slaves largely held on large plantations, and whites who had finished their indentureship concentrated with small landholders in the marginal agricultural areas. The social gap between plantation society and poor whites was already evident in an early description cited in Tree (1972: 16): "This Iland is the dunghill whar our England doth cast forth its rubidg." "Rodgs and Hors and such like peopel" became the poor whites. A useful description of the eventual linguistic outcome of this social gap is provided by Blake (1997).

The second half of the 1600s saw a consolidation of plantation society. Due to massive importation of slaves, the black population rose to 46,000 by 1684. The remaining white servants tended to be employed as "overseers, artisans, book-keepers and other non-field occupations" (Beckles 1990b: 32). The overall white population fell from 23,000 in 1655 to 12,500 in 1712 (Beckles), with most of the loss due to emigration to Jamaica, Guyana, and South Carolina. Barbadian small landholders and their slaves are often held to have played a large role in the formation of creoles in those areas (see Cassidy 1980 vs. Hancock 1980). Although a resolution of that debate is well beyond the scope of this paper, we might wish to note a reminder from Beckles (1990b) that the great majority of the whites who left the island were poor ex-servants, not slaveholders. Similarities between Bajan and Gullah, then, may be due to similar ecology (Mufwene 1999) and substrate input, and identical "superstrate" (poor white) input.

Did the social conditions for the establishment of a widespread basilectal plantation creole exist in Barbados in the 1600s? The high proportion of whites in the colony, and the slow growth of the slave population from 1627 to 1640, would argue against it (see Mufwene 1999, Hancock 1980). The conditions between 1640 and 1700, however, were more suited to pidgin/creole formation, especially if the majority of the white population was marginal to plantation society. Ligon (1657: 46) describes slaves in Barbados in 1647–50 in textbook Pidgin/Creole origin terms: "They are fetch'd from several parts of *Africa*, who speak several languages, and by that means, one of them understands not another: For, some of them are fetch'd from *Guinny* and *Binny*, some from *Cutchew*, some from *Angola*, and some from the River of *Gambia*." Although the precise African origins of Barbadian slaves cannot be traced, it is likely that most were from the Ga, Ibo, Ashanti, Ewe, Edo, Fanti, Adangme, Dahomey, and Yoruba peoples, from what is now Ghana, Togo, Dahomey, and western Nigeria (Beckles 1990b: 32–33). If a widespread basilectal creole did develop in Barbados, the century between about 1650 and 1750 would have seen its widest use.

The chances of basilectal features being introduced to Barbados after about 1750 are remote indeed. Although plantation life was brutal, Barbados became more or less self-sufficient in labor (and has remained so to this day). This is partly due to an accident of geography: the island's coral base ensured relatively disease-free water. By the late 1700s, Barbados (and St. Kitts) had the fewest African-born slaves of any place in the West Indies (Beckles 1990b: 55). Although pre-1834 slave exports probably consisted largely of transshipments of recently-arrived Africans (Mufwene 1999), Barbadians have been seeking work elsewhere since emancipation.

It is highly unlikely that there was any large-scale importation of labor from Sierra Leone, for example, to introduce basilectal features, as suggested in Hancock (1980). Barbadian laborers actually went *to* West Africa. Letters from Liberia in the 1860s (American Colonization Society) describe the arrival of a shipload of well-educated Barbadian workers. In addition, it is unlikely that anything more than the occasional lexical item would have been introduced by adult Barbadians returning from work elsewhere in the Caribbean or from Panama. Beckles (1990b: 142–146) points out that these workers, especially the "Panama men," were responsible for the growth of the black middle class, and strongly encouraged formal education for their children. If anything, this group would have hastened decreolization.

The establishment of many church-run schools in the early 1800s (Tree 1972: 88–90) and the acknowledged literacy of leaders of the 1816 slave rebellion (Beckles 1990: 81) might suggest widespread access to the standardizing forces of education throughout the history of Barbados. Beckles (1990b) points out that this is not especially true. Although Barbados had 213 schools by the 1834 Emancipation, five or fewer admitted blacks (90). Despite a post-Emancipation hunger for education and government committee recommendations of compulsory education in 1878 and 1896, a 1905 planters' newspaper editorial exemplifies the views of the elite: "Handl[ing] the negro properly... would involve, amongst other things, the giving of a sound *practical* education. Some book learning is of course essential, but the mistake [of giving too much literacy] must be avoided" (cited in Beckles 1990b: 138). As mentioned above, it was money earned abroad that after 1910 led to the growth of the black middle class, political mobilization, and access to education. From slavery until less than a century ago, then, we see two parallel streams: a somewhat educated group, largely made up of free coloreds and their descendants, and a working-class group with limited or no access to education. This situation could easily lead to the concurrent existence of a standard-like Barbadian English and the somewhat basilectal creole whose features are described here and elsewhere.

Data collection

The data that will provide the examples cited in this paper were collected in Barbados in the summer of 1998, as baseline data for a possible future investigation of language change among Barbadian-Canadians. The recordings were made by a Barbadian-born Canadian interviewer through an extension of the friend-of-a-friend technique. In this case, the informants were friends-of-friends (or of relatives) of the interviewer herself. The recordings range in length from a half an hour to an hour, although in each case the interviewer spent between three and six hours in conversation with the informants before the tape rolled. The topics of conversation are those typical of the sociolinguistic interview, plus the Bajan concerns of that summer: youth violence, Kadooment, best nightclubs, and dark cake. As Table 1 indicates, the nine informants cover a wide spectrum of Bajan society. From left to right, informants range in age from 80 down to 17, from rural working class to urban upper middle class, from partial elementary school to university education. Youth, education, urbanization, and high socioeconomic status correlate. The speakers' normal lects correlate with this demographic data, with the least creole-like speech found toward the right of the table.

Table 1. Barbadian informants: age, socioeconomic status, urbanization, and education

	Granny	Mr. F	Mr. P	Mrs. S	Aunt M	Mrs. J	Aunt R	Mr. C	Ms. X
Age	80	71	70	68	61	55	51	31	17
SES	Low	Low	Low	Low	Mid	Mid	Mid	Hi Mid	High
Urban	no	no	no	part	part	part	part	part	yes
Educ.	<prim	prim	prim	H. S.	H. S.	H. S.	H. S.	Univ	to Univ

I deliberately use the term "normal lect," because Barbadians have long been known for their tendency to switch to their most formal speech when outsiders are listening or when the tape is rolling. See Blake (1997: 76–78) for Bajan exemplification of the observer's paradox. I have met two of these nine informants since the recordings were made, and have noticed creole features in their speech that are not found in the recordings. One advantage of the present data collection technique is that the long pre-interview conversations let the interviewer gauge the degree to which each informant switched up lects while being recorded. As one might expect, the most switching happens in the middle of the table (upper working and lower middle class). As those speakers use the familiar Bajan dialect, the phenomenon does not affect the features I intend to describe here. I will concentrate on the informants at either end of the continuum, partly because we seem to have tapped into extremely informal speech and partly because this is where we hear speech that is the least like mesolectal or constructed Bajan. This seems to be the most efficient way to build a list of basilectal features. Note a similar strategy in Rickford (1992).

Granny is the informant with the most basilectal speech. She is 80 years old, lives in St. Michael parish near the boundary of St. George, has a small farm, and is the unofficial grandmother of her neighborhood. The postman and local policeman still drop by almost every day for lunch, joining the 17 children for whom she cares. In the sample of her speech presented in (3), we note unmarked past, *dem* in subject position, negative concord, copula deletion, and *ain't*, as well as such typical Bajan phonological features as diphthong nucleus raising, interdental stopping, and full rhoticity.

(3)   [an sʌmtajmz de keːm fə dɛɹ fɹɛnz an wɛn dɛm bitin ɹawn di buʃ ʌj tɛl ʌʔʌ ʌjm ovɚhiɹ dəm jə noː jə noː jəs so a təl ʌʔʌ ʌj ɛ̃ bɔɹn bɪg fɹɔm smal ʌj gɹoː ʌp dʒʌs lʌjk dɛm tə… so ɛ̃ nʌθin de ɛn kʌm tə ful mi wɪd de fulɪn dɛɹsɛlf ɹʌjt bikaz aj tol əm ʌj dɪn bɔɹn bɪg ɹʌjt soː sʌmtʌjm bifɔɹ dɛm si tɪŋz ʌj ɑlɹɛdi tɛl dɛm soː an so ɪz di kes]

'And sometimes, they came for their friends. And when them beating around the bush, I tell, "uh-uh." I'm overhear them, you know. You know. Just so. I tell them, "uh-uh, I ain't born big. From small, I grow up just like them too… So ain't nothing they ain't come to fool mi with. They fooling their self. Right. Because I told them, I didn't born big. Sometimes before them see things, I already tell them so and so is the case' (Granny 207–245).[3]

Creole features

The following is a list of putative creole features of Bajan, accompanied where possible with examples from my data, generally from Granny, and a discussion of the lectal range, relative rarity, and possible provenance of each feature.[4]

Tense/aspect

1.   Preverbal anterior *bin*

(4)   [ʌj go wɚʔ kʌ baʔ kʊk fud dʌn beːðɛm ən ɛvɹi so ʌðɚ θiŋ tʃɛk ðɛm bʊks bɪn ansɚ ðɛm pɹɛɹz]

"I go work, come back, cook food, done bathe them, every so other thing, check them books, *bin* answer them prayers" (Granny 3001).

Rickford (1992: 188) points out that historical attestations of Bajan anterior *bin* are usually dismissed as being "of questionable authenticity" (Morrow 1984: 10), or the form is said to have "disappeared" (Alleyne 1980: 182). While it is exciting to note the continued existence in Bajan of preverbal *bin*, it is safe to say that the form is rare, even in basilectal speech. Like Rickford (1992: 189), I found only one unquestionably preverbal token in my data. This feature is certainly not part of the mesolect. In fact, when a Barbadian author recently rendered a text of mine "more Bajan," she *removed* preverbal *bin*.

2. Habitual *da*

(5) [ɛvɹi mɔɹnin de də wɜ·k]
    "Every morning they *da* work" (Granny 2149).

(6) [ʌj ē no: wɪtʃ ɹo:d hi də wɑk ɪn bʌʔ i dɪn wɑk ɪn di ɹʌjt ɹo:d]
    "I ain't know which road he *da* walk in, but he didn't walk in the right road" (Granny 1138).

In mesolectal Bajan, the habitual marker *does* is among the most frequent non-Standard features, and has acquired something of a totemic quality. "Constructed" dialect texts almost always highlight *does*, Rickford (1992: 189) describes it as "a classic mesolectal creole form;" Schneider (1990: 90) lists it as the Barbadian habitual marker; Collymore (1955: 39) decries it as a "monstrous solecism;" and Burrowes (1983: 42) says, "/doz/ is a common feature of Barbadian speech — all ages." It is interesting, then, that this feature does not occur in Granny's speech at all. Her only habitual preverbal marker is the basilectal *da*, which she uses five times during the recording. Most of the examples are with past temporal reference.

3. Continuative *da*

Continuative *da* does not occur in Granny's speech. Schneider (1990: 90) does not list a *da*-type continuative for Bajan, and Burrowes (1983: 42) describes the form as "possibly restricted to St. George and St. Philip." The examples given can also be read as habitual, as in "hii *da* wok mis G grong?" (Rickford 1992: 187), or as historical examples of periphrastic *do* (Burrowes 1983: 42, Fields 1995: 97). The status of continuative *da* in Bajan seems questionable.

4. Anterior *did*

(7)   [de dɪd waz kɑlɚˈɹə]
      "De *did* was cholera." = There was/had been cholera (Granny 1755).

Preverbal *did* used to mark the earlier of two past events is described as "quite a common feature in Bajan and other Creoles" by Burrowes (1983: 43), and "the most common creole tense aspect marker in this sample" by Rickford (1992: 188). The above example is its only occurrence in Granny's speech, although it is also used by Mrs. Orleans, a working-class speaker whose speech is less basilectal than Granny's: [dɛm pipəl dɪd stɪŋk] "Them people *did* stink!" (Mrs. Orleans 615). Note the use of *did* with anterior statives in these examples. The interaction of anteriority and habituality (and perhaps emotional involvement) in this context might be worthy of further study, especially given the phonetic similarity between *did* and the (present or past) habitual *da* form. The specific combination of *did* and *was* in Granny's example is also found in Collymore (1955: 39).

5. Completive *don*

(8)   [ɪʔ dʌn sɛt sɪns las jiɹ]
      "It *done* set since last year" (Granny 2630).

This form is mentioned as part of Bajan by Burrowes (1983: 43), Rickford (1992: 187), and Schneider (1990: 90), but without elaboration. This may be due to the feature's limited use as a creole diagnostic, as it is also found in other varieties of English, notably vernacular speech of the American south (see e.g. Feagin 1979). In my data, *don* usually acts as both a completive and an emphatic, which is also typical of its use elsewhere.

6. Anterior *had*

The almost total overlap between "creole" anterior marker *had* and "StdE" past perfect *had* (Tagliamonte 1996) suggests that we should have no trouble uncovering such a form in supposedly-mesolectal Barbados. This does not appear to be the case. The form does not occur in my data; Schneider, Burrowes, and Fields do not mention it; and Rickford (1992: 188) and Blake (1997: 160) indicate that it is considerably less common in their data than anterior *did*. *Did* may be the (lower) mesolectal form, with *had* in the upper mesolect and acrolect behaving much like StdE *had*. The occasional use of non-standard or bare participles in this context (e.g. "hii *had* went," Rickford 1992: 187) is also a widespread feature of non-standard English.

7.   Third person present -*s* absence

(9)   [di lɔɹ dõ:n don wɜ˞k dat kʌjn ə we: i sɛnd sʌmbʌdi]
"The Lord don't- don't work that kind of way... he *send* somebody" (Granny 1250).

Burrowes (1983: 41) describes this as a "general Creole feature," and Rickford (1992: 187) gives an example. Other authors do not mention it. Perhaps it is seen as too common to be worth comment. Its relative rarity in my data may be due to the rarity of third-singular contexts in Granny's speech. It seems unlikely that –s marking in Granny's speech represents a decreolized form of a mesolectal *does* habitual marker (Schneider 1990). Her speech is generally *more* basilectal than that of *does* users, and the example shows there is no privative association of –s marking and habituality.

8.   Unmarked past tense

(10)   [tu de: bifɔɹ ʃi pasəwe: ʌj tɛl ɜ˞ tə staɹt krʌjin nʌw]
"Two day before she *pass* away, I *tell* her to start crying now" (Granny 1605).

Fields (1995: 96), Rickford (1992: 187), Blake (1997: 148–161), Burrowes (1983: 40), and Schneider (1990: 90) are among those identifying unmarked past tense as a feature of Bajan. Like habitual *does*, this is a feature that is salient, across the continuum, and frequent. Its frequency suits it to quantitative study: Blake (1997) found high rates of zero marking, ranging from 84% to 97%, depending on phonological and verb-type factors. She also describes a lexical effect, whereby *go* and *have* are almost always marked, while *do* and *say* are almost always unmarked.

9.   *Gonna/gon* future

(11)   [ɪʔ gʌ̃ə fomɛ̃ʔ]
"It *gonna* ferment" (Granny 2727).

This form, described in Schneider (1990: 90) as a "going" future and by Fields (1995: 97) as irrealis "go," seems to be the *going to* form widespread in English, accompanied by auxiliary deletion (see copula deletion, below). Granny's speech shows two surface realizations: a form halfway between *gonna* and *gon'* and the form [gwɪn], which is not far from the "gwine" of constructed dialect.

10. *Fo(r)* infinitive markers

These forms, as in "He been want *fa* ruin my poor pick'nee too" (Fields (1995: 97), are not found in my data, nor mentioned by Rickford. The only suggestion I have found that they occur at all in contemporary Bajan comes from Burrowes (1983: 43).

Copula and related forms

11. Copula absence

(12) [de gʌ̃ə lambeːst ju tu]
___ *gonna:* "They *(0)* gonna lambaste you too" (Granny 805).

(13) [ʌj doːən lʌjk haw i plē: di geːm]
___ V-in: "I don't like how he *(0)* playin' the game" (Granny 849).

(14) [ʃɪ lʌki da a ē tɹo ɪt an ɚ]
___ adjectives: "She *(0)* lucky that I ain't throw it on her" (Granny 1025).

(15) [aldo dɛ hav dɛɹ oːn kɪdz dɛm hiɹ]
___ locatives: "Although they have their own kids, them *(0)* here" (Granny 201).

(16) [naʔ ʃi ʃi də datɚ]
___ NP: "Not she, she *(0)* the daughter" (Granny 2023).

Copula absence is, of course, a frequently discussed feature of Caribbean creoles and of African American Vernacular English, mentioned for Bajan by Rickford (1992: 187, 190–193), Blake (1997: 100–140), Schneider (1990: 90), and Fields (1995: 96). Granny deletes copulas before all five of the grammatical categories traditionally considered in this context. This is a broader copula deletion context than described in Schneider (1990: 90), where *be* forms are listed before locatives and noun phrases. The broad context, and high overall rates, agree with the findings of Rickford (1992), Blake (1997), and Rickford & Blake (1990), as does the general "creole" hierarchy of deletion rates: *gonna* > V-in>adj/loc>NP. Like Rickford's Mrs. Thankyou and Grateful, Granny always deletes before *gonna*. Readers seeking a more detailed description of Bajan copula deletion are directed to Blake(1997), which also includes a description of past tense copula deletion, as in Granny's pre-adjectival sentence above.

12. *De/di(d)* true copulas (non-preverbal)

Only Rickford (1992: 186–188) describes the *de* form, which is infrequent in his data. Fields (1995: 96) describes a *dere* for historical Bajan ("Who *dere?*"), but this form is indistinguishable from English *there* with Bajan phonology and copula deletion. Rickford (1992: 187) describes the *did* copula as frequent and found before adjectives and locatives, while Schneider (1990: 90) limits its occurrence to locatives with third-person plural subjects. Burrowes (1983: 43) describes a general *did* past tense marker, and one of her examples ("dat *did* a gud piksha") is pre-NP. There are no clear-cut occurrences of either form in Granny's speech, although it could be argued that an attempt to integrate at least one of them into an otherwise English-like sentence is responsible for [de dɪd waz kalɚ.ɪə] "De did was cholera" (Granny 1755). Of the two forms, *did* is clearly more robust, and even shows up occasionally in constructed dialect texts.

13. *Bin* true copulas (non-preverbal, past)

(17)   [de bɪn ɪn mʌj gjaɹdɪn]
       "They *bin* in my garden" (Granny 510).

Like preverbal *bin*, this form is found only once in my data, described elsewhere only by Rickford (1992: 188–189), and is rare even there. These forms may have an anterior-like quality, or may result from extension of the participle to preterite use, as we find with *seen* and *done* elsewhere. The historical example in Fields (1995: 96) looks like *have been* with deleted *have*.

14. *De* adjectival copulas

(18)   [ʃɪ dʊ lʌki da ʌj dɪn tɹo ɪt an ɚ]
       "She *de* lucky that I didn't throw it on her" (Granny 1030).

This form occurs only twice in Granny's recorded speech, and does not appear to be mentioned elsewhere. It may be a semantic extension from the locative *de* form (Rickford 1987: 188) or a reduction of the *did* form. As with other rarely-occurring basilectal forms (*bin*, locative *de*), the odds of collecting enough data to permit a more complete description are remote. The form also occurs in Guyanese (Schneider 1990: 90).

15. *Is* topicalization

Described only by Schneider (1990: 90), this form does not occur in my data. Given the general reduction of *it is* to *is* in Bajan, as in [kɑz ɪz tɹu] 'Cause *is* true' (Granny 636), it is unclear how this form would be distinguished from the StdE *it is.*

16. Existential *it is/it woz*

This form, mentioned only by Rickford (1992: 187; "*it woz* a lak outsaid"), does not occur in my data.

17. Existential *they got*

(19)   [de gɑʔ ə paɹʔ dʌn ɛɹ əs kɑld gʌn hɪl]
       "*They got* a part down there that's called Gun Hill" (Granny 858).

This form is listed by Rickford (1992: 187), and widespread in my data. It is not mentioned elsewhere, perhaps because it is also widespread in non-Standard English.

18. Passives: zero-marked, *get*

Zero-marked passives are described by Rickford (1992: 187) ("plantation *(0)* sel out") and Burrowes (1983: 43). They might be seen as an extension of copula deletion. *Get* passives, a widespread feature of non-Standard English, are attributed to Bajan by Burrowes (1983: 43). Neither feature occurs in my sample of Granny's speech.

Negation and question formation

19. *Ain't*

(20)   [dɛm ɛn spikɪn tə mi]
       "Them *ain't* speaking to me" (Granny 432).

(21)   [ɪt eːn kɑnsɚn ju]
       "It *ain't* concern you" (Granny 452).

(22)   [dɛm bʌsəl ɑʌ hʌsəl ən en pe ju nʌ mʌjn]
       "Them bustle and hustle and *ain't* pay you no mind" (Granny 653).

(23) [ʃɪ dʊ lʌki da ʌj en tɹɔ ɪt an ɝ]
"She de lucky that I *ain't* throw it on her" (Granny 1030).

This form, usually represented as *en* or *in,* is described for Bajan by Rickford (1992: 187), Burrowes (1983: 43), and Schneider (1990: 92). The form, widespread in Barbados, is a marker of constructed dialect, and is, of course, found in non-Standard English world-wide. What is of note in Granny's speech is that *ain't* behaves in a particularly creole manner, as an invariant negator. In non-Standard Englishes, including early African American English (Howe 1995, Howe & Walker 1999), *ain't* is largely restricted to present-tense *be* and *have* contexts. This restriction has existed for over 300 years (see Miege 1688). The examples above show that Granny uses *ain't* in a far wider range of contexts, including places where StdE would use *doesn't, don't,* or *didn't.* In fact, the only situation in which Granny prefers another verbal negator, *don't,* is for negative imperatives, actual [dõn mɪs dɛm sɛpɹətli] "Don't mince them separately" (Granny 2707) or implied [di lɔɹ dõːn don wɝk dat kʌjn ə we] "The Lord don't- don't work that kind of way [and neither should you]," (Granny 1250).

20. *Din (didn't)*

(24) [de dɪn wan de fal dʌwn ovɝ sẽ tɑməs]
"They *didn't* want they fall down over St. Thomas" (Granny 1403).

This form is mentioned by Schneider (1990: 92) alone, and described as an anterior negator, although the StdE equivalent sentence given ("She didn't sing") suggests a broader past context. Granny appears to prefer the basilectal *ain't,* as previously described. She does, however, use *didn't* twice in creole anterior (past-before-past) contexts, as well as in the highly non-Standard [ʌj dɪn bɔɹn bɪg] "I *didn't* born big" (Granny 237), which is an emphatic repetition of her earlier [ʌj ɛ̃ bɔɹn bɪg] "I *ain't* born big" (Granny 223).

21. *Na, no* preverbal markers

Fields (1995: 97) gives historical examples, but the example in Rickford (1992: 187), "de *na* gud," seems more like a deleted copula with a negated complement, and is certainly not "preverbal." Granny does not use the form.

22. Negative concord

(25)   [dɛm bʌsəl ən hʌsəl ən en pe ju nʌ mʌjn]
       "Them bustle and hustle and *ain't* pay you *no* mind" (Granny 653).

Negative concord, like *ain't*, is a stereotype of non-Standard English world-wide. As such, its existence in Bajan should come as no surprise. It is mentioned in Fields (1995: 97) and Rickford (1992: 187).

23. Negative inversion

(26)   [ē nʌθɪn de ɛn kʌm tə ful mi wɪd]
       "Ain't nothin' they ain't come to fool me with" (Granny 230)

This feature is not described elsewhere for Bajan, and this is the sole such example in Granny's speech. Although the example could also represent a deleted existential ("There ain't nothin'…"), the possibility of negative inversion in Bajan requires notice, as it is generally associated with AAVE and non-creole non-Standard English (Howe 1995).

24. Non-inverted questions

The examples in both Burrowes (1983: 43) and Fields (1995: 97) are yes-no questions, which can avoid inversion in most varieties of English (Van Herk 2000). Granny uses no questions except tags in this data set, but non-inversion in WH-questions is common across the Barbadian lectal spectrum.

The noun phrase

25. Unmarked plural nouns

(27)   [de θɑʔ de tʊk ɑl daʔ gʌn]
       "They thought they took all that *gun*" (Granny 1857).

Burrowes and Schneider both qualify their description of Bajan unmarked plural nouns. Schneider (1990: 93) describes "variable usage" of the suffix, even in conservative varieties. Burrowes (1983: 41) says, "In Barbadian Creole this feature is only very residually manifested today." Granny's speech appears to share with many Barbadians and other West Indians a broader definition of non-count nouns than do speakers of other varieties, as in "all that gun(0)" above or "dee iit di keen(0)" in Rickford (1992: 187).

26. Unmarked possessive nouns

(28) [jə no: sʌm pipəl ke:k jə kʌt ɪʔ hiɹ jə fʌjn ə lʌmp]
"You know some people*(0)* cake, you cut it here, you find a lump"
(Granny 2721).

This feature is described by Burrowes (1983: 42), Schneider (1990: 92), Rickford (1992: 187), and Fields (1995: 96). It is also part of constructed Bajan.

27. Pluralizing/deictic *dem*

(29) [bəʰn dɛm ɹɛdwʊdz ka de ē bʌjn ɛsɛlvz]
"Burn(t) *them* redwoods, `cause they ain't burn(ing) theirselves"
(Granny 2955).

This feature is mentioned by Rickford (1992: 187) and Fields (1995: 95), although all examples appear more deictic/demonstrative than pluralizing. In other words, this appears to be the stereotypical *them/those* alternation of non-Standard English world-wide.

28. Subject pronouns as objects

(30) [ʌj ē mʌjn ʃɪ ʌj də wɛnʔ]
"I ain't mind *she*, I de went" (Granny 1205).

This feature is mentioned by Rickford (1992: 187), Burrowes (1983: 41), Schneider (1990: 94), and figures in the title of Blake (1997) "All o' we is one." It occurs only with *he*, *she*, and *we*, although in Granny's recorded speech no *we* contexts surface. This is a highly salient feature of mesolectal Bajan and constructed dialect.

29. Object pronouns as subjects

(31) [bʌʔ ɪf ju gã ʃʌwʔ ən ju gwɪn skɹim dɛm ã wã ə hiɹ ju]
"But if you gon' shout and you gon' scream, *them* ain't want to hear you"
(Granny 740).

Them in subject position is mentioned by Schneider (1990: 94) and Burrowes (1983: 41), and alternates with /de/ in Granny's speech. Fields (1995: 95–96) and Burrowes (1983: 41) describe *me* in subject position in descriptions of earlier Bajan and in songs, but the form's stereotypical identification with pidgins and creoles may render such early attestations less trustworthy than those for other features.

30. Subject and object pronouns as genitives

(32)   [tɛl mi kʊd dɛɹ titʃ͡ɚ lʊk ɪn i bʊk ɔɹ pe: ɛni tɛnʃɔ̃]
       "Tell me, could their teacher look in *he* book or pay any attention?"
       (Granny 3212).

(33)   [ka dɛm mɛ̃ʔ tə pʊʔ dɛm hand]
       "Because them meant to put *them* hands" (Granny 2928).

This is mentioned by Schneider (1990: 94), Rickford (1992: 187), and Burrowes (1983: 41) as part of a general process of absence of case marking, whereby the *she*, *he*, *we*, and *them* forms spread across all three cases (subject, object, genitive). As with subject pronouns as objects, subject pronouns as genitives are a highly salient feature of mesolectal Bajan and constructed dialect.

31. *Wunna/Unna*

The second person plural pronoun *wunna*, often proposed since Turner (1949) to be of West African origin, is mentioned by Schneider (1990: 94), Burrowes (1983: 41), and Collymore (1955: 115). Although the form is extremely salient in Barbados, and a clear marker of constructed dialect, it does not occur in Granny's speech. This is likely due to the absence of favorable contexts, as the form is nowadays specifically associated with negative affect,[5] especially exasperation, especially directed toward "hard-ears" children. Note Collymore's example, even 35 years ago: "*Unna* ain't got no manners?" In contemporary Bajan, *wunna* is the preferred of the two forms.

32. Neutral third singular *um/om*

Burrowes (1983: 41) describes this form as used across all three cases and "quite common in Bajan." Her example refers to a young child. Granny does not use this form, but she does use neutral *it* to refer to a young child: [ʌj kal jɚ tʃɪlən ən laʃ ɪʔ an tɛl ɪt wʌj ʌj laʃ ɪʔ] 'I call your children and lash *it* and tell *it* why I lash *it*' (701). Other authors do not describe the form for contemporary Bajan. The historical example in Fields (1995: 96) sounds more like the reduced English third person plural `*em*, especially as it has plural reference: "me no tief *um*."

33. Third singular gender neutralization

(34)   [ɔɹ ɪf i kʌm ʃi pas tɹu di hʌws ən ʃi go bak ʌwtsʌjd]
       "Or if *he* come, *she* go on through the house, and *she* go back outside"
       (Granny 942).

Here, the *he*, pronounced [i] has the same referent as the *she* later in the sentence. Only Burrowes (1983: 41) mentions the form, which she describes as "usually associated with Christ Church [parish], but also heard in St. George." Granny lives in St. Michael parish, near the boundary with St. George.

Phonology

Burrowes (1983), Blake (1997: 31–34), and Collymore (1955) briefly discuss phonology. Burrowes points out that "very particular work needs to be done" (1983: 40). That particular work is not done here, as I mention only the most widespread and salient features.

34. Interdental fricatives become stops

This feature is widespread across the Bajan lectal range and highly salient. In fact, the infrequency or absence of stopped fricatives among my most "acrolectal" (young, urban, educated, upper-class) informants came as a surprise. As Collymore (1955: 89) points out, however, even well-educated Bajans often prefer *da* for "the."

35. Consonant cluster reduction

This feature is also widespread, especially with word-final stops after nasals or fricatives. Burrowes (1983: 40) gives "ask" as one example, but almost all my informants (and almost all Barbadians I've ever met) prefer the "metathesized" or archaic form *aks*.

36. Palatalization

Burrowes (1983: 40) gives the best-known examples: [gyardin], [kyar]. This is perhaps not quite as widespread or salient as the previous two features. Given that Collymore (1955: 117) and Haynes (1973: 5) also represent palatal glides *before* velars in words like "bag" and "egg," and that some earlier Bajans represented "come" as "cuom" (Fitzherbert 1770), it might be productive to investigate whether this form actually represents velar consonants influencing (all) low vowels.

37. /ai/ raising

(35)   [nʌjn ɪz mʌjn]
        "Nine is mine" (Granny 002).

In Granny's speech, the nucleus of the diphthong in words like "mine" and "nine" is usually raised, especially before nasals. The informants described in Blake (1997: 34, 177) either raise or back the nucleus. Collymore (1955) describes both this (117) and the opposite process, with "anoint" becoming *'nint* (74). Granny also sometimes raises and backs the nucleus in words like "out" to roughly the same low-mid relatively back articulation as the nucleus in "mine."

38. Glottalization of voiceless stops

Blake (1997: 34) suggests that Bajan voiceless stops /p,t,k/ become glottal stops in syllable-final position. In Granny's speech, in particular, there is a good deal of variation in the amount of glottalization: /t/ is usually fully glottalized, while /k/ retains a good deal of its velar quality. The *da* article hypothesized by Fields (1995: 95) appears to be the word "that" with glottalization and interdental stopping.

39. Rhoticity

Unlike some of its Caribbean neighbors, Bajan is fully rhotic, and if anything, more rhotic than North American StdE. Blake (1997: 34, after Wells 1982: 584–5) suggests that "speakers of other Caribbean English Creoles... stereotype BCE [Bajan] speakers by their r-fullness."

40. Long vowels

Bajan /o/ and /e/, as in most of the English Caribbean, are often lengthened rather than diphthongized. Collymore (1955: 117) represents the most extreme forms when he renders "pay for the goat" as "pay-uh for the go-aht." These forms are also occasionally found in Granny's speech.

Lexical items, word coining, and other markers

Even the less frequent of the following features are salient in Bajan, and often feature in constructed dialect. None (except the omnipresent *chupse*; see 44 below) surface in Granny's speech, but even a casual listener can amass a collection in Barbados in a short time. Collymore (1955) is a useful source for the older of these (*c'dear, duppy, hard-ears,* etc.).

41. Reduplication

Burrowes (1983: 44) mentions reduplication for intensity ("sik sik"), while Collymore (1955: 33) mentions verb coining from reduplicated adjectives, whereby "out out," for example, means, "to extinguish."

42. Two-part nouns

These are what Collymore (1955: 33) describes as "compound redundants" for combinations like *sparrow-bird, sow-pig,* and *ram-goat.* Many seem to involve defining the sex of an animal or employee. Perhaps they are related to the *man rat* or *wuman kondukta* examples in Burrowes (1983: 42).

43. Onomatopoeic forms

Bajans appear to have great license in coining these, especially for sounds of destruction: *bronalong* (Burrowes 1983: 44), *baddarax, bruggadung,* etc. (Collymore 1955: 43).

44. Chupse

Also known as stupse, or sucking of teeth, the chupse is extremely widespread. It can indicate amused tolerance, disdain, disgust, among other meanings. Collymore (1955: 30–31) is especially thorough in his description of "the universal language of the West Indies, the passport to confidence from Jamaica to British South America." All nine informants use this feature.

Basilectal Bajan, mesolectal "dialect," acrolectal external norms

It is clear that the features presented here and elsewhere collectively constitute a language variety closer to the basilect than what is generally described for Barbados, even by Barbadians. The sociohistorical evidence suggests that such a lect may have existed in Barbados for several centuries. At the same time, it is clear that Barbados has long had a fairly well-educated population, speaking a language variety substantially closer to English (Standard or dialectal) than the vernacular of other Caribbean islands. We are left with the original contradiction: How can these basilectal forms survive without Bajan being identified as a full creole ("creole for true," in Morrow's words)? Perhaps more strikingly, given that Barbados is small, lacks marronage areas, and is relatively wealthy and well-educated, how has such a basilect survived at all?

We have, of course, no way at this point of determining what percentage of the population, now or earlier, controlled such a basilect. I would suggest that for at least the last century, and perhaps even throughout the history of Barbados, the basilect-speaking population has been relatively small. It is also possible that basilectal features have been stigmatized across such a wide range of classes that the traditional restriction of such forms to private use has been even stronger on Barbados than elsewhere. The result in either case would be the same. As each generation sees a reduction in the size and number of basilectal communities, and a restriction of the domains of basilectal use, a smaller percentage of the population has access to such forms, or even aware-ness of their existence.

Some (mesolectal) creole forms, however, have taken on the functions of group identity markers, and as such carry less stigma (although some Barba-dian schoolteachers might disagree). These features clearly include habitual *does*, unmarked past tense, copula deletion, most phonological features de-scribed above, and a range of lexical items, notably *wunna*. These features are, in fact, the most common non-standard features in the speech of most Barba-dians. They persist into the high mesolect at least, although at higher levels they are more clearly marked as things to do when one is "being Bajan." As such, I have described this cluster of features as "constructed" dialect, although no connotations of artificiality are necessarily attached.

One interesting result of the wide (social) range of dialect use, and the small basilect-speaking population, is that contemporary urban Barbadian youth do not have access to the basilectal variety for the purposes of identity creation, as they might in other creolophone areas (or as youth do in much of the world). The linguistic choices easily available to them are the dialect, identified with their parents' generation, and Standard (Caribbean) English — in other words, the poles of the Barbadian continuum, as it is traditionally described. Young Barbadians, then, might be expected to seek exogenous target varieties. The results can be heard in the speech of Ms. X, the "right-most" (young, urban, wealthy, educated) of my informants. Ms. X was seven-teen at the time of the recordings, living along Barbados' "Gold Coast" and preparing to go to a prestigious British university. Like Granny, Ms. X has lived her entire life in Barbados, and has no relatives from other English-speaking areas. In the same way that Granny's speech is not what is expected of dialect, Ms. X's is not really the Caribbean Standard English of previous generations. The excerpt in (36) shows the absence of creole features, especially compared to Granny's speech in (3).

(36) [ʃiz fɛɹli bɹutəl sow ʃI tʌk af ɚ ʃu ən staɹɹed biɾiŋ ɚ ɪtwəz lajk wənə ðoz platfɔɹm ʃuz jənow lajk wənwəðə tal hilz jənow lajk jənow ðə wʌnz wɪðə tal hil ən ðən ðə bɪg platfɔɹm ʃiwəz holənət baj ðə hi:l ənjʌs klʌbɪŋ hɚ wɪθɪt an ðə gɹawn an ʃi wəz bɪg pɹɛgnənt ðɪs tajm ʃiz bɪg pɹɛgnənt stɹaɾəlɪŋ ðɛ gɚl an biɾɪŋ ɚ wɪθ ðə ʃu]
      "She's fairly brutal, so she took off her shoe and started beating 'er. It was, like, one of those platform shoes, y'know, like, one with the tall heels, y'know, like, y'know, the ones with the tall heel and then the big platform. She was holding it by the heel, and just clubbing her with it, on the ground! And she was big pregnant this time, she's big pregnant, straddling the girl, and beating her with the shoe!" (Ms. X 1831–1856).

The transcription indicates exogenous youth speech features like *y'know* and *like,* as well as the almost complete absence of Barbadian phonology, even of unstigmatized features, in Ms. X's speech. Even though this is a very relaxed, unmonitored conversation, the only vaguely Barbadian features audible in this passage are slightly centralized low front vowels and slightly more stress on the second syllable of "platform" than a North American norm would indicate. Overall, Ms. X's speech is close to middle-class African-American, and even closer to second-generation Caribbean-Canadian. She, like her friends, does not use (Bajan) dialect to construct identity. Their identification is young, black, middle-class, and North American. Non-standard features that do surface in their speech are as likely to be North American as Bajan. This phenomenon is now becoming widespread enough to feature in Barbadian public debate, with this "Canadian" accent apparently associated with high status and/or snobbery. If the trend continues, we may in the future see a reinforcement of Bajan and non-standard North American (especially AAVE) features. For example, the habitual *be* now occasionally heard in acrolectal young Bajan may be borrowed from AAVE, but reinforced by older Bajan habitual *does (be)*.

The future of the clearly basilectal features which I have described is less certain. Most of them seem to occur rarely in speech, and their use appears to be limited to elderly Barbadians. These facts, combined with strong Barbadian sensitivity toward stigmatized features, makes collecting these forms extremely difficult. On the other hand, basilectal Bajan, like many other minority languages and lects, appears to have survived for several centuries, against all odds. There may be life in the old features yet.

Notes

1. Winford (2002), perhaps one of the most substantial discussions of Bajan and its history to date, only came to my attention after the present article was finished.

2. In a (post-) creole language continuum, language varieties are described as more (basilectal) or less (acrolectal) creole, with middle varieties described as "mesolectal" (Bickerton 1975). These terms are used both to compare creoles (e.g. "Barbadian is mesolectal, compared to Jamaican"), and within a specific linguistic situation (e.g. "Bajan basilect").

3. Examples of Bajan speech from my own data follow International Phonetic Alphabet transcriptions, followed by a gloss that represents syntactical and morphological features only and identification of speaker pseudonym and tape counter number. Examples from other written sources maintain the source transcription.

4. Much work remains to be done describing and analyzing the linguistic and social factors conditioning the use of these features, not to mention building larger data sets. Blake (1997) takes just such an approach to past marking and copula deletion in rural Bajan.

5. Thanks to John Rickford (p.c.) for bringing this to my attention.

Eastern Caribbean suprasegmental systems

A comparative view with particular reference to Barbadian, Trinidadian, and Guyanese

David Sutcliffe
Universitat Pompeu Fabra, Barcelona

1. Introduction

The approach taken in this chapter is basically the one adopted by Carter (1987) in her analysis of Guyanese and Jamaican Creole suprasegmentals and by Devonish (1989) in his study of Guyanese suprasegmentals. (*Suprasegmentals* are defined here as pitch patterns mapped onto syllables or phrases, creating intonation and tonal patterns.) That is, we show that Caribbean English-derived Creoles can be analyzed as having tonal systems, even if somewhat evolved in the direction of mainstream English. By tonal systems we mean those that organize the melodic pitch used by speakers into two or more pitch phonemes or tones (contrasting high and low in the case of two-tone systems). In such systems, moreover, "both pitch phonemes and segmental phonemes (vowels and consonants) enter into the composition of at least some mor-phemes" (Welmers 1973: 80). It is important to note that in such systems, morphemes may consist of significant pitch alone, so that for example the tense marker may be a pitch phoneme mapped onto a syllable much like an inflec-tion. As a natural result of these conditions, word stress is assigned indepen-dently from tone, as we shall see. That is to say, two words may have stress on the same syllable, but differ in their pitch patterns.[1]

Maurice Holder (Holder 1984, 1998, 1999) approaches the topic from a different angle, arguing that Guyanese, Bajan and related varieties can be described as pitch-accent languages. The latter are language varieties which could loosely be described as tonal, but which differ from the latter in that pitch contours belong to the word rather than the syllable (Trask 1997). It could be argued that the two views are complementary and that, depending on the approach adopted, many suprasegmental features can be described as forming part of a tonal system or as forming part of a pitch-accent system. After all, the first or Founder speakers of the Creoles in question were overwhelmingly speakers of the main languages of the Ghanaian and Dahomean coast: Twi, Fante, Ga-Adangme, Ewe, Fongbe.[2] These languages, and the minor languages alongside them that make up the intricate West African linguistic mosaic, are all tone languages. We can assume, consequently, that the Founder speakers attempted to do what speakers of tone languages in West Africa do when either speaking English, or adopting English words into their languages — that is, to reinterpret English word stress as tone (see Amayo 1980). As we shall see, the most usual pattern was for English word stress to be reinterpreted as high tone. This is what happens in West African Pidgin (Carter 1989). West African Pidgin [WAP] is a recognized tone language and the modern-day descendant of the English trading pidgin that many of the first slaves may have learned to speak while they were in captivity, waiting to be shipped to the Americas.

On the other hand, it is equally true that the very first African speakers on Caribbean soil would have had ample exposure to the specific European language in question. The years in question here are the 1630s and 1640s and the place Barbados, the entrepot from where many African slaves were subsequently distributed throughout the Caribbean. The first African slaves into Barbados would have worked for, and often alongside, speakers of English. The outcome of the resulting language contact, which laid the foundations for the emerging creole, must necessarily have involved a readjustment between two major types of system, the African tonal systems, on the one hand, and English stress and intonation on the other. As such, it would not be surprising to find that the system can be "read" as either a tonal or a pitch-accent one — the latter being less tonal, as it were, and closer to typical European intonation systems. Carter (1987) regards pitch-accent as a form of tone, further closing the gap between the two views.

In this chapter, I set out to provide a systematic account of Eastern Caribbean suprasegmental features, taking a broad theoretical approach similar to Carter's, but in addition relating my findings to information drawn from a variety of other sources, ranging from Allsopp (1996) to Sylvain's pioneering work (1936) on Haitian Creole. After an initial look at the most distinctive features of Eastern Caribbean intonation (in Bajan, Trinidadian and Guyanese) and the way that these can be transcribed as exponents of a tonal system, I situate Bajan, Trinidadian and Guyanese suprasegmental systems within the wider context of Caribbean and Caribbean-rim varieties. The latter include Saramaccan at one extreme and African American Vernacular English (AAVE) at the other. Lexical tone, in the sense of distinguishing one word from another, is seen to be particularly developed in the Eastern Caribbean, compared with the other areas to the west and north.

I proceed to look at the main sentence types, in terms of typical tonal juncture features such as *downstep* (a high tone which is literally a step down from an immediately preceding high tone), and *downdrift* (the progressive lowering of high tones towards the end of the sentence, a process in which high tones are automatically lowered after a low tone). I also look at the distinctive sentence final rising intonation so typical of Bajan and Guyanese in terms of these same tonal juncture rules.

We see that downstep plays an important role on the syntactic and discourse levels of the varieties under consideration. Another feature that I examine is the tonal marking of the focus in front-focusing movement and elsewhere. Front-focusing is where a word is highlighted by being shifted to the beginning of the clause, as, for example, *tell* in "iz TEL shi tel mi" or *that* in "iz DAT mi waant," and so on. The intersection between high tone on the focus and grammatical downstepping is seen to account for a significant part of the workings of the system. Lastly, I look at compound-noun formation where compounds take predictable tone patterns. Basically, as we shall see, the high tone of the first of the two nouns — the modifier noun — is replaced by a low tone. We refer to this as initial low tone (ILT) replacement. Thus *fàlá* ("follow") plus *fàshán*, combined, becomes: *fàlàfáshàn* ("imitate", "imitation"). There is an important distinction between these compounds with their low-tone replacives, and other noun phrases that take a simple downstepping pattern. There are a number of interesting implications here, not least the possibility that increased knowledge in this area of tonal and post-tonal systems may afford increased insights into the processes of creole genesis.

2.   Geographical variation in the Anglophone Caribbean and Caribbean rim

2.1   The Eastern Caribbean

Bajan, the vernacular speech of Barbados, constitutes a distinctive variety within the range of the English-lexis Creoles of the Eastern Caribbean. This is evident on the suprasegmental and other levels. The characteristic pitch patterns of Barbados speech are a recognizable hallmark which mark this variety out as clearly distinctive, when heard together with certain other phonological traits such as the "hoy toid" ("*high tide*") diphthong where schwa + /ɪ/ is used for standard /aɪ/, or the extensive use of glottal stops to replace other consonants. Glottal stops, of course, are the sound heard in standard Englishes in *uh-uh!* ("no" or "don't!"), *oh-oh!* ("oh, no!") or indeed the place-name *Hawai'i* (as pronounced by locals). It is important, however, to note that where suprasegmentals are concerned, there are basic features of the system that indicate its connection with that of other Eastern Caribbean varieties. The relationship between Bajan and Guyanese on the suprasegmental level is particularly obvious: both share a substantial list of lexical minimal pairs, mostly disyllables, which are differentiated by pitch patterns alone. *Síster* for example (with the pitch pattern / ‒ _ /) means female sibling, whereas *sistér* (with the pitch pattern / _ ‒ /) denotes a nun or sister in the religious sense. *Wórker* (with pitch pattern / ‒ _ /) is one who works, while *workér* (with the pitch pattern / _ ‒ /) means seamstress or needlewoman (Sutcliffe 1982: 111). This is a feature of both Bajan and Guyanese, but not so far attested for any other Caribbean creole. Note, too, that this feature is not to be explained as a shift in stress, such as we would find in English elsewhere. In these words the pitch alone changes, while the stress remains in the same place (on the first syllable). Similarly, both Bajan and Guyanese commonly have a characteristic rising final intonation at the end of a sentence — or, more exactly, a suppression of the expected falling intonation or downturn:

(1)   Fàin táim !án màrìd-mán táim: Fàin táim bétúh dàn màrìd-mán táim / _ _ ‒‒ / (market stallholder, Georgetown Guyana, 1994). "You have married-man thyme and fine-thyme. Fine-thyme is better than married-man thyme."[3]

(2)   Hì músí ^dín !éebl tù **gèt úhp.** / _ ‒‒ / (Bajan: BS/B/40/99) "He must not have been able to get up."

(3) Àn dì k′òrlz díd kòm óut àn ít ᴧdín lúk vèrì náis. / _ _ – – / (British Bajan:
    M./UKL/10/75)
    "And the curls came out and it didn't look very nice."

Of course, many varieties of creole, including those of the Eastern Caribbean,
do in fact have a final downturn at the end of Wh-questions and at least some
statements. This is known as *final cadence* or *final crumbling*. However, as we see
in (1), (2) and (3), this intonational feature may be frequently overridden in
Bajan and Guyanese, as a stylistic option, perhaps associated with pragmatic
function and affective meaning. Note that the stallholder's utterance, discussing two types of thyme, is mildly contrastive, although not emphatic.

We find no examples of this "Guyanese rise" anywhere in our Trinidadian
data from Dulcie C., although the other two Trinidadian consultants, Ella F.
and Lilly H. use it frequently. Further afield to the north, we find it as a common
variant in Gullah, as Turner himself pointed out (1949: 252). In the Western
Caribbean, basically Jamaica, the rise occurs sporadically (for reasons un-
known) but appears to be the common or unmarked variant only on the north
coast, including the Montego Bay area (John Figueroa,p.c.).

2.2 The wider geographical matrix

There are wider pan-Caribbean affiliations that extend beyond the Eastern
Caribbean. Carter (1987), Sutcliffe (1998), and Holder (1999) all agree that
there are major differences precisely on this level between Bajan and Guyanese,
on the one hand, and Jamaican on the other. That has to be made very clear.
Nonetheless, in all three Caribbean varieties, distinctive pitch patterns enter into
the composition of lexical and grammatical morphemes and as such are assigned to tone-bearing units consisting of vowels or continuants (consonants
that may constitute syllables). Furthermore, in all these varieties, such pitches
can be transcribed as being contrasting high and low tones, modified in actual
use when incorporated into an utterance by downstep, downdrift and other
intonation-like features (more exactly, juncture features) which are typical of
tone languages. Tone-bearing units consisting of vowels can be short or long;
they are reflexes of the historically short and long vowels in the lexifier language.[4]

Interestingly, the intonation of AAVE can *similarly* be transcribed as a two-
tone system showing certain features in common with those of the Eastern and
Western Caribbean. AAVE also has long and short vowels — as a physical
rather than abstract feature — even though most other varieties of American

English have lost contrastive vowel length (Sutcliffe 1998: 160). This suggests there is an even wider grouping here, including *all* varieties which emerged out of the contact between African languages and English during the time of the slave trade in and around the Caribbean and along the Atlantic seaboard.

This does not necessarily mean that all these language varieties are unambiguously tonal, but at the very least that their suprasegmental features can be transcribed using tonal notation. In fact, Herskovits (1941: 291) noted long ago that the "music" of United States African American speech was reminiscent of African tone languages. He assumed, however that these suprasegmental patterns were no longer "functional" — that is, no longer the exponent of a functional tonal system. Lorenzo Turner (1949: 248–249) assumed the same of Gullah, illustrated by the range of examples he provided. At the other extreme we have Saramaccan and Ndyuka (and sister languages such as Kwinti) on one side of the Atlantic and Krio and West African Pidgin on the other. These languages formed largely outside the plantations — more or less out of reach of the alleged effects of decreolization — and all are unambivalently and clearly tonal languages (Devonish 1989, Sutcliffe 1992).

Fully tonal (Southern)	Intermediate (Eastern)	Intermediate (Western) (Western Atlantic)	Residual/ post-tonal (Northern)
Saramaccan, Kwinti, Ndyuka, and other creoles of inland Suriname	Bajan, Guyanese, (Trinidadian) and other Eastern Caribbean varieties Gullah (Bahamian)	Jamaican/ Western Caribbean (Haitian creole)	19th Century AAVE Modern AAVE
Monosyllabic function words have L. Polysyllabic nouns with only L tones occur.	*Monosyllabic function words have L. No polysyllabic nouns with only L tones occur.*	*Monosyllabic function words have H. No polysyllabic nouns with only L tones occur.*	*Monosyllabic function words have L. Possible grammatical tone.* *Falsetto/ register shift for emphasis.*
Lexical minimal pairs. Grammatical tone.	*Lexical minimal pairs. Grammatical tone.*	*Lexical minimal pairs. Grammatical tone.*	
Tonal sandhi	*Downstepping and other tonal juncture patterns.*	*Downstepping and other tonal juncture patterns.*	*Downstepping and other tonal juncture patterns.*

Notes (exemplification)

Cf. Ndyuka *bùkù* (LL: "fungus"), *sàbàkù* (LLL: "wading bird").

Cf. Ndyuka *bùkù* (HL:"book") v. *bùkù* (LL: "fungus"); *ákísì* (HHL: "ask") v. *àkísì* (LHL: "axe")(Goury 2001).

Saramaccan has minimal pairs: *fíì* (HL: "feel") v. *fíí* (LH: "free"), *béè* (HL: "family") v. *bèè* (LL: "reddish") (Voorhoeve 1961).

Saramaccan has *mì*, (L: "I", subject) and *mí* (H: "me", oblique). Also tonal sandhi reflects grammatical relations: *tàtá* ("father") *mí tátá* ("my father") (Voorhoeve 1961, Rountree 1972).

Saramaccan's sister language Ndyuka has *nà mì píkìn* ("it's my child") v. *ná mì píkìn* ("it's not my child") (Goury 2001).

The only words with fixed low tone are certain monosyllabic function words. Devonish (1989).

Lexical minimal pairs: see Dalphinis (1989: 80–81,70–71) for Guyanese; see Roberts (1988: 94) for Barbadian.

Barbadian focus marked by high tones (see below). Compounding shows tone rules (see below, also Allsopp (1996) for Eastern Caribbean: *bàd hánd*, "an injured arm) v. *bád hànd* "bad hand" (cards), *lòng-tíme* ("formerly") v. *lóng tìme* ("long since").

For Guyanese see Devonish (1989: 100). Also Carter (1987, 1989) on tone in reduplication and grammatical function of downstep in Guyanese.

See also James (2001) for grammatical tone in Tobagonian.

No polysyllabic words in JC have low tone only; monosyllables may have low tones derived from underlying high tones (Devonish 1989: 135). Similarly Gullah texts such as Stoddard (1949) have no LL(LL) words (personal research).

A few minimal pairs of the *sìstá* v. *sísta* type so far attested in JC (Shelome Gooden, p.c.). (Lawton 1984 gives a few minimal pairs: *dédhòus* "mortuary" v. *dèdhóus* "inherited house" [compound v. non-compound?]).

Grammatical tone in JC: focus has H, followed by DH; L tone replacives on "subjunctive" verbs; embedded pronouns take H (Sutcliffe 1998). Tone rules in compounding (DeCamp 1960, Lawton 1963).

Haitian Creole has certain pitch patterns signalling grammatical distinctions (Sylvain 1936).

Tonal or "post-tonal" grammatical patterns may exist in AAVE. Candidates would be "tone" rules in compounding (and reduplication) and grammatical downstep in embedded clauses (Sutcliffe 1997).

Falsetto, also raised pitch and vowel lengthening for emphasis in AAVE (Sutcliffe 1998, Feagin 1997).

AAVE downstep (Sutcliffe 1998) also downdrift, although more restricted (Sutcliffe 1992, Foreman 1996).

Some of these pitch patterns are found also in Southern White Vernacular English (Feagin 1997; Rebecca Larche Moreton, p.c.) as a result of contact and areal diffusion.

Figure 1. Range: degrees of tonality in New World Creoles and Englishes

2.3   Conventions used for marking tonal features

In the examples that follow, relative high tone (H) is marked with an acute accent (é), relative low tone (L) with a grave accent (è). There is also the downstepped high tone (DH) which (as it name suggests) consists of a high which is a step down from the directly preceding H. This is marked with an acute accent and prefixed with an exclamation mark (!é), a notation used for example by Carter (1982, 1987) and Sutcliffe (1982, 1992). The opposite effect, the upstepped high tone (raising of a high tone, after an immediately preceding high tone) also occurs, and this is marked with a prefixed "up" arrow, thus (^é).

Phonetically, at least, Bajan could be said to have a third or mid-tone, neither high nor low. This "tone" (M) may be heard for instance immediately preceded by a low tone and followed by a high, or followed by a low and a high. The elegant solution here is to take this as a depressed high tone, occurring before a fully high tone. The impression this gives (and which may turn out to be unfounded) is of a system that once had three functional tones. If so, this was long ago re-interpreted as a two-tone system (a system with two basic tonemes), bringing it in line with all other tonal systems so far analyzed in Atlantic Creoles.

2.4   Data and data sources

2.4.1   *Eastern Caribbean and related material*
Most of the data examined here were recorded in the course of the Bedford survey[5] (see Sutcliffe 1982: 35–37, 138–140, 162–164; 1992; 1998: 144–148). This data contained some two hours of recordings of a Trinidadian-born adolescent, Dulcie C. (referred to as *Dorita* in Sutcliffe 1982). There were also recordings of four Bajan-speaking adolescents, two of whom I recorded in Luton, while the other two were recorded by Viv Edwards in Reading and kindly supplied to me (Sutcliffe 1982: 139). The two Luton speakers, aged 15 at the time, were able to switch between Bajan and an approximation to local Luton speech, but used demonstrably full Bajan phonology — that is, with the recognized Bajan sound system — in the conversations in question. The speakers from Reading were aged 12–13 years at the time, and belonged to the large Reading Bajan community, and again used Bajan phonology and talked about their Bajan culture during the conversations that were recorded. In addition, a presentation by Bajan poet Bruce St John was taped from the radio (1981). Then, during the preparation of this chapter, a Bajan linguist kindly

supplied me with a further recording made in Barbados of a deep vernacular speaker with full Bajan phonology, and a longer recording of a Bajan sports commentator. Finally the Trinidadian material was supplemented by a further recording, this time of Trinidadian adult speakers Ella F. and Lilly H. who were recorded in conversation in Barcelona.

2.4.2 Other material

Western Caribbean: Jamaican data drawn on for comparison is actually British Jamaican, from the 1974–75 Bedford Survey and the 1982–1983 Dudley Survey, the latter jointly carried out with Viv Edwards. Northern area: The AAVE data is from the Ex- slave Recordings 1935–1944 from the Archive of Folk Song at the Library of Congress, and the Gullah data is from Stoddard (1949). The other sources of crucial importance, of course, are the abundant data contained in the work of other scholars drawn upon here: above all Allsopp (1972, 1996), Carter (1987, 1989, 1993), Devonish (1989), Lawton (1963), Roberts (1988), Sylvain (1936) and Welmers (1973).

2.5 The data and methodological issues

The question of methodology needs to be addressed here. The taped speech data analyzed in this chapter was recorded either by me or by other linguists who were closely involved with the speech communities in question. However, a substantial part of the material was recorded not in the Caribbean, but in England, from first- or second-generation immigrants. The question arises, then, can the "Bajan" of British-born speakers properly be taken to be the same language as that spoken by their Barbados-born parents? The answer, of course, is that some differences are evident. However, it would appear to be the lexical levels of a given language that are most subject to change. Thus to take British Jamaican as an example, we find that even fluent British-born speakers have lost most of the vocabulary of putatively African origin that their parents and grandparents used (Sutcliffe 1978). In terms of lexico-phonology (the assignment of phonemes to lexis) we also find differences. Finally, where language contact is intense, and use of the ethnic language weakens, syntax may start to modify under the influence of other languages (in this case varieties of British English).

The suprasegmental level — the one involving intonation, stress, and tone — is evidently much more resistant to change. For example, Celtic Englishes (Englishes spoken where there was or still is a Celtic language spoken) have characteristic intonation systems that are markedly different from other Englishes, even those spoken in close proximity to them. This might, paradoxically, suggest rapid change. The highly distinctive intonation, however, is actually a result of resistance to change, and the retention of the intonational systems used in the original Celtic mother tongues. In general, it is fair to say that transplanted varieties are subject to at least as much change as non-transplanted varieties, particularly on the lexical and segmental phonology levels. Fortunately, for our purposes here, change is much slower or structurally resisted on the suprasegmental level.

Having prepared the ground, we can now move on to looking at the specific areas of the suprasegmental systems of Eastern Caribbean varieties, analyzed as potential or putative tonal systems, beginning with a brief overview of research up until the present.

3.   Tonal analyses

3.1   Background

A tendency to tonality has been noticed by scholars of Caribbean Creoles for some time, as has the tendency for tone patterns to coincide with word-stress patterns or syllable types. Le Page and DeCamp (1960) revealed several instances in Jamaican Creole where noun phrases with distinct grammatical structure and meaning were distinguished by pitch-patterns alone. Lawton (1963) provides a full-length treatise on the suprasegmentals of Jamaican. Lawton's view was that the system was tonal, with high, falling and low tones, and that these tones were predictable for lexical reasons and were closely associated with syllable type. Lawton observed that every syllable in the language bore a tone or predictable relative pitch.[6] This is an important point. It means that all words in the language without exception have their own pitch patterns, i.e., contrastive pitch (or "tone") is entered into the lexicon. Lawton's observation can be seen to hold true for many (probably all) English-derived Atlantic Creoles (see Carter 1987; Sutcliffe 1992: 108–109, 117–118).

Lawton also contended that Jamaican was a language in which tone patterns trigger word stress and not vice versa. Accordingly, he found that native speakers did not easily recognize words that were assigned the correct stress but incorrect tonal marking. Furthermore, while trisyllables were always stressed on the first syllable, they could have high-high-low or high-low-high, depending on the word, e.g. kásádà (HHL, 'cassava') but kótàkú (HLH 'basket'). The significance of this is that in much instances, Jamaican is clearly and unequivocally behaving like a tone language, since the pitch pattern and the word stress are working independently. Bajan and Guyanese have many more examples where significant pitch patterns (or tone) and stress part company. In the Eastern Caribbean, Allsopp did pioneering work (1972), noting the pitch pattern L-H as the favored one for disyllables in those varieties. Additionally, Allsopp (1996) contains a small but valuable number of references to grammatical tone marking. Even earlier than these pioneers for Caribbean English, Haitian linguist Suzanne Sylvain (1936) noted examples of fixed pitch patterns in Haitian in compound formation and other morphosyntactic processes. It is precisely in their role in these areas of the grammar that, as Carter points out (1987), creole suprasegmentals differ most obviously from their European lexifier language while agreeing with each other and, to an extent at least, with their African substratum languages.

We will proceed now to look in more detail at some of the specific suprasegmental features of Bajan and related Eastern Caribbean varieties. As stated above, we shall be treating these as exponents of a system which is typologically tonal or which shares many of the features of typical tonal systems. This approach will also allow us to pinpoint some of the highly characteristic features of the "Bajan voice."

3.2 Lexical tone

The lexical or inherent tones of a word are the "dictionary entry" tones, entered in the lexicon and used in its citation form. It is important to note that tonal morphology rules may operate on these lexical tones, logically enough since such grammatical tone changes are the equivalent of inflection in inflected languages such as Latin or Russian. Finally, intonational rules are applied after the rules for lexical and morphological tone (Carter 1987; Ham 1999). In other words, a word may have one tone pattern when in cited in isolation, and another (derived from the first) when used in a particular grammatical slot in a sentence. Lastly, this derived pattern may be further altered by intonational rules — for instance when in the final downturn of sentence intonation. For example, in Jamaican, *Ràstá* (LH, 'Rastafarian') becomes *Rástá* (HH) in vocatives. And when this vocative occurs utterance finally, it is realized as HL, as in *A we yaa go, Rástà?* ('Where are you going, Rasta?'). Since the lexical or citation tonal patterns of a word may be modified in the way we have just seen, they are best elicited in a frame such as *frésh brèdfrúut (is good.) Bàrbéedós (is good)* where the item concerned is in a particular syntactic frame and in non-final position. This frame, of course, is for adjectives and nouns. Inherent tones of verbs, reduplicated adjectives, adverbs, and function words similarly have to be elicited in non-final position and the syntactic frame carefully controlled.

Caribbean Creoles from all parts of the Caribbean and Caribbean rim may be said to have lexical tone patterns, since contrastive pitch or tone is entered into the lexicon, and attached to syllables — more exactly, attached to mora (tone-bearing units). However, in the Eastern Caribbean varieties Bajan and Guyanese, the situation is particularly interesting. We have already seen that the pattern LH or LLH (as in "get-up," "fine thyme," "very nice") may be realized as such even at the end of a phrase or sentence. This pattern is in contrast to other Creoles and indeed other tone languages where the final downturn of the intonation would bring the high tones down. In both Bajan and Guyanese, disyllabic nouns, adverbs and adjectives can have one of two tonal patterns: depending on the word, they may have either a LH or a HL.

This leads to the occurrence of minimal pairs marked purely by pitch-patterns (word stress is assigned independently and falls on the first syllable). We have already mentioned *wórker* (/ − _ /) but *workér* (with the pitch pattern / _ − /) meaning seamstress or needlewoman (Sutcliffe 1982: 111, quoting Bruce St. John). It is important to be clear that this feature is *not* the same thing as the many minimal pairs in English distinguished by their stress patterns, such as *insult* (noun) versus *insult* (verb) or *desert* meaning "arid region" versus *desert* meaning "abandon." In Bajan there is no shift in stress, but rather a change in pitch pattern that applies independently of word stress.

Roberts (1988) makes this point more or less explicitly and supplies further Guyanese and Bajan examples of this type including titles, names and occupations such as *fármer,* (occupation), contrasting with *Farmér (surname).* This is a typological feature that is possibly restricted to Guyanese and Bajan in the Eastern Caribbean, and perhaps lacking from the otherwise closely related English-derived creole varieties of Grenada and Trinidad. Certainly this feature is restricted, if it exists at all, in western Caribbean varieties (e.g. Jamaican) or in northern varieties such as Bahamian and Gullah. Crucially, however, it does also occur in Krio, the creole of Sierra Leone and the Gambia (Sutcliffe 1992: 109). We shall return to this point below.

a.	múhda	'mother, i.e. female parent'
	mùhdá	'female head of a religious order or organization'
b.	fáada	'father, i.e. male parent'
	fàadá	'priest'
c.	sísta	'sister, i.e. female sibling'
	sìstá	'female member of a religious order'; 'nursing sister'
d.	brúhda	'brother, i.e. male sibling'
	brùhdá	'male member of a religious order'
e.	fárma	'one who farms'
	fàrmá (Fàrmér)	surname
	béeka	'one who bakes'
	bèeká (Bàkér)	surname

Figure 2. Noun minimal pairs in Bajan
(adapted from Roberts 1988: 94)

Disyllabic surnames with initial stress have LH as their basic pattern in all instances, even in surnames like *Wilson* or *Walcot* (or many others) where there is no equivalent name of an occupation. Roberts explains that this pattern undergoes modifications depending on the context: for example, the disyllabic surnames change pattern to HL when they are prefixed by a title or first name: *mìstèr Líncòln, Tònì Bákèr*. The LH religious respect words (mùhdá, fàadá, sìstá, brùhdá, etc.) similarly change to HL when followed by a name: *múhdà Wílsòn, sístà Bàtes, brúhdà Shàw*.

Roberts also states that in Bajan and Guyanese *úgly, béautiful*, etc. are adjectives, while *Uglý, Beautifúl, etc.* (with final high tone) are descriptive epithets or nicknames. It seems likely that these latter examples are vocatives in origin. Unlike the surnames, their tonal patterns do not alter when combined with titles like "Miss" or "Mister" in a complex Noun Phrase.

a.	práblem	'problem'
	pràblém	'a mathematics problem'
b.	sìngín	'singing practice'
	síngin	'singing' (verb)
c.	wàshá	'washing machine'
	wásha	'one who washes'
d.	rìidá	'reader (text book)'
	ríida	'someone who reads'

Figure 3. Noun minimal pairs in Guyanese
(Devonish 1989)

In Figures 2 and 3 we have contrasting minimal pairs. In many other instances we have only one pattern or the other (HL or LH). The LH pattern is less common than the HL one, but nevertheless applies to a substantial number of words (see Holder 1999 for an extensive list). According to Hubert Devonish, these instances of LH with the L falling on the stressed syllable are, in Guyanese at least, derived from what were historically the reverse, i.e. a sequence of HL with H on the stressed syllable. If we look at instances where West African tone languages have incorporated English loan words into the language, we find that word stress on the English stressed syllable is regularly and consistently interpreted as high tone.[7] This is not so much a peculiarity of this or that tone language. Rather, it is a predictable reaction of tone language-speakers when confronted with non-tonal English. This in turn can be explained by the fact that in most (not all) varieties of British and American English, word stress coincides, most often, with raised pitch. Thus for example in Efik we find nàikíryà (LHL) 'Nigeria,' sídìng (HL) 'shilling,' bénì (HL) 'penny,' mótò (HL) 'motor car,' tósìn (HL) 'thousand,' and s′wòp (HL) 'soap.' There seem to be no counterexamples. Hausa has súkàr 'sugar,' ìngìlà (HLL) 'England,' sákándàrè (HHLL) 'secondary school,' ófìs (HL) 'office,' fénsìr (HL) 'pencil,' tíchà (HL) 'teacher.' Yoruba has sígà (HL) 'cigar,' Sátidé (HMH) 'Saturday,' and wáyà (HL) 'wire, telegraph' (Welmers 1968 for Efik, Kraft and Kirk-Greene 1973 for Hausa, Rowlands 1969 and Salami 1972 for Yoruba).

In his analysis, therefore, Devonish refers to all such stressed low tones as Underlying High Tones (UHT). This is because a) the equivalent syllables in the neighboring Suriname Creoles have high tone, and b) many other words in Guyanese still have high tone assigned to the stressed syllable. Devonish's UHT analysis can be applied to Bajan, since we have basically the same pattern there, affecting the same words. What is interesting from the point of view of the system's origins is that Krio and West African Pidgin, unlike Jamaican, also have words with the UHT, and indeed the list of such words is very similar to the Guyanese-Bajan one (Chris Corcoran, p.c.).

In Jamaican, we find that stress on low tone on the stressed syllable is actually the usual pattern for the lexical or citation form, though this changes in certain syntactic contexts. What this means is that the Jamaican system is different in this respect from all the other systems mentioned here. So there are undoubtedly clues here as to the route creole genesis took, in linguistic and social space, perhaps beginning on the coast of West Africa and immediately spreading to Barbados in the 1630s and 1640s. From there the process, already at an advanced stage, fanned out to other Eastern Caribbean islands. However, some major new factor must have intervened at some point before the settlement of Jamaica was begun by the English and their slaves from the late 1650s onwards. This factor could have been a change in the African language input (with perhaps Ga becoming less important) associated with a shift of locus of slaving operations from the original slavers' castles described in McWhorter (1995).

Devonish (1989: v) explains that it was this UHT pattern that initially drew his attention to the suprasegmentals of Guyanese:

> In spite of the shared lexicon, the supra-segmental features of [British and American] English are radically different from those of Guyanese creole. One observation often made is the absence in the metropolitan varieties of items that Guyanese often describe as being "sung." These are words with low-falling pitch on the first syllable and high pitch on the second in Guyanese Creole.

The so-called "sung" effect — the LH sequence — is not confined to the word-level, but applies equally to the intonational architecture of the language. That is to say, words that unexpectedly have LH at word-level continue to do so when occurring sentence finally. For example, *in dì wàátá* (L L LLH) is pronounced / _ _ _ _ – /, even at the end of the sentence and there is no downturn to the intonation. What happens on the word-level happens on the sentence level, and produces the Guyanese and Bajan rise, mentioned above, and looked at in more detail below.

3.3 Sentence types and suprasegmentals

One of the main functions of suprasegmentals in European languages, and indeed in many West African languages, is to differentiate the various sentence types of the language, e.g. statements from questions. When these languages are tonal, or at least marginally so, as in the case of Bajan, the intonation marking sentence types acts like an overlay imposed on basic pitch patterns. More exactly, it constitutes a principled modification to basic pitch patterns that can be expressed as a set of rules. We have already seen this, in fact, with regard to eliciting words (*breadfruit, Barbados*) within a frame such as *frésh brèdfrúut (is good), Bàrbéedós (is good)*. The discussion below will make this clearer.

Bajan, like Guyanese, Jamaican and other Caribbean Creoles, marks both questions and statements with a descending contour. In statements, this is achieved by *final cadence* and *downdrift* — intonational features that are characteristic of tonal languages and which may also be termed tonal juncture rules. Final cadence [FLC] cuts in at the end of a tone sequence to give the final rounding down with a drop in pitch to near baseline (the lower limit of the pitch range). We shall return to this point below. Downdrift affects the overall contour of the tone sequence and (as we have said) literally involves a progressive lowering of successive tones. Any high tone (H) that immediately follows a low tone (L) is automatically flattened or lowered slightly in pitch, relative to any preceding high tones. This process may occur repeatedly depending on the length of the sequence. Let us take a sequence HLHLHLH (HL…). The first H will be fully high, the second H will be a little lower than the first, the third a little lower than the second, and so on progressively until the last HL sequence in the sentence. The interval involved will tend to be constant in a given context and register (overall pitch of voice chosen by speaker) but will vary from speaker to speaker. All is relative, of course, so that at the end of such a sequence, or *tone group*, H tones may actually be realized on a pitch that is lower than the L tones at the beginning of the sequence:

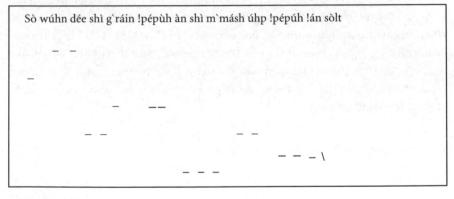

Figure 4.   Pitch diagram

(4)   Àn hé wàs ál!só ábóut tó !gó tó !CéeBéeCèe.
      (Bajan: Barbados, LH/40/99)
      'And he was also about to go to CBC.'

(5)   Hì músí ∧dín !éebĺ tù gèt-úp. (Bajan: Barbados, BS/40/99)
      'He must have not been able to get-up.'

(6)   Sò wúhn dée shì gŕáin !pépùh àn shì m̀másh úhp !pépúh !án sòlt.
      (Trinidadian: Dulcie C./UKB/10/73).
      'So one day she ground pepper and she pounded pepper and salt.'

(7)   Óolà dèm gèt só fràitń á !h´òu wáià dí mùhdáz mék!ín dì chíljrén stèe-òut
      só lèet. (Trinidadian: Dulcie C./UKB/10/73)
      'All of them are astonished at the way the mothers let the children stay out
      so late.'

High tones following low tones are automatically lowered in examples such as these, where downdrift is applied. Highs following highs are not automatically lowered — although they may be, as we shall see. We find instances in Bajan where the expected downdrift is *not* applied:

(8) Ìt lúk tù míi làik **dát** *wùhz wà* **hápnín** *wì dì* **déez, náù.** (Bajan: Barbados, BS/40/99) 'It looks to me like that is what is happening with the days now.'

Figure 5. Pitch diagram

Downdrift is normal in statements, as we have seen. It is natural to ask why downdrift is suspended here, but no definite answer can be given at this point. Possibly it is because of the affect being expressed here, something like mild surprise and complicity ("strange, isn't it?..."), but this question would bear further investigation. The rhythm is also notable, for being almost stress-timed, in that the short unstressed low toned syllables, in italics above, are at least twice as fast in delivery as the more stressed high toned syllables, indicated in bold type. However it is important to note that Guyanese and (to a lesser extent perhaps) Jamaican can also have this kind of change of rhythm (cf. Kelly and Local 1981). This phenomenon is something which is not well-understood at this point, but it seems to be based in the first place on the interaction of syllable length (phonemic in these three varieties) with word stress. Notice that the distinction between syllable- and stress-timing has proved to be one that eludes non-impressionistic definition (cf. Roach 1981).

These are complex issues that are not well-understood, and, in any case, go beyond the scope of this article. Let us limit ourselves here to observing that Caribbean Englishes would appear to exploit the range between different types of timing. At all events, there may be a higher-level organizational system for the prosodic level (timing and rhythm) which can handle or "take in" the apparent changes in timing. This indeed seems to be the idea behind the proposal put forward by Kelly and Local (1981) that Anglophone Caribbean creoles are neither simply syllable-timed nor stress-timed, but rather *pulse* timed. The pulse-timing concept can be explained briefly as follows: the "music" of a given stretch of speech will have a tempo that can be described as so many pulses or beats per minute (i.e. running at an even rate). Some of these pulses are, at any one point, selected by the speaker while others are not. This notion neatly allows for the micro-changes in rhythm or apparent changes in tempo.

3.4   Downstepping contours after peaks

In both direct and indirect Wh-questions (and relative clauses) there are additional modifications, in that the descending contour achieved by downdrift is further modified by a *downstepping* or descending terraced pattern. Some examples will make this clearer.

(9)   Whìch Chàrles yóu !talking ábòut? (Trinidadian: EF/TT/92)

(10)   Sò whát !háppén ìs Í hèard ít mýsèlf. (Bajan: Barbados, LH/40/99)

(11)   Yù núo ^wé ^mí á !táak bòut. (British JC: Pauline/UKD/21/83)
       "You know what I'm talking about")

In these sequences there is a descending stepping contour after a peak earlier in the sentence. The symbol ! marks downstepped high tones. Such downstepped highs originate from underlying lows. What are L tones underlyingly are raised to the level of the following H, in effect "filled in," to form a downstep relative to previous high. Thus (specifically in Wh-questions) the semicategorical rule is HLH(LH) > H!HH(!HH) in the context Wh /___ where !H marks the downstepped high after the initial Wh- word on a high tone. As the rule indicates, this downstepping pattern begins with the first (underlying) L following the Wh-word. Its extension to words later in the utterance may actually depend on the syntax.

3.5   Final cadence and final rise

Final cadence [FLC], as we have seen, cuts in at the end of a tone sequence to give the final rounding down with a drop in pitch to on or near baseline (the lower limit of the pitch range). In tonal terms the last two syllables are affected: the penultimate tone, if low, becomes downstepped high, and the final syllable is realized as a low, whether it is lexically low or not. Here are examples from Bajan, Jamaican, and AAVE:

(12)   Wél ^éf À lív À wùd láik tù. Éf À lív À wùd láik tù [tones prior to application of FLC: *láik tú*] (Bajan: BS/40/99)
       "Well, if I live, I would like to. If I live I would like to."

(13) Thát shóuldñ bè á !próblèm. [tones prior to application of FLC: *próblèm* - unchanged]. (Trinidadian: EF/TT/92)
"That shouldn't be a problem."

(14) Ì jús hòllér thát hòllér ^yóu !héar mé ùh hóllér àn hé dùh ánswér mè wá::y òvér !yóndèr. [tones prior to FLC: *yòndér*].
(AAVE, Ex slave Bob Ledbetter, AFS/ESR/*EBE* 47, Louisiana 1940.)
"I'd just holler that field holler you heard me hollering, and he would answer me, wa-a-ay over there."

We can now look at the typical Bajan and Guyanese final rise, the tell-tale intonational trait of these speech varieties, in greater detail. At word level this is the non-application of final cadence. The words in question have the tones they would have before the application of the final cadence rule. High stays high, downstepped high stays downstepped and low remains low:

(15) Yù gát màrìd-mán táim **àn fàin táim**. Fàin táim bétá !dán màrìd mán tàim.
(Georgetown Guyana, 1994. Market stallholder, recorded by hand).[8]

This rise has the following variant in Bajan, where the final high is extended and the tone dips slightly. This can be analyzed as a high followed by downstepped high tone extension: that is, *é!é(é)*, where *é* represents the tone on the nucleus and *!é(é)* represent tones on the extension. There is no final drop to baseline, just a slight dip or scoop.

(16) Yù síi àutsáid? ìt óol náis àn ti!íng. (British Bajan: J./UKR/VE/75).

Final low tone becomes level (that is, with no fall to baseline) and may be transcribed as a downstepped high tone:

(17) Oo, Ai gon kuk shi up som ^gúd kùkú !mán. [tones prior to rule application: *kùkú mán*] (British Bajan: J/UKR/VE/75)
"Oh, I'm going to cook some good coucou [vegetable and cornmeal balls] for her, man"

(18) Ài nóo, bùt... Ái kún hèlp ít !mán... [tones prior to rule application: *ít màn*]
(British Bajan: J/UKR/VE/75)
"I know but...I couldn't help it, man".

(19) Ìt lúk !rán!stíd. (British Bajan: B/UKL/10/75)
"It [your hair] looks "rancid" [i.e. a mess]."

Bajan and Guyanese speakers use final cadence, although less frequently than in other Caribbean varieties. Accordingly, the rise and its different variants can be seen as stylistic options. The Bajan example of final cadence in (12) seems to be associated with greater emphasis or finality: *Wél ^éf À lív À wùd líke tù. Éf À lív À wùd líke tù* (second *tú* falls to baseline).

In the sports commentator's Bajan, the rise occurs in less than half the available sites (that is, tone-group final in statements). Factors here may include the narrative style he employs as much as his educated middle class background. Example (4) above shows a classical instance of downdrift ending in final cadence with *no* Bajan rise: Ân hé wàs ál!só ábóut tó !gó tó !CéeBéeCèe (Bajan: Barbados, LH/40/99).

Other Eastern Caribbean speakers, including some Trinidadians like Dulcie C., would seem not to have this final rise in statements. In any case, it should be remembered that in all the Creoles considered in this chapter, including Bajan and Guyanese, speakers consistently have final cadence in Wh-questions. Here are Trinidadian examples with final cadence in statements:

(20)   So shi wuhz evuh so angri bikuhz dì súkúnyá [soucouyen[9]] !súhkín èvrì béebí !thát shí hàv. (Trinidadian: EF/TT/92).
"So she was ever so angry because the vampire woman was blood-sucking every baby that she had."

(21)   Lídĺ !pígíz, lídĺ !pígíz ópń !yó dòo — àn sháutín !'ìt! (Trinidadian: Dulcie C./ UKB/10/73)
"Little piggies, little piggies, open your door — and he was shouting it."

3.6   High rise intonation

As in many languages in both Europe and West Africa, total or "yes-no" questions in Bajan, Guyanese and Trinidadian, are indicated by a level or upturning intonational contour. This is achieved by eliminating downdrift (the overall downward contour of the sentence; see below) raising the overall pitch register (to varying degrees, depending on the affect) and introducing an upturn (an upstepped high tone) on the final H tone of the sequence. Any following L will be realized as an upstepped H.

(22)   Yù síi òutsáid? / _ – – _ ^ – – / (British Bajan: J/UKR/VE/75)
"Do you see outside?"

(23)   Yù wén tù Lánd^n? / _ – _ – – ^ – – / (British Bajan: J/UKL/10/75)
"Did you go to London?"

3.7 Emphasis

Emphasis is handled in tone languages and post-tone languages[10] in a variety of ways that differ predictably from what we find in purely intonational languages like mainstream English. The typical resources of English such as placing nuclear stress on the focused and potentially contrasted item, e.g., *John* will pay for that (not you), are in effect ruled out. Quite simply, pitch is not available to be used to stress or emphasize because it is tied to specific syllables for lexical and syntactic reasons. Instead, other strategies are used. One strategy we look at in the next section is fronting of the focused or emphasized item, a device common in African languages as well as in Atlantic Creoles. Another device is *en bloc* shifting to a higher pitch register, including falsetto (common in Caribbean creole and AAVE heightened styles). Yet another device is lengthening, which may be applied to the tone-bearing vowel (or mora), as in:

(24) …àn hé dùh ánswér mè **wá::y** òvér !yóndèr. (AAVE, Ex-slave Bob
       Ledbetter, AFS/ESR/*EBE* 47 Texas1940)
       "…and he would answer me, far away over there."

This lengthening device may also be applied to consonants in certain Caribbean Creoles, and there are many examples from Jamaican and Trinidadian. Word-initial fricatives, sonorants, continuants, and even voiced plosives become geminate or double consonants. The onset is treated as a prefix and assigned low tone: gr̀áin !pépúh, m̀másh úp !pépúh ("*grind* pepper", "*pound* pepper") (Trinidadian: Dulcie C./ UKB/10/73).

3.8 Grammatical tone

3.8.1 *Focus marking*
David Lawton raised a crucially important point (p.c., 1985) which he never mentioned in any published article. Jamaican Creole consistently makes a tonally marked distinction between topic and focus in the formal subject of the sentence. The focus is marked with high tones which replace the lexical tones of the focused item, whereas the topic retains the lexical tones unaltered. So for example in my British Jamaican data, a Rasta says: "*dís* ∧*DÁATÀ bén´!á rìid dí !b´áib`l*" ("this young woman [+Focus] was reading the Bible") (see Sutcliffe 1992: 74). One definition of focus is "special prominence which is given to some element in a sentence to mark it as expressing the most important new information or to contrast it with something else" (Trask 1997). Notice that

the distinction between topic and focus includes the distinction between old and new information, except that the focus selects the most important or contrastive new information. Another point is that in WH-questions the focus regularly falls on the question word (*who*, *where*, *what*, *why*, etc.), which *substitutes* for new information. This distinction was followed up in Sutcliffe (1992) where it was seen as a key to understanding the overall Jamaican tonal system from both synchronic and historical points of view. The following example from basilectal Jamaican will make this clearer: after the low-toned focus markers *à* (or *ìz*) and *nò*, the focused item, whether noun or subject pronoun, takes a high tone replacive:

(25) Nò TÚOS yú !á dù. (British Jamaican: M/UKB/15/75)
"*toast* is what you were making (to be sure!)."

In such examples, low-toned *no* before high tone is taken to be emphatic assertion rather than negation. We find comparable examples from Bajan, showing basically the same pattern. That is, there is high-toned focus after low-toned *tìz* and *sò* focus markers:

(26) Lídí !bóy hía !tel míi tìz FRÁID ʌÍ (Bajan: BS/40/99)
("the little boy, here, told me it was *Friday*" — not Thursday).

(27) Sò THÁT !ís !whé're Í tòok òvér (Bajan: LH/40/99)
("So *that* is where I took over").

We find the same pattern in Trinidadian. In the following instance, the focused item has high tone, as before, but there is no prefixed focus particle or marker:

(28) Dòon pík mì, ʌMÁMÍ !pláan mí hìa. (Trinidadian: Dulcie C./ UKB/10/73)
"Don't pick me, (it was) Mammy (who) planted me here."

In this case, as in the others, the focus ʌ *Mámí* is marked by high tones (marked extra high by the prefixed ʌ up-arrow) and followed by downstep.

There is a significant instance of tonally marked focus-shift altering the meaning of a sentence noted in Jamaican (Roberts 1988: 287). Roberts shows that *aal* can have two distinct readings in Jamaican, even when inserted into apparently the same linguistic frame. It can mean "even" (adverb, as in "even the bad times are good"), or alternatively, it can mean "all" or "the total quantity (of)" (adjective, as in mainstream English). When *aal* means "even", it precedes and introduces the focus of the sentence, whereas in the other case it is actually *in* the focus, marked by high tone replacives (high tones replace lexical tones). We have supporting examples of this in our Eastern Caribbean data in Trinidadian:

(29)   Òol dì SÚKÚNYÁ, !wén shí tékóut húh skín àn shì ẁwént-òut...
       FOCUS
       (Trinidadian: Dulcie C./UKB/10/73)
       "So even the *soucouyen* [vampire woman], when she took off her skin and went out..."

Compare this pattern with the contrasting pattern in example (9) above, reproduced here for convenience:

(30)   ÓOLÁ dèm get so fraitn at hou waia di mudaz mekin di chiljren stee out
       FOCUS
       so leet.
       (Trinidadian: Dulcie C./UKB/10/73)
       "All of them were so amazed at the way mothers let their children stay out so late."

3.8.2. *Grammatical downstep*

In Bajan, Guyanese, and Trinidadian, downstep in fact plays a major role in the marking of syntactic relations in the system. As well as marking sentence types as shown above, it also has at least three other functions of this sort. In the first place, downstep occurs between verb and the NP complement of the verb. In example (24), above, there are two instances: *gřínd !péppér* and *m̀másh úp !péppér*

Secondly, downstep occurs in relative constructions; that is, relative clauses are introduced by a downstepped H tone. This downstep immediately follows the H on the (focused) subject of the relative clause in question:

(31)   **Wá !háppen** ìs Í hèard ìt mýsèlf. (Bajan: LH/40/99)
       what DH-REL happen...
       "What happened is that I heard it myself."

(32)   ...dì súkúnyá !súhkín èvrì béebí !**thát shí hàv.** (Trinidadian: Dulcie C./UKB/10/73)
       ...the soucouyen sucking every baby DH-REL she have.
       "... the vampire woman was sucking every baby she [the mother] had."

We have already seen that downstepped H (!H) is obligatory in Wh-questions after the H of the (focused) interrogative pronoun. What we can now say is that the latter (Wh-questions introduced by such interrogative pronouns) constitute a particular instance of relativization. In fact, in Caribbean Creoles generally, and in many of the West African languages that provided their substratum, *any* fronted and focused word, whether a Wh-Question word or not, is followed by implicit or explicit relativization.

In Jamaican, for example we have: á hít !mí !díil ínà ("*that* is what I relate to") (British Jamaican: Everton, Dudley/DS. England, 1983). Here, as before, we see the pattern of H on the focus (*hít*), followed by downstep on the implicitly relativized item. Front focus is inherently associated with relativization not only in Caribbean and other Atlantic Creoles but in characteristic substratum African languages such as Yoruba (Rowlands 1969: 90), Hausa (Kraft and Kirk-Greene 1973: 105–106), Igbo (Welmers 1973: 147), kiKongo (Hazel Carter, p.c.). Interestingly enough, Igbo, one of the more important of the substratum languages, actually employs downstep to mark (at least some) relativization,[11] as we see in the following examples (Welmers 1973: 143):

(33) a. ònyé   wépùtàrà   yà
          person bring-out-PAST it
          "the person brought it out."

      b. ònyé !   wépùtárá   !ya
          person DH-REL bring-out-PAST it
          "the person who brought it out."

The high-toned continuative particle *ná* is downstepped before the verb to express relativization, producing a pattern apparently identical to the one we are describing for Caribbean Creoles (Welmers 1973: 145):

(34) a. ònyé   nà   èrí !rí
          person CONT eat food
          "The person is/was eating."

      b. ònyé !ná   èrí !rí
          person DH-REL CONT eat food
          "The person who is/was eating."

The last function of grammatical downstep we will mention here is in NP between the attributive adjective and the noun it qualifies and similarly between ADJ (or ADV) and ADJ in a string.

(35) Dì lídí !bói wén pík ùh pépùh
      "The little boy went to pick a pepper.")
      (Trinidadian: Dulcie C./ UKB/10/73).

Carter (1987) gives a series of examples from the speech of academic Dennis Craig and other Guyanese speakers including the polysyllabic *distríbútíve !meáning, morphológícál !prócesses*. In Bajan, we similarly find *fírs !time, t'rée !Súndáy mornings, twó !children, tóo !Báján'y, líd'l !bóy hére*. In all instances it will be seen that the adjective + noun strings consist of lexical tones on modifier (adjective) followed by downstepped high on the head noun. Recall that by lexical tones we mean the inherent or "dictionary entry" tones unaltered by grammatical tone rules. As we shall see in the next section this tonal pattern contrasts with the one used for compound nouns in Guyanese and Bajan.

3.8.3 *Compounds and non-compounds*
Compounding is an extensively used device in Caribbean Creoles and Atlantic Creoles generally. We already have a body of evidence in the literature to support the idea that such NP structures in Creoles are marked by tonal morphology. For example, Sylvain (1936: 42) looked at the structures of Haitian Creole and their similarities on the one hand to spoken varieties of French, and on the other to the Kwa language Ewe (Ewe-Fon, spoken in Ghana, Benin, and Dahomey). In the course of this comparison, she noted the use of contrastive pitch patterns in certain word collocations in Haitian Creole. For instance, *yún màmàn shá* / − _ _ − / "a mother cat" (compound noun) had a different suprasegmental pattern from the otherwise homophonous *yún mámá'n shá* / − - \ -/ "an enormous cat." Morgan Dalphinis (p.c.) notes this same distinction in the French Creole of St. Lucia, but in his analysis he treats it as a phenomenon of stress (or stress accent).

DeCamp (1960) noticed basically the same minimal pair for Jamaican, differentiated by pitch or tone alone. He observed that the compound word for "foal" (literally child-horse) had the pattern *pìknì háas,* / _ _ − − / whereas the non-compound form *píkní hàas* (meaning 'child's horse') had the pattern / − − _ _ /. The compound versus non-compound pattern discussed here is found in the Eastern Caribbean and is very clear in Guyanese. For example, *fìne thýme, màrrìed-mán th'yme, bàd-hánd* ('injured arm or hand') and *bàd-fóod* ('food to which a potion has been added') are compounds, tonally marked as such by the low tone replacives (lowering of high tone to low) on the mora(s) of the first morpheme (the morpheme before the head noun). Accordingly, the lexical tones of the simplex form of the words (i.e. before compounding) would be *bád, hán(d)* and so on. Similarly, the compound *bàd-fóod* would be *bád !fóod* / − _ / if used as uncompounded adjective-plus-noun collocation meaning 'spoiled food.' We refer to this as the initial low tone [ILT] rule.

Allsopp (1996: 353) reveals the following examples: *lòng-tíme* (LH) the compound adjective meaning 'of days gone by,' 'old-fashioned,' versus *lóng-!time* (H !H or HL) the adjective phrase meaning 'a long time ago,' 'some time ago.' Carter (1987) gives a series of tonally marked compounding in Guyanese, including *bàllòt-páper, sèa-wáter, flòor-mánager*. In our Bajan data, we have *lòve-bírd, yòuth méeting, sùntán, brèdfrúit*; and the following, which are probably also compounds: *mìstèr Jàmes Ólívér, Tònì Báss, Pètèr Sháw, tòok-óvér, còme-dówn*.

When we turn to our Trinidadian data (from Dulcie C.) we find *only* the downstepping variant, and she has no initial lows in compounds at all. The explanation may be that in Dulcie's grammar, sequences like *péppér !trée* ('pepper plant'), *púppúh !trèè* ('pawpaw tree'), *bróthér !bróther* ('brother's brother') and *wífe !múddúh* ('wife's mother'), are actually being treated not as compounds but rather as adjective-plus-noun (modifier + head) collocations where, of course, the grammatical downstep pattern would be expected.[12] It is possible that the apparent variation noted here may be lexically predictable, although more information is needed to be sure. In any case, we need to take account of the fact that some words behave exceptionally in compounding. David Lawton (1963) drew attention to the fact that in Jamaican some words had unalterable tones under compounding and thus our ILT Compound Rule did not apply. For example, *pàasń* 'parson' remains unaltered in compounds such as *pàasń bróun* (type of yam), and *jàkás* ('jackass') remains the same in a number of noun-noun compounds. Allsopp (1996) indicates very much the same kind of pattern: the usual compound pattern has ILT, but in some specific lexical instances it does not. That is, some first elements of compounds remain unaltered. Hence *lòng-táim* ('long ago'), *bàd-hánd* ('injured arm'), *fàlà-fáshán* ('imitate'), *còw-támbrín* ('wild tamarind') are all altered (ILT applies), but, exceptionally, *fràitén-fràidí*[13] ('timorous person') is unaltered (ILT not applied).

A mention of the African background to this may also be apposite here. Carter is rightly cautious about attributing African origins. However, it is worth noting that noun compounding (a common feature in English, e.g. *bookcase, goldsmith, rainbow, firebrand*, etc.) is also used very extensively in many West African languages and typically involves tone changes. So Bini (Nigeria) for instance, combines *àmè* ("water") and *èhý* ('pepper') to form *àmé èhý* ('pepper water') and *òwè* ('leg') and *òsà* ('chimpanzee') to form *òwé òsà* ('chimpanzee's leg'). Notice that there are tone changes in each case. Generally in African linguistics (since Welmers 1973) this compounding (whether or not it involves tone changes) is referred to as the associative construction. It is given this distinctive label because it accounts for not only modifier + noun collocations but also possessive constructions like the 'chimpanzee's leg' example just given. Associative or compounding constructions are attested for a long list of African languages including Twi, Igbo, Kpele (Welmers 1973); Efik (Welmers 1968); Ewe (Westermann 1930); Yoruba (Rowlands 1969); Hausa (Kraft and Kirk-Greene 1973); Bini (Amayo 1976); Ibibio (Urua 1995); Etsako (Elimelech 1978); Yekhee (Elugbe 1989); Isoko (Donwa 1982); and Emai (Egbokhare 1990).

In view of the variation we have mentioned between downstepping and initial low tone replacement [ILT] it is significant that we find cross-linguistic variation on this score in the most important African substratum languages. For example, Igbo has grammatical downstep in associative constructions: *úló !ányí* ('our house') (Welmers 1973: 147) while on the other hand Yoruba, Kpelle[14] and Twi have the ILT pattern (Rowlands 1969: 100, Welmers 1973: 147). For example, Twi has *ǹkàtí* ('peanuts') + *ǹkwán* ('soup') forming the compound *ǹkàtì-ǹkwán*, and *dénkyém* ('crocodile') + *òbú* forming the compound *dènkyèm-bú* ('diamond'), thus showing ILT replacives on the modifier with unchanged tones on the head noun, exactly as in the most common Caribbean Creole pattern.

3.8.4 *Reduplicated adjectives with intensive or distributive force*

Sylvain (1936: 33) also noticed an interesting tone distinction in Haitian Creole, in the reduplication of adjectives. She noted that a reduplicated form like *píké-pìkè* "very sharp," which she represented as / – – _ _ / had a tonal shape that conveyed intensity, while a contrasting pattern *pí`kè-píké* that she indicated as / \ _ – – / conveyed an attenuated or diffuse meaning "rather sharp" or "sharp here and there." This pattern ties in well with what we find not only in Guyanese and Bajan in the Eastern Caribbean, but also in Jamaican, including British Jamaican, and indeed in African languages such as Yoruba (Rowlands 1969: 207). Hazel Carter (1987, 1989) drew our attention to these forms in Caribbean varieties and found that the intensive was formed by iteration (unmodified repetition of the simplex form) while the distributive or diffusive had altered tones (ILT applied as in compounding). Further information based on machine analysis will soon be available on these tonal patterns in Jamaican (see Gooden 2001). The closeness of the parallel with Yoruba is particularly striking (see Ola 1995, Akinlabi 1986, Pulleyblank 1986), although we have no information on intensive and distributive/diffusive patterns in other African languages.

Meanwhile we can provide the following rather limited but suggestive comparisons across Western Hemisphere Creoles and African languages in Figure 6. Yoruba data in the table is from Ola (1995); Hausa examples are from Kraft and Kirk-Greene (1973); the situation in Hausa is more complex than shown, however, and Kirk-Greene gives no minimal pairs. Data in the table for Guyanese, Bajan, Jamaican, and Trinidadian are from sources credited above.

	Intensive or Iterative	Distributive or Compound
Guyanese	táll !táll 'very tall'	tàll-táll 'rather tall'
	hóléy!hólèy 'very holey'	hòlèy-hóléy 'rather holey'
Bajan:	níce-!níce 'very nice'	[nìce-níce?]
Trinidadian	láte-!láte 'very late'	[làte-láte?]
Jamaican	líttle-!líttle 'very little'	pàchi-pátchí 'rather patchy'
_		òne-óne 'one by one'
Haitian Creole	píké-pìkè 'very sharp'	pí'kè-píké 'rather sharp'
Yoruba	gbèm-gbè?m 'heavy & soft'	gbèm-gbem 'unevenly soft'
	rògòdò-rògòdò 'round and big'	rògòdò-rogodo* 'unevenly round'
Hausa	mázá-mázá (>mázá)	tsàllé-tsàllé (>tsálléé)
	'very quickly'	'various types of jump'

Figure 6.   Intensive and distributive reduplicated adjectives
* unmarked vowels have midtone

Note that there is no entry in the table for AAVE. The fact is that the pitch marking of compounds in AAVE has not been studied in any detail, let alone reduplication to express intensive and distributive force. Looking at nineteenth century AAVE data we find such compounds as *péach !órchárd, péach !órchárd !trée, slóppín !róom* (Laura Smalley; Bailey et al. 1991: 66, 66, 63), *frittér !tree, grócerý !stóre* (Charlie Smith; Bailey et al. 1991: 109, 111), *níggér!trádér, cáb´le!cár* (Hughes; Bailey et al. 1991: 33, 37).

4.   Conclusions

Over the course of this article the evidence we have looked at suggests that Bajan and other Eastern Caribbean English-derived speech varieties have specific, distinctive suprasegmental patterns that can be transcribed and described in terms of a tonal system. Tonal notation captures their characteristic pitch patterns, and provides a key to their systematized study.

Nonetheless, the Eastern Caribbean varieties described here arose out of seventeenth-century contact between African languages on the one hand and non-tonal varieties of regional English on the other. As a result, their putative tonal patterns (i.e., the pitch patterns here described in tonal terms) can be viewed as closely reflecting or *shadowing* the prosodic patterns of British Isles English varieties. Compare the way English loan words in African languages are assigned tones but at the same time reflect the prosodic pattern of the original non-tonal word. We have already looked at examples like Yoruba *sìgá* 'cigarette,' *Sátidé* 'Saturday'; Hausa has *súkàr* 'sugar' *sákándàrè* 'secondary school' to give only a few examples. In Caribbean English Creoles, English-derived words constitute more than 90% of the lexis, and so are not usually regarded as loans. Even so, the process is essentially the same, with just two provisos. Firstly, as we have seen, the same English word (or cognate) may have two lexical tone patterns in Eastern Caribbean varieties like Bajan and Guyanese. Thus, tonal processes are actively part of the resources of the language. The second proviso is that shadowing (copying with reinterpretation) of English prosodic patterns extends to the phrase level, as we have said, so that varieties of English sentence intonation are similarly copied and reinterpreted. Even the Bajan or Guyanese Rise that we have commented on as so typical may well be modeled on the so-called Celtic rise of Cornish English and other British Englishes. The Celtic Rise (a high rise on a non-question) is an intonational feature of many areas of the British Isles where the Celtic languages spoken *in situ* or brought to the cities by nineteenth century migrants left their intonation as a lingering substratum feature (see Cruttendon 1986).

In any case, we have to recognize that the analysis of Eastern Caribbean suprasegmentals presented here is the result of working from this researcher's viewpoint and, of course, there are others. As Sutcliffe (1994) and Bailey et al. (1991) point out, the observer's effect on data can never be removed. Working from a more Anglicist viewpoint (or one interpreting the system in a non-tonal way) would necessarily produce different results. The interesting thing is that this different approach might, if not too narrowly Anglicist, succeed in revealing the other side of the diachronic picture. By that I mean the process by which the first native English speakers in Barbados became actively involved in a (*non*-tonal) reinterpretation of African (*tonal*) reinterpretations of native (*non*-tonal) English. This suggests a series of dynamic reinterpretations.

There is certainly good evidence that African linguistic reinterpretation was a powerful force in the negotiation of linguistic form-function during relevant formation periods for each respective English-derived system.[15] Apart from the very general fact that the resultant suprasegmental systems yield to tonal analysis, there are also the specific parallels between particular features in

West African languages on one hand and Caribbean Creoles (and other Atlantic Creoles) on the other. Languages in both groups have tonal relative markers introducing relative clauses that are also inserted after focused Wh-words and other front-focused items; both have tonal marking of compounds, and in some West African languages, there is the same kind of low-tone replacive in such compounds. Yoruba in particular has the same tonal distinction between intensives versus distributives as found in Caribbean Creoles. Even the *sísta* v. *sistá* series in Bajan and Guyanese has a small but suggestive parallel in Yoruba where there is at least one such pair: *bàbá* (HL) 'father' versus *baba* (MM) 'senior, master.' Yoruba is often used in comparisons with Caribbean Creoles, as a representative of the old Eastern Kwa division of West African languages. The possibility of its actually being involved in the seventeenth century period of creole formation tends to be dismissed, since Yoruba people were not present in the Americas in significant numbers until the nineteenth century. Notwithstanding, it is possible that we have an unexplored connection here between Yoruba or a language very much like it (a transplanted variety, or perhaps a second language version of Yoruba) and the incipient pidgin-creoles that were possibly transported to the Caribbean.

It should be emphasized, of course, that we have only been able to look at a limited number of Eastern Caribbean varieties within the scope of this article. For comparative reasons we have also looked briefly at Western Caribbean and North American varieties and their equivalent features. What this evidence suggests is that the Eastern Caribbean Creoles like Bajan and Guyanese are the most tonal of all the Creoles in the Americas other than Saramaccan, Ndyuka and adjoining varieties in the Suriname region. Bajan can be considered distinctive within the Eastern Caribbean group. Indeed it is more distinctive than we have been able to bring out here. For example, one characteristic feature of Bajan tonal juncture that should be looked at in the future is the phonetic impression it gives of a three-tone system. We have seen, too, that Trinidadian suprasegmental phonology is different from both Bajan and Guyanese in certain respects. The differences we have noted here are the use of downstepping and the consistent application of final cadence rather than final rise.

Even limiting ourselves to these three Eastern Caribbean varieties it is evident that considerably more work remains to be done if we are to have a representative and robust description of their suprasegmentals. Ideally, we need to know much more about details of prosody, syllable-timing versus stress-timing (and perhaps other types of timing), varieties of cadence and other partly or wholly intonational features. A closely linked consideration, since it neatly bridges tonality and intonation, is the necessary introduction of tone group rules, associated with syntactic units within the sentence, as discussed by Devonish (1989: 110) and Carter (1987: 36). Additionally, we need to go beyond the type of description given here and apply other powerful explanatory approaches, and this process is already underway (see Ham 1999; Holder 1998, 1999). Finally, the question of modeling creole genesis by combining "opposing" researcher approaches, as raised above, is an intriguing one that could well bear investigation in the future. The practical logistics involved in doing this are daunting, but from a theoretical standpoint Le Page's notion of focusing and diffusion, and acts of identity (Le Page 1975) surely would provide a promising point of departure.

Notes

1. The reverse is also possible in Caribbean creoles. Thus in Jamaican, *mì dí-dè* with stress on *dè* can only mean, "I was there" (I PAST locative-COP). If the same sequence is used with the same pitch pattern but with stress shifted back to *di*, *mì dí-dè*, the phrase becomes untensed, as in *mí wàan fí dí-dè* "I want to be there". Where *dí* is stressed it cannot be the past marker clitic ("did") since clitics are unstressed, and has to be interpreted as an allomorph of the locative copula *de*.

2. The concept of Founder speakers and the Founder Principle is from Mufwene (1996) from an original proposal in biology by Hampton Carson; see also Sutcliffe and Wright 2001.

3. This data was recorded by hand on the spot. Pitch patterns of *fine-thyme* and *married-man thyme* checked against Allsopp 1996, where the latter is entered as *married-man pork* (pitch-pattern: 1.1.2.1; that is, LLHL).

4. British English may be losing the physical distinction between long and short vowels, too, particularly in southern England. Note that in the Anglophone Caribbean, Grenadian and other varieties that have been influenced by French Creoles have only short vowels.

5. Funded by a grant from the Economic and Social Science Research Council of Great Britain, for which I would like to express my thanks.

6. At least one "tone" per lexical word is specified (by the lexicon). Remaining (unspecified) syllables are assigned pitch by later rules.

7. Not all tone languages interpret European language stressed syllables as high tone, especially in the case of three-tone systems. In Yoruba, some English stressed syllables become mid tones (Devonish 1989).

8. Recorded by hand on the spot. See footnote 3.

9. Dulcie consistently says *sukunya* and not *soucouyen*. Interestingly, the Sininke language (West Africa) has *sukunya* meaning 'witch' or 'sorcerer' (Aub-Buscher 1989: 8).

10. By "post-tonal" I mean a language that was once a tone language earlier in its history, but now has evolved in the direction of a non-tonal model such as mainstream English. The tonal features will have become either reinterpreted as intonation or perhaps camouflaged as such.

11. Downstep is used in relative clauses in Igbo after the head, where the head is the subject of the relative clause. When it is the object, as in *the man whom I saw*, other rules apply (Welmers 1973: 145).

12. Similarly, there is some downstepping in compounds in what appears to be a possible English-derived creole that has survived in the Mississippi Delta, though I only have data from a single speaker in the form of a recording made by McClung (1997; kindly supplied to me by John McWhorter). Here we find, for example, *dáy-!cléan* ("dawn", "first light"), *Tíi-!tíi* (name) and *Túu-!túu* (name). But there is also the (compound?) word *nàmà-yámá*, which shows the initial low tone rule: *tɔrn-af di dam ting, ít tèk mì nàmà-yámá.* ("Turn off [the tape recorder], it takes/will take my *nama-yama!*"). The authenticity of this recording still remains to be established beyond doubt.

13. Both Lawton's and Allsopp's pitch marking is adapted here (Allsopp numbers the pitch levels: *bàd-péoplé* 1.2.2, *còw-támbrín* 1.2.2, *frìghtén-Frìd´y* 1.2.1.2.

14. In Kpelle, the head word comes first so that it is the second word in the compound that has low tone replacive: *tóu* (palm nut) + *wúlo* (oil) → *tóu-wùlo* (palm oil) (Welmers 1973: 134).

15. For example, see Lumsden 1999.

References

Abrahams, Roger D. 1967. "The Shaping of Folklore Traditions in the West Indies." *Journal of Inter-American Studies* 9: 456–480.

———. 1973. "Christmas Mummings on Nevis." *North Carolina Folklore Journal* 1:120–131.

———. 1983. *Man of Words in the West Indies: Performance and the Emergence of Creole Culture.* Baltimore: Johns Hopkins University Press.

Aceto, Michael. 1995. "Variation in a secret creole language of Panama." *Language in Society* 24: 537–60.

———. 1996. "Syntactic innovation in a Caribbean creole: The Bastimentos variety of Panamanian Creole English." *English World-Wide* 17: 43–61.

———. 1998. "A new creole future tense marker emerges in the Panamanian West Indies." *American Speech* 73: 29–43.

———. 1999. "Looking beyond decreolization as an explanatory model of language change in creole-speaking communities." *Journal of Pidgin and Creole Languages* 14: 93–119

———. 2002a. "Going back to the beginning: Describing the (nearly) undocumented Anglophone creoles of the Caribbean." In Glenn G. Gilbert, ed. *Pidgin and Creole Linguistics in the 21st Century.* New York: Peter Lang, 93–118.

———. 2002b. "Barbudan Creole English: Its history and some grammatical features." *English World-Wide* 23: 223–250.

———. fc.a. "Progressive aspectual constructions in regional dialects of English and English-derived Creoles."

———. fc.b. "St. Eustatius Creole English: Why did an English-derived creole emerge in a Dutch colony?"

Akinlabi, Akinbiyi. 1986. "Tonal Underspecification and Yoruba Tone." Unpublished Ph.D. dissertation, University of Ibadan.

———, ed. 1995. *Theoretical Approaches to African Linguistics. Trends in African Linguistics, 1.* Trenton, NJ: African World Press.

Albury, Paul. 1975. *The Story of the Bahamas.* London: Macmillian.

Allen, J. 1994. "Sainte-Lucie: Relexification, Décréolisation, Recréolisation, ou Adlexification?" Unpublished mémoire de D. E. A. des sciences du langage, Université Lumière Lyon II.

Alleyne, Mervyn C. 1961. "Language and society in St. Lucia." *Caribbean Studies* 1:1–10.

———. 1971. "Acculturation and the cultural matrix of creolization." In Dell Hymes, ed. 1971: 169–186.

———. 1980. *Comparative Afro-American: An Historical-Comparative Study of English-Based Afro-American Dialects of the New World.* Ann Arbor, MI: Karoma.

Allsopp, Richard. 1972. "Some suprasegmental features of Caribbean English." In *Papers from the Conference on Creole Languages and Educational Development*. St. Augustine, Trinidad: University of the West Indies, 120–133.

———. 1996. *Dictionary of Caribbean English Usage*. Oxford: Oxford University Press.

Amastae, J. 1979. "Dominican Creole English phonology: An initial sketch." *Anthropological Linguistics* 21: 182–204.

Amayo, M. A. 1976. "A Generative Phonology of Edo (Bini)." Unpublished Ph.D. thesis, University of Ibadan.

———. 1980. "Tone in Nigerian English." In *Papers from the 16th Regional Meeting of the Chicago Linguistics Society*. CLS, University of Chicago, 1–9.

American Colonization Society (ACS), letters to. Series I. Incoming Correspondence, 1819–1917. B. Letters from Liberia, 1833–1917. Containers (volumes) 11, 12, 13. 22 Oct 1860–15 Dec 1866. Unpublished documents held at the Library of Congress, Washington, D. C.

Andersen, Roger. ed. 1981. *New Dimensions in Second Language Acquisition Research*. Rowley, Massachusetts: Newbury House.

———. ed. 1983. *Pidginization and Creolization as Language Acquisition*. Rowley, MA: Newbury House.

Andrews, William L., Frances Smith Foster, and Trudier Harris. 1997. *The Oxford Companion to African American Literature*. New York: Oxford University Press.

Archer, William. 1904. *Real Conversations*. London: W. Heinemann.

Arends, Jacques, Pieter Muysken and Norval Smith, eds. 1995. *Pidgins and Creoles: An Introduction*. Amsterdam, Philadelphia: John Benjamins.

Ash, Sharon. 1996. "Freedom of movement: /uw/ fronting in the Midwest." In Jennifer Arnold, Renée Blake, Brad Davidson, Scott Schwenter, and Julie Solomon, eds. *Sociolinguistic Variation: Data, Theory, and Analysis*. Stanford, CA: CSLI Publications, 3–25.

Ayres, Harry Morgan. 1933. "Bermudian English." *American Speech* 8: 3–10.

Bailey, Beryl L. 1966. *Jamaican Creole Syntax: A Transformational Approach*. Cambridge, England: Cambridge University Press.

Bailey, Guy, Natalie Maynor and Patricia Cukor-Avila. 1991. *The Emergence of Black English: Texts and Commentary*. Amsterdam, Philadelphia: John Benjamins.

Baker, Philip. 2000. "Theories of creolization and the degree and nature of restructuring." In Ingrid Neumann-Holzschuh and Edgar W. Schneider, eds. 2000: 41–63.

———. 1998. "Investigating the Origin and Diffusion of Shared Features among the Atlantic English Creoles." In Philip Baker & Adrienne Bruyn, eds. *St. Kitts and the Atlantic Creoles: The Texts of Samual Augustus Mathews in Perspective*. Westminster Creolistics Series 4. London: University of Westminster Press, 315–364.

——— & Adrienne Bruyn, eds. 1998. *St. Kitts and the Atlantic Creoles: the texts of Samual Augustus Mathews in perspective*. Westminster Creolistics Series 4. London: University of Westminster Press.

Bakhtin, Mikhail. 1981. *The Dialogic Imagination*. Austin: University of Texas Press.

Bakker, Peter and Maarten Mous, eds. 1994. *Mixed Languages*. Amsterdam: IFOTT.

——— and P. Muysken. 1995. "Mixed languages and language intertwining." In Jacques Arends et al., eds. 1995: 41–52.

————, Mark Post, and Hein van der Voort. 1995. "TMA particles and auxiliaries." In Jacques Arends et al., eds. 1995: 247–58.

Barclay, Alexander. 1826. *A Practical View of the Present State of Slavery in the West Indies*. London: Smith Elder.

Barnett, Sheila. 1978–9. "Pitchy patch." *Jamaica Journal* 43: 19–32.

Beckles, Hilary McD. 1986. "From land to sea: Runaway Barbados slaves and servants, 1630–1700." In Gad J. Heuman, ed. *Out of the House of Bondage: Runaways, Resistance, and Marronage in Africa and the New World*. London: Frank Cass, 79–94.

————. 1990a. "A 'riotous and unruly lot:' Irish indentured servants and freemen in the English West Indies, 1644–1713." *The William and Mary Quarterly* 48: 505–522.

————. 1990b. *A History of Barbados: From Amerindian Settlement to Nation-state*. Cambridge: Cambridge University Press.

Benítez-Rojo, Antonio. 1996. *The Repeating Island: The Caribbean and the Postmodern Perspective*. Translated by James E. Maraniss. Durham and London: Duke University Press.

Berglund, David C. 1995. *Shipwrecks of Anguilla 1628–1995*. Basseterre, St. Kitts: The Creole Publishing Company.

Bernstein, Cynthia, Thomas Nunnelly, and Robin Sabino, eds. 1997. *Language Variety in the South Revisited*. Tuscaloosa: University of Alabama Press.

Berry, Jack. (no date). *The Pronunciation of Ewe*. Cambridge: Heffer.

————. (no date). *The Pronunciation of Ga*. Cambridge: Heffer.

Bethel, Patrick. 1995. *Growing up in Cherokee: 1935–1950*. Abaco, Bahamas: Self-published.

Bettelheim, Judith. 1979. "Afro-Jamaican Jonkonnu Festival: Playing the Forces and Operating the Cloth." Unpublished Ph.D. dissertation, Yale University. University Microfilms International.

Bickerton, Derek. 1975. *Dynamics of a Creole Continuum*. Cambridge: Cambridge University Press

————. 1981. *Roots of Language*. Ann Arbor, MI: Karoma.

Bilby, Kenneth M. 1983. "How the 'older heads' talk: a Jamaican Maroon spirit possession language and its relationship to the creoles of Suriname and Sierra Leone." *New West Indian Guide* 57: 37–88.

Black, Ian. 1997. "Britain finds it hard to shake off DTs." *Guardian Weekly*, June 29, 7.

Blackshire-Belay, C. 1993. "Foreign workers' German: Is it a pidgin?" In Francis Byrne and John Holm, eds. *Atlantic Meets Pacific: A Global View of Pidginization and Creolization*. Amsterdam, Philadelphia: John Benjamins, 431–440.

Blake, Renée. 1997. "All o' We is One? Race, Class, and Language in a Barbados Community." Unpublished Ph.D. dissertation, Stanford University.

————. 2000. "Past tense marking in Barbadian Creole English." Paper presented at SPCL (Society for Pidgin and Creole Linguistics) annual meeting, Chicago, Jan. 7–8, 2000.

Boultbee, Paul G. 1991. *Turks and Caicos Islands, Vol. 137*. Oxford and Santa Barbara: Clio Press.

Brana-Shute, R. (with the assistance of Hoefte, R.) 1983. *A Bibliography of Caribbean Migration and Caribbean Immigrant Communities*. Gainesville: Reference and Bibliographic Department, University of Florida Libraries, in cooperation with the Center for Latin American Studies, University of Florida.

Brinkley, Frances Kay. 1978. "An Analysis of the 1750 Carriacou census." *Caribbean Quarterly* 2: 4–60.

Brousseau, Anne-Marie. fc. "The prosodic system of Haitian Creole: the role of transfer and markedness values." In Ingo Plag, ed. fc..

Burrowes, Audrey (in collaboration with Richard Allsopp). 1983. "Barbadian Creole: A note on its social history and structure." In Lawrence Carrington et al., eds. 1983: 38–45.

Burton, Richard D. E. 1997. *Afro-Creole: Power, Opposition, and Play in the Caribbean.* Ithaca: Cornell University Press.

Carr, Andrew T. 1956. "Pierrot Grenade." *Caribbean Quarterly* 4: 281–314.

Carrington, Lawrence. 1969. "Deviations from Standard English in the speech of primary school children in Dominica and St. Lucia: A Preliminary Survey, Parts I and II." *International Review of Applied Linguistics in Language Teaching* 7: 165–184 & 259–281.

————. ed. (in collaboration with Dennis R. Craig and Ramon Todd-Dandaré) 1983. *Studies in Caribbean Language.* St. Augustine, Trinidad: Society for Caribbean Linguistics.

————. 1984. *St. Lucian Creole: A Descriptive Analysis of its Phonology and Morpho-Syntax.* Hamburg: Helmut Buske Verlag.

————. 1992. "Images of creole space." *Journal of Pidgin and Creole Languages* 7: 93–99.

————. 1993. "Creole space — A rich sample of competence?" *Journal of Pidgin and Creole Languages* 8: 227–236.

————, J. Marquez, and P. Aquing. 1976. "Basilect, Mesolect, and Corrective Pressure in the Speech of some Trinidadian Children." Paper presented at the conference of the Society for Caribbean Linguistics, 11–14 August, University of Guyana.

Carter, Hazel. 1987. "Suprasegmentals in Guyanese: Some African comparisons." In Glenn G. Gilbert, ed. 1987: 213–263.

————. 1989. "Three creole pitch systems." In Isabelle Herik, ed. *Papers from the 18th Conference of African Linguistics.* Montreal: University of Quebec at Montreal, April 1987, 27–44.

———— and David Sutcliffe. 1982. "Pitch patterns of a Jamaican speaker." Paper presented to the Conference of the Society for Caribbean Linguistics, Suriname, August 1982.

Carty, Brenda and Colville Petty. 1997. *Anguilla.* London: Macmillan Education Ltd.

Cassidy, Frederic G. 1961. *Jamaica Talk: Three Hundred Years of the English Language in Jamaica.* London: Macmillan.

————. 1980. "The place of Gullah." *American Speech* 55: 3–15.

————. 1986. "Barbadian Creole — Possibility and probability." *American Speech* 61: 195–205.

C. I. A. World Fact Book. 1999. http://cliffie.nosc.mil/~NAWFB/ factbook/ tk-p.html.

Chambers, J. K. and Peter Trudgill. 1998. *Dialectology* (2nd ed.) Cambridge: Cambridge University Press.

Chaudenson, Robert. 2001. *Creolization of Language and Culture.* London: Routledge.

Childs, Becky. 2000. "The role of contact in isolated transplant communities: The case of consonant cluster reduction in the Bahamas." Paper presented at Southeastern Conference on Linguistics 62. Oxford: University of Mississippi.

Christaller, J. G. 1933. *Dictionary of the Asante and Fante language called Tshi* (2nd) *ed.*

Basel: Evangelical Missionary Society.

Christian, Ijanya, ed. 1993. *Dictionary of the Anguillian Language.* The Valley, Anguilla: The Anguillian Printers.

Christie, Pauline. 1968. "A Sociolinguistic Study of Some Dominican Creole Speakers." Unpublished Ph.D. dissertation, University of York.

————. 1982. "Language maintenance and language shift in Dominica." *Caribbean Quarterly* 28: 41–50.

————. 1983. "In search of the boundaries of Caribbean creoles." In Lawrence Carrington et al., eds. 1983: 13–22.

————. 1986. "Evidence for an unsuspected habitual marker in Jamaican." In Manfred Görlach and John Holm, eds. 1987: 183–90.

————. 1987. "Dominica: A sociolinguistic profile." *Working papers in Linguistics.* UWI, Mona: Department of Language, Linguistics and Philosophy, 50–73.

————. 1989. "Questions of standards and intra-regional differences in Caribbean examinations." In Ofelia García and Ricardo Otheguy, eds. 1996: 243–262.

————, ed. 1996. *Caribbean Language Issues Old and New.* Kingston: The Press University of the West Indies.

Collymore, F. A. 1955. *Notes for a Glossary of Words and Phrases of Barbadian Dialect.* Bridgetown: Advocate Company.

Comrie, Bernard. 1976. *Aspect: An Introduction to the Study of Verbal Aspect and Related Problems.* Cambridge: Cambridge University Press.

Cooper, Vincent. 1980. "On the notion of decreolization and St. Kitts Creole personal pronouns." In Richard R. Day, ed. 1980: 39–50.

Craig, Dennis. 1976. "Bidialectal education: Creole and standard in the West Indies." *International Journal of the Sociology of Language* 9: 93–134.

Craton, Michael, and Gail Saunders. 1992. *Islanders in the Stream: A History of the Bahamian People* (2 Vols). Athens: University of Georgia Press.

Crowley, Daniel J. 1956. "The traditional masques of Carnival." *Caribbean Quarterly* 4: 194–223.

Cruttenden, Allen. 1997. *Intonation.* Cambridge: Cambridge University Press.

Dalphinis, M. 1985. *Caribbean and African Languages: Social History, Language, Literature and Education.* London: Karia Press.

David, Christine. 1985. *Folklore of Carriacou.* Wildey, St. Michael, Barbados: Cole Printery Limited.

Day, Richard R. 1980. *Issues in English Creoles: Papers from the 1975 Hawaii Conference.* Heidelburg: Julius Gross Verlag

De La Beche, H. T. 1825. *Notes on the Present Condition of the Negroes in Jamaica.* London.

Dean, Ernest. 1997. *Island Captain: The Autobiography of Mail Boat Captain Ernest Dean of Sandy Point, Abaco, Bahamas.* Decatur, IL: White Sound Press.

DeCamp, David. 1960. "Four Jamaican Creole texts." In R. B. Le Page, ed. *Jamaican Creole* (*Creole Language Studies,* Vol 1). London: Macmillan, 129–139.

————. 1961. "Social and geographical factors in Jamaican dialects." In R. B. Le Page, ed. *Proceedings of the Conference on Creole Language Studies (Creole language studies II)* New York: Macmillan, 61–84.

————. 1971. "Toward a generative analysis of the post-creole continuum." In Dell Hymes, ed. 1971: 349–370.

DeGraff, M. 1993. "A riddle on negation in Haitian." *Probus* 5: 63–93.

————. ed. 1999. *Language Creation and Language Change. Creolization, Diachrony, and Development.* Cambridge, MA: The MIT Press.

Devonish, Hubert. 1986. "The decay of neo-colonial official language policies: The case of the English-lexicon creoles of the Commonwealth Caribbean." In Manfred Görlach and John Holm, eds. 1987: 25–51.

————. 1989. *Talking in Tones: A Study of Tone in Afro-European Creole Languages.* London and Barbados: Karia Press and Caribbean Academic Publications.

Di Pietro, R. J. 1971. "Multilingualism in St. Croix." *American Speech* 43: 127–37.

Dixon, R. M. W. 1997. *The Rise and Fall of Languages.* Cambridge: Cambridge University Press.

Dodge, Steve. 1995. *Abaco: A History of an Out Island and its Cays.* Decatur, IL: White Sound Press.

Donnelly, Janet. 1996. "Basilectal Features of Bahamian Creole English." Paper presented at 11th Biennial Conference of the Society for Caribbean Linguistics, St. Maarten.

Donwa, S. O. 1982. "The sound system of Isoko." Unpublished Ph.D. thesis, University of Ibadan.

Dookhan, Isaac. 1994. *A History of the Virgin Islands of the United States.* Jamaica: Canoe Press.

Dubois, Sylvie and Barbara M. Horvath. 1998. "From accent to marker in Cajun English: A study of dialect formation in progress." *English World-Wide* 19: 161–188.

Dunn, Richard. 1969. "The Barbados census of 1680: Profile of the richest colony in English America." *William and Mary Quarterly* 26: 3–30.

Edwards, John. 1994. *Multilingualism.* London: Routledge.

Egbokhare F. 1990. "A phonology of Emai." Unpublished Ph.D. thesis, University of Ibadan.

Elimelech, Baruch. 1978. *A Tonal Grammar of Etsako.* Berkeley: University of California Press.

Elugbe, Ben O. 1989. *Comparative Edoid: Phonology and Lexicon.* Port Harcourt: University of Port Harcourt Press.

Elworthy, Frederic. 1879. "The grammar of the dialect of West Somerset." *Transactions of the Philological Society 1877–88–89*, 143–256.

Farquhar, Bernadette. 1974. "A Grammar of Antiguan Creole." Unpublished Ph.D. thesis, Cornell University.

Fase, W., K. Jaspaert and S. Kroon. 1992. "Maintenance and Loss of Minority Languages: Introductory Remarks." In W. Fase et al. eds. *Maintenance and Loss of Minority Languages.* Amsterdam, Philadelphia: John Benjamins, 3–14.

Fasold, Ralph W. 1972. *Tense Marking in Black English: A Linguistic and Social Analysis.* Washington, D.C: Center for Applied Linguistics

Faul, Michelle. 1996. "Turks and Caicos Islands coping with Haitian influx." *The Los Angeles Times*, Aug. 4, 24.

Fayer, Joan M. 1999. "Neagar Business: A Christmas Folk Performance in Nevis." Paper presented at the conference The Islands in Between: Language, Literature, and History of the Eastern Caribbean, Hillsborough, Carriacou.

———. 2000. "African Influences on the Carriacou Shakespeare *Mas'*." Paper presented at the Twelfth Triennial Symposium on African Art, St Thomas, U. S. Virgin Islands.

——— and Joan F. McMurray. 1994. "Shakespeare in Carriacou." *Caribbean Studies* 27: 224–249.

——— and Joan F. McMurray. 1999. "The Carriacou *Mas'* as `syncretic artifact.'" *Journal of American Folklore* 112: 58–73.

Feagin, Crawford. 1979. *Variation and Change in Alabama English: A Sociolinguistic Study of the White Community.* Washington, D. C.: Georgetown University Press.

———. 1997. "The African contribution to Southern States English." In Cynthia Bernstein et al., eds. 1997: 59–71.

Fercharson, Richard. 1770. Bridgetown, Barbados, to William FitzHerbert. Letters to the FitzHerbert family. FitzHerbert collection (D239), Derbyshire Record Office, Derby, UK.

Fields, Linda. 1995. "Early Bajan: Creole or non-Creole?" In Jacques Arends, ed. *The Early Stages of Creolization.* Amsterdam, Philadelphia: John Benjamins, 89–112.

Fitzherbert family, letters to. 1770. Richard Fercharson, Bridgetown, Barbados, to William Fitzherbert. Fitzherbert collection (D239), Derbyshire Record Office, Derby, UK.

Fontaine, M. and P. Roberts. 1991. *Dominica's Diksyone.* Barbados: The Folk Research Institute, The Konmite Pou Etid Kwéyòl (KEK) and The Department of English and Linguistics, UWI.

———. 1999. *A Visitor's Guide to Kwéyòl.* Dominica: Marcel Fontaine.

Foreman, Christina. 1996. "Boundary tones and focus realization in African American English intonation." Paper given at the autumn 1996 ASA and ASJ 3rd joint meeting, Hawaii.

Frank, D. 1993. "Political, religious, and economic factors affecting language choice in St. Lucia." *International Journal of the Sociology of Language* 102: 39–56.

García, Ofelia and Ricardo Otheguy, eds. 1989. *English across Cultures, Cultures across English: A Reader in Cross-Cultural Communication.* Berlin: Mouton de Gruyter.

Garrett, P. B. 2000. "'High' Kwéyòl: The emergence of a formal creole register in St. Lucia." In John H. McWhorter. ed. *Language Change and Language Contact in Pidgins and Creoles.* Amsterdam, Philadelphia: John Benjamins, 63–101.

Georgia Writers' Project. 1940. *Drums and Shadows.* Athens: University of Georgia Press.

Gibson, Kean. 1986. "The ordering of auxiliary notions in Guyanese Creole." *Language* 62: 571–585.

Gilbert, Glenn G., ed. 1987. *Pidgin and Creole Languages: Essays in Memory of John E. Reinecke.* Honolulu: University Press of Hawaii.

———, ed. 2002. *Pidgin and Creole Linguistics in the 21st Century.* New York: Peter Lang.

Givón, Talmy. 1984. *Syntax: A Functional-typological Introduction* (Vol.1). Amsterdam, Philadelphia: John Benjamins.

Glassie, Henry. 1975. *All Silver and No Brass.* Bloomington: Indiana University Press.

Goffman, Erving. 1981. *Forms of Talk.* Philadelphia: University of Pennsylvania Press.

Good, Jeff. fc. "Saramacan tone raising." In Ingo Plag, ed. fc..

Gooden, Shelome. 2001. "The role of "tone" in Jamaican Creole reduplication." Paper presented at the conference of the Society for Pidgin and Creole Languages. Washington, D. C.

Görlach, Manfred and John A. Holm, eds. 1986. *Focus on the Caribbean*. Amsterdam, Philadelphia: John Benjamins.

Goury, Laurence. 2001. "Synchronic and diachronic aspects of tonology in Ndyuka." Paper presented at the conference of the Society for Pidgin and Creole Languages. Washington, D. C.

Gramberg, Anne-Katrin, and Robin Sabino (trans.) 1998. Pontoppidan, Erik. (1881). "Some notes on the creole language of the Danish West Indian islands." *Journal for Ethnologie* 13: 130–8. http://www.ling.su.se/Creole/Archive/Pontoppidan-1881-Eng.html, retrieved 04/04/01.

Great Britain Colonial Office. 1966. *Annual Report on the Turks and Caicos Islands*. London: H. M. Stationery Office.

Gumperz, John J. and Robert Wilson. 1971. "Convergence and creolization: A case from the Indo-Aryan/Dravidian border." In Dell Hymes, ed. 1971: 151–167.

Guy, Gregory R. 1980. "Variation in the group and the individual: The case of final stop deletion." In William Labov, ed. *Locating Language in Time and Space*. New York: Academic Press, 1–36.

Hackert, Stephanie. 2001. "'I did done gone': Typological, sociolinguistic and discourse-pragmatic perspectives on past temporal reference in urban Bahamian Creole English." Unpublished Ph.D. dissertation, University of Heidelberg.

Ham, William. 1999. "Tone sandhi in Saramaccan." *Journal of Pidgin and Creole Languages* 14: 45–91.

Hancock, Ian. 1980. "Gullah and Barbadian: Origins and relationships." *American Speech* 55: 17–35.

———. 1986. "The domestic hypothesis, diffusion and componentiality: An account of Atlantic Anglophone creole origins." In Pieter Muysken and Norval Smith, eds. *Substrata Versus Universals in Creole Genesis*. Amsterdam, Philadelphia: John Benjamins, 71–102.

———. 1987. "A preliminary classification of the Anglophone Atlantic creoles, with syntactic data from thirty-three representative dialects." In Glenn G. Gilbert, ed. 1987: 264–334.

Handler, Jerome S. & Frederick W. Lange. 1978. *Plantation Slavery in Barbados*. Cambridge, MA: Harvard University Press.

Hannah, Dawn. 1995. "Copula absence in Samaná English." Ph.D. Qualifying paper, Dept. of Linguistics, Stanford University.

Haynes, Lilith M. 1973. "Language in Barbados and Guyana: Attitudes, Behaviours, and Comparisons." Unpublished Ph.D. dissertation, Stanford University.

———. 1982. "Rural and urban groups in Barbados and Guyana: Language attitudes and behaviours." *International Journal of the Sociology of Language* 34: 67–81.

Heine, Bernd, Ulrike Claudi, and Friederike Hunnemeyer. 1991. *Grammaticalization. A Conceptual Framework*. Chicago: The Chicago Press.

Herskovits, Melville J. 1941. *The Myth of the Negro Past*. New York and London: Harper Brothers.

Hill, Donald R. 1973. "'England I Want to Go.' The Impact of Immigration on a Caribbean Community." Unpublished Ph.D. Dissertation, Indiana University.

———. 1977. *The Impact of Migration on the Metropolitan and Folk Society of Carriacou, Grenada.* New York: Anthropological Papers of the American Museum of Natural History.

———. 1980. *The Big Drum and "Ting": Ritual and Social Music of Carriacou.* Bloomington: Folklore Institute, Indiana University.

Hoffman, Barbara. 2001. *Griots at War: Conflict, Conciliation and Caste in Mande.* Bloomington: Indiana University Press.

Holder, Maurice. 1984. "The compound stress rule in Guyanese English." Paper presented at the conference of the Society for Caribbean Linguistics, Jamaica, 1984.

———. 1998. "A proposal regarding prosodic features and levels of representation in Guyanese English." Paper given at the conference of the Society for Pidgin and Creole Linguistics. New York.

———. 1999. "Accent tonal en Anglais Est-Caribéen: Une Breve Esquisse." Paper given at the Colloques des Etudes Creoles. Aix-en-Provence.

Holm, John. 1980. "African features in white Bahamian speech." *English World-Wide* 1: 45–65.

———. 1988–89. *Pidgins and Creoles* (two volumes). Cambridge: Cambridge University Press.

——— and Stephanie Hackert. fc. "Southern Bahamian: Transported AAVE or transported Gullah?" In John Lipski, ed. *African-American English and its Congeners.* Amsterdam, Philadelphia: John Benjamins.

——— and Alison Shilling. 1982. *Dictionary of Bahamian English.* Cold Spring, NY: Lexik House.

Honychurch, Lennox. 1984. *The Dominica Story.* Roseau: The Dominica Institute.

Huber, Magnus and Mikael Parkvall, eds. 1999. *Spreading the Word: The Issue of Diffusion among the Atlantic Creoles.* Westminster Creolistics Series 6. London: University of Westminster Press.

Huttar, George. 1988. *Notes on Kwinti, A Creole of central Suriname.* Society for Caribbean Linguistics Occasional paper no. 20. St. Augustine, Trinidad: University of the West Indies.

Hymes, Dell. ed. 1971. *Pidginization and Creolization of Languages.* Cambridge: Cambridge University Press.

International Population Census for Latin American and the Caribbean. Jamaica, 1881–1943.

———. Turks and Caicos, 1960, 1970, 1980.

Isaac, M. F. 1986. "French Creole Interference in the Written English of St. Lucia Secondary School Students." Unpublished M. A. thesis, University of the West Indies at Cave Hill.

James, Winford. 2001. "The noun phrase in Tobagonian." *Society for Caribbean Linguistics Occasional Papers Series*, No. 28. St. Augustine, Trinidad: University of The West Indies.

Janson, Tore. 1984. "Articles and plural formation in creoles: Change and universals." *Lingua* 64: 291–323.

Jesse, C. 1994 [1956]. *Outlines of St. Lucia's History*. Castries: St. Lucia Archaeological and Historical Society.

Jones, S. B. 1936. *Annals of Anguilla*. Belfast: Christian Journals Ltd.

Kachru, B. B. 1983a. *The Indianization of English: The English Language in India*. Oxford: Oxford University Press.

———. 1983b. *The Other Tongue: English across Cultures*. Oxford: Pergamon.

Kautzsch, Alexander & Edgar W. Schneider. 2000. "Differential creolization: Some evidence from Earlier African American Vernacular English in South Carolina." In Ingrid Neumann-Holzschuh and Edgar W. Schneider, eds. 2000: 247–274.

Keane-Dawes, Jennifer. 2000. "The spirits of Christmas." *The Weekly Gleaner (N. A.)*, *Dec.30-Jan.5, 2000*, 12. Jamaica, NY: The Weekly Gleaner.

Kelly, John, and John Local. 1981. Is creole pulse timed? University of York, manuscript.

Kephart, R. 1991. "Creole French in Carriacou, Grenada: Texts and commentary." *Florida Journal of Anthropology* 16: 81–89.

———. 1992. "Reading Creole English does not destroy your brain cells." In J. Siegel, ed. 1992: 46–62.

———. 2000. *Broken English. The Creole Language of Carriacou*. New York: Peter Lang.

Knight, Franklin, ed. 1997. *General history of the Caribbean, 6 vols*. London: UNESCO Publishing.

Kozy, Charlene Johnson. 1991. "Tories transplanted: The Caribbean exile and plantation settlement of Southern loyalists." *Georgia Historical Quarterly* 75: 18–42.

Kraft, Charles, and A. H. M. Kirk-Greene. 1973. *Teach Yourself Hausa*. London: Hodder and Stoughton.

Kuiper, K. and D. Tan Gek Lin. 1989. "Cultural congruence and conflict in the acquisition of formulae in a second language." In Ofelia García and Ricardo Otheguy, eds. 1989: 281–304.

La Ban, Frank.1971. "From Cockney to Conch." In Juanita Williamson ed. *A Various Language: Perspectives on American Dialects*. New York: Holt, Rinehart, and Winston, 301–309.

Labov, William. 1969. "Contraction, deletion, and the inherent variability of the English copula." *Language* 45: 725–762.

———. 1972a. *Language in the Inner City: The Black English Vernacular*. Philadelphia: University of Pennsylvania Press.

———. 1972b. *Sociolinguistic Patterns*. Philadelphia: University of Pennsylvania Press.

———, Paul Cohen, Clarence Robins, and John Lewis. 1968. *A Study of the Non-Standard English of Negro and Puerto Rican Speakers in New York City*. US Office of Education Final Report, Research Project 3288.

Lawton, David. 1963. "Suprasegmental Phenomena in Jamaican Creole." Unpublished Ph.D. Dissertation, University of Michigan.

———. 1984. "Tone structure and function in Jamaican Creole." Unpublished ms., Central Michigan University.

Le Page, Robert B. 1957/8. "General outlines of Creole English dialects in the British Caribbean." *Orbis* 6: 373–391; 7: 54–64.

———. 1975. *Projection, focussing and diffusion, or steps towards a sociolinguistic theory of language.* University of York: York Papers in Linguistics.

———. 1977. "De-creolization and re-creolization: A preliminary report on the sociolinguistic survey of multilingual communities Stage II: St. Lucia." *York Papers in Linguistics* 7: 107–128.

———. 1998 (1992). "'You can never tell where a word comes from': Language Contact in a Diffuse Setting." In Peter Trudgill and Jenny Cheshire, eds. 1998: 66–89.

——— and David DeCamp. 1960. *Jamaican Creole: Creole Language Studies Vol 1.* London: MacMillan.

——— and A. Tabouret-Keller. 1985. *Acts of Identity: Creole-Based Approaches to Language and Ethnicity.* Cambridge: Cambridge University Press.

Lévi-Strauss, Claude. 1969. *The Elementary Structures of Kinship.* Boston: Beacon Press.

Ligon, Richard. 1657 (1970). *A True & Exact History of the Island of Barbadoes.* London: Frank Cass & Co.

Lippi-Green, Rosina. 1997. *English with an Accent: Language, Ideology, and Discrimination in the United States.* London, New York: Routledge.

Long, Edward. 1828 (1774). *The History of Jamaica.* London: T. Lowndes.

Louisy, P. and P. Turmel-John. 1983. *A Handbook for Writing Creole.* Castries: Research St. Lucia Publications.

Lumsden, John. 1999. "The role of lexification in creole genesis." *Journal of Pidgin and Creole Languages* 14: 225–258.

Lyons, John. 1977. *Semantics Vol 2.* Cambridge: Cambridge University Press.

Marshall, M. M. 1982. "Bilingualism in southern Louisiana: A sociolinguistic analysis." *Anthropological Linguistics* 24: 308–324.

McClung, Yolanda. 1998. Unpublished audio recording of Yansa A. California: Berkeley University. Courtesy of John McWhorter.

McDaniel, Lorna. 1998. *The Big Drum Ritual of Carriacou.* Gainesville: University of Florida Press.

McDavid, Raven I., Jr. 1955. "The position of the Charleston dialect." *Publication of the American Dialect Society* 23: 35–50.

McMurray, Joan F. 1999. "Cowboys and Indians in Nevis: An interview with Mr. Samuel Hanley." *Nevis Historical and Conservation Society Newsletter*, 4–5.

McWhorter, John H. 1997a. "It happened at Cormantin: Locating the origin of the Atlantic English-based creoles." *Journal of Pidgin and Creole Languages* 12: 1–44.

———. 1997b. *Towards a New Model of Creole Genesis.* New York: Peter Lang.

———. 1998. "Identifying the creole prototype: Vindicating a typological class." *Language* 74: 788–818.

———. 1999. "A Creole by any other name: Streamlining the terminology." In Magnus Huber and Mikael Parkvall, eds. 1999: 5–28.

———. 2000. *The Missing Spanish Creoles: Recovering the Birth of the Plantation Contact Languages.* Berkeley: University of California Press.

Meditz, Sandra W. and Dennis M. Hanratty. 1989. *Islands of the Commonwealth Caribbean: A Regional Study.* Washington D. C.: Library of Congress.

Mertz, Elizabeth. 1996. "Linguistic ideology and praxis in U. S. law school classrooms." Reprinted in Bambi B. Schieffelin, Kathryn A. Wollard, and Paul V. Kroskrity, ed.

Language Ideologies: Practice and Theory. Oxford: Oxford University Press, 149–162.

Mesthrie, R. 1992. *English in Language Shift: The History, Structure and Sociolinguistics of South African Indian English.* Cambridge: Cambridge University Press.

Michaelis, Susanne. 2000. "The fate of subject pronouns: Evidence from creole and non-creole languages." In Ingrid Neumann-Holzschuh and Edgar W. Schneider, eds. 2000: 163–183.

Midgett, D. 1970. "Bilingualism and linguistic change in St. Lucia." *Anthropological Linguistics* 12: 158–170.

Miege, Guy. 1688/1969. *The English Grammar.* Menston, UK: Scolar Press.

Mills, Frank L., S. B. Jones-Henrickson and Bertram Eugene. 1984. *Christmas Sport in St. Kitts-Nevis: Our Neglected Heritage.* n.p.

Mufwene, Salikoko. 1986a. "Number delimitation in Gullah." *American Speech* 61: 33–59.

———. 1986b. "Les langues créoles peuvent-elles être définies sans allusion à leur histoire?" *Etudes Créoles* 9: 135–150.

———, ed. 1993. *Africanisms in Afro-American Language Varieties.* Athens, GA: University of Georgia Press.

———. 1994. "New Englishes and criteria for naming them." *World Englishes* 13: 21–31.

———. 1995. "Gullah's development: Myths and socio-historical facts." In Cynthia Bernstein et al., eds. 1997: 113–122.

———. 1996. "The founder principle in creole genesis." *Diachronica* 13: 83–134.

———. 1997. "Jargons, pidgins, creoles, and koines: What are they?" In Arthur K. Spears and Donald Winford, eds. *The Structure and Status of Pidgins and Creoles.* Amsterdam, Philadelphia: John Benjamins, 35–70.

———. 1999a. "Accountability in descriptions of creoles." In John R. Rickford and Suzanne Romaine, eds. *Creole Genesis, Attitudes and Discourse.* Amsterdam, Philadelphia: John Benjamins.

———. 1999b. "Some sociohistorical inferences about the development of African American English." In Shana Poplack, ed. 1999: 233–263.

———. 2000. "Creolization is a social, not a structural, process." In Ingrid Neumann-Holzschuh and Edgar W. Schneider, eds. 2000: 65–84.

Murdock, George Peter. 1949. *Social Structure.* New York: The Free Press.

Mutaka, Ngessimo. 1990. "Syllables and morpheme integrity in Kinande reduplication." *Phonology* 7: 73–119.

Myers-Scotton, Carol. 1993. *Social Motivations of Codeswitching.* Oxford: Oxford University Press.

Neumann, Ingrid. 1985. *Le Créole de Breaux Bridge, Louisiane: Etude Morphosyntaxique, Textes, Vocabulaire.* Hamburg: Helmut Buske Verlag.

Neumann-Holzschuh, Ingrid and Edgar W. Schneider, eds. 2000. *Degrees of Restructuring in Creole Languages.* Amsterdam, Philadelphia: John Benjamins.

Newman, Paul & Martha Ratcliff, eds. 2001. *Linguistic Fieldwork.* Cambridge: Cambridge University Press.

Nicholls, Robert W. 1998. *Old Time Masquerading in the U. S. Virgin Islands.* St. Thomas: The Virgin Islands Humanities Council.

Niles, Norma A. 1980. "Provincial English Dialects and Barbadian English." Unpublished

Ph.D. dissertation, University of Michigan.

Nunley, John W. 1988. "Masquerade mix-up in Trinidad Carnival: Live once, die forever." In John W. Nunley and Judith Bettelheim, eds. *Caribbean Festival Arts*. Seattle: The Saint Louis Art Museum and The University of Washington Press, 85–119.

Ola, Olanikẹ. 1995. "Proper headedness and binarity: prosodic words in Yoruba." In Akinbiyi Akinlabi, ed. 1995: 273–293.

Olwig, Karen Fog. 1985. *Cultural Adaptation and Resistance on St. John: Three Centuries of Afro-Caribbean Life*. Gainesville, FL: University of Florida Press.

Packwood, Cyril Outerbridge. 1975. *Chained on the Rock: Slavery in Bermuda*. New York; Hamilton, Bermuda: Eliseo Torres.

Parkvall, Mikael. 1997. "The Rise and Fall of French Creole on the Commonwealth Lesser Antilles." Unpublished manuscript, Stockholm University.

———. 2000. "Reassessing the role of demographics in language restructuring." In Ingrid Neumann-Holzschuh and Edgar W. Schneider, eds. 2000: 185–213.

———. 2001. "Creolistics and the quest for creoleness: A reply to Claire Lefebvre." *Journal of Pidgin and Creole languages* 16: 147–151.

Parsons, Elsie Clews. 1969 (1933). *Folk-lore of the Antilles, French and English*. 26, Part 2. Millpond, NT: Kraus Reprint Co. 16: 147–151.

Patrick, Peter. 1994. "Functional pressures on plural-marking in Jamaican Patwa." A paper presented at the 10th biennial conference of the Society for Carribean Linguistics. Georgetown, Guyana.

———. 1996. "The urbanization of Creole phonology: Variations and change in Jamaican." In Gregory R. Guy, Crawford Feagin, Deborah Schiffrin, and John Baugh, eds. *Towards a Social Science of Language: Papers in Honor of William Labov*. Amsterdam, Philadelphia: John Benjamins, 329–55.

Patterson, Orlando. 1969. *The Sociology of Slavery: An Analysis of the Origins, Development, and Structure of Negro Slave Society in Jamaica*. Rutherford, NJ: Fairleigh Dickinson University Press.

Payne, Nellie. 1990. "Grenada *Mas'*: 1928–1988." *Caribbean Quarterly* 36: 3,4.

Plag, Ingo. 2001. "The nature of derivational morphology in creoles and non-creoles." *Journal of Pidgin and Creole languages*, 16: 153–160.

———, ed. fc. *Proceedings of the Siegen 2001 International Workshop on the Phonology and Morphology of Creole Languages*.

——— & Christian Uffmann. 2000. "Phonological restructuring in creole: The development of paragoge in Sranan." In Ingrid Neumann-Holzschuh and Edgar W. Schneider, eds. 2000: 309–336.

Pollard, Velma. 1990. "The speech of the Rastafarians of Jamaica in the Eastern Caribbean: The case of St. Lucia." *International Journal of the Sociology of Language* 85: 81–90.

Poplack, Shana. 1981. "Syntactic structure and social function of code-switching." In Richard P. Duran, ed. *Latino Language and Communicative Behavior*. Norwood, NJ: Ablex Publishers, 169–184.

———. 1998 (1988). "Contrasting patterns of code switching in two communities." In Peter Trudgill and Jenny Cheshire, eds. 1998: 44–65.

———, ed. 1999. *The English History of African American English*. Oxford: Blackwell,

———— and David Sankoff. 1987. "The Philadelphia story in the Spanish Caribbean." *American Speech* 62: 291–314.

Proudfoot, M. J. 1950. *Population Movements in the Caribbean.* Port-of-Spain: Caribbean Commission Central Secretariat, Kent House.

Pulleyblank, Douglas. 1986. *Tone in Lexical phonology.* Dordrecht: Reidel.

Radford, Andrew. 1997. *Syntax. A Minimalist Introduction.* Cambridge: Cambridge University Press.

Redhead, W. A. 1970. "Truth, fact and tradition in Carriacou." *Caribbean Quarterly* 16: 61–63.

Reinecke, John E. 1937. "Marginal languages: A sociological survey of the creole languages and trade jargons." Unpublished Ph.D. dissertation. Yale University.

————, et al. 1975. *A Bibliography of Pidgin and Creole Languages.* Honolulu: University Press of Hawaii.

Reubens, E. P. 1961. *Migration and Development in the West Indies.* University College of the West Indies, Jamaica: Institute of Social and Economic Research.

Richardson, B. 1974. "The overdevelopment of Carriacou." *Geographical Review* 65: 390–99.

Rickford, John R. 1986a. "Social contacts and linguistic diffusion: Hiberno-English and New World Black English." *Language* 62: 245–89.

————. 1986b. "Some principles for the study of black and white speech in the South." In Michael Montgomery and Guy Bailey, eds. *Language Variety in the South: Perspectives in Black and White.* Tuscaloosa: University of Alabama Press, 38–60.

————. 1987. *Dimensions of a Creole Continuum: History, Texts, and Linguistic Analysis of Guyanese Creole.* Stanford: Stanford University Press.

————. 1992. "The creole residue in Barbados." In Joan H. Hall, Nick Doane and Dick Ringler, eds. *Old English and New: Studies in Language and Linguistics in Honor of Frederic G. Cassidy.* New York: Garland Publishing, 183–201.

————. 1998. "The creole origins of African-American Vernacular English: Evidence from copula absence." In Salikoko Mufwene, John Rickford, Guy Bailey and John Baugh, eds. *African American English.* New York: Routledge, 154–200.

———— and Renee Blake. 1990. "Copula contraction and absence in Barbadian English, Samaná English, and Vernacular Black English." *Proceedings of the Sixteenth Annual Meeting of the Berkeley Linguistics Society* (BLS 16), 257–268.

———— et al. 1991. "Rappin on the copula coffin: Theoretical and methodological issues in the analysis of copula variation in African-American Vernacular English." *Language Variation and Change* 3: 103–132.

———— and Jerome S. Handler. 1994. "Textual evidence on the nature of early Barbadian speech, 1676–1835." *Journal of Pidgin and Creole languages* 9: 221–255.

Rivera-Castillo, Yolanda. 2001. "Tone-shifting and syntax in two Atlantic Creoles." Paper presented at the conference of the Society for Pidgin and Creole Languages. Washington, D. C.

Rizzi, Luigi. 1999. "Broadening the empirical basis of universal grammar models: A commentary." In Michel DeGraff, ed. *Language Creation and Language Change. Creolization, Diachrony, and Development.* Cambridge, MA: The MIT Press, 453–472.

Roach, Peter. 1982. "On the distinction between "stressed-timed" and "syllable-timed" languages." In David Crystal, ed. *Linguistic Controversies*. New York: Academic Press, 73–79.

Roberts, Peter A. 1988. *West Indians and Their Language*. Cambridge: Cambridge University Press.

Robertson, Ian. 1982. "Redefining the post-creole continuum: Evidence from Berbice Dutch." *Amsterdam Creole Studies* 4: 62–78.

————. 1996. "Language education policy (1) Towards a rational approach for Caribbean states." In P. Christie, ed. *Caribbean Language Issues Old and New*. Kingston: The Press UWI, 112–19.

Roy, John D. 1984. "An Investigation of the Processes of Language Variation and Change in a Speech Community in Barbados." Unpublished PhD dissertation, Columbia University.

————. 1986. "The structure of tense and aspect in Barbadian English Creole." In Manfred Görlach and John Holm, eds. 1987: 141–156.

Rountree, S. C. 1972. "Saramaccan tone in relation to intonation and grammar." *Lingua* 29: 308–325.

Rowlands, E. 1969. *Teach Yourself Yoruba*. London: Hodder and Stoughton.

Sabino, Robin. 2000. "How much Scots do they speak in the Bahamas?" Paper presented at Southeastern Conference on Linguistics 62. Oxford, University of Mississippi.

———— and Gramberg, Anne-Katrin (trans.). 1998. Pontoppidan, Erik. (1887). "The Danish West Indian Creole Language." *Tilskueren*. 4: 295–303, http://www.ling.su.se/Creole/Archive/Pontoppidan-1887-Eng.html, retrieved 04/04/01.

Sadler, H. E. 1977. *Turks Islands Landfall*, (7 vol.). Grand Turk: B. W.I (The Author).

Salami, A. 1972. "Vowel and consonant harmony and vowel restriction in assimilated English words in Yoruba." *African Language Studies* 13: 162–181.

Scheffer, Johannes. 1975. *The Progressive in English*. Amsterdam: North Holland.

Schilling-Estes, Natalie. 1998. "Investigating "self-conscious" speech: The performance register in Ocracoke English." *Language in Society* 27: 53–83.

Schneider, Edgar. 1990. "The cline of creoleness in English-oriented creoles and semi-creoles of the Caribbean." *English World-Wide* 11: 79–113.

————. 1997. "Earlier Black English Revisited." In Cynthia Bernstein et al., eds. 1997: 35–50.

Sellers, Jason. 1999. "A Sociolinguistic Profile of Cherokee Sound, Bahamas: Analysis of an Out Island Community." MA thesis. Raleigh, North Carolina State University.

Seymour, Chanti, Cecilia Cutler, and Stefanie Hackert. fc. "Bermuda and the Bahamas area — The Turks and Caicos Islands." To appear in Peter Trudgill, ed. *Sociolinguistics Handbook*. Berlin: Mouton de Gruyter.

Shields, Kathryn. 1989. "Standard English in Jamaica: A case of competing models." *English World-Wide* 10: 41–53.

Shilling, Alison. 1980. "Bahamian English: A non-continuum?" In Richard R. Day, ed. 1980: 133–146.

Siegel, Jeff, ed. 1992. *Pidgins, Creoles, and Nonstandard Dialects in Education*. Applied Linguistics Association of Australia.

Simmons-McDonald, H. 1988. "The Learning of English Negatives by Speakers of St. Lucian French Creole." Unpublished Ph. D. Dissertation. Stanford University.

————. 1994. "Comparative patterns in the acquisition of English negation by native speakers of French Creole and Creole English." *Language Learning* 44: 29–74.

————. 1996. "Language education policy (2): The case for Creole in formal education in St. Lucia." In P. Christie, ed. *Caribbean Language Issues Old and New*. Barbados, Jamaica, Trinidad and Tobago: The University of the West Indies Press, 120–142.

Singler, John Victor. 1984. "Variation in Tense-Aspect-Modality in Liberian English." Unpublished Ph.D. dissertation. UCLA.

————. 1989. "Plural Marking in Liberian Settler English, 1820–1980." *American Speech* 64: 40–64.

————. 1990. "On the use of sociohistorical criteria in the comparison of creoles." *Linguistics* 28: 645–659.

————. 1991a. "Liberian Settler English and the ex-slave recordings: A comparative study." In Guy Bailey, Natalie Maynor & Patricia Cukor-Avila, eds. *The Emergence of Black English: Text and Commentary*. Amsterdam, Philadelphia: John Benjamins, 249–274.

————. 1991b. "Copula variation in Liberian Settler English and American Black English." In Walter F. Edwards and D. Winford, eds. *Verb Phrase Patterns in Black English and Creoles*. Detroit: Wayne State University Press, 129–164.

————. 1993. "African influence upon Afro-American language varieties: A consideration of sociohistorical factors." In Salikoko Mufwene, ed. *Africanisms in Afro-American Language Varieties*. Athens, GA: University of Georgia Press, 235–53.

————. 1996. "Theories of creole genesis, sociohistorical considerations, and the evaluation of evidence: The case of Haitian Creole and the relexification hypothesis." *Journal of Pidgin and Creole Languages* 11: 185–230.

————. 1998. "What's not new in AAVE." *American Speech* 73: 227–256.

Sivertsen, Eva. 1960. *Cockney Phonology*. Oslo: Griegs Boktrykkeri.

Smith, L. E. and M. L. Forman, eds. 1997. *World Englishes 2000*. Honolulu: University of Hawaii Press.

Smith, M..G., 1962. *Kinship and Community in Carriacou*. New Haven: Yale University Press.

Smith, Norval S. 1987. "The Genesis of the Creole Languages of Surinam." Unpublished Ph.D. dissertation, University of Amsterdam.

Smith, Raymond T. 1996. *The Matrifocal Family: Power, Pluralism, and Politics*. London: Routledge.

St. George's Chronicle and Grenada Gazette. August 24, 1833, 273.

St. Lucia government reports:

1918, 1919, 1920, 1922, 1931. *Report of the Inspector of Schools on the Education Department*. Castries: Government Printing Office.

1921. *Report on the Census of the Colony of St. Lucia*. Castries: Government Printing Office.

1966. *St. Lucia Annual Statistical Digest*.

1980–81. *Population Census of the Commonwealth Caribbean: St. Lucia, Vol. 1*. Caricom.

Stoddard, Albert. 1949. *Animal Tales Told in the Gullah Dialect* (record albums and mimeo transcriptions). Washington, D. C.: Library of Congress.

Sutcliffe, David. 1978. "The Language of First and Second Generation West Indian Children in Bedfordshire." M. A. thesis, University of Leicester.

———. 1982. *British Black English.* Oxford: Basil Blackwell.

———. 1992. *System in Black English.* Avon: Multingual Matters.

———. 1994. "The observer and the data." Paper given at the conference of the Society for Caribbean Linguistics. Georgetown, Guyana.

———. 1998 "African American Vernacular English: Origins and Issues." Unpublished Ph.D. thesis, University of Reading.

———. fc. "African American English tone: A study of tonal patterns in United States Black English." In Ingo Plag, ed. fc..

Sylvain, S. 1946 [1936]. *Le Créole Haitien: Morphologie et Syntaxe.* Port-au-Prince: Imprimerie de Meester.

Tagliamonte, Sali T. 1996. "Has it ever been perfect? Uncovering the grammar of early Black English." *York Papers in Linguistics* 17: 351–396.

——— and Shana Poplack. 1993. "The zero-marked verb: Testing the creole hypothesis." *Journal of Pidgin and Creole Languages* 8: 171–206.

Taylor, Douglas. 1955. "Phonic interference in Dominican Creole." *Word* 11: 45–52.

———. 1977. *Languages of the West Indies.* Baltimore: Johns Hopkins University Press.

Thomas, Erik R. 2001. "An Acoustic Analysis of Vowel Variation in New World English." *Publication of the American Dialect Society* (85). Durham: Duke University Press.

——— and Guy Bailey. 1998. "Parallels between vowel subsystems of African American Vernacular English and Caribbean Anglophone creoles." *Journal of Pidgin and Creole Languages* 13: 267–296.

Thomason, Sarah Gray. 1993. "On identifying the sources of creole structures: A discussion of Singler's and Lefebvre's papers." In Salikoko Mufwene, ed. *Africanisms in Afro-American Language Varieties.* Athens, GA: University of Georgia Press, 280–295.

———, ed. 1997. *Contact Languages: A Wider Perspective.* Amsterdam, Philadelphia: John Benjamins.

——— and Terrence Kaufman. 1988. *Language Contact, Creolization, and Genetic Linguistics.* Berkeley: University of California Press.

Trask, R. L. 1997. *A Student's Dictionary of Language and Linguistics.* London: Arnold.

Travis, Carol, ed. 1990. *A Guide to Latin American and Caribbean Census Material.* Boston: G. K. Hall.

Tree, Ronald. 1972. *A History of Barbados.* London: Rupert Hart-Davis.

Trevor, Jack C. 1949. "First drafts of the Virgin Islands tales and proverbs with notes on their collection and recording." Ms.

Trudgill, Peter. 1990. *The Dialects of England.* Cambridge, Oxford: Basil Blackwell.

——— and Jenny Cheshire, eds. 1998. *The Sociolinguistics Reader, Volume 1: Multilingualism and Variation.* London: Arnold.

———, Daniel Schreier, Daniel Long, and Jeffrey Williams. In press. "On the reversibility of mergers: /w/, /v/, and evidence from lesser-known Englishes." *Folia Linguistica Historica.*

Turner, Lorenzo D. 1949. *Africanisms in the Gullah dialect.* Chicago: The University of Chicago Press.

Urua, Eno. 1995. "The status of contour tones in Ibibio." In Akinbiyi Akinlabi, ed. 1995: 329–344

U. S. Census Bureau, International Data Base. 2000. www.census.gov/ipc/idbsum/tksum.txt

Valdman, Albert. 1988. *Ann Pale Kreyòl: An Introductory Course in Haitian Creole.* Bloomington: Creole Institute.

Van Herk, Gerard. 2000. "The question question: Auxiliary inversion in early African American English." In Shana Poplack, ed. 1999: 175–197.

Veatch, Thomas C. 1991. "English Vowels: Their Surface Phonology and Phonetic Implementation in Vernacular Dialects." Unpublished Ph.D. dissertation. Philadelphia: University of Pennsylvania.

Voorhoeve, Jan. 1961. "Le ton et la grammaire dans le Saramaccan." *Word* 17: 146–163.

Warner-Lewis, Maureen. 1991. *Guinea's Other Sons. The African Dynamic in Trinidad Culture.* Dover, MA: The Majority Press.

Warrack, Alexander. 2000. *The Scots Dialect Dictionary.* New Lanark, Scotland: Waverley Books.

Wekker, H. Chr. 1976. *The Expression of Future Time in Contemporary British English: An Investigation into the Syntax and Semantics of Five Verbal Constructions Expressing Futurity.* Amsterdam: North Holland.

Wells, J. C. 1982a. *Accents of English 1: An Introduction.* Cambridge: Cambridge University Press.

———. 1982b. *Accents of English 2: The British Isles.* Cambridge: Cambridge University Press.

———. 1982c. *Accents of English 3: Beyond the British Isles.* Cambridge: Cambridge University Press.

Welmers, William E. 1968. *Efik.* Ibadan, Nigeria: University of Ibadan Press.

———. 1973. *African Language Structures.* Berkeley, California: University of California Press.

Westermann, Dietrich. 1930. *The Ewe Language.* London: Missionary Society.

Wilkinson, Henry. 1950. *Bermuda in the Old Empire.* London: Oxford University Press.

Williams, Jeffrey P. 1985. "Preliminaries to the study of the dialects of white West Indian English." *Nieuwe West-Indische Gids* 59: 27–44.

———. 1987. "Anglo-Caribbean English: A study of its sociolinguistic history and the development of its aspectual markers." Unpublished Ph.D. dissertation, The University of Texas at Austin.

———. 1988. "The development of aspectual markers in Anglo-Caribbean English." *Journal of Pidgin and Creole Languages* 3: 245–263.

———. ms. "Verbal -s and habitual aspect in West Indian Anglophone white enclave communities." Department of Anthropology, Cleveland State University.

Winer, Lise. 1981. "A Description of Errors in the Written English Compositions of Trinidadian English Creole Speakers." Unpublished Ph. D. dissertation, University of the West Indies at St. Augustine.

———. 1984. "Early Trinidadian Creole: The Spectator texts." *English World-Wide* 5: 181–210.

———. 1993. *Trinidad and Tobago.* Amsterdam, Philadelphia: John Benjamins.

————. 1995. "Penny Cuts: Differentiation of creole varieties in Trinidad, 1904–1906." *Journal of Pidgin and Creole Languages* 10: 127–155.

Winford, Donald. 1993. *Predication in Caribbean English Creoles.* Amsterdam, Philadelphia: John Benjamins.

————. 1994. "Sociolinguistic approaches to language use in the Anglophone Caribbean." In Marcyliena Morgan, ed. *Language and the Social Construction of Identity in Creole Situations.* UCLA: Center for Afro-American Studies, 43–62.

————. 1997. "On the origins of African American Vernacular English — A creolist perspective." *Diachronica* 14: 305–344.

————. 2000. "'Intermediate' creoles and degrees of change in creole formation. The case of Bajan." In Ingrid Neumann-Holzschuh and Edgar W. Schneider, eds. 2000: 215–246.

Wolfram, Walt. 1969. *A Sociolinguistic Description of Detroit Negro Speech.* Washington, D. C.: Center for Applied Linguistics.

————. 1974. *Sociolinguistic Aspects of Assimilation: Puerto Rican English in New York City.* Washington, D. C.: Center for Applied Linguistics.

———— & Donna Christian. 1976. *Appalachian Speech.* Arlington, VA: The Center for Applied Linguistics.

————. 1980. "Dynamic dimensions of language influence: The case of American Indian English." In Howard A. Giles, W. Peter Robinson, and Philip M. Smith, eds. *Language: Social Psychological Perspectives.* Oxford, New York: Pergammon Press, 377–388.

————. 1984. "Unmarked tense in American Indian English." *American Speech* 59: 31–50.

————, and Natalie Schilling- Estes. 1998. *American English: Dialects and Variation.* Malden, Oxford: Blackwell.

———— and Jason Sellers. 1998. "The North Carolina connection in Cherokee Sound." *North Carolina Literary Review* 7: 86–87.

————, Becky Childs, and Benjamin Torbert. 2000. "Tracing English dialect history through consonant cluster reduction: Comparative evidence from isolated dialects." *Southern Journal of Linguistics* 24: 1–24.

————, Erik R. Thomas, and Elaine W. Green. 2000. "The regional context of earlier African American speech: Evidence for reconstructing the development of AAVE." *Language in Society* 29: 315–355.

————. fc. "The Sociolinguistic Construction of Remnant Dialects." In Carmen Fought et al., eds. *Identities and Place: Sociolinguistic Approaches.* Oxford University Press.

World Book Multimedia Encyclopedia. 1998. Q.v. Tape Recorder.

Wright, Laura and Sutcliffe, David. 2001. "Unlikely though it be. Reflexes of early modern English and African subjunctives in African American English." Paper given at the Conference of the Society for Pidgin and Creole Linguistics. Washington, D. C.

Zuill, William Sears. 1951. "Bermuda, salt and the Turks Islands." *The Bermuda Historical Quarterly* 8: 162–68.

Index

G30. ACETO, Michael and Jeffrey P. WILLIAMS (eds.): *Contact Englishes of the Eastern Caribbean*. 2003.

G31. THOMPSON, Roger M.: *Filipino English and Taglish. Language switching from multiple perspectives*. N.Y.P.

T1. TODD, Loreto: *Cameroon*. Heidelberg (Groos), 1982. Spoken examples on tape (ca. 56 min.)

T2. HOLM, John: *Central American English*. Heidelberg (Groos), 1982. Spoken examples on tape (ca. 92 min.)

T3. MACAFEE, Caroline: *Glasgow*. 1983. Spoken examples on tape (ca. 60 min.)

T4. PLATT, John, Heidi WEBER & Mian Lian HO: *Singapore and Malaysia*. 1983.

T5. WAKELIN, Martyn F.: *The Southwest of England*. 1986. Spoken examples on tape (ca. 60 min.)

T6. WINER, Lise: *Trinidad and Tobago*. 1993. Spoken examples on tape.

T7. MEHROTRA, Raja Ram: *Indian English. Texts and Interpretation*. 1998.

T8. MCCLURE, J. Derrick: *Doric. The dialect of North-East Scotland*. 2002.

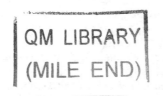